OUT of the BLUE

. . . "It looked as if the down-coming masses would suffocate every single life on the ground. . . ." (near Grave, Holland, September 1944)

OUT of the BLUE

U.S. Army Airborne Operations in World War II

by James A. Huston

Purdue University Studies
West Lafayette, Indiana
1972

Library of Congress Catalog Number 76-186530
International Standard Book Number 0-911198-31-8
Printed in the United States of America

Preface

Concepts and strategic doctrine of airborne warfare forged in the crucible of World War II retain a pointed relevancy more than a quarter of a century later. Now the Air Force provides bigger and more powerful troop carrier aircraft, and the glider has disappeared, replaced in a sense by the helicopter, but the essentials of airborne warfare remain closely identified with the World War II experience. Of yet more general applicability is the way in which these ideas developed, and the pressures for and against the introduction of a new way of warfare. Aside from the importance which this experience may have for current training activities and for current doctrine, there remains the question of the significance of airborne warfare in World War II itself.

This is an effort to survey that experience and to weigh its significance. After an introductory account of the greatest airborne operation of the war, the air invasion of Holland in September 1944, as a case study, it goes back to the rather more pedestrian matters of conception, organization, and training, and then to brief summaries of the other airborne operations.

Perhaps the result is more of a history textbook of airborne operations than a sweeping narrative. But hopefully it will be of interest to the general reader as well as to the veteran "who was there," and as much to the current student of airborne warfare as to the student of World War II.

Though all statements remain entirely my own responsibility, I owe a great deal to those who have assisted. Above all I must acknowledge my debt to the late Kent Roberts Greenfield, formerly chief historian, Office of the Chief of Military History, Department of the Army, under whose guidance these studies began. I am grateful for the continuing assistance and cooperation of the General Reference Branch and others concerned in the Office of the Chief of Military History, and of the staff of the Washington National Records Center of the National Archives. For assistance in typing and in preparing the manuscript for the publisher I wish to thank Mrs. Doris Collins, Mrs. Joyce Good, Mrs. Kitty Bush, Mrs. Betty Pizzagalli, Mrs. Charlene Clemens, Mrs. Grace Dienhart, and Miss Helen Shepard. Further thanks are due the editor, Mrs. Diane Dubiel. Maps are from the official records and histories. The photographs are from the files of the U.S. Audio-Visual Agency, Department of Defense.

James A. Huston

Where is the Prince who can afford so to cover his country with troops for its defense, as that ten thousand men descending from the clouds, might not, in many places, do an infinite amount of mischief before a force could be brought together to repel them?

—Benjamin Franklin, 1784

Contents

Chapter I

"Out of the Blue Sky"

A Case Study

"It was early on the Sunday afternoon of 17 September. The cinemas in the small Dutch towns were slowly filling up, and the streets and highways, along the canals and small streams, were crowded with young people on bicycles. And then out of the blue sky roared several hundred enemy fighter-bombers. Their aim was to attack the German defensive positions and locate the flak positions. Barely had they disappeared beyond the horizon when, coming from the west across the flooded coastal area, appeared the planes and gliders carrying regiments and brigades of the enemy's airborne army . . . . The troops bailed out from a very low altitude, sometimes as low as 60 metres. Immediately after that the several hundred gliders started to land. In those first few minutes, it looked as if the down-coming masses would suffocate every single life on the ground . . . .

"Shortly after the landings of the British and American divisions, our reconnaissance troops went into action. By searching the countless forests and large parks in that area, cut by numerous small streams, they had to ascertain where the enemy intended to concentrate his forces; only then could a basis for our counter-attacks be established. The telephone lines were cut. The reconnaissance cars could move forward only slowly. Some of the enemy dug themselves in near their landing places and brought weapons into position. Others moved up to the houses and barricaded themselves, using the furniture inside the buildings. From there they tried to dominate the bridges and beat back our counter-attacks. Elements of the Dutch population assisted the enemy in their task."[1]

So wrote a German war reporter who happened to find himself in the midst of the great Allied airborne invasion of Holland in 1944.[2]

D Day in Holland

Masses of troop carriers and gliders flew in steady streams regardless of intense flak which appeared here and there. On the northern route 1,033 troop carrier planes – 408 of them towing gliders – carried American and British troops toward Nijmegen and Arnhem. On the southern route another 494 planes – 70 with gliders – flew north of Eindhoven. A fleet of 821 B-17 bombers had struck flak positions and defense installations with over 3,000 tons of bombs. Fighters – 313 P-51's, 201 P-47's, 36 P-38's – escorted the airborne columns. Appearance of flak was the signal for fighter-bombers to dive on the positions and beat it down. Though fighters encountered two groups of enemy planes near the Rhine, none ventured to intercept the columns. Another 371 fighter-bombers of the Royal Air Force (RAF) made cannon attacks on barges, motor vehicles, and flak positions, while 102 medium and light bombers attacked barracks at Arnhem, Nijmegen, and Ede, and 221 bombers of the Bomber Command made diversionary sweeps.[3] No evasive action now broke up the airborne formations as had been the case earlier; now troop carrier pilots flew unswervingly to the drop zones, slowed to the proper speed, and jumped their "sticks" of paratroops in compact patterns.* Within an hour and twenty minutes, 6,000 to 8,000 paratroops dropped in each division area, and they landed in good concentrations on their drop zones (DZ's). Unit commanders in each division considered it

* Two examples which illustrate something of the way the troop carrier pilots held to their courses are these:

(1) "September 17, 1944 . . . When we passed over the British Second Army and into hostile territory the flak commenced raining on us from Eindhoven. My plane was hit in the left engine and left tail section and some of it came through the floor at the front of the plane where no one was seated. The fire became so intense that the motor cut out and we had to jump prematurely. However, the pilot held on so tenaciously that we were able to jump within the edge of the DZ. The crew chief jumped out after we had gone (I saw him in Zon later) but the plane went down in flames. I have not learned about the pilot, co-pilot and navigator, but I'm afraid they didn't make it – perhaps because they stuck it out for us." From the diary of Lt Col H. W. Hannah, Division G-3, quoted in Leonard Rapport and Arthur Northwood, Jr., *Rendezvous with Destiny,* p. 420 n.

(2) "On Tuesday or Wednesday, I am not sure which day it was, I saw three planes hit and catch fire, and the pilots, instead of saving themselves, calmly circled again, dropped their cargo, and crashed in flames." From a letter by 1 Lt Bruce E. Dabis (GGI controller who accompanied British glider troops to Arnhem), to CG Ninth AF, 15 Oct 44, sub: Rpt on Arnhem Opn 18-25 Sep. Ninth AF 373.2. In FAAA 322 (MARKET) (Microfilm roll No. 3).

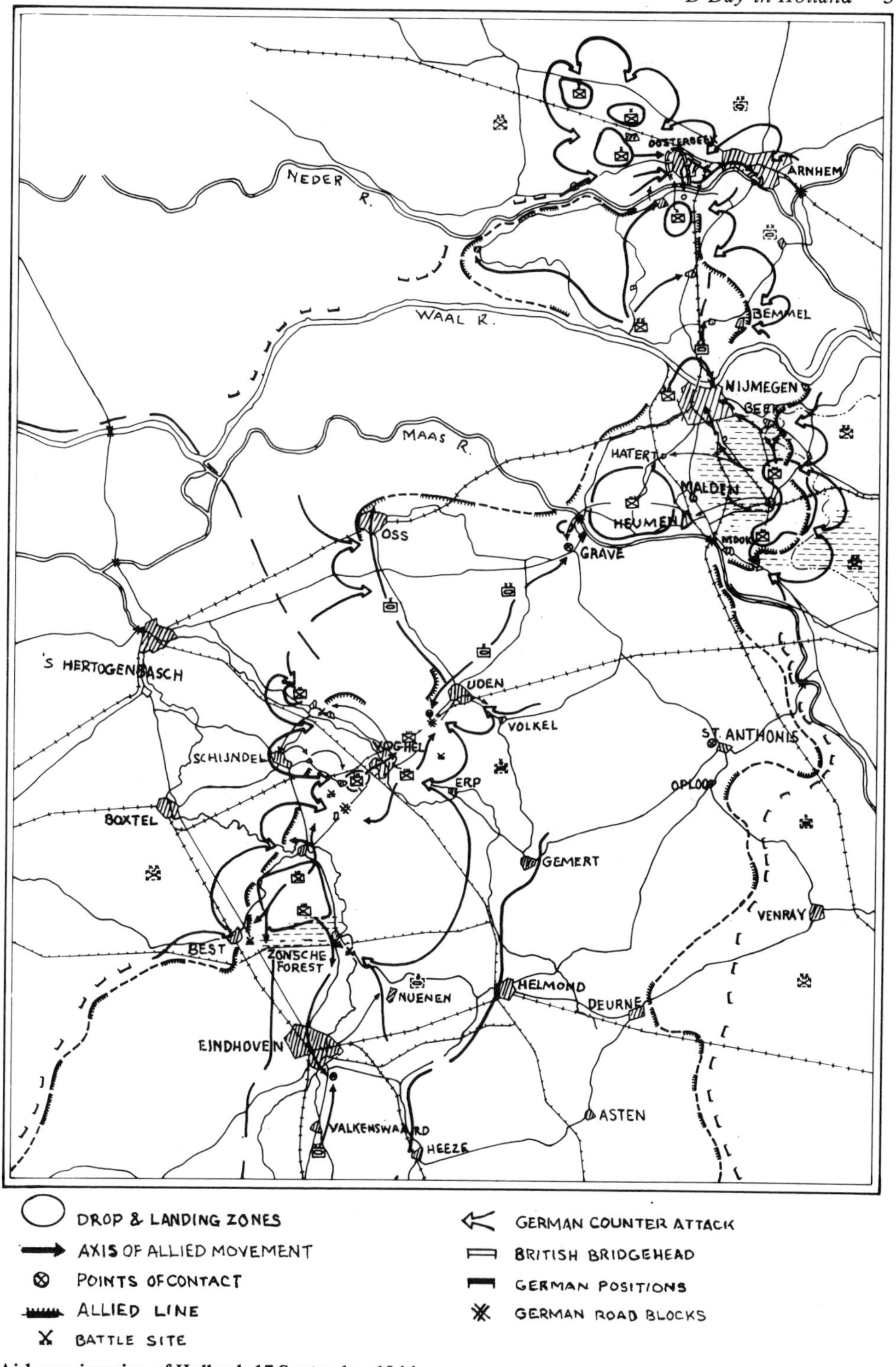

Airborne invasion of Holland, 17 September 1944.

the best drop in their history. This did not mean complete perfection – a battalion of the 101st Airborne Division landed three miles northwest of its drop zone (but in good formation) and some units of the Eighty-second dropped in the wrong zone, but it was more nearly perfect than any previous drop, and about as nearly so as anything can be in warfare. In this moment, when great airborne fleets were arriving at the right place at the right time, and units were dropping in concentrations where they could attack quickly, in this moment seemed full justification for all the hours of planning and months of training which had preceded it.

Once on the ground, troops moved quickly toward their immediate objectives. Landing without opposition on DZ "A" west of Veghel, the 401st Parachute Infantry (101st Airborne Division), minus the First Battalion, went for the bridges in and near that town. By 1500 the regiment had seized intact all four bridges – two highway bridges and two railway bridges each over the Willems Vaart Canal and the Aa River. The First Battalion, scheduled to drop on DZ "A-1" on the opposite side of the canal, had landed three miles to the northwest. It ran into some scattered enemy resistance, but reached Veghel at 1700. The engineer detachment immediately began building a second bridge across the canal in order to permit two-way traffic if necessary.

More scattered in their drop (some units assembled by mistake on the smoke of the 506th Regiment), all battalions of the 502d Parachute Infantry were not assembled until 1500. Again enemy opposition failed to develop at the DZ, and the First Battalion moved north to St. Oedenrode where, after a short skirmish, it seized the town and its objective, the bridge over the Dommel River, intact. Company H of the Third Battalion[4] hurried to the southwest and took intact the highway bridge near Best. However, a strong enemy counterattack recaptured that bridge before nightfall. The other companies of the battalion then joined H Company and prepared for another attack on the bridge the next morning. The remainder of the 502d went into division reserve a mile north of Zon.

Without waiting for formal assembly on DZ "B," companies of the First Battalion, 506th Parachute Infantry – each represented by a small group of fifteen to twenty-five men – hustled southward with the hope of getting to the three bridges over the Wilhelmina Canal near Zon before they could be blown. The battalion was to by-pass the town to the west, and then attack the bridges in a flanking movement along the canal. The First Battalion marched toward Zon down the main road with the Second following. The First Battalion came under mortar fire as it approached Zon from the west, but it reached the canal and attacked eastward toward the main highway bridge. Fire from an 88-mm. gun then held up the advance until riflemen killed or captured all the members of the crew. No opposition appeared in front of the Second Battalion until it reached the

Parachute serials arrive over Holland, 24 September 1944.

One paratrooper lands on his head.

Waves of reinforcements make a massive jump on 24 September.

outskirts of Zon. There a surprised German soldier rode a bicycle right into the midst of the paratroops. But then an 88-mm. gun set up in the center of the town fired two quick rounds down the main street. A slight curve in the street protected the column while the advance party – one platoon – moved to the right, and under the protection of surrounding houses, walked up to within fifty yards of the gun. One round from a bazooka put it out of action, and a paratrooper's submachine gun killed the crew members. Then, as the two battalions were converging on the bridge, hardly a hundred yards away, it went up in a resounding blast before their eyes. (The other two bridges had been blown several days before.) Some of the leaders jumped into the canal and swam across. Most of the First Battalion got across then on rowboats. Engineers, building upon the central pillar which remained, improvised a bridge of ropes, thin boards, and barn doors, so that the remainder of the regiment could march across in single file. It was nearly midnight before the regiment was in position on the other side, and the commander decided to wait until morning to resume the march on Eindhoven.

The gliders, following the parachute serials to landing zone "W," encountered intense flak. This was the way of an airborne operation – often it was worse for the tail than for the head. Five gliders were lost between the initial point and the drop zone when the two ships exploded. Several gliders dropped prematurely, over the English Channel or over the Continent, and others landed deep behind enemy lines. Nevertheless the 53 (out of 70 dispatched) gliders that landed safely on the landing zone (LZ) brought in 252 officers and men, 32 jeeps, and 13 trailers. No artillery came with the first lift. Headquarters detachments and equipment arriving on the gliders joined advance elements who had jumped with the 502d Parachute Infantry and moved into Zon to set up the initial command post.

Meanwhile the British Guards Armored Division had jumped off at 1400 to attack toward Eindhoven from the south. Unexpectedly stiff opposition, however, had stalled its attack and at nightfall it still was six miles short of that city.

During this time paratroops in the area of the Eighty-second Airborne Division – about twenty miles to the northeast – were going about their tasks with dispatch.

Objectives for the 504th Parachute Infantry were separated by four miles, so that the battalions dropped on separate zones to be nearer assigned objectives. Half an hour after dropping on DZ "O" west of Overasselt, enough men of the Second Battalion had collected to set out for its objective, the 640-foot bridge over the Maas at Grave. Company E of that battalion dropped on the other side of the bridge west of Grave and worked through the ditches and canals toward the bridge from that direction. Snipers and fire from emplaced 20-mm. antiaircraft guns harassed the attackers, but a party of eight men went for the bridge. They got into a flak tower at the north end of the bridge – the gun shield had been cut by strafing aircraft, but the gun was still operative – and turned the weapon against one remaining German gunner who was covering the bridge from the flat. At 1630 Company E fired green flares to signal that it controlled the south end of the bridge, and half an hour later men were crossing back and forth. The Second Battalion captured Grave and established a bridgehead to the south. The Third Battalion set up a defense to the north. The First Battalion, landing to the east of the Second, went after the bridges over the Maas-Waal Canal to the east of the drop zone. The bridges near Malden and Hatert had been blown, but the battalion captured the sites and seized intact the southernmost canal bridge at Heumon.

Except for the Second Battalion and regimental headquarters, the 505th Parachute Infantry landed on the assigned DZ "N" southeast of Groesbeek. It came down almost on top of some German flak batteries, and quickly wiped out the crews. The Second Battalion came down on DZ "T" (assigned to the 508th) north of Groesbeek, but, assembling quickly, it lost no time in seizing Groesbeek as it moved southward. The battalion then assembled in reserve in the woods west of Groesbeek, and one platoon moved westward to the Heumon Bridge where it contacted the 504th Parachute Infantry. Detachments of the First Battalion held Mook (where a railway bridge had been blown) and set up road blocks to protect the landing zone and to protect the British Airborne Corps Headquarters in the woods west of Groesbeek.

The 508th Parachute Infantry, after landing northeast of Groesbeek on DZ "T," moved immediately toward Nijmegen. One battalion cleared the landing zone for gliders against considerable enemy resistance, and another occupied the wooded hill southeast of the city against moderate opposition. This ground – the highest in Holland – had been recognized as a key terrain feature from the beginning. On the basis of a Dutch report that Nijmegen and the bridges were lightly held, a company was sent directly for the bridges. This move brought violent reaction, however, and at 2000 the attack stopped 400 yards short of the main highway bridge; the attackers pulled back to prepare for another attempt the next day.

The 376th Parachute Field Artillery Battalion dropped on DZ "N," assembled its ten howitzers, displaced one thousand yards to its assigned positions, and at 1800 fired its first mission on call of the 505th Parachute Infantry.

The glider serial for the Eighty-second Airborne Division brought in eight 57-mm. antitank guns (distributed two to each parachute infantry regiment and two in reserve near the division command post), twenty-four jeeps and seven trailers, and 209 officers and men. Two gliders were destroyed, one dropped over the English Channel, and one landed eighty-five miles southwest of the area, but all the others of the fifty which took off arrived at or near the landing zone – though only thirty-three arrived undamaged.

Troops of the British First Airborne Division were coming down on drop zones and landing zones five to eight miles west of Arnhem. As soon as assembled, two battalions of the First Parachute Brigade started by separate routes toward the bridges. Following a road near the river, the Second Battalion got through. The railway bridge had been destroyed, but the highway bridge remained intact. One battalion got to the bridge, disarmed the demolitions, and established itself in nearby houses where it could command the northern half of the bridge. The other battalion ran into strong resistance in the outskirts of Oesterbeek, and only the survivors of one company got through to the bridge. Troops of the First Airlanding Brigade – actually their gliders had begun landing *before* the paratroops dropped[5] – had their hands full in protecting the drop zones and landing zones.

Glider serials take off (17 September).

Gliders with men and equipment of the 101st Airborne Division land near Zon, Holland.

A victim of German flak, a transport plane plunges to earth near gliders already landed near Zon (23 September).

One glider crashed in a Dutch cow pasture.

British Airborne Corps was unable to establish signal communications with either the 101st Airborne Division or the British First Airborne Division. Both the Eighty-second and 101st Airborne Divisions, as well as Airborne Corps, did make radio contact quickly with their respective rear bases in the United Kingdom.

Lt. Gen. Lewis H. Brereton sent a message to Supreme Headquarters Allied Expeditionary Forces (SHAEF) to report that radio contact had been established with the Operation Market task force headquarters at 1700; then he added: "In my opinion operation conclusively proves fighter action against flak can reduce it to negligible quantity in airborne operations."[6]

A troop carrier fleet of 1,544 airplanes and 478 gliders, American and British, had carried approximately one-half the strength of three airborne divisions (two of them over-sized divisions) to widely separated areas and delivered them simultaneously. No German aircraft had intercepted the column, and the supporting air action against antiaircraft positions had been highly successful for the most part. No British aircraft had been lost to enemy action, but flak had claimed thirty-five American troop carrier planes and thirteen gliders. Pathfinders had functioned well, serials had arrived over their drop zones and landing zones close to schedule, and parachute drops and glider landings had been in good formation. Not all of the units had hit their designated drop zones precisely, but in most cases they had been massed and control could be established quickly. That night the 101st Airborne Division held Veghel, St. Oedenrode, and Zon with a bridgehead south of the Wilhelmina Canal. The Eighty-second Airborne Division was in possession of the bridge over the Maas at Grave and the bridge over the Maas-Waal Canal at Heumen, the high ground southeast of Nijmegen and that south and southwest of Groesbeek. One force was in Nijmegen fighting toward the south end of the important highway bridge over the Waal. The British First Airborne Division had encountered some bitter resistance, but its First Parachute Brigade controlled the north end of the main bridge over the Lower Rhine at Arnhem.

German reaction had been feeble in most places. Although German commanders had considered the possibility of Allied airborne landings in Holland, they had regarded such an effort more likely against the German homeland.[7] Increasing aerial activity, O.B. West noted on 16 September, had suggested the possibility of an attack in the Netherlands.[8] Nevertheless the timing and the magnitude of the operation did catch the enemy by surprise. The Allied air preparation beginning about three hours before the landings might have disclosed the intentions, but the Germans thought the air activity not greatly above normal, and they thought that the attacks against their antiaircraft positions were attempts to destroy the bridges.[9] Army Group B had its command post, at the beginning of the operation, in a hotel at Oesterbeek within view of a British landing zone; but the two to three hours which it took for the British to assemble allowed the German headquarters enough time to move to Terborg.[10] German Army Group B had a conglomeration of troops with which to face the Allied assaults. Its strongest units probably were those assigned to the Fifteenth Army, but they were committed to holding the Scheldt Estuary and the islands in order to deny to the Allies the use of Antwerp as a supply port, and therefore were not available to strengthen appreciably the defenses to the east. A weakened First Parachute Army defended the line against the thrust of the British Second Army. No reserves were immediately available to it. Disposed to protect various key points in Holland were numbers of "combined" units – fortress troops, SS reserves, depleted units from the Eastern Front, naval land units for coastal defense – of the Military District of the Netherlands.[11] The first forty-eight prisoners taken by the British at Arnhem yielded twenty-seven different unit identifications.[12] This was the great advantage of airborne operations: a drop deep behind enemy lines would encounter only weak, disorganized rear area units without an organized defense or sufficient strength for rapid counterattacks. One circumstance, however, spoiled this condition for the British. It just happened that, unknown to the Allies, the II Panzer Corps, with its two rather depleted panzer divisions, was in the area north and northeast of Arnhem for rehabilitation.* By 1640 orders were going out for the employment of elements of II SS Panzer Corps as well as for small units of the Military District of the Netherlands.[13]

Prior Planning

First mention of plans for Operation Market at Headquarters, First Allied Airborne Army had come in a telephone call at 1430, 10 September, from Lt. Gen. F. A. M. Browning, deputy Airborne Army commander and commander of British Airborne Troops, to Brig. Gen. Floyd H. Parks, Airborne Army chief of staff. Browning had just returned to England from a visit at Twenty-first Army Group Headquarters on the Continent. He had said then that Eisenhower and Montgomery wanted an airborne operation in the same general area as that planned for Operation Comet – Arnhem, Nijmegen and Grave – except that the area should extend farther south. The force to be employed should be enlarged to that

* "Enemy chooses for airborne landings areas where there are few troops. II SS Panzer Corps was a nasty surprise to him. Here his intelligence service, in spite of the best agent connections, failed him." Translation of German analysis of airborne landings at Arnhem. German postwar study, Action in Belgium and Holland Sep-Dec 1944. MS No. T-122.

contemplated for Operation Linnett – three, and possibly four, divisions plus the Polish Parachute Brigade.[14]

That evening twenty-seven officers, commanders, and staff officers of airborne and troop carrier units assembled at Sunninghill Park to consider Browning's tentative plan and to discuss major questions on which decisions had to be made in order to permit early completion of detailed planning. Lt. Gen. Lewis H. Brereton, commanding general of the First Allied Airborne Army, announced that Browning, with Headquarters, Airborne Corps (British), would command the initial task force including the British First Airborne Division and Polish Parachute Brigade, U.S. Eighty-second Airborne Division, U. S. 101st Airborne Division, and supporting troops. Maj. Gen. Paul L. Williams, commander of the U.S. IX Troop Carrier Command, would command all troop carrier forces (including the British Thirty-eighth and Forty-sixth Groups) in the operation. A second echelon – including Headquarters, U.S. XVIII Corps (Airborne) and the British Fifty-second (Lowland) Division (Airportable) – would go in if and when conditions permitted. Presumably the American divisions then would come under tactical control of XVIII Corps (Airborne), while the British Airborne Corps would continue to exercise control over the British divisions. Upon making contact with ground forces, the airborne troops would come under the command of Twenty-first Army Group. Brereton considered the question of timing of greatest importance. The date for the operation would depend upon obtaining adequate air photo coverage and maps of the target area, whatever air preparation might be necessary, and time required for detailed planning, as well as the tactical situation on the ground. Ready date (Y Date) was set for 15 September.[15] This allowed little time for making decisions and detailed planning.

The first question was whether this operation should follow the pattern of Sicily and Normandy in being another night operation, or whether an attempt now should be made to conduct a major airborne operation in daylight. Difficulties of navigation and of assembly of troops on the ground in darkness were well known, and this would be a period of no moon. At the same time the German night fighter force, relatively intact (it was estimated that one hundred effective enemy night fighters were within range), might be more formidable than the day fighters – and it would be more difficult for escorting fighters to protect the column at night. Antiaircraft fire could be expected at night as well as in daylight, (and that it could be effective had been demonstrated in Sicily, when friendly ground fire had destroyed over 25 percent of participating troop carrier aircraft on one night's operation).[16] Moreover, IX Troop Carrier Command had not been practicing night glider assemblies in formation for the last three months, and therefore gliders probably should be taken in during daylight (the morning after a night parachute drop) in any case. On the other hand enemy flak doubtless would be far more accurate in daylight. Flak was a primary concern for the slow, low-flying troop carriers. Overwhelming air support against flak and against enemy fighters seemed essential for a daylight airborne operation. Brereton believed that sufficient air support was at hand, and he believed that the air forces could knock out flak positions in advance and beat them down during the operation. He decided for a daylight operation.

Another question to be decided was that of the routes which the troop carriers should follow to the target areas. Several factors, not always compatible, had to be taken into account. Aside from following prominent terrain features which would simplify navigation, the route should be the shortest and most direct possible; it should respect traffic control patterns of IX Troop Carrier and RAF units; it should avoid barrage balloon and antiaircraft areas in Great Britain; it should avoid turns over water; it should make landfall over prominent, irregular coastlines; it should proceed the shortest possible distance over hostile territory. Preliminary studies suggested two possible routes. The most direct route was one which went across the North Sea from Orford Ness, passed over the Dutch Islands, and turned northeast near Hertogenbosch; this route required a flight over enemy-held territory of some eighty miles. A more southerly route would go east from North Foreland to Belgium, turn northward near Gheel, cross the ground force front line and pass over a maximum of sixty-five miles of enemy-held territory. General Williams recommended that both routes be used – the 101st Airborne Division to follow the southern, and the British First and U.S. Eighty-second to follow the northern. If only one route were used in the initial lift, the column would be so long that the enemy might be alerted in time to bring effective fire against the rear elements, or the aircraft would have to fly in parallel columns so broad that all could not avoid known flak locations. Another advantage in having two routes would be that on subsequent days reinforcing and resupply lifts could be routed either way if weather or enemy action ruled out one while the other remained open. Browning's original plan had called for the 101st Airborne Division to go into the Grave-Nijmegen area, and the Eighty-second into the Eindhoven-Uden area, but the use of two routes as outlined by General Williams, with respect to the location of the troops in England, made it desirable to transpose the objectives of those two divisions to avoid crossing routes. Brereton accepted the recommendations, and changed the divisions' missions accordingly.[17]

No problem was more important from the point of view of airborne commanders than the selection of drop zones for the parachute drops and landing zones for the gliders. After careful examination of terrain studies and enemy defense overprints, the troop carrier commander and the airborne commanders made the initial selections at a conference the next morning. They had to consider accessibility to assigned objectives, ground formations, avoidance of flak and enemy defenses, and concentration of the airborne forces. Again compromise was necessary. It generally was desirable for paratroops to drop directly on an objective, or as close to it as possible. In this case, however, drop zones could not be close to the main bridges because flak concentrations protected those bridges. For the same reason cities had to be generally avoided. Rivers and canals might be hazardous for parachute troops, but streams and ditches in the target area also were a great advantage: they were effective antitank obstacles.

Maj. Gen. Maxwell D. Taylor, commander of the 101st Airborne Division, was dissatisfied with Browning's original plan for disposition of his division. That plan would have spread the division in seven separate areas along an axis some thirty miles long. Taylor was anxious to concentrate his forces. Sharing his views, Brereton observed: "Such dispersion destroys its tactical integrity, renders it incapable of fighting as a division, and presents insurmountable problems of resupply. Each small group is susceptible of being destroyed in detail."[18] The Airborne Army commander raised further objections from the air point of view: the difficulty of making accurate drops on the numerous small drop zones, the problem of finding suitable drop zones in each of the areas, and exposure of the air lifts to hostile fire over a large area. Finally Taylor received permission to discuss the problem with Lt. Gen. Sir M. C. Dempsey, the commanding general of the British Second Army, under whose command (through Thirty Corps) the 101st Airborne Division would operate on the ground. As a result, the proposed seven areas for the 101st parachute drop were consolidated into two general areas.[19] Another factor influencing selection of drop zones appeared when General Williams determined that it would be inadvisable to drop parachutists south of the Wilhelmina Canal because of flak concentrations around Eindhoven. This meant that the nearest drop zone would be about eight miles from that objective. Taylor estimated that it would take two hours for a regiment to assemble after landing, and another three hours – a total of five – for it to reach the city.[20] The principal concentration of 101st Airborne Division troops would be in the area designated LZ "W" between Zon and St. Oedenrode west of the main highway. One regimental drop zone, DZ "B," would be in the south part of this area about a mile and a half northwest of Zon. Another regimental drop zone, DZ "C," was chosen in the north part of the area about a mile south of St. Oedenrode. All gliders for the division were to land on LZ "W." The third regimental drop zone, DZ "A," was about five miles north of DZ "B," southwest of the Willems Vaart Canal near Veghel. Actually Taylor agreed to divide this regiment's drop zones so that one battalion could come down about three miles to the northwest in

DZ "A-1" on the opposite side of the canal and astride the small Aa River. This disposition might facilitate quick seizure of the bridges in that area from both sides.

All drop and landing zones for the Eighty-second Airborne Division, with the exception of one rifle company drop zone just west of Grave, were north of the Maas River. Drop zone "O," for two battalions less one rifle company, was immediately north and west of Over Asselt and about a mile and a half east of Grave; the drop zone for the other battalion of that regiment was about a mile and a half east of the main DZ "O." The whole area comprised LZ "O" for gliders. Drop zones and landing zones "N" and "T" were about six miles east of this area. Drop Zone and Landing Zone "N" were south of Groesbeek and DZ and LZ "T" were north of that town. (Groesbeek was about seven miles southeast of the Nijmegen highway bridge.) The area lay between a large woods and ridge line on the west, and a hilly, partly-wooded region called the Reichswald just across the boundary in Germany on the east.

Drop zones and landing zones selected for the British First Airborne Division, all north of the Lower Rhine, lay from five to eight miles west of Arnhem; DZ "K" for the First Polish Parachute Brigade (attached to the First Airborne Division and scheduled for the third lift) was south of the Lower Rhine immediately opposite Arnhem.

While detailed planning proceeded, it appeared for a time that D Day would not be before 23 September. Once more the now familiar pattern of operations planned and then postponed or cancelled seemed to be taking shape. After a visit of Lt. Gen. W. Bedell Smith, SHAEF chief of staff, to Twenty-first Army Group, however, Field Marshal Montgomery announced on 12 September that he had advanced the date six days: D Day would be 17 September.[21]

Problems of logistics – of getting up the necessary equipment and supplies for maintaining units in combat – are often decisive in any kind of warfare. These problems become especially acute and complex in airborne operations. It was anticipated that air resupply would continue for units in Operation Market for as long as ten days. General Williams decided that the distance to the target areas and the reduced hours of daylight would make it possible for troop carriers to fly only one lift a day.[22] The distance also ruled out the use of gliders in double tow, in Williams' judgment.[23] Brig. Gen. James M. Gavin, now commanding the Eighty-second Airborne Division, expressed special concern about getting in supplies. If troop carriers could not fly more than one lift a day, it would be D plus 2 before the three air lifts for the troops could be completed, and supplies could not then come in until D plus 3 which, in Gavin's opinion, would be too late. He asked that First Allied Airborne Army make every effort to arrange with the Eighth Air Force for B-24

Liberator bombers to drop supplies on D plus 2. Williams pointed out that a lift of about 200 gliders could be flown on D plus 2 even if supplies were also flown on that day. Need of aircraft for resupply made it unlikely that the Fifty-second (Lowland) Division (Airportable) could go in before D plus 4 or 5.[24]

No doubt it would have been desirable to cut down on distance and to lessen the hazards of unfavorable weather by flying supply missions from bases on the Continent. This was not possible, however, because tactical air forces occupied most of the suitable airfields, and few continental bases were available in time to base airborne operations on them.[25]*

Because of the nature of the organization of Headquarters, First Allied Airborne Army, and the recency of its formation, many of the supply functions ordinarily performed by an army headquarters were in this case undertaken by the corps. British Airborne Corps would be responsible for all administrative arrangements for the British units, and it would "have the same responsibility for the supply, maintenance, and evacuation of U.S. forces as a normal U.S. Corps has in the field when it operates under a Field Army."[26]** The U.S. XVIII Corps (Airborne) would be responsible for detailed arrangements for all supplies by air to the American forces. Plans for supply to the American divisions were based on the assumption that they would be withdrawn very soon after link-up with the ground forces:

> It is the intention that as soon as the ground forces have joined up with the airborne troops the two U.S. divisions will be withdrawn. No arrangements have therefore been made for the supply of ammunition, rations, or POL for these divisions in a fighting role. As soon as these divisions have been withdrawn, 21 Army Group will be responsible for providing such rations and POL

* Gen. Brereton recommended that after the conclusion of Operation Market that nine airfields in the vicinity of Reims, France, be allocated to IX Troop Carrier Command for basing troop carrier groups, and that the Eighty-second and 101st Airborne Divisions, as well as the 878th Airborne Engineer Battalion (Aviation) remain on the Continent and be billetted near the troop carrier airdromes. Letter from CG FAAA to SCAEF, 14 Sep 44, sub: Bases for Two A/B Divs and Tr Carrier Wings on the Continent. In FAAA 322 (MARKET) (Microfilm roll No. 3).

** "The corps commander, when the corps is part of an army, ordinarily is not a link in the chain of supply . . . He supervises the expenditure of class V supplies (ammunition) for elements of his command. When items of any other class are in short supply, he supervises their allocation or priority of issue to elements of his command." FM 100-10, Field Service Regulations: Administration, Sept 1949, par 142.

as they require from British sources and for making all the necessary arrangements for their evacuation to the UK.[27]

Supplies would be dropped automatically to all divisions and the Polish brigade; the first full supply drop now was scheduled for D plus 1. Supplies would continue to be dropped by parachute until landing strips could be prepared.

The Eighth Air Force did agree to furnish 252 B-24 bombers, with ball turrets removed, for resupply missions. Crews to handle the supplies on the bombers had to be trained quickly and arrangements made for moving supplies to Eighth Air Force bases. Supplies were to move to those bases on 16 September in 110 trucks and trailers to be furnished by the supply services. Men from the services of supply would accompany the loads to the airfields, supervise loading in the aircraft, and accompany the planes to eject the bundles.[28]

Shortage of organic transportation and administrative units in airborne divisions – even including their seaborne tails which would arrive after ground contact had been established – made it necessary to obtain additional supporting units for them. First Allied Airborne Army on 14 September requested, as "essential," that four quartermaster truck companies, one quartermaster service company, two graves registration platoons, a medical clearing company, an ambulance company, and an evacuation hospital (400 beds) be concentrated in the Brussels area on 17 September and be available to join the American divisions any time after D Day.[29] It was confirmed the next day that Communications Zone and Twelfth Army Group would coordinate in alerting and dispatching the units requested.[30]

Casualties would have to be retained by division medical units until supporting forces arrived. It was planned that when airfields in the division areas had been secured, division medical units would establish advance casualty air evacuation centers, and evacuation of casualties to the United Kingdom in returning supply aircraft would begin.[31]

According to the airfield plan, engineer officers were to accompany Thirty Corps until contact had been established to permit their reconnaissance of airfields near Tilburg, Eindhoven, Uden, and Arnhem. It was planned to construct one airfield as quickly as possible and a second and third if necessary. The 878th Airborne Engineer Battalion (Aviation) was briefed on all four fields. Priority would be determined after ground reconnaissance. On D minus 3, Headquarters, British Airborne Troops decided that the airfields would have to be north of Arnhem in order to avoid adding to the heavy traffic on the roads to the south.[32]

The country into which the airborne troops would go was low flatland, virtually without a ridge system except one pronounced north-south ridge about five miles long between Groesbeek and Nijmegen.

This ridge rose two hundred to three hundred feet above the surrounding polders (a polder is a plot of ground which has been reclaimed from the sea and protected by dikes). Much of the land was below sea level, and with hundreds of dikes and ditches and small patches of woods breaking its surface, most fields were not more than two to three hundred yards long. It was a densely populated country, and a number of sizeable towns and cities lay within division objectives. Eindhoven had a population of nearly 120,000; Nijmegen, over 98,000, and Arnhem about the same.[33]

Another element which had special importance for airborne operations was the weather. It was recognized that the weather in this area was very unreliable and subject to rapid change, though conditions were supposed to be at their best during summer and early autumn. During this time of year land fogs might be expected in the early morning as well as sea fogs over the English Channel. There should be light winds and little rain, but visibility might be poor over the sea and coast lands.[34]

Since the disintegration of German defenses before the rapid advances of the Allied Armies across France and Belgium during the summer, Allied leaders could hope now to strike a blow before the enemy had had an opportunity to organize new positions. But in spite of their disorganization, German infantry, supported by Tiger tanks and self-propelled guns, was putting up stubborn resistance against the British Second Army.[35] The only defensive works known in the Nijmegen-Arnhem area – and they were not considered formidable – were west and south of Nijmegen. There was no indication that this position had been occupied since April.[36] Intelligence estimates suggested that the German high command had assigned first and second priorities to the stopping of the U.S. Third and First Armies, and thus Holland had been left generally free of armor. It was known that the German Fifteenth Army, comprising the 245th, 711th, 712th, 346th, and 70th Divisions was withdrawing from the Ghent gap (in the area to the west of the British Second Army's forward positions), but it was not known whether the withdrawing troops would be used on the Albert Canal line to keep open the escape route, or whether they were digging in on a river line to the north. Both the Fifteenth and Seventh Armies were considered to be short of equipment and manpower and to include weak remnants of many units.[37] Airborne Corps estimated that enemy forces defending the line of the Albert and Escaut Canals had fifty to one hundred tanks, mostly Mark IV, and that those forces were made up of remnants of some good divisions, including parachute divisions, but that they had few reserves. There were signs that the enemy was strengthening defenses of the river lines through Arnhem and Nijmegen, especially with antiaircraft guns sited for both antiaircraft and ground roles, but the troops manning them were thought to be few and of poor quality.[38] This growth in flak defenses was of most immediate concern. Continuous study of the general area during the period 6-11 September showed an increase of 20 percent in gun defenses – a development which was to be expected to continue as the enemy had opportunity to regroup his batteries. "Such an air landing operation performed in daylight against the flak defenses shown is considered from the flak point of view a hazardous one . . . . But accepting the risks involved, it is believed that if sufficient surprise, flak neutralization, and continuous air cover are available, this operation appears to have the necessary chances for successful accomplishment."[39] On D minus 2 two squadrons of RAF Spitfires flew a special flak reconnaissance patrol. Flying at 1000 feet in line abreast extending five to eight miles, they covered the whole length of the northern route to Arnhem.[40]

By 13 September decisions had been made sufficiently firm for formal orders to be issued, though all missions had not yet been precisely defined. Instructions of British Airborne Corps confirmed the assignments for the divisions:

> *1 British Airborne Division.*
> Will land to capture the ARNHEM Bridges, with sufficient bridgeheads to pass formations of Second Army through.
>
> *82 US Airborne Division.*
> Will seize and hold the bridges at NIJMEGEN and GRAVE with the same object in view. The capture and retention of the high ground between NIJMEGEN and GROESBEEK is imperative in order to accomplish the Division's mission.
>
> *101 US Airborne Division.*
> Will seize bridges and defiles on 30 Corps' main axis of advance to ensure the speedy pass-through of that Corps to the GRAVE-NIJMEGEN and ARNHEM crossings. Definite locations will be notified shortly.
> It is the intention to evacuate 82 and 101 Airborne Divisions as soon as the ground situation permits.
>
> *52 (L) Division.*
> Will be flown in NORTH of ARNHEM as soon as airstrips are available and will concentrate in reserve nearby, in accordance with orders which will be issued on landing.[41]

Advance headquarters of Airborne Corps would go in with the Eighty-second Airborne Division.

While over-all plans were being completed, detailed planning was proceeding simultaneously in the subordinate units. Division plans were confirmed in field orders on 13 and 14 September. Continuation of attachment of additional parachute regiments (except for the withdrawal of the 507th Parachute Infantry from the Eighty-second Airborne

Division) since the Normandy operation, and modification of the glider organization left the two participating American airborne divisions with infantry elements including three parachute regiments and one glider regiment each. (Official tables of organization still called for an infantry organization of one parachute and two glider regiments.) Infantry elements of the British airborne divisions included two parachute brigades (equivalent to American regiments) and one airlanding (glider) brigade.

Changes in the 101st Airborne Division's original drop zones and specific missions delayed that unit's field order until 14 September. It directed the 506th Parachute Infantry, with a platoon of Company C, 325th Airborne Engineer Battalion and a detachment of the division reconnaissance platoon attached, to drop on DZ "B" (farthest south) and to seize the three crossings of the Wilhelmina Canal near Zon immediately on landing. The regiment was to be prepared to move on Eindhoven (five miles south of Zon) within two hours after landing in order to secure stream and canal crossings there. Dropping on DZ"C," the 502d Parachute Infantry was to assemble in division reserve, but its immediate tasks were to block the Zon-St. Oedenrode Highway and to send detachments to the highway and railroad bridges over the Wilhelmina Canal south and southeast of Best (three and four miles west of Zon.) The 502d should be prepared to take over the bridgehead of the 506th at Zon and to support the latter regiment in its move on Eindhoven. It would secure LZ "W" for the D Day glider lift, and division headquarters would jump with the 502d.

The third parachute infantry regiment, the 501st, with two platoons of engineers attached, was to drop on DZ "A" (later modified to allow one battalion to drop on DZ "A-1") and secure the crossings of the Willems Vaart Canal and the small Aa River in the Veghel area (five miles northeast of St. Oedenrode). Glider lifts on D plus 1 and D plus 2, including artillery, the 327th Glider Infantry, and special units would assemble and await orders.[42]

In the area assigned to the Eighty-second Airborne Division, the 504th Parachute Infantry, with Company C, 307th Airborne Engineer Battalion attached, was directed to jump on DZ "O" near Over Asselt (one company would jump on the other side of the river, west of Grave) to seize the main highway bridge across the Maas north of Grave and crossings of the Maas-Waal Canal east of the drop zone (four miles east of the Grave bridge.) The 505th Parachute Infantry was to drop on DZ "N." It was to clear, secure, and mark LZ "N" for subsequent glider and supply lifts, to seize and hold the key terrain south and southwest of Groesbeek, and to capture the town of Groesbeek (four miles east of the Maas-Waal Canal.) From DZ "T" (north of Groesbeek) the 508th Parachute Infantry was to hold the key ridge in the area southeast of Nijmegen and be prepared to move on order to seize the main highway bridge across the Waal at Nijmegen. It was to deny hostile movement southward from the line Hatert-Klooster. Although the 376th Parachute Field Artillery Battalion had been trained to drop, with its 75-mm. pack howitzers, by parachute, it never had gone into combat in that manner. On this occasion, however, it was to go in by parachute. In this case the decision hinged upon the necessity of conserving aircraft and of limiting air space. While a glider field artillery battalion required ninety-five C-47 airplanes as tugs, plus an equal number of gliders, and occupied fifteen minutes of air space, a parachute battalion could be dropped from forty-eight C-47's, taking up only four minutes of air space.[43] After dropping on DZ "N," the 376th was to mass its fires on Groesbeek in direct support of the 505th Parachute Infantry. A battery of antitank guns, the reconnaissance platoon, signal company, and additional headquarters personnel and equipment would go in on the division's one glider serial scheduled for D Day. The remainder of the artillery would go in by glider with the second lift (D plus 1). The 325th Glider Infantry, on arrival with the third lift (scheduled for D plus 2), would assemble in division reserve and prepare to attack Nijmegen.[44]

In the Arnhem area the First Parachute Brigade, British First Airborne Division, had as its first responsibility the capture of the main road bridge over the Lower Rhine, and secondly, to seize a pontoon bridge a short distance downstream. The First Airlanding Brigade was to protect the drop and landing area until the arrival of the second lift on D plus 1, and then was to form a perimeter defense line on the western outskirts of Arnhem. The Fourth Parachute Brigade, to arrive on the second lift, was to move eastward and continue the perimeter line along the high ground just north of Arnhem. The attached First Polish Parachute Brigade, in the third lift, was to land south of the river, opposite Arnhem, to cross the river by the main bridge, and occupy a position on the eastern outskirts of Arnhem. Thus it was hoped to establish a firm bridgehead at the tip of this long corridor which would project northward from the Escaut Canal in Belgium.[45]

From beginning to end, of course, all planning of the airborne divisions had to be coordinated closely with troop carrier forces. Beyond those major decisions already agreed upon, the detailed planning of assignment of airplanes, of scheduling departure fields, and adjusting units to frequent change made continuous collaboration necessary. It was impossible to maintain complete integrity of both the troop carrier and the airborne units. In general, airborne troops were assigned to planes in a way to coincide with the tactical air formations which the troop carrier commander desired. Serials were modified, however, when the result would have been a too extreme breaking up of airborne tactical units.

Since dispositions had already been made for the Linnet and Comet operations, only minor changes in troop locations now were necessary. The 101st Airborne Division was in the Newbury area (in Southern England), close to IX Troop Carrier Command fields; the Eighty-second was near Nottingham (in the Midlands), also close to troop carrier fields; the British First Airborne Division was still at fields in the Seindon area, and the First Polish Parachute Brigade was in the Grantham area. Troops began moving to the take-off fields (seventeen fields were being used for the American units and seven for the British) 15 September and were sealed in at daylight the next day.[46]

Troop carrier arrangements included rather elaborate plans for navigational aids. Even though the operation was to be conducted in daylight, navigational aids would be used to insure identification of routes and drop zones. Eureka (radar) and compass beacon equipment was set up at wing assembly points; departure points on the English coast were marked by Eureka, compass beacons, and occult (light flashing a code letter); midway across the North Sea marker boats, with Eureka and green holophane lights sending code letters, provided a reference point. Aircraft on the southern route would pass over a white panel T and yellow smoke five thousand yards before reaching enemy lines after turning at the initial point near Gheel. Pathfinders would precede the columns to each division area (a pathfinder team from the Eighty-second Airborne Division would mark DZ "O" and two teams from the 101st Division would mark DZ "A" and DZ "B"). Pathfinder aircraft would carry special radar equipment (SCR 717-C and GEE) by which the crews would find their way to the target areas from the boat markers. The division pathfinder teams would mark the drop zones and landing zones with Eureka, compass beacons (on the American zones), colored panels, and colored smoke (color combinations to identify the respective drop zones).[47]

Troop carrier officers gave a great deal of consideration to the keeping of column time length short in order to have the greatest protection from escorting fighters and in order to have carriers over enemy-held territory the shortest time possible. Formation intervals could be tightened over that which had been used in night operations, and troop carrier plans provided that aircraft might fly in three streams – the right and left each separated from the center by one and a half miles. (Actually RAF planes sometimes formed a fourth stream a thousand feet above the center.)[48]

Air formations had to allow a certain amount of maneuverability, and, at the same time, give good concentration for paratroops and gliders on the ground. The C-47's were to fly in nine-ship elements in V of V's comprising serials of up to forty-five aircraft, in trail, with four-minute intervals between leading aircraft of each serial. Glider columns would form into pairs of pairs echeloned to the right, in serials of up to forty-eight airplanes towing gliders, in trail, with seven-minute intervals between heads of serials. Altitudes had to be decided with a view to avoiding small arms as well as heavy antiaircraft fire, to dropping troops and releasing gliders at minimum safe altitudes, and to assuring clearance of incoming aircraft with those returning from the target area. Troop carriers were to fly at 1,500 feet on the flight out, descend to 500 feet over drop zones and landing zones, and return at 3,000 feet. Speeds for the aircraft to fly were set as follows: pathfinders, going out, 150 miles per hour; parachute aircraft in the main serials, 150 miles per hour to the initial point (IP), 120 from the IP to the DZ, and not more than 110 miles per hour for the parachute drop. Tugs would tow gliders at 120 miles per hour. All aircraft would return at 150 miles per hour.[49] Maximum payloads for the operation were: for parachute aircraft, 5,850 pounds; for Horsa gliders, 6,900 pounds; for the CG-4A, 3,750 pounds, and for tug aircraft, nil.[50]

Timing was of the essence in successful airborne-troop carrier coordination. Troop carrier planning had to time the elements of the air columns in such a way as to assure a safe interval between serials while maintaining the shortest possible column time length. It had to allow enough time on the ground for servicing aircraft and for resting crews between missions while exploiting fully any advantage gained by surprise. It had to get parachute troops in early enough ahead of the gliders to seize glider landing zones, and it had to get a certain number of gliders in as early as possible to provide artillery support.[51] The air movement table annexed to the troop carrier field order included detailed plans through the fifth lift, (D plus 4) which was scheduled to carry the British Fifty-second (Lowland) Division. The table showed the make-up of each serial – the number of airplanes and/or gliders it was to include and the troop carrier group to furnish them – elements of which airborne division or other unit it was to carry, the take-off airfield, the drop zone or landing zone which was its destination, and the time for dropping or landing. Space was left to note for each serial at what time the aircraft and gliders were available for loading, what time loading of equipment was completed, when the aircraft and gliders were ready for emplaning, what time emplaning of troops was completed, and the take-off time.[52] A time schedule followed which showed the time that each serial, from A 1 to A 92 (fourth lift on D plus 3) was to cross the departure point, the initial point, arrive at the drop zone or landing zone, and return. One schedule gave all the times in clock-time, according to the H-hour (1300) which had been announced; a second gave all times on the basis of H-hour, that is, H plus so many hours and minutes, so that it would be a simple matter to make necessary adjustments in the event of a change in the announced H-hour.[53] Thus serials A 1, A 2A, and A 2B, of two planes each, were to take off from Chalgrove Airfield carrying pathfinder teams of the Eighty-second and 101st Airborne Divisions, and to drop them on their respective drop zones at 1245.[54] Serial A 3, forty-five aircraft of the 313th Troop Carrier Group, would take off from Folkingham Airfield with a battalion of the 505th Parachute Infantry (Eighty-second Airborne Division), cross the departure point, Orford Ness, on the northern route at 1119, cross the initial point near Hertogenbosch at 1247, and arrive over DZ "N," south of Groesbeek, at 1300; on the return the planes were to re-cross the initial point at 1314, and the departure point at 1436. The first serial of the main body over the southern route, A 4, forty-five aircraft of the 434th Troop Carrier Group, was to take off from Aldermaston Airfield with a battalion of the 501st Parachute Infantry (101st Airborne Division), cross the departure point, North Foreland, at 1140, pass over the initial point, near Gheel, at 1242, and arrive over DZ "A," west of Veghel, also at 1300; returning planes of the serial were to pass over the initial point at 1319, and over the departure point at 1421. The last parachute serial for the 101st Airborne Division (a battalion of the 502d Parachute Infantry) was to arrive over DZ "C" at 1334. The last parachute serial for the Eighty-second Airborne Division (the 376th Parachute Field Artillery Battalion) was to arrive over DZ "N" at 1340. The last three serials, A 28, A 29, and A 30, were to be for gliders – fifty for the Eighty-second Airborne Division in one serial, and thirty-five for the 101st in each of the other two serials. The last serial of the D Day lift was planned to arrive at the landing zone at 1346.

Commanders briefed the air crews to take no evasive action between the initial points and the drop zones so that troops on the ground could have the best possible concentrations. Wing and group commanders had the responsibility of enforcing the established troop carrier-airborne policy that no paratroops or gliders were to be returned to bases, but all were to be dropped or released in the target area.[55]

Another major aspect of the planning for Operation Market involved the coordination of air support. In a preliminary conference on 12 September at the headquarters of the Allied Expeditionary Air Force at Stanmore, and a larger meeting on 15 September, representatives of all participating air forces and commands, together with officers of First Allied Airborne Army, agreed upon measures of coordination and the assignment of specific tasks. Initially the division of responsibility was to be as follows: Eighth Air Force, escort of troop carrier columns and attack of flak batteries along the route between the initial points and the drop and landing zones, and a resupply mission on D plus 1 with B-24 bombers; Ninth Air Force, air support to the airborne troops after the drop; Air Defense of Great Britain (RAF), escort and anti-flak from landfall to the initial points; Coastal Command (RAF), diversionary raids; Bomber

Command (RAF), diversionary dummy parachute drops and bombing of enemy installations; Second Tactical Air Force (RAF), photo reconnaissance of the target areas.[56] The IX Troop Carrier Command established an advanced command post at Eastcote, and all air commanders concerned used it as a combined headquarters from which all activities could be directed. After coordination through his G-3 and the Combined Headquarters at Eastcote, the commanding general, First Allied Airborne Army, made all final decisions regarding routes, air support, and weather.[57]

All Allied agencies – army, navy, air forces – were informed of the detailed flight plan for the troop carrier columns. The commander of the British Second Army issued orders to all Allied troops in the area of the routes and targets that they should fire on *no* aircraft until further notice.[58]

Troop Carrier planes continued to haul freight for ground units until three days before D Day. Then on 14 September SHAEF notified the Army groups that aircraft of the First Allied Airborne Army would not be available for supply lift after that date until further notice.[59]

For this operation there was no opportunity for large-scale training exercises or rehearsals. Between the claims on aircraft for supply of ground armies and the almost constant alerts of airborne troops for one expected operation after another, there was little chance for any training at all during the six weeks before D Day. Indeed no other major American airborne operation of the war was launched with the benefit of so little specific training.[60]

At 1630 on 16 September staff weather officers issued their weather prediction for the period 17-20 September. A high pressure area was approaching from the southwest which probably would bring early morning fog, but the outlook was for generally fair through the 20th (D plus 3). The 17th should be fair; fog would limit visibility to 500 yards early on the 18th, but it should clear by late morning. Fair weather should continue on the 19th, but there probably would be fog over the target area in the morning.[61]

By 16 September the detailed plans for all aspects of the operation had been worked out. That evening the weather outlook was favorable and at 1900 hours the commanding general gave the word to lay the operation on.[62]

The Attack is On

At 1040, 17 September 1944, a fair day, with light winds and slight haze, the pathfinder serials of the 101st and Eighty-second Airborne Divisions took off from Chalgrove airdrome, circled, and followed a course generally east to the coast. There the two planes of the second serial

Paratroopers of the Eighty-second Airborne Division board a plane in England for the invasion of the Netherlands.

Loaded down with jump equipment, American paratroopers await the First Allied Airborne Army's jump into Holland.

Airborne troops organize on the ground while a Dutch boy comes out to greet them.

circled twice to kill time, and then followed the route of the leading pair. The first two teams were to mark DZ "A," west of Veghel, and the other two were to mark DZ's "B" and "C," between Zon and St. Oedenrode. P-47 fighters contacted the flight over the English Channel to furnish escort. The pathfinders bore north near Bourg-Leopold. Orange smoke, marking the front lines, mushroomed below. Heavy antiaircraft shells began bursting around the formations. The pilots took no evasive action, but they increased speed to 180 miles per hour. Near Patie, Belgium, heavy flak caught one of the C-47's. Fragments tore through the left engine and wing tank, and flaming, the plane fell into a steep dive. Only four parachutes appeared from the plane before it crashed and exploded in a sheet of flame. Ten minutes later the other plane of that serial was approaching the railroad which ran generally west to east into Veghel. At this point the pilot swung to a course paralleling the tracks, slowed the plane almost to a stall (85-90 miles per hour), and the pathfinder team jumped exactly on the target. The time was just ten seconds before 1245. No enemy resistance developed immediately on the drop zone, and the Eureka was assembled and operating within one minute, and the panel "T" and panel letter "A" were out within 2½ minutes. The antenna for the radio beacon gave some trouble, but it was operating within five minutes. The two teams of the other serial jumped side by side on DZ's "B" and "C" and had all their aids operating within four minutes. The main body came into view just three minutes off schedule, and the pathfinders set off their red smoke.[63] Similarly, the Eighty-second Division's pathfinders, who had continued northward, were arriving over DZ "O" at the same time. A flak tower and flak wagon at Grave brought heavy fire on the pathfinders as they jumped, but escorting fighters promptly attacked and neutralized the enemy fire. The two teams dropped side by side, and since there had been no losses, the second team provided local security while the first set up its aids. Radar and radio were operating and panels were out within three minutes. Serials flying to all the drop zones in the Eighty-second area were dependent on the aids set up on DZ "O". Those going to DZ's "N" and "T" would fly over "O" and then find their respective drop zones. Pathfinders of the 505th Parachute Infantry would drop with the first serial on DZ "N," and a team from the 325th Glider Infantry would drop with the 508th Parachute Infantry on DZ "T" to mark the landing zone for the gliders.[64]

A well planned and executed airborne operation, like a surprise river crossing or beach landing, is likely to meet light resistance at first, but to have its most difficult fighting later, after the enemy has had a chance to recover from the initial shock and to organize his forces for counterattacks. The critical time for Operation Market would come after D Day.

Success and Failure

During the next nine days troop carrier aircraft flew resupply and reinforcing missions while the troops on the ground fought vigorously to consolidate the narrow corridor which would threaten the German position in Holland. An air fleet almost as great as that of D Day brought additional troops and equipment on D plus 1, and later the same day 252 B-24 bombers of the Eighth Air Force dropped 782 tons of supplies.

When the meteorological staff predicted (accurately) that rain and low clouds spreading across Belgium would affect the southern, but not the northern route, First Allied Airborne Army G-3 recommended that all troop carriers follow the northern route on the second lift. Necessary orders were issued within the hour, but fog delayed the take-offs until between 1000 and 1100 – the time when the planes and gliders were supposed to be over their drop and landing zones.

Most of the 327th Glider Infantry and 146 more jeeps and 109 trailers arrived on the landing zones, and 428 (of 450 which took off) gliders reached the 101st Airborne Division safely.

The Eighty-second Airborne Division used the 454 gliders assigned to its second lift to bring in the remaining three artillery battalions. They arrived at the landing zones in the midst of a fire fight, and quickly went into action. Germans had attacked from the Reichswald and seized a part of the landing zone. A mid-morning attack had driven them off the zone

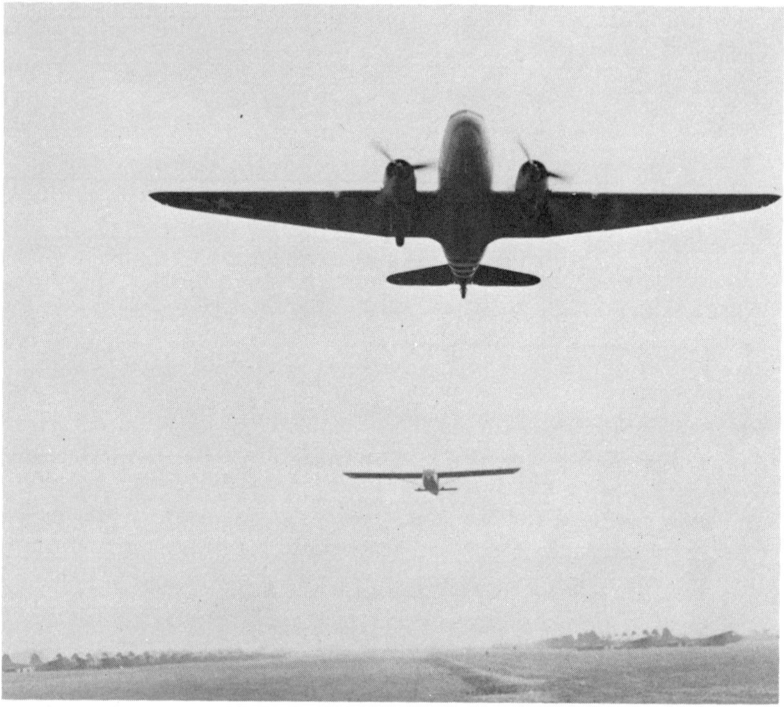

A C-47 tow plane takes off with a glider for Holland.

Horsa gliders in the foreground and CG 4A gliders in the background are massed on an airfield in England, awaiting take-off for Holland, 17 September.

but they still had much of it under fire. General Gavin had sent a message to rear base in an effort to have glider pilots notified to land on the west side of the landing zone.* The message arrived too late for new briefings, however, and a number of gliders which landed near the Reichswald came under intense and damaging fire.[65] In the midst of the landings of several hundred gliders on the correct landing zone, twenty-five gliders of the 319th Field Artillery Battalion continued over the landing zone beyond the Reichswald, and landed about five miles inside Germany; about half the men got back to the division within a few days.**

Reinforcements for the British First Airborne Division on D plus 1 included the Fourth Parachute Brigade, in 127 American planes, and other troops in 296 British gliders. Another thirty-three British aircraft dropped supplies.

The Eighth Air Force bombers went in at low altitudes to drop their 782 tons of supplies to the 101st and Eighty-second Airborne Divisions, but variations in their release points scattered the bundles considerably.[66] Since neither enemy action nor poor visibility had hampered the drop, and inasmuch as the bombers flew at the correct altitude, the number of bundles reported to have dropped anywhere from one to eight miles from the drop zone suggested the need for a quick-release mechanism to make uniform the time required to get the panniers out of the ball turret openings and bomb bays.[67]

A total of 1,360 airplanes and 1,200 gliders had flown the second lift. Then bad weather sharply curtailed air operations for four successive days.

The force of the 101st Airborne Division which had crossed the Wilhelmina Canal at Zon the previous evening – the 506th Parachute Infantry – advanced toward Eindhoven early on the morning of 18 September. Held up by enemy fire about a mile north of the city, it outflanked the defenses to the east and won control of most of the city by 1300. British reconnaissance patrols had by-passed the city to contact the airborne troops to the north shortly after noon, and the main body made

* The procedure of selecting alternate drop zones and landing zones which had been used during the Tennessee maneuvers of the 101st Airborne Division in 1943 had not been applied in combat, as it seemed to complicate unduly an already complex undertaking; but this is an instance when an alternate landing zone might have been very useful.

** The glider pilots explained that they had failed to get a green light signal from the tugs, and thought they should not release. (Standard procedure was for the glider pilots to cut loose on signal from the airplane pilot, but if the glider pilot failed to release his glider in a reasonable time, then the airplane pilot was supposed to cut loose the glider near the landing zone.) (SHAEF Op Memo No. 12).

firm contact just south of the city at 1900. Tanks of the Guards Armored Division passed through Eindhoven quickly and reached the Wilhelmina Canal at 2100. There engineers immediately began building a bridge. That task completed during the night, the British armored division began crossing at 0615 (19 September). Racing on through St. Oedenrode and Veghel, it was approaching the sector of the Eighty-second Airborne Division by 0645. While other troops of the 101st Airborne Division fought to strengthen their hold on the corridor, the main axis became a mass of vehicles streaming northward. After an attack on the preceding day, and another on this, to regain the bridge near Best had failed, and now increasing commitments of the 502d Parachute Infantry there threatened to weaken dangerously the defenses of St. Oedenrode, a final assault at 1800 won even that objective – and over a thousand German prisoners. A third glider lift that afternoon brought in more troops of the 327th Glider Infantry, antitank guns, and artillery. The antitank guns arrived just in time to help drive off a German tank attack against the bridge at Zon that evening. That night German planes bombed Eindhoven heavily. When the threat to Zon continued to grow during the night and the next day (20 September), two battalions of the 506th, with British tanks, returned northward from Eindhoven to join with a battalion of the 327th Glider Infantry in repelling the attacks.

Meanwhile the Eighty-second Airborne Division was being extended in defending itself against attacks coming from the Reichswald in the southeast, and continuing attacks of its own to the north. While other units attacked to clear the landing zones on D plus 1, platoons from the 504th and the 508th Parachute Infantry Regiments converged on the canal bridge of the main Grave-Nijmegen highway near Neerbosch and captured it. This bridge was damaged, but would carry light traffic. One company of the 508th returned for another try at the main highway bridge at Nijmegen, and with the assistance of members of the Dutch Resistance, again got to within 400 yards of the objective. But then after fighting until 1500 without any further advance, it was withdrawn. Arrival of the Guards Armored Division the next day (19 September), by way of Grave (it contacted the 504th Parachute Infantry there at 0820) and Heumen, added new strength for another assault on the Nijmegen bridges, though strong enemy attacks from the Reichswald still kept other units there defending to the south and east. The Second Battalion, 505th Parachute Infantry, was attached to the British division for the new attempt. Near the center of the city, one company of the 505th, with seven tanks, turned northwest to attack the railroad bridge, while the rest of the battalion and the remaining tanks of the Second Battalion, Grenadier Guards, together with a British armored infantry company, attacked directly for the highway bridge. Once more the attackers got to within 400 yards of the objective, and then were stopped. Violent combat continued through the evening and the night, but the German defenses held. The whole success of the operation might depend upon getting that bridge intact. Corps and division commanders agreed upon a bold maneuver: a river crossing by boat. While infantry and tanks continued to attack the south end of the bridge, the 504th Parachute Infantry, with the Second Irish Guards attached, moved up on the west and cleared an area to the river. After instruction in the use of British assault boats, at 1500 the parachute regiment started across about a mile downstream from the railroad bridge. It had only enough boats to take one battalion at a time, but they got across and then moved over several hundred yards of flat ground under fire from an old fort. After some hard fighting the paratroops reached the north end of the railroad bridge at 1800. When they reached the north end of the highway bridge, the troops on the opposite side stormed the south end of the bridge. Shortly thereafter, the first tank of the Grenadier Guards rolled across. At dawn they would go for Arnhem.

The delays which had slowed the advance of the British Thirtieth Corps – the defense south of Eindhoven, the building of a bridge at Zon, German attacks against the road near Zon, the fight for the Nijmegen bridge – these delays were having serious consequences for the British First Airborne Division at Arnhem. And there enemy reaction was relatively stronger and swifter than elsewhere. By the time the Fourth Parachute Brigade had arrived on D plus 1, several hours late because of the weather, the Germans had the time to build up effective counter forces. By evening the Germans had cut the route between the landing zones and the troops at the bridge, and had the British forces cut into three parts – one between the landing areas and Oesterbeek, one in the western outskirts of Arnhem, and one at the north end of the bridge. Moreover, the division had been unable to maintain effective communications.* Attempts of the battalions in the outskirts of Arnhem to break through to the bridge the next day failed. Glider elements of the Polish Parachute Brigade arrived in the midst of a fire-fight (D plus 2), but the Polish paratroops could not go in as planned on D plus 2, or on D plus 3,

* On 29 September a pigeon message was relayed to FAAA. It was from the commander of the Second Parachute Battalion addressed to Rear Headquarters, Airborne Corps, dated 18 September: "2nd Parachute Battalion captured north end of main bridge at 17 2000 and are now holding perimeter of 300 yard radius from bridge. Enemy defense of town light. 20 armored cars crossed bridge in last half hour. Destroyed 10. Ammunition especially required." A penciled note was scribbled on the bottom of the copy of the message at FAAA Headquarters: "CG – If only we could have gotten this in time!" In FAAA 322 (MARKET) (Microfilm roll No. 3).

because of the bad weather. Resupply missions failed on both days when nearly all the bundles fell into enemy hands. Without supplies, and facing increasingly stronger German infantry and heavy tank attacks, the troops at the bridge were in a perilous position. The houses which they occupied were burned out one by one, and when they tried to get into alternate positions outside they came under direct tank fire. No shelter remained for the wounded, and three hundred of them had to be surrendered. Out of ammunition, the band of 140 survivors early on 21 September split up into small parties to try to filter back to the main body. None made it. A force, numbering 500 at its maximum, had held out at the key Arnhem bridge for more than three days, without resupply, against determined enemy tanks. Now, at almost the hour that tanks of the Guards Armored Division were starting north from the Nijmegen bridgehead, their last remnants were being eliminated. Other elements of the division continued to hold a steadily contracting area to the west of Arnhem. Holding to the terminus of the Heaveadorp ferry, they hoped that the Polish Brigade might be able to drop there. The bad weather on D plus 3, however, prevented that.

Though the spearheads of the ground forces now had moved northward toward Arnhem, fighting in the south continued as vigorously as ever. Troops of the 101st Airborne Division in turn warded off enemy attacks against St. Oedenrode and themselves attacked and seized Schijndel. That had to be given up, however, when stronger German attacks against Veghel (22 September) actually cut the main highway and held it until the next day.

As the Eighty-second Airborne Division fought back against strong counterattacks in its sector, all the way from Mook in the southeast to Beek and Ubbergen (east of Nijmegen) in the northeast, the fact that the 325th Glider Infantry had not been able to join the division became a serious matter.

In spite of the unfavorable weather on D plus 4 (21 September), the plight of the British First Airborne Division made it almost mandatory to try to get the Polish Parachute Brigade in anyway. American troop carriers took off at 1400 with about half of the brigade in 110 planes. Loss of the Arnhem bridge now made use of the drop zone originally selected for the Polish paratroops, south of the bridge, impractical. Therefore they should be dropped near Driel, on the south bank of the river opposite the area still held by the British. They then could cross the river on the Heaveadorp ferry. Unfortunately the weather was so bad that forty-one aircraft returned without dropping their paratroops, three landed at Brussels, thirteen were missing; only fifty-three reached the area of the drop zone, and they dropped about 750 men. By the time these troops assembled and reached the river bank, however, they found that the ferry had been sunk, and the Germans controlled the north bank at that point. The attack of the Guards Armored Division, meanwhile, was bogged down before an effective antitank screen near Rossen.* Tanks were unable to operate off roads in this country during the rainy weather, and on 23 September the British Forty-third Division passed through the Guards Armored Division to make an infantry attack toward Arnhem. Armored cars of the Household Cavalry Regiment moved northward from the Nijmegen bridge at dawn, by-passed enemy resistance at Elst, and drove to Driel to link up with the First Polish Parachute Brigade at 0800 (22 September). The main attack was unable to get beyond Elst on the road to Arnhem, but another battalion, mounted on tanks, followed the route of the armored reconnaissance corps and reached the Driel area before nightfall. More troops, bringing amphibious trucks (DUKW's) loaded with ammunition and supplies for the First Airborne Division, arrived in the area before midnight. But the DUKW's could not get through the mud along the river bank, and could not be launched. A few improvised rafts did carry about fifty Poles across the river during the night.

No troop carrier operations at all had been possible on D plus 5, but with improved weather the next day, the largest lift since D plus 1 took off. It also was the day of greatest reaction from the German Air Force. Gliders took in more artillery and jeeps for the 101st Airborne Division, and the 325th Glider Infantry was at last able to join the Eighty-second Airborne Division (their gliders landed on what had been DZ "O" near Over Asselt.) More Polish parachutists flew to the area of the Eighty-second Airborne Division in forty-one American aircraft, and British Stirlings and Dakotas – 115 of 123 reached the drop zone – and planes dropped supplies for the First Airborne Division, but again nearly all of them fell into enemy hands. That night 150 to 250 more Polish troops ferried across the river to try to reinforce the First Airborne Division. But already British Second Army had given permission to withdraw all the forces then north of the Lower Rhine should it become necessary.

German forces in the south still had not given up their attacks against the 101st Airborne Division near Veghel. In fact on 23 September an enemy force probed between the regiments holding St. Oedenrode and Veghel, and once more cut the corridor. The 506th Parachute Infantry, with British tanks, raced back southward from Uden and the British Fiftieth Division attacked from the south. The combined forces were unable to reopen the road until 26 September, but this time it was permanent.

* According to a German report, only two battalions and two antiaircraft units were able to oppose the Allies on the Nijmegen-Arnhem highway. Postwar German Study, Action in Belgium and Holland, Sep-Dec 1944.

Strong pressure continued against the Eighty-second Airborne Division, and on 25 September about forty German planes bombed the Nijmegen Bridge; one hit damaged it. But by 25 and 26 September airborne troops again were attacking to broaden their area along the Waal.

Attempts to reinforce the shrinking British First Airborne Division continued through 24 September. Another 300 to 400 men of the Forty-third Division ferried across the river that night, but the next day Thirty Corps made the decision to withdraw the First Airborne Division. At first it was hoped that the Forty-third Division might be able to establish a new bridgehead east of Renkum, but finally even that had to be given up. That night, 25-26 September, survivors of the First British Airborne Division, together with Poles and British infantrymen who had only recently joined them, withdrew to the south bank of the Lower Rhine (a few returned the next night).

The air phase of Operation Market had about ended. Some plans had been made to use fighter-bombers to resupply the British First Airborne Division. Believing that the speed, maneuverability, and fire power of fighter-bombers, together with their ability to drop accurately on a small drop zone, would make an effective means for emergency supply, air officers arranged to have Typhoons and Mosquitoes drop supplies in belly tanks released from bomb racks on D plus 8 and 9. However, supplies could not be packed in available containers before the division had been withdrawn.[68] On D plus 4 intelligence reported a German airfield, not previously noted, in a big bend of the old Maas River bed west of Grave. It was found to be an excellent grass field, but with no marking and poor road access (the Germans had not used it as an operational field.) Immediately Airborne Corps had asked permission of Second Army to use the airfield to bring in the U. S. 878th Airborne Engineer Battalion (aviation), the British Airborne Forward Delivery Airfield Group, and the British Second Light Antiaircraft Battery, to be followed by supplies and possibly the Fifty-second (lowland) Division (airportable.) On D plus 9 (26 September) 209 C-47's landed the Airborne Forward Delivery Airfield Group (AFDAG) and most of the personnel, but not their Bofurs guns, because poor weather ruled out the use of gliders, of the Second Light Antiaircraft Battery. All the planes landed, unloaded, picked up American glider pilots to be evacuated, and took off in just three hours and fifty minutes. Guiding on a pathfinder team flown in the preceding day, all aircraft arrived safely. The next day a column of 125 trucks of the RAF Eighty-three Group (Tactical Air Force) drove up to the field. Apparently "83 Group seemed to be under the impression that they had marked and prepared it for their own use."[69] Just as AFDAG had prepared to receive much-needed ammunition and supplies, higher headquarters had decided to use the airfield as a fighter base because of the noticeable strengthening of the Luftwaffe in the area. Now, without any visit or communication with Airborne Corps, Eighty-three Group suddenly arrived to take over the field. Under the circumstances the 878th Airborne Engineer Battalion (aviation) and the guns of the Second Light Antiaircraft Battery were not brought in; AFDAG was removed from the field and dispersed within Second Army to perform ordinary ground duties.[70] The final troop carrier missions for the operation were on D plus 12 and D plus 13 when small numbers of C-47's (six out of eleven arrived on the one day and all of twenty-two on the next) landed supplies on the strip near Grave. Earlier, planes had landed the remaining troops of the 327th Glider Infantry and 907th Glider Field Artillery Battalion (101st Airborne Division) at Brussels in time for them to join their units by D plus 10. Seaborne tails had sailed from Southhampton on D plus 2, landed at Omaha Beach on D plus 3, and arrived in the areas of the 101st and Eighty-second Airborne Divisions on D plus 4, 5, and 6. The sea echelon for the 101st Airborne Division alone included 1,077 officers and men, 176 2½-ton trucks, 9 1½-ton trucks, 44 ¾-ton trucks, 71 jeeps, 133 trailers, 2 bulldozers, 2 motorcycles, and 7 ambulances.[71]

On conclusion of the airborne phase of the operation the inevitable struggle to extricate the airborne divisions from continuing ground action developed. What remained of the British First Airborne Division left Nijmegen for England on 28 September, and those of the First Polish Parachute Brigade returned on 7 October. Two days later Headquarters, British Airborne Corps moved back to England. But the 101st and Eighty-second Airborne Divisions – whose early evacuation had been anticipated in plans and orders – were left behind for several weeks more of intensive combat. Though frequently violated, it was supposed to be an accepted principle that airborne troops, because of their special training and equipment and the difficulty of replacing casualties, should be relieved from ordinary ground operations as quickly as possible. Such continued employment prevented the preparation of further airborne operations in the immediate future in which they might be needed. At the same time it could not be expected that a ground commander would release airborne divisions until the tactical situation permitted it, or until they could be replaced. Repeatedly General Brereton asked that the American airborne divisions be relieved. SHAEF agreed that it should be done as soon as possible, but Montgomery held that the situation would not yet permit it.[72] The divisions were not relieved until November. On relief by the Second Canadian Corps, 11-13 November, the Eighty-second Airborne Division moved to Sissone, near Reims. Relieved by the British Thirty-first Division 25-27 November, the 101st Airborne Division moved to Mourmelon-le-Grand, also in the Reims area.

Operation Market was an airborne operation of unprecedented magnitude. A total of 34,876 troops had gone into the battle by air – 20,190 by parachute, 13,781 by gliders, and 905 by airplane on a prepared landing strip. In addition airplanes and gliders had carried more than 5,200 tons of supplies, including 568 artillery pieces and 1,927 vehicles.[73]

Casualties among airborne troops through D plus 30 were reported as follows:

	Killed	Wounded	Missing	Total
1 Airborne Division (British)	322	240	6424	6986
1st Polish Parachute Brigade	34	142	207	383
82 Airborne Division	336	1912	661	2909
101st Airborne Division	573	1987	378	2938
Total	1265	4281	7670	13216[74]

In addition airmen of IX Troop Carrier Command suffered 454 casualties and those of RAF Thirty-eighth and Forty-sixth Groups, 294.[75]

Conclusions

In many ways Operation Market was a remarkable and spectacular success. The nearness which it came to complete and unqualified success made all the more disappointing the failure of the ground forces to link up with the British First Airborne Division at Arnhem. The appraisal of the operation by First Allied Airborne Army Headquarters was as follows:

> The Airborne troops accomplished what was expected of them. It was the breakdown of the Second Army's time table on the first day – their failure to reach Eindhoven in 6 to 8 hours as planned – that caused the delay in the taking of the Nijmegen bridge and the failure at Arnhem.
>
> The airborne operations proceeded not only according to plan but with much less loss than expected. Daylight airborne operations over enemy territory heavily defended by flak have been considered excessively hazardous. "Market" has proved this view erroneous. The great dividends in accuracy of drop and landing and in quick assembly of troops which may be had from daylight operations were enjoyed to the full. Three factors are chiefly responsible: (1) Strong supporting air forces were available and were skillfully employed to knock out flak positions in advance, to beat flak down during the

> airborne operations themselves, and to protect the troop carriers from hostile aircraft. (2) Excellent staff work so organized the movement of troop carriers, their protection by the supporting air forces, and the drop and landing of troops as to achieve the maximum of surprise. (3) Thorough training of both troop carrier and airborne personnel produced almost perfect accuracy in the drops and landings. Weapons were rapidly retrieved and units quickly formed up for the accomplishment of their initial missions.
>
> From D plus 2 until D plus 6 weather seriously hampered resupply and reinforcement efforts, yet on the whole they too were accurately effected. It is true that higher rates of loss were suffered in these succeeding days, but this must be, and was, expected in view of increasing enemy resistance.[76]

Actually to what extent the "breakdown of the Second Army's time table on the first day – their failure to reach Eindhoven in 6 to 8 hours as planned" was responsible for the failure to reach Arnhem, and to what extent it was due to conditions which the airborne divisions themselves might have altered is problematical. If the Second Army would have reached Eindhoven in six to eight hours, that is by 2200 on D Day, troops of the 101st Airborne Division would not yet have arrived there to meet them. At that hour, the 506th Parachute Infantry still was crossing the Wilhelmina Canal in Zon. It also had been anticipated (in General Taylor's letter to General Dempsey) that troops of the 101st Airborne Division would reach Eindhoven within about five hours after landing. Moreover all the bridges at Zon had been blown before paratroops could seize them, and the wait for engineers to build a bridge would have occurred anyway.

When the Guards Armored Division did reach Nijmegen, on D plus 2, the Eighty-second Airborne Division had not completed its assigned task of seizing the bridge. Not until late the next day were tanks able to cross the bridge.

Therefore while it is conceivable that the operation might have been a complete success if the British Second Army could have moved more quickly, it is also conceivable that the ground army could have moved rapidly enough to complete the junction at Arnhem in time if the airborne divisions had been able to capture Eindhoven more quickly, had seized the bridge at Zon intact, and had seized the bridge at Nijmegen before the armored spearheads approached.

Many factors contributed to the outcome of Operation Market-Garden. A change in any one of them might have brought a quite different result. The operation might have been completely successful if good fortune or insight could have changed any *one* of a series of conditions which happened to prevail. The outcome *might* have been completely successful if: (1) the British had been able to concentrate their drops nearer the objective, and to drop or land troops near the south end of the Arnhem Bridge on D Day; (2) the weather had permitted the Polish Parachute Brigade and the 325th Glider Infantry to be dropped and landed on D plus 2 as planned; (3) the weather had not delayed the arrival of the Fourth Parachute Brigade from morning till afternoon on D plus 1; (4) II SS Panzer Corps had not happened to be refitting near Arnhem, or at least if Allied intelligence had been aware of its location; (5) communications had been adequate with the British First Airborne Division so that Airborne Corps and First Allied Airborne Army might have been aware sooner of the seriousness of the situation at Arnhem; (6) it had been possible to deliver the entire airborne strength of the three divisions in not more than two lifts instead of over such a long period of time; (7) American glider pilots had been organized and trained to make a more effective contribution to ground combat.

Arrival of the First Polish Parachute Brigade on D plus 2 at the drop zone originally intended near the south end of the Arnhem bridge, at the time when British troops still were firmly intrenched at the north end, could have been decisive. The 325th Glider Infantry might have provided just the extra strength which the Eighty-second Airborne Division needed to seize the Nijmegen bridge while defending itself against attacks from the south and east. Had the British Thirtieth Corps been able to speed across that bridge as soon as it arrived, it might yet have reached the Lower Rhine in time to relieve the First Airborne Division. Or even the arrival of the Fourth Parachute Brigade a few hours earlier, as scheduled, on D plus 1 might have been enough for the 1st Airborne Division to consolidate in a strong position before German troops had had time to build up such strong counterattacks. All these things depended upon the weather, and good weather failed to continue. Yet an airborne operation hardly could be planned on the assumption that the weather – a condition far more critical for airborne than for ordinary ground operations – would be more favorable than usual for that region in that time of year. Weather was poor, but it was no worse than could have been expected: "While the weather encountered could not be termed ideal, it would be termed 'above average' in favor of the operation for this time of year."[77]

That the German II SS Panzer Corps was refitting near Arnhem was a fortuitous circumstance. It was the kind of condition which might be encountered in any airborne operation. Actually an intelligence trace had noted that armored divisions might be refitting in the area of the Reichswald,[78] but that seemed to have little direct influence on planning. It is doubtful that a similar notation for the Arnhem area would have made a great deal of difference either, though precise information might have brought some effective tactical air strikes. Possibility of armored counterattack always was of the greatest concern for an airborne division.

One of the greatest failings in the operation was that of communications. Airborne Corps was not aware of the seriousness of the situation of First Airborne Division at Arnhem until forty-eight hours too late. In response to an offer by the commander of the Fifty-second (Lowland) Division to send a force in gliders to aid the First Airborne Division, General Browning had sent (on D plus 5) the following message. "Thanks for your message but offer not repeat not required as situation better than you think. We want lifts as already planned including Poles. Second Army definitely require your party and intend to fly you in to Deelen airfield as soon as situation allows."[79] If communications had been adequate, Airborne Corps might have arranged to accept that offer, or it might have issued orders to the First Airborne Division to move westward to the area of Renkum when such a movement was yet possible; in that area a good bridgehead might have been held until Thirtieth Corps could cross relatively unopposed.[80] After the operation First Allied Airborne Army gave a great deal of attention to the correction of communication inadequacies.[81]

From the moment that airborne forces landed they faced three conflicting tasks: the accomplishment of their assigned missions – a task which became progressively more difficult as the enemy recovered from his initial surprise; the continued protection of drop and landing zones as long as additional air lifts were to come, and the blocking or fending off of enemy reserves moving up to interfere with the mission. All this suggests that airborne troops should be used in mass and the rate of their build-up must be rapid.[82] If all the Allied airborne troops used in the invasion of Holland could have been committed on the first two days, the final outcome might have been different. A much greater initial force, or very rapid reinforcement, might have made possible complete and permanent control of the Arnhem bridge as well as earlier seizure of the Nijmegen bridge. A German analysis concluded that the Allies' chief mistake was in failing to land the entire First Airborne Division at once rather than over an extended period, and in not landing another airborne division (perhaps the U.S. Seventeenth Airborne Division, known to be in the United Kingdom) where it could have added possibly decisive strength at Arnhem. First Allied Airborne Army did not have at its disposal enough aircraft to carry the airborne divisions in greater mass than they did. Aside from acquiring more aircraft another possibility might have saved the situation: the basing of at least a sizeable part of the troop carrier and airborne forces on the Continent. If the operation, at least in good part, could have been mounted from airfields in Belgium and northern France, it might have been possible to fly two lifts on a single day instead of one, double glider tows might have been used for the shorter distance, and much of the bad weather – that which interfered with operations over England but not over the Continent – might have been avoided. Tactical air forces, however, occupied all the suitable airfields. The question of providing adequate troop carrier bases on the Continent was one which would have had to be anticipated in strategic planning long in advance of operations. (The statement of policy which the Combined Chiefs of Staff had issued in February 1944 – CCS 496 – had emphasized that airborne troops should be kept well forward.) It was another case when tactical air forces took priority over troop carriers to the exclusion of the latter, when closer planning might have provided adequately for both.

Conceivably, gliders might have been taken in double tow anyway, or two missions might have been flown as was done in southern France. Greater use of bombers and earlier discovery and exploitation of the airfield near Grave might have made a considerable difference.

Another German study suggested that if the airborne operation had been timed to take place well *after* the armored attack on the ground had gained momentum, the results might have been decisive, for then no German reserves would have been left to turn against the airborne troops.[83]

If the glider pilots available to the Eighty-second Airborne Division on D plus 1 had been organized and trained to participate effectively in ground combat, those pilots might have been assigned a defensive sector for the time being along the Reichswald front. This might have released parachute troops there for an attack on the Nijmegen bridge. Such an attack conceivably could have resulted in the earlier capture of the bridge and the relief of the British First Airborne Division at Arnhem.[84] British Airborne Corps considered the British system under which glider pilots were assigned to the Army rather than the Air Force, and were organized into the equivalent of battalions, companies, and platoons, and trained to fight as infantry, to be far superior to the American. It reported that the stand made by the First Airborne Division, and its subsequent withdrawal across the Lower Rhine, would have been impossible without the assistance given by the organization and training of the 1,200 glider pilots. Commanders of both the Eighty-second and 101st Airborne Divisions expressed a need for better organization and control of glider pilots after landing. It was a problem which had been anticipated in maneuvers, it had appeared in operations in Sicily, Italy, and Normandy, and after repeated recommendations for improving the situation, the problem was as evident as ever in Holland. General Gavin described it in this way:

> . . . One thing in most urgent need of correction, is the method of handling our glider pilots. I do not believe there is anyone in the combat area more eager and anxious to do the correct thing and yet so completely, individually and collectively, incapable of doing it than our glider pilots.

> Despite their individual willingness to help, I feel that they were definitely a liability to me. Many of them arrived without blankets, some without rations and water, and a few improperly armed and equipped. They lacked organization of their own because of, they stated, frequent transfer from one Troop Carrier Command unit to another. Despite the instructions that were issued to them to move via command channels to Division Headquarters, they frequently became involved in small unit actions to the extent that satisfied their passing curiosity, or simply left to visit nearby towns. In an airborne operation where, if properly planned, the first few hours are the quietest, this can be very harmful, since all units tend to lose control because of the many people wandering about aimlessly, improperly equipped, out of uniform, and without individual or unit responsibilities. When the enemy reaction builds up and his attack increases in violence and intensity, the necessity for every man to be on the job at the right place, doing his assigned task, is imperative. At this time glider pilots without unit assignment and improperly trained, aimlessly wandering about cause confusion and generally get in the way and have to be taken care of.
>
> In this division, glider pilots were used to control traffic, to recover supplies from the LZ's, guard prisoners, and finally were assigned a defensive role with one of the regiments at a time when they were badly needed.
>
> I feel very keenly that the glider pilot problem at the moment is one of our greatest unsolved problems. I believe now that they should be assigned to airborne units, take training with the units and have a certain number of hours allocated periodically for flight training.[85]

General Ridgway, commander of XVIII Corps (Airborne) did not go along with the proposal to place glider pilots under the command of division commanders for full-time ground training. "British practice to the contrary notwithstanding," glider pilots, General Ridgway thought, were where they belonged: in the troop carrier squadrons. They could receive whatever ground training they needed with their associated airborne divisions.[86] This apparently was no change from the policy which had created the problems which were of so much concern to the airborne division commanders.

While it may be true that a change in only one of a number of unfortunate conditions might have resulted in success for the whole operation, doubtless it is also true that less fortunate circumstances – any one of several – might have spelled complete disaster. Success might have been much less if: (1) the enemy, instead of being disorganized as the result of long and rapid retreats, had been in well-organized positions with command and control completely reestablished; (2) the enemy air force had been able to come out in greater force; (3) the civilian population had been hostile instead of actively helpful; (4) German troops had blown all the bridges before Allied paratroops could reach them; (5) the weather had been even worse; (6) more reserves, especially in armor, had been available to the enemy; (7) the British Thirtieth Corps had failed to link up as soon as they did. Airborne commanders pointed out that this had been a "marginal performance," and they expressed the fear that their very success might lead in the future to commitment in less favorable circumstances and the sacrifice of their divisions in an effort beyond their capabilities.[87]

The problem of resupplying the troops by air had not yet been solved satisfactorily in Operation Market. Airborne commanders were agreed that resupply by parachute should be regarded only as an emergency expedient. The scattered drops meant that the fighting strength of the division had to be weakened to provide recovery details, and many bundles were lost. Gliders, when they could get in, were of course much more reliable, but the use of one-way gliders, each requiring a pilot, was an expensive means. Supposedly the "approved solution" was to prepare a forward delivery airfield where supplies could be landed by airplane. But that procedure would depend upon the situation – how long it was expected that airborne troops would need resupply by air, and whether enough troops were at hand to clear and defend a forward airfield. In this operation one field had been put to use briefly, but then a conflict had developed with the tactical air forces. British Airborne Corps presented the airborne point of view: "There is no doubt that this conflict is inevitable and changing conditions during the battle (e.g. in this case the strengthening of the Luftwaffe in the area) may upset pre-arranged priorities. It is not agreed, however, that priority for all airfields everywhere must go to the tactical air forces on all occasions." In his report the engineer officer concluded that one or more airfields should be among the primary objectives in any airborne operation, and that an airfield should not be given a secondary priority after bridges or town, because the airfield might be indispensable to the holding of other objectives, coordination then should be made effective on a high level.[88] This generally had been the assumption in airborne maneuvers, though statements of doctrine had not made that procedure mandatory. General Ridgway thought that the generalization that landing strips should always be constructed was not justified.[89] Better communication might have improved the supply situation. A troop carrier air control party with each division, equipped to communicate with troop carrier headquarters and with the planes, could have prevented some of the drops into enemy territory.[90]

Airborne commanders after Operation Market generally agreed as to the soundness of airborne doctrine as laid down in War Department Training Circular No. 113. General Ridgway wrote: "I cannot too strongly urge the study, the mastery, and the application, by all upon whom devolved any degree of responsibility for the employment of airborne forces, of the principles enunciated in War Department Training Circular No. 113, 9 October 1943."[91] Probably the operation's greatest contribution was its demonstration of the feasibility, and advantages, of a major airborne operation in daylight under the conditions then prevailing. But the results seemed to cool some of the sentiment which had been expressed from time to time for a long-range strategic envelopment and prolonged action from an independent airhead. The Germans found a general opinion among Allied prisoners whom they captured that ground forces must make contact with airborne troops within three days. From this Army Group B drew the conclusion that far-reaching airborne landings in the future were unlikely. It was expected that the next airborne attacks would be in conjunction with ground attacks or seaborne landings. The German view was that the next airborne operation would not likely take place behind sections of the West Wall remaining intact, because the Allies probably would not think it possible for a ground attack to break through there within three days.[92] General Brereton wrote as follows: "[The enemy] has the ability to reinforce any threatened area quickly. Therefore, it is vital that the Airborne thrust be joined with the ground thrust in a minimum of time to avoid undue losses. The armament of airborne troops does not permit sustained operations against a prolonged attack by heavy weapons and armored forces."[93]

Operation Market unquestionably was the best planned and the most skillfully executed large-scale airborne operation thus far. The experience of earlier operations played an important part in that achievement, but it is not unlikely that the existence of an over-all coordinating agency in the First Allied Airborne Army helped in large measure to make it possible. This centralized control of all airborne and troop carrier forces, together with the direction of all associated air forces, was the culmination of a trend which had been developing since the Sicily operation.

Faulty organization still seemed to be evident in the airborne division. Both the Eighty-second and the 101st Airborne Divisions had continued to depart from the published tables of organization and equipment in effecting a more practicable organization. Both commanders repeated their recommendations for reorganization.

Although the failure at Arnhem had tended to overshadow the real success of the airborne and troop carrier units themselves, Operation Market had demonstrated the feasibility of mass airborne operations in daylight. The mission was not the kind which would have appealed to airborne officers as the most desirable kind, for the units on the ground had been widely separated along a narrow corridor which made consolidation and holding difficult. But on the whole the airborne divisions had gained their assigned objectives, and they had demonstrated something of the potentially decisive influence which airborne operations might have. The effectiveness of the joint operation, aside from the planning and coordination which had gone into it, was a tribute to the training of the participating units. As the troop carrier report put it, "Training should never be allowed to bog down when results are so gratifying."[94]

Chapter II

A New Approach in Warfare

Development of an Idea

Possibly the first serious plan for the employment of parachute troops in combat operations was that of Brig. Gen. William Mitchell when, in October 1918, he won acceptance for a proposal to capture Metz by parachuting from Allied bombers a strong part of an infantry division in the rear of the German defenses. To work out the details of the plan he called upon the future commander of the First Allied Airborne Army (Lt. Gen. Lewis H. Brereton), then a young Air Service staff officer. But the Armistice came before the plan could be put into effect.[1]

Such plans received little consideration in military circles during the years immediately following World War I. It was for the Russians to arouse widespread general interest in the possibilities of airborne warfare with their maneuvers and demonstrations during the 1930's. In what probably was the first use of parachute troops in a major tactical exercise, a lieutenant and eight men jumped in the Moscow area during Red Army maneuvers in 1930. The Red Army organized an "Airlanding Corps" in 1935, and transported a whole airborne division from Moscow to Vladivostok. A Russian propaganda film on the subject that same year further kindled interest in other countries. Foreign observers at maneuvers near Kiev in 1936 became missionaries for this new kind of warfare. They watched two battalions, with sixteen light field guns and 150 machine guns, land in eight minutes, and immediately occupy the town which was their objective. In the United States and other countries, the idea found favor with some, but others rejected it with scorn. Significantly, it aroused the most immediate enthusiasm in Italy and Germany.[2] The United States had experimented briefly with parachute troops as early as 1928. In one test a formation of four two-place observation planes dropped three men and a machine gun at Brooks Field, Texas; the men assembled the gun, and had it in operation within a few minutes. However, little enthusiasm developed, and the experiments had been discontinued.[3]

Problems of airborne warfare first appeared in the curriculum of the Command and General Staff School at Fort Leavenworth in 1938.[4] Later, exercises at the school would raise many of the questions of doctrine which were to demand answers in organizing an airborne effort, and officers associated with studies there were to play an important part in developing that doctrine.[5]

But the Germans made the first effective use of airborne troops in major combat operations. The descent of parachutists in Norway, Holland, and Belgium to pave the way for the capture of airfields and reduction of fortifications in 1940 startled anew a world not yet recovered from the accounts of air-ground blitzkrieg in Poland and Scandinavia. Spearheading the German drive through the low countries in May, a small force of 500 parachutists captured the crossings of the Albert Canal intact. Two officers and seventy-eight men arrived by glider atop the broad roof of the great Belgian fort, Eben Emael, and held the garrison at bay until mechanized infantry arrived the next day. In April 1941 Germans used gliderborne troops in the seizure of Corinth. Less than a month later they offered their final demonstration that airborne troops were "here to stay" – the parachute, glider, and airlanding assault of Crete. The capture of that strategic island in the eastern Mediterranean left a lasting impression on Allied armies.[6]

Ironically, while the spectacular German success at Crete urged the Allies to new efforts, it was so costly to the attacker that it was the last major airborne operation that the Germans attempted in the war.* While the British recoiled in dismay, and anticipated where next the dreaded German airborne forces might strike, Hitler was saying, "Crete proves that the days of the paratroopers are over." The British and Commonwealth land and sea forces lost over 4,000 men killed. But so did the German airborne forces. Indeed the German losses by the end of the first day were greater than those for any other single day up to that time in the war.[7a] Although the Crete operation gave impetus to the program already being organized in the United States, it was recognized as being no more than a

* The Germans undertook only two tactical parachute attacks after the Crete invasion. Both were of battalion size. One was at Leros (a Greek island of the Dodecanese group) in the fall of 1943, and the other was in the Ardennes in December 1944. Translation of Airborne Operations: A German Appraisal, written after the war by Hellmuth Reinhardt, a former German staff officer, in collaboration with the German ex-officers, p. 34. In the Foreign Studies Section, OCMH. MS # P-051.

point of departure. When, about a year later, Army Ground Forces circulated copies of the German instructions for that operation, it was with the direction that they were being sent only for historical purposes, as an example, and were not to be accepted as illustrative of American methods.[7]

Inauguration of the Airborne Effort

At first, American leaders generally had limited their conception of airborne warfare to an assumption that parachutists would operate primarily in small combat groups against key communication and supply installations in enemy rear areas.

From the beginning of airborne activity, Maj. Gen. Lesley J. McNair, commanding general, and other officers of the Army Ground Forces had held to a concept of using standard infantry divisions in airborne operations. Even after the activation of airborne divisions this idea remained, and in 1942 the Airborne Command had proceeded with the training of the Second Infantry Division in air transportation. Such training not only would prepare additional divisions for the exploitation of airborne assaults, but it would lend a greater strategic flexibility in any employment. An ability to shift divisions by air would be the equivalent of adding divisions to a commander's total force.

In May 1942 Field Manual 31-30, "Tactics and Technique of Airborne Troops," appeared. It was difficult to say that parachute troops "generally" perform in a certain way when no American airborne troops had as yet participated in any kind of an operation, but much of what the publication presented remained valid in the test of combat, and much was retained in later statements of policy and doctrine. Really fundamental statements of doctrine were, of course, outside the scope of the field manual, and that area remained void for the time being. Parachute troops were considered "the spearhead of a vertical envelopment or the advance and guard element of air landing troops or other forces." The concept of airborne warfare generally was one which envisaged the seizure of suitable landing areas by parachute troops, and then their reinforcement by troops arriving by glider or airplane. But a whole series of possible objectives for parachute troops was listed: river and canal crossings, defiles, establishing bridgeheads; attack of defended positions by landing on flank or in rear, or within the perimeter; destruction of enemy supply and communication installations; consolidation and holding of ground taken by armored forces until the arrival of other ground units; and assistance to ground offensives by vertical envelopment.[8] It pointed to the need for thorough preparation and advance planning for any operation – reconnaissance, liaison with air transport units, pilot-jumpmaster conferences, desirability of rehearsal

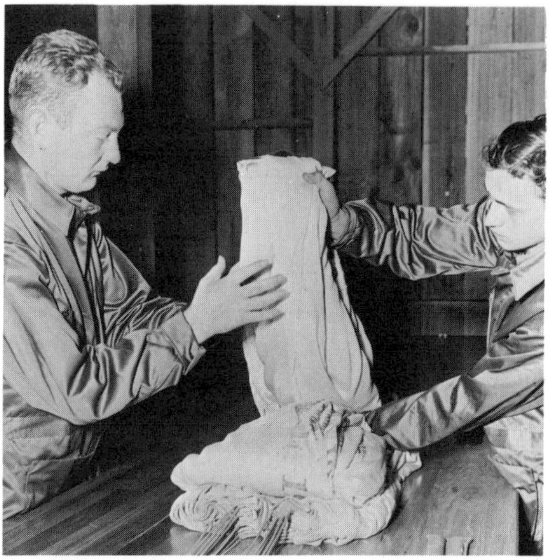

Members of the 501st Parachute Battalion learn to pack a parachute at Fort Benning, April 1941.

During early training of infantry for airlanding, members of the Ninth Infantry (Second Division) load an antitank gun into a C-47 transport at Fort Sam Houston, January 1941.

of the operation.[9] One section was devoted to operations to seize airfields.[10]

Many details remained yet to be worked out. By August 1942 it was clear to the Airborne Command that some standardization in procedure was necessary. It proposed, therefore, that a board of air and ground officers be appointed to recommend standard techniques in such matters as staff planning, troop loading, resupply, mutual identification and communication, control, formations, and pilot-jumpmaster coordination. The proposal won the approval of all concerned.[11] It did not take many exercises to demonstrate the desirability of working out other standard operating procedures for airborne-troop carrier operations. One of the first requirements was to agree upon a prescribed altitude for parachute jumping. The decision was that the novice paratrooper's first jump was to be at 1500 feet. A minimum altitude of 1200 feet was set for the early stage of parachute training. In transition to operational training, an altitude of 800 feet was prescribed, and it was found that operational jumps should be at altitudes of 500 feet or less.[12] In April 1943 a joint airborne-troop carrier board reported its recommendations for a standard technique for parachute jumps and procedure for planning parachute operations: It was agreed that planes should fly at speeds no less than 100 miles per hour and no greater than 120 miles per hour for a parachute jump. Ten minutes out from the drop zone pilots were to sound an alert signal. Two minutes out, the pilot was to flash the red light over the door as the signal for the men to stand, and move toward the door. At the drop zone the pilot was to flash the green light which was the signal for the leading man to jump. In night operations the alert signal would be sounded fifteen instead of ten minutes before arrival over the drop zone.[13]

Among those most concerned with the development of a far-reaching airborne doctrine were the chief of staff and the secretary of war themselves. Visiting General Eisenhower in Algiers while the North African campaign was in progress, General Marshall discussed the idea "that in the proper development of airborne operations lies one field in which we have real opportunity and capability to get ahead of the enemy."[14]

After a conversation with Secretary of War Henry L. Stimson on 2 October 1943, G. H. Dorr, special assistant to the secretary, reduced to writing the questions which had been raised – questions which again went to the heart of the whole problem:

> 1. Have we overcome the inherent difficulty in effectively knitting together Air and Ground functions (a) in provision of equipment, (b) in training and (c) in tactics in air borne operations?
>
> a. The Air Forces part in this function both as to equipment and operation is a diversion from the straight line of the Air Forces job of direct attack.

> b. While the operation becomes ultimately a Ground Force operation, the equipment for transport, the actual transport and the protection are furnished by another force over which they have no control.
>
> 2. Were the questions raised by analysis of airborne maneuvers in this country taken account of in the Sicilian operations? Is the organizational set up such that the lessons of both and of the efficient New Guinea operation will be given effective application in prospective operations?[15]

At the top of the memorandum was this notation:

> To OPD and AGF. I have had the query raised to me before. I should like to know if the subject is receiving any attention.
>
> H. L. S.

Statement of Doctrine

Such immediate concern was not always evident among those directly responsible for airborne development. In Field Manual 100-20, the Air Forces' "Declaration of Independence" published 21 July 1943, little attention was given to troop carrier aircraft or to the role of the Air Forces in airborne operations. In a statement devoted to a presentation of the case for concentrated air action under air commanders, mention of troop carrier activity was confined to a definition: "Troop carrier (including gliders) is the term applied to air units which carry parachute troops, airborne troops and cargo."[16] True, that was another subject, but the spirit of independence indicated in the publication of this field manual suggested little immediate interest in troop carrier-airborne operations. Indeed the definition which it offered for troop carrier aviation did little to clarify the confusion already apparent between activities of the Troop Carrier Command and the Air Transport Command.

On this point a board of officers headed by Maj. Gen. Joseph M. Swing sought to define the functions more clearly:

> After the combat zone becomes incorporated in the communication zone the Air Transport Command assumes the function of air transportation. Troop Carrier Units are combat units and as such, while they are not participating in actual combat operations, they should be in training in preparation for such combat operations and should not be diverted to freight handling which might prevent their proper training for combat.[17]

This was ideal from the point of view of airborne and troop carrier units, but it ran against demands for delivering supplies by air, and from that point of view it meant an uneconomical use of airplanes. As long as training was regarded as something which could be done without, and as long as commanders – in particular, commanders of ground armies – regarded immediate supply difficulties as more important than future airborne operations, the recommended procedure was one not likely to be attained.

No satisfactory airborne program could be expected without the attention – and the imagination – of all concerned in its development. Imagination in the early period seemed to be confined to a few enthusiasts who became active in the program, but it faced the deterrent of apathy elsewhere. In October 1943 Col. Josiah T. Dalbey, Airborne Command chief of staff, wrote:

> One of our basic troubles has been the failure to properly evaluate this new weapon, from topside down; I speak feelingly in this regard from experience in G-3, where it was an up-hill struggle, and from trying to run this outfit the past year. Both RAF in England and the AAF here are extremely apathetic toward anything airborne. I was at British Airborne Headquarters the day after the Sicily landing and that morning eight general officers from the British war office descended on the place to find out what-in-hell was this parachute glider thing that had appeared suddenly in the news reports. A similar visit in these parts would not have been inappropriate. Our AAF Chief has been too busy to give the personal prod to troop carrier developments in this country until about two months ago.[18]

Dalbey went on to say that although here was a military weapon of widest capability, it seemed that it might "suffer through lack of use or intentional abuse." He felt strongly that thinking should go beyond plans for use of airborne troops in connection with the amphibious assault against Europe, that plans should be contemplating widespread use of airborne units in subsequent European operations and in the Pacific. He saw good indications in the greater interest which General Arnold had been taking recently, in the informal acceptance by General Devers of the idea of setting up an airborne section on his staff in the European theater, and in the calling of a conference by Maj. Gen. Ray E. Porter (War Department G-3) for the ironing out of differences. He suspected that in the conference the non-existence of a suitable tactical doctrine would "come to life." He felt that there was a need for an airborne forces equivalent to Field Manual 100-20.

A statement of doctrine did in fact follow. A new War Department training circular, "Employment of Airborne and Troop Carrier Forces" was approved on 9 October, and advance copies of the circular, bearing the notice: "This Advanced Copy Training Circular will be distributed to all airborne units in the continental United States the size of a company or larger," were sent out on the 12th. General Marshall personally directed that copies be sent to theater commanders.[19] Later the document was published as Training Circular 113, 9 October 1943.

The circular defined troop carrier units as: "Army Air Forces units which are specially organized, trained, and equipped to transport airborne troops and supplies into combat. Troop carrier units should not be confused with elements of the Air Transport Command which have the primary mission of transporting personnel, supplies, and mail between theaters."[20] The principle was laid down that airborne units should not be employed unless necessary for the accomplishment of the mission of the force as a whole, nor for missions which could be performed more economically by other troops. The doctrine called for the employment of airborne troops in mass, but stated: "Airborne troops should not be employed unless they can be supported by other ground or naval forces within approximately 3 days, or unless they can be withdrawn after their mission has been accomplished."

The need for training was emphasized: "Realistic and thorough joint training for all units participating in an airborne operation should be conducted. Thorough training in technical aspects is not sufficient. Training for specific missions must cover all details and contingencies, and culminate in a rehearsal of the operation with conditions approximating as closely as possible those of the actual operation."[21]

The listing of missions suitable for airborne troops followed generally those which had been given in Field Manual 31-30, though there was no longer the underlying assumption that seizure of airfields and reinforcement by airlanding troops would be the normal procedure – the limitation of "approximately 3 days" for independent action without support from ground or naval forces seemed to rule out the strategic employment of airborne troops deep within enemy territory with dependence solely on air support. One important consideration was added: that was the use of airborne forces "as a constant threat by their mere presence in the theater of operations thereby causing the enemy to disperse his forces over a wide area in order to protect his vital installations."[22] Here was a new application of the naval concept of the "fleet in being."

Section III of the training circular defined the troop carrier commander's responsibilities, the airborne commander's responsibilities, and the airborne and troop carrier commanders' joint responsibilities.

Doctrine Reaffirmed

Airborne and troop carrier leaders and higher commanders and general staff officers looked anxiously to airborne operations in combat for guidance in establishing or improving doctrine, developing new equipment, drawing up better tables of organization and equipment, and improving training. Sometimes changes which seemed to commanders in the theaters obvious improvements were long in coming, but clearly those recommendations and the reports of observers in the theaters had great impact on the development of future forces and future operations. These efforts for improvement continued right on to the end of the war and afterward.

From the area which had seen the major airborne operations thus far in the war, the Northwest African Air Forces recorded its "complete accord" with Training Circular 113, with two exceptions. Suggesting that there might be instances when small groups could accomplish the desired mission, it objected to the impression that airborne troops could be employed only in mass. The other objection was to a statement in the circular that night airborne operations were not feasible unless a quarter moon or better were assumed. The development of pathfinder units in the future might well extend the possibilities of night operations.[23] Allied Force Headquarters and War Department Operations Division concurred in those views.[24]

On the basis of the experience of the Eighty-second Airborne Division in Sicily and Italy., Maj. Gen. Matthew B. Ridgway, its commander, generally supported the War Department's statement of policy. His recommendation was that the airborne division be committed as a whole rather than piecemeal. He re-emphasized the need for exact planning, for careful coordination with other troops including air and naval, and the need for several weeks of training for each specific operation.[25]

Field Manual 101-10, "Staff Officers' Field Manual, Organization, Technical, and Logistical Data," published 18 October 1943, included a section on movement by air transport. It outlined the procedure, orders to respective commanders, initial studies, conference between commanders, plans and orders of the cooperating units.[26] This manual defined troop carrier units as follows:

> These are combat units organized, equipped and trained for tactical employment as combat carriers in active operations in the combat zone. Their primary mission is to carry combat troops and auxiliary combat equipment to effective locations in the combat zones from which to begin active combat operations. Their secondary mission is to maintain combat supply and resupply to units in the combat zone and to evacuate casualties and other personnel and material from such zones.[27]

Much of the difficulty of the airborne program grew out of a conflict between demands for the primary and for the secondary missions, or perhaps more exactly, a conflict arising from airborne-troop carrier training needs, on the one hand, and too broad an interpretation of maintaining "combat supply . . . to units in the combat zone," on the other.

Meanwhile a study of airborne policy undertaken by the Combined Chiefs of Staff pointed in a similar direction, but went further. The Combined Staff Planners considered current policy for the employment of airborne forces sound, but noted that up to that time such forces had not been employed *en masse.* They recognized the need for close coordination among land, sea, and air forces. They felt that possibilities for the use of airborne forces were of broader scope than had been indicated generally. They were convinced that airborne forces could be employed *en masse* in independent operations to attack and hold ground. Limitations on such employment would be the availability of transport aircraft, the firepower furnished by supporting combat aircraft, and the weapons, supplies, and reinforcements that could be brought in by air.[28] They held it to be essential that either airborne troops or airlanding troops, or both, be maintained as a reserve and a threat in each major theater of operations.[29]

The study continued through the early months of 1944. The United States Joint Chiefs of Staff found the material presented by the Combined Planners to be "a valuable compilation of information," but it brought no significant change in policy. In fact it was found that in many cases events had overtaken the recommendations. The Joint War Plans Committee (JWPC) recommended in January 1944 that capable troop carrier and airborne advisers should be included on the immediate staffs of theater and air commanders in theaters where airborne operations were contemplated. More specifically it recommended an expansion of the airborne effort in the Pacific, and urged that the Air Forces be prepared for rapid redeployment of troop carrier groups to the Pacific upon the defeat of Germany.[30]

The army members in February restated most of those recommendations in a proposed report to be presented by the Combined Planners to the Combined Chiefs of Staff.[31] The Combined Planners accepted the recommendations, in general, in a report circulated for approval by the Combined Chiefs. The report reaffirmed the soundness of the principles stated in War Department Training Circular 113, 9 October 1943, but it noted that higher commands generally had failed to follow the policies as established. The result was a serious gap between established policy and training methods, on the one hand, and operational execution on the other. But the report went further. Referring to the German operation against Crete as proof that it was practicable to use airborne troops *en masse* in independent offensive operations, the Combined Staff Planners pointed out that the Allies so far had failed to undertake any similar operation even though their airborne potential and capability was far greater than the enemy's. "Apparently we have lacked the boldness of thought and execution essential to airborne operations on a large scale."[32]

The report noted that the use of parachute and glider troops as a team in which the former seize landing zones for the latter had not yet been attempted, but it reaffirmed the far-reaching potentialities in that concept. Another criticism was the length of time which had been required to plan an airborne operation and the consequent failure to use airborne troops to exploit success. It was suggested that one cause might have been the basing of airborne troops and troop carrier aircraft too far to the rear. It was recommended, therefore, that they be kept well forward. The report recommended further study of the problems of supply by air for large-scale airborne operations, and suggested the use of bombers and of transport planes ordinarily assigned to other missions. It recommended continued study of the problems of troop carrier navigation and the possible use of pathfinders. Finally, the paper noted troop carrier units too often were being assigned to theaters on a semi-permanent basis regardless of the need for them for airborne operations. It suggested that both troop carrier and airborne troops should be shifted from one theater to another as needed. But airborne troops, designed primarily for use whenever the opportunity might arise,should not be used in roles for which other units were suited and available.[33]

In a meeting of the Joint Chiefs of Staff, General Marshall explained that he had sent his own views on the employment of airborne troops to Eisenhower and that their proper employment was well understood. Admiral Leahy raised the question whether the report was necessary if the commanders already were planning the employment of airborne troops as recommended in the report, but Arnold thought that the report would serve a useful purpose, and the Joint Chiefs agreed to recommend its approval.[34] The Combined Chiefs of Staff, after Marshall had explained Eisenhower's reaction to his proposal for strategic use of airborne forces, approved the report.[35] Thus the highest strategic planning agency of the Western Allies had concurred in a far-reaching statement of airborne doctrine which could be interpreted only as an action aimed at the expansion of the airborne effort toward greater things. Operations Division sent nineteen copies of the report to the adjutant general for dispatch to the various theater and air commanders.[36]

Already, in December 1943, staff officers of the chief of staff to the supreme Allied commander (COSSAC), with the advice of Brig. Gen. James M. Gavin, had begun the preparation of a statement of policy to govern the use of airborne troops in the Overlord operations.[37] Published in January as a memorandum of Supreme Headquarters, Allied Expeditionary Force (SHAEF), the statement of principles followed generally the pronouncements of War Department Training Circular 113 and paralleled the report then being considered by planners for the Combined Chiefs of Staff. But beyond its agreed generalities and appeals for coordination, the memorandum anticipated the possible use of airborne troops in purely ground roles: "If appropriate opportunities to employ airborne troops on airborne missions do not appear imminent, or if sufficient aircraft to permit employment of the Division as a whole are not available, the Division should be unhesitatingly employed as a whole as a light infantry combat division with missions appropriate to its fire power and combat strength."[38] Recognizing the limitations of airborne organizations, the memorandum added that additional motor transportation and medical, engineer, signal, and quartermaster support must be provided when the division was assigned to a ground role. Similar additions should also be made, it stated, when airborne divisions were to be employed for sustained mobile operations after landing.

The memorandum called for general joint training and for special training to prepare for each specific operation. However, it repeated the principle that airborne troops, especially trained and equipped to accomplish specific tasks, should not be used on missions which could be performed more economically by other forces.[39] The supreme commander was responsible for the employment of all airborne and troop carrier units. After a decision to use those forces, the supreme commander would issue orders to the commander in chief, Allied Expeditionary Air Force (who controlled the troop carrier units and was responsible for the planning and execution of the air aspects of an airborne operation), and to the army group commander under whom the airborne troops would operate. Orders and joint planning then would proceed through lower units.[40] Publication of a standing operating procedure for airborne and troop carrier units followed in March. It outlined the duties of liaison officers who were to be exchanged upon the receipt of directives or orders to participate in joint training or combat missions, staff procedures, operating procedures, joint responsibilities of airborne and troop carrier commanders, responsibilities of troop carrier units, responsibilities of airborne units, a schedule of planning for airborne operations, and a special appendix setting forth rules for navigation and the use of pathfinder units.[41]

Meanwhile Arnold continued to be concerned about the lack of long-range planning for more extensive use of airborne forces. In February 1944 he directed the Army Air Forces Board to "institute a study immediately which will outline the possible future airborne operations not only in the European Theater but also in the China-Burma-India Theater and the Southwest Pacific Theater."[42]

In April the Air Forces Board reported: "The conception of airborne operations has been too limited in scope to permit treatment of large scale operations on other than broad lines . . . Unfortunately, because of other obvious higher priorities, it had not been possible to provide the necessary air force personnel and equipment required for the rapid and extensive development of troop carrier aviation."[43] The board concluded that current tactical doctrine was inadequate for large scale operations. Other difficulties were that the tactical employment of gliders had not been definitely determined, and that troop carrier and airborne organization and tactical requirements were not "clearly matched." It was suggested that gliders were expensive in aircraft needed, time and space taken, and low battlefield recovery, and should be used only for missions which could be accomplished in no other way.

Colonel Dalbey, commanding the Airborne Center, raised a number of questions about the Air Forces report. Noting a recommendation that the document be published as an Army Air Forces manual, he questioned the advisability of issuing a separate field manual on tactical doctrine of troop carrier aviation which would divorce it from the airborne troop element. He pointed out that already the Airborne Center, on instructions from the War Department and Army Ground Forces, was preparing a manual under the suggested title, "Employment of Airborne and Troop Carrier Forces," and that that project would be coordinated with the Army Air Forces. Dalbey agreed with the desirability of extending general appreciation of the potentialities of airborne operations, but he doubted the usefulness of submitting such a study to the chief of the Army Air Forces.

Certain specific statements to which the Airborne Center commander took exception related to the proposals about large scale operation and organization. He believed that the planning and execution of large scale airborne operations had been precluded not by any lack of conception, but by the limitations of troop carrier aviation. He noted that troop carrier and airborne tactical unity would be desirable, but he said that preservation of separate organizations was understandable. Organization and tactical requirements of troop carriers would be relatively definite regardless of airborne organization and tactical requirements, and the airborne forces were interested only to the extent that aircraft were provided in sufficient numbers. Dalbey agreed on the lack of tactical doctrine for the employment of gliders, but he pointed out that so far only the CG 4A had been made available, and further experience would be necessary to determine best results. But he objected strongly to the suggested curtailment of the use of gliders. He emphasized that glider troops could go into combat with better armament and with better unit organization on landing than could parachutists.[44] Enclosing a copy of his letter to General Eubank, Colonel Dalbey wrote to General Evans at I Troop Carrier Command:

> It is my belief that the Troop Carrier Command and Airborne people have been agreed on most ideas relative to airborne operations up to date, and I regard it as highly important that the Army Air Forces Board does not charge off on a tangent without a

> thorough discussion on the part of all concerned. I am personally curious to know just how much coordination was effected between the Air Forces Board and your headquarters prior to the preparation of their study.[45]

War Department Training Circular 113, 9 October 1943, remained the basis for airborne doctrine throughout the remainder of the war. Other publications were largely duplications, restatements, or summaries of the circular.

Field Manual 100-5, "Field Service Regulation, Operations," published in June 1944, retained in general the statements of the training circular in the chapter on airborne operations.[46] Perhaps of greatest significance in these statements was the retention of the training circular's definition of missions for troop carrier units. The field service regulation repeated the statement, "Troop carrier forces are air forces which are specially organized, trained, and equipped to transport airborne troops and supplies into combat. They should not be confused with elements of the Air Transport Command."[47] But, like the training circular, it also defined the missions of troop carrier units as including, as secondary mission, the transportation of supplies in other than airborne operations.[48] Demands for transport planes for supply missions had an important bearing on the availability of troop carriers for airborne operations and training.

An Air Force study prepared for publication on the Holland airborne operation was referred to AGF for comment. AGF officers objected to a statement that it was axiomatic "that airborne units should not be committed when the commander has offensive mobility in a potentially decisive area of continuous front." They did not concur in the Air Forces statement that "all well conceived airborne operations will resemble bold gambles." Another objection was to the statement, "Troop Carrier lift should be used for emergency purposes." They said that this was a relative statement, and that the day was near when air transport should be considered the normal method of supplying troops. But here it appears that they may have been falling into the same confusion which had appeared so frequently – failure to distinguish between troop carriers and air transport in general.[49]

Still in 1947, in the publication of FM 71-30, "Employment of Airborne Forces," the doctrine of War Department Circular 113 was to remain without very much change. The same definitions of primary and secondary missions for troop carriers were there, and the missions given for airborne troops were essentially the same.[50] About the only additions were these further possible uses:

> To counter enemy airborne attacks by landing close to or on top of the enemy airborne forces.

> To land closely following the action of combat aviation and attack the rear of an enemy front line position before it can recover from the air attack.
>
> To fill or strengthen gaps in positions where this action is difficult for other ground forces to accomplish.[51]

And contrary to the statements of some of the war-time leaders, the assumption remained, "As a rule, airborne forces are not employed independently but are used in coordination with other ground, sea and air forces."[52]

In March 1945 Army Air Forces announced a policy of "air transportability" which had for its objective the development of the means to transport by air any combat or service unit of a division, corps, or army. Noting that thus far the designers of aircraft and of ground equipment had progressed independently, it suggested "that both AGF and AAF designers should make compromises to weld into a perfect entity the airplane and the cargo it is designed to carry."[53] The Air Forces urged that air transportability be included in specifications for new equipment. Its definition of air transportability, for the time being, would be a desired capability of being loaded, with least possible disassembly, within the limitations of the C-46, and a minimum capability of being loaded within the limitations of the C-82 aircraft. While concurring in the general objective of air transportability, Army Ground Forces insisted that battlefield performance should continue to be the governing criterion for the design of any piece of ground forces equipment. AGF held that it would be inadvisable to tie ground equipment to any particular type of airplane. Rather it would be preferable to hold to a general policy of modifying designs – to the extent necessary and without compromising battlefield characteristics – to permit the easy and rapid disassembly of the equipment into the smallest practicable loads.[54]

Strategic Planning

Underlying the training program of any military unit is the employment which is planned for it. This was especially important with regard to airborne troops, for they had no traditional role to play. A great deal of vagueness surrounded the possible employment of airborne units at the time their organization began. This is understandable. At that time plans for employment of most military units in the war effort had not become very precise. In the beginning, the development of a major airborne program was more the result of the impression which the Germans had made in their airborne invasion of Crete than it was of any concrete notions about the probable employment of airborne divisions in some future invasion of Europe. In other words, there was a conviction that some airborne troops would be "handy to have around." Perhaps this is reason enough to justify a military organization, for hardly ever can definite missions be foretold very far in advance. But until strategic planning anticipated the employment of airborne units in specified theaters of operations, those units could not be expected to enjoy a very high priority in training and equipment. When airborne units did appear in such plans, on the other hand, it was reasonable to expect that they would be granted the facilities to prepare for those missions. As early as May 1942, the Operations Division of the War Department General Staff, in its preliminary forecast for the 1943 Troop Basis, allowed for seven airborne divisions. In the Troop Basis as approved by the War Department this figure was reduced to five.[55]

Already in April 1942 initial plans were being laid for an invasion of Western Europe, and those plans included the use of airborne troops.[56] At that time plans were based upon a cross-channel operation scheduled for April 1943 or, under a modified plan, for September 1942. It was expected that one airborne division would be used for the 1943 offensive, or four parachute battalions would be used under the modified plan for September 1942.[57]

Although as of 13 April 1942 only one parachute regiment (less one battalion) had been designated for planned operations, Operations Division anticipated that all parachute regiments would be used in offensive operations before 1 June 1943, and it was expected that the demand for parachute units would exceed the number provided for in the 1942 Troop Basis; therefore it was recommended that the Parachute School continue to operate at full capacity throughout that year.[58] The Troop Carrier Command (designated Air Transport Command at that time) was expecting to move overseas in August or September.[59]

Changes inevitably accompanied further consideration of plans for a 1943 cross-channel operation against Western Europe, but an airborne plan remained a part of them. Plans in May 1942 called for a force to be built around eight infantry divisions. This force was to include an airborne division as well as four separate parachute regiments.[60] A tentative movement schedule prepared a few days later showed eleven infantry divisions, but the airborne division still was one of them. "The development of current War Department plans for the European Theater," it was noted, "is based on the utilization of an airborne division in the initial phase of the operation."[61] This would appear to have been sufficient impetus to the airborne effort to permit a training program which would provide effective airborne troops for those plans. But at the very moment when plans were being circulated and movement schedules being prepared which called for the inclusion of an airborne division, G-3 issued a memorandum which stated: "No units other than parachute units and special task and test units will be organized solely for airborne operations."[62] In other words, the War Department was saying in effect that an airborne division should participate in the planned invasion of Europe in April 1943, but no airborne division should be organized and trained. The explanation is apparently that it was expected that a standard infantry division would be used in the airborne role.

In Operations Division, on the other hand, the feeling was growing that airborne troop requirements for the invasion forcce had been underestimated. Col. J. E. Hull favored the organization of two airborne divisions and the continued operation of the Parachute School at full capacity.[63] General McNair approved a recommendation to redesignate the Eighty-second and 101st Divisions as airborne divisions,[64] and a memorandum prepared for War Department G-3 gave 15 August as the date for the planned activation of the airborne divisions, adding: "The airborne divisions must be organized and equipped without delay if they are to be ready for their announced task."[65]

By April 1943 plans called for a total of twelve airborne divisions, plus separate units. One airborne division, the Eighty-second, was projected for North Africa during 1943; four airborne divisions were projected for the United Kingdom by June 1944, and a parachute infantry regiment (the 503d), already was in the Southwest Pacific. There were, of course, a number of other airborne units; but there were also a number of troop carrier units, with C-47 airplanes and gliders, in theaters where no airborne troops were present or projected.[66] This was about as definite as could be expected at that stage, and it was the kind of information which was indispensable for intelligent planning.

General Arnold was continuously urging an expansion of airborne operations. In October 1944, after the operation of the First Allied Airborne Army in Holland, he wrote to General Brereton:

> There has at all times been in the Air Staff a very strong interest and belief in Airborne operations. It was their organization here which initiated efforts to convince theater planners to try bold airborne employment before OVERLORD and also before ANVIL. Nevertheless I regret to say that my Staff feel that they sense a reluctance in the theater to consider advice or suggestions regarding airborne operations or to accept observers from Washington. . . .
>
> From the limited data available here I would offer one conclusion on your initial operation. . . . It appears to me that the success of the Air Commando operations in Burma, and to some extent the inability of your British First Airborne Division to achieve its objective, indicate that the key to the success of large-scale airborne operations lies in the seizing of airfields or landing strips in the initial phases of such operations. From this

> viewpoint . . . it seems clear that an airborne force cannot rely completely on the advance of any ground force.[67]

A few weeks later the Army Air Forces chief wrote, "We are still groping for the principles which must be used as guides whenever large airborne forces are employed."

Chapter III

Command and Control

First proposals for an airborne organization in the U.S. Army came from the Office of the Chief of Infantry. On 6 May 1939, the executive in that office proposed the organization of a small detachment of air infantry. A general staff study on the subject led almost at once to differences of opinion over control of the project. The chief of engineers contended that inasmuch as parachutists would be used primarily as demolition teams and saboteurs, they ought to be trained and employed by the engineers. The chief of the Air Corps maintained that logically they should be "Marines of the Air Corps"; he proposed that they be placed under jurisdiction of the Air Corps and designated "Air Grenadiers." The chief of infantry, whose initial responsibility was being challenged, held that parachute troops would fight on the ground as infantry and, to be effective, they would have to be trained as infantry; air simply was to be regarded as a means of transportation to take them to the battlefield.

In June 1940, the War Department G-3 Division recommended that the program be taken out of the hands of the chief of infantry and be placed directly under G-3. Shortly thereafter the Miscellaneous Section of the G-3 Division came up with a new proposal to place it under the chief of the Air Corps. This proposal quickly won the strong support of that chief, Maj. Gen. Henry H. Arnold. But Brig. Gen. Lesley J. McNair, chief of staff of the newly organized General Headquarters, objected vigorously. He insisted, as had the chief of infantry before, that air transport was only another means of transportation, and that the primary mission of parachute troops was ground action. A later G-3 proposal offered the suggestion – and it seemed a logical one since the airborne program would cut across traditional branches – that the project be placed directly under

GHQ. The matter came to a head with a prolonged discussion on 27 August in the office of Maj. Gen. William Bryden, deputy chief of the War Department General Staff; at the conclusion General Bryden announced that the project would continue under the infantry.[1]

Meanwhile, the chief of staff directed GHQ to give attention to the "organization, equipment, and tactical employment of parachute and air-transported infantry." Early organization progressed from a test platoon under the commandant of the Infantry School, Fort Benning, Georgia (directed 25 June 1940), to the activation of the First (later redesignated the 501st) Parachute Battalion (authorized 16 September 1940), the supervision of additional battalions under a Provisional Parachute Group Headquarters (activated 10 March 1941), the extension of the authority and functions of the provisional group headquarters to those of a regiment (1 July 1941), the establishment of the Parachute School at Fort Benning (30 April 1941), the consolidation and expansion of the original battalions into regiments (February 1942), the activation of the First Parachute Infantry Brigade (30 July 1942), to the activation of the Eighty-second and 101st Airborne Divisions (15 August 1942).[2]

The first airlanding unit in the United States Army was the 550th Infantry Airborne Battalion, which was activated 1 July 1941 at Fort Kobbe, in the Canal Zone, under the command of Lt. Col. Harris M. Melaskey. Shortly afterward, Company C of the 501st Parachute Infantry Battalion, which had completed its parachute training at Fort Benning, arrived in the Canal Zone for attachment to the new airlanding battalion.[3]

The Airborne Command

Clearly the expansion of the airborne program would raise further questions of control and coordination. With the formation of combat teams it would be necessary to effect coordination with the field artillery and the engineers as well as with the Army Air Forces. Late in 1941 the War Department revived the idea of placing all airborne troops under the Army Air Forces – this time under the Air Support Command. Counterproposals called for the creation of a unified command to include all airborne and participating Air Corps troops under GHQ or the chief of staff, or the formation of a parachute force, including air transport, similar to the Armored Force. The reorganization of the War Department of 9 March 1942 and the creation of the Army Ground Forces cleared the way for unification of the control of training of ground elements. The activation on 21 March 1942 of the Airborne Command, under the Army Ground Forces, provided the agency for centralized control of those ground elements, but it omitted the final step – inclusion of the air elements under a common headquarters.[4]

The provisional Parachute Group Headquarters became the headquarters of the Airborne Command, and Col. (later Maj. Gen.) William C. Lee, group commander, who, as an officer in the Office of the Chief of Infantry, had been largely instrumental in bringing the airborne idea to fruition, became first commanding officer of the new organization. With Headquarters and Headquarters Company, Airborne Command, the 501st Parachute Infantry (less one battalion, inactive); the 502d Parachute Infantry; the 503d Parachute Infantry (less one battalion, inactive), then at Fort Bragg, North Carolina, and the Eighty-eighth Infantry Airborne Battalion (glider), the new command began its activities. Initially at Fort Benning, the Airborne Command headquarters moved, subsequently, first to Fort Bragg, North Carolina (9 April 1942), and later to its new training area, Camp Mackall, North Carolina (4 April 1943). The Parachute School, remaining at Fort Benning, came under the Airborne Command in May 1942.[5]

"The Father of U.S. Airborne Forces," Lt. Col William C. Lee was commander of the Provisional Parachute Group at Fort Benning, Georgia (July 1941); later became a major general and first commander of the Airborne Command, and then was made first commanding general of the 101st Airborne Division. (A heart condition forced him to give up command before entering combat.)

Primarily a training organization, the Airborne Command was to give unit training to organizations under its jurisdiction and to others as AGF directed; it was to activate airborne units under the direction of AGF; it was to make recommendations on airborne doctrine and equipment. In addition it would control the allocation of airplanes made available by the Army Air Forces and would coordinate its activities and requirements with the troop carrier units concerned.[6] These functions became more specific with additional instructions shortly after activation. The Airborne Command would undertake collaboration and maintain liaison with the Army Air Forces on the development of new types of troop carrier aircraft, the control and protection of airborne troop convoys while in flight, combat aviation support of airborne troops after landings, and air supply. Collaboration and liaison with the Navy would be necessary on problems growing out of airborne-seaborne joint operations.[7]

A month after activation of the Airborne Command, its opposite number appeared in the Army Air Forces. Known originally as the Air Transport Command, the new air force organization in June 1942 was redesignated Troop Carrier Command, and a month later it became the I Troop Carrier Command. It should not be confused with the later Air Transport Command which was formed out of the Air Forces Ferrying Command and the Air Cargo Division of the Air Service Command. The I Troop Carrier Command continued throughout the war as the training agency of the Air Forces in airborne operations.[8] It was "to organize and train Air Transport units for all forms of Air Transport with special emphasis on the conduct of operations involving the air movement of airborne infantry, glider troops, and parachute troops, and to make such units available to other elements of the Army Air Forces to meet specified requirements for Air-borne forces."[9] As defined in June 1942, "the primary mission of troop carrier units was to provide transportation for parachute troops, air-borne infantry, and glider units."[10]

In May 1943 Maj. Gen. Elbridge B. Chapman, then commanding the Airborne Command, had recommended the establishment of an airborne board "to insure continuity and consistency in the development of organization, armament, equipment and tactical doctrine in accordance with policies prescribed by the commanding general, Airborne Command." He was trying to broaden the scope of the test section of four officers then existing in the command. But at this time Army Ground Forces held to the test section as being adequate for its purpose, and saw matters of organization and doctrine as being within the province of other staff sections.[11]

Late in 1944, however, an Airborne Board was organized at Camp Mackall. Army Ground Forces assigned the president of the board (in December 1944 Lt. Col. Chester B. DeGavre was named to that post) and the Airborne Center assigned all other personnel. Its principal function was to correlate developments with requirements. Absence of such an agency had necessitated much improvisation in the theaters of operation while the Airborne Center remained ill-informed on requirements. When hostilities ended the board had detachments in both major theaters of operations – there to assist the highest airborne commanders in development projects, to notify the Airborne Board, through AGF, of airborne requirements, and to transmit information on airborne developments from the United States to interested commanders in the theaters. It sent liaison officers to the Army Air Forces Board at Orlando, Florida, and to the Air Technical Service Command at Wright Field.[12]

It was the well-established policy of General McNair to keep overhead in personnel down to a minimum, and whenever an organization or agency had reduced responsibilities, he was ready to reduce the size of the organization. Early in October 1943 he raised the question of replacing the Airborne Command with a small Airborne Center.[13] Noting that all airborne units then contemplated were overseas or in combined training, with the exception of a few which were scheduled to complete individual and unit training by 1 January, General McNair suggested that it would be desirable to effect the change in the Airborne Command about 1 January. The Airborne Center would be concerned primarily with the air training of all airborne units – including those directly under its command, and those brought in from corps and army. "In general the Airborne Center would be the link betweeen the airborne units and the Troop Carrier Command from AAF."[14] He decided to shift General Chapman to the command of an airborne division, and then to name a brigadier general as his successor at the Airborne Command.[15]

A Quest for Unity of Command

Airborne organization in the United States never achieved unity at the top level. There never was developed any equivalent of the German XI Air Corps. The first stage in airborne organization had been the formation of parachute regiments. The Germans had achieved the second stage of organization in 1939 when three parachute regiments, with additional special troops, were incorporated as the Seventh Division of the Air Force. In February 1941 they achieved the final stage when the airborne elements were joined with the air transport fleet in the XI Air Corps.[16]

When General Chapman proposed, in August 1943, the organization of an airborne task force headquarters and headquarters company, the reply of Army Ground Forces was, "Present plans and demands on manpower do not permit activation of additional units at this time." It was General Chapman's thought that the Airborne Task Force Headquarters would consist of approximately three officers and seventy-five enlisted men. Its mission would be to undertake the detailed preparation, combined staff work, and coordination between air and ground elements for the joint training of airborne divisions with troop carrier units. In case of necessity, he suggested that the organization would be available for shipment overseas where it might perform similar functions in combat operations. But AGF replied that maneuvers would be conducted under the supervision of an Army headquarters.[17]

Nonetheless, maneuvers soon demonstrated the need for such an organization, and the nearest that American forces ever came to achieving the stage of unified air-ground command in this country was in the *provisional* Airborne-Troop Carrier Maneuver Headquarters. But there were other advocates for unified command at the top. Colonel Dalbey, Airborne Command chief of staff, listed as one of the important shortcomings of the airborne operations in Sicily the "failure to appreciate the necessity of placing airborne troops and troop carrier elements under central control for a proper period of training prior to the operation."[18]

Appreciation of this necessity gained first acceptance in overseas theaters. Just as in the case of other developments in air-ground cooperation, it required the exigencies of combat to give effect to procedures which escaped the planners and organizers in the United States. Again, Colonel Dalbey pointed to the example in the Southwest Pacific of "Brothers MacArthur and Kenney exercising centralized command, assigning appropriate missions, and thoroughly training all participating elements."[19] And there were indications of more effective coordination in the European theater when, in November, Brig. Gen. James Gavin of the Eighty-second Airborne Division arrived in Great Britain to act as airborne adviser on the staff of Army Group. He had full authority "to deal directly with both the Troop Carrier Command and the airborne division in order to get best results."[20] Here was a first step which would culminate in a unified command, in a later period, in the formation of an airborne army.

Imaginative thinking extended as well to officers of the I Troop Carrier Command. In a statement in February 1945, Brig. Gen. W. D. Old, then commanding I Troop Carrier Command, called for the creation of an "airborne forces," which would include airborne, troop carrier, and auxiliary agencies, to be co-equal to AAF, AGF, and ASF. With the development of troop carrier aircraft, he foresaw the possibility which had been a vain hope in 1944 – the employment of entire airborne armies deep in strategic areas of enemy territory, with reinforcement, supply, and maintenance entirely by air.[21]

The Airborne Command, after coordination with the I Troop Carrier Command, drafted three additional standard operating procedures in the fall of 1943.[22] The first outlined procedure for a parachute operation. It directed that each airborne element operating from a separate airfield should designate a liaison officer to work with troop carrier units operating from that field, and it specified the liaison officer's duties. Instructions for jumpmasters and pilots outlined duties before emplaning, the duties immediately before and during the drop, and provided a detailed aircraft inspection list whose observance was largely a joint responsibility of jumpmaster and pilot. The second of these procedures covered glider and airlanding operations, again with instructions for airborne personnel – liaison officers and commanders of tactical loads – and for troop carrier personnel – glider, tow plane, and airlanding plane pilots and crew chiefs. The third was a procedure for an airborne operation. It traced the specific steps in planning, from the essential orders from higher headquarters, the initial studies by airborne and troop carrier commanders, to the conference between the two commanders and their individual and joint responsibilities.

While in flight, control of airborne troops was the responsibility of the commander of the supporting air task force. After landing, the control of these troops reverted to their own commander.[23]

The report of the Combined Staff Planners to the Combined Chiefs of Staff in February 1944 suggested that a great shortcoming of the airborne effort had been the failure of higher commanders to provide themselves with capable airborne and troop carrier staff advisers. Some commanders had relied solely on air force members of their staff for airborne guidance, and had disregarded the fact that airborne troops were ground forces, and that the air trip was only their initial phase of combat. In other cases, airborne-troop carrier staffs had been organized only after the arrival of airborne troops in the theater, when they should have been organized in the beginning, because "airborne planning must be anticipatory and continuous. Neither will it ever work well to take senior officers from the airborne or troop carrier tactical units to act temporarily in a high staff capacity; to do so may seriously cripple the combat efficiency of the tactical unit concerned."

The Combined Planners frowned on the tendency of higher commanders to delegate to a lower headquarters the responsibility for achieving the necessary coordination among land, sea, and air forces during an airborne operation, and they emphasized that the decisions effecting such coordination should be made by the commander having direct control of all forces involved.

Airborne Divisions

Early plans had had no place for the airborne division as such. It was thought a violation of the rule of economy of force to organize divisions solely for airborne operations. Rather it was assumed that such specialized organization and training would be confined to parachute units and special task and test units, while all infantry divisions, within the limitations of available troop carrier aircraft and gliders, would be trained for airborne operations before their departure for an overseas theater.[24] This was based upon the concept which saw airborne operations principally as the action of troops landed by airplane or glider in areas seized by the parachutist spearhead. Army Ground Forces on 28 May 1942, had stated: "Airborne divisions should not be designated as such. They should be organized as infantry divisions and trained for airborne operations." But within a month it was being advised in AGF that that statement of policy should be ignored, and that specifically designated and organized airborne divisions should be activated.[25]

Inasmuch as the plans for the invasion of Europe in 1943 contemplated the use of an American airborne division, General Lee was sent to Great Britain to study the problem of airborne organization. He returned with the recommendation that special airborne divisions be organized and trained.[26] His recommendations, together with those of Major William P. Yarborough, Airborne Command intelligence officer, became the basis for the new divisional organization.[27] By 19 June 1942 General McNair was prepared to accept the airborne division as a specialized organization.

That there should be two glider regiments and one parachute regiment in the division was another manifestation of the earlier concept that the parachutists should be merely the spearhead for airlanding troops. On the basis of British organization, General Lee recommended two parachute regiments and one glider regiment, but General McNair could find no valid reason for the British organization. Further inquiry suggested that the British organization was one of necessity rather than one based on long-range plans. No German table of organization could be found which combined parachute and glider troops in one division. It seemed that the German practice had been to organize special task forces for each operation – the parachute troops were part of the air force, and the glider troops were from the ground forces. The training section of AGF G-3 recommended that the emphasis be on flexibility so that the number of parachute and glider regiments might be varied to meet specific requirements.[28] In view of plans for a European invasion within less than a year, then, General McNair recommended that the training of standard infantry divisions in air transportation continue, and that two airborne divisions be formed. They were to be constituted from the Eighty-second Division, then a motorized division finishing its individual training, with the addition of the necessary parachute units.

The proposed organization amounted to a miniature infantry division of 504 officers and 8,321 enlisted men. It called for one parachute and two glider infantry regiments plus division artillery, an engineer battalion, a medical company, signal company, and quartermaster company. It was suggested that the number of parachute and glider regiments might be changed as needed.[29] The proposals won prompt approval in the War Department, and General Eisenhower, then commanding the European theater, expressed the hope that he might have these divisions in his forces by 1 April 1943.[30]

Following this plan, the Eighty-second and the 101st Airborne Divisions were activated on 15 August 1942 under the respective commands of Brig. Gens. Matthew B. Ridgway and William C. Lee. Both divisions were activated under Third Army. The plan initially was to have them assigned to the Airborne Command for airborne training only, but General McNair felt that this division in training responsibility would lead to confusion and unsatisfactory results. Consequently they were placed under the Airborne Command for both basic and airborne training, and were attached to the Second Army for administration and supply.[31]

Before the Sicily operation in 1943 the Eighty-second Airborne Division was authorized to change its organization to include two parachute and one glider infantry regiments. When it went to the United Kingdom, the 101st Airborne Division still had the one parachute, two glider infantry regiments arrangement. But for the Normandy operation the Second Battalion, 401st Glider Infantry (the glider regiments had only two battalions) was attached to the 325th Glider Infantry, Eighty-second Airborne Division, and the remaining battalion was attached to the 327th Glider Infantry, 101st Airborne Division. Thus each division had, in effect, one three-battalion glider regiment. Then two additional parachute regiments were attached to each division for that operation. Except for one of the parachute regiments for the Eighty-second Division, these attachments continued for the Holland operation so that both had three parachute and one glider infantry regiments, each of three battalions. Modifications which the Eighty-second Airborne Division made included the formation of a provisional fourth company in the engineer battalion to support the attached parachute infantry regiment, the conversion of one of the three antiaircraft batteries of the airborne antiaircraft battalion into an antitank battery so that the battalion had four antitank and two antiaircraft batteries, the organization of a provisional reconnaissance platoon, and the organization of a provisional parachute maintenance company out of the packing sections which the various parachute units were authorized.[32] The division artillery included one parachute and three glider battalions. The 376th Parachute Field Artillery Battalion and the 456th Glider Field Artillery Battalion each had three firing batteries, each with four 75-mm. pack howitzers; the 319th Glider Field Artillery Battalion had two firing batteries of six 75-mm. howitzers, and the 320th had two firing batteries of six 105-mm. M3 howitzers. The 101st Airborne Division had made similar modifications.[33]

Another important factor which taxed the division strength and brought out other shortcomings in tables of organization was the disposition which the division commander found it necessary to make for the Holland operation as well as for the earlier missions. This disposition was as follows: (1) an element of the airborne division had to remain in the billet or bivouac area to guard and maintain the housing area, certain motor vehicles, and organizational equipment not needed for the operation; (2) a rear base installation to handle details at the departure field; (3) a seaborne or ground (if airborne bases had been located on the Continent) echelon with heavy equipment which could not be air transported and which was to join the division after contact with attacking ground troops; (4) the airborne echelon which in turn was divided into the normal rear installations of a division for administration and the forward elements for combat.[34] Moreover the nature of the combat in which airborne troops engaged demonstrated other needs in organization.

On the basis of this experience and the repeated recommendations of division and corps commanders, First Allied Airborne Army in November asked that a new table of organization and equipment be approved for American airborne divisions. In general these recommendations repeated those which had been made, and disapproved by the War Department on the ground of the shortage of manpower, after the Normandy operation, and they represented the principal changes which the Eighty-second and 101st Airborne Divisions had in fact made before being committed to combat. Predicated on the assumption of two parachute infantry regiments and one glider infantry regiment for the division, the recommendations sought to bring division organization into line with that arrangement, and to overcome shortcomings which had become evident in the Normandy and Holland operations.

Because of the wide separation of the division in three or more echelons, and the need for liaison with each part, with higher headquarters,and with the troop carrier command, airborne officers asked for an expansion of the division general staff. An air support party also would be added as an organic part of the staff. Airborne warfare had raised major problems in civilian population control, traffic control, and handling prisoners of war; consequently a traffic section and an additional police squad were asked for the military police platoon. The nature of airborne operations in unfamiliar terrain against potentially greater forces demanded rapid reconnaissance before the enemy could organize a counterattack; therefore airborne officers asked that their division reconnaissance platoons be authorized in a table of organization. A command post defense platoon was asked for addition to the division headquarters company. Airborne officers had found the basic doctrine of triangular

Maj. Gen. Maxwell D. Taylor, commanding general of the 101st Airborne Division, waves from his plane before take-off.

employment tactically sound, and therefore again recommended a third squad for the parachute infantry platoon, and a third battalion for the glider infantry regiment. They recommended the substitution of an additional parachute engineer company in the engineer battalion in lieu of a glider company, and the addition of a third platoon to the glider infantry company in order to conform to the recommended infantry organization. Other recommendations were for reorganization of the signal company to that found in a standard infantry division, addition of a litter bearer section to each platoon of the medical company, an additional transportation section for the quartermaster company, and the addition of a second parachute field artillery battalion as direct support for the second parachute infantry regiment and the equipping of the glider field artillery battalion for general support with 105-mm. howitzers, M3, in lieu of 75-mm. pack howitzers.[35] In December the War Department asked that an officer from XVIII Corps (Airborne) be sent to Washington to discuss the proposed changes in the airborne division tables of organization and equipment. For this mission the corps commander chose Maj. Gen. Maxwell D. Taylor, commander of the 101st Airborne Division.[36]

The War Department authorized most of the requested changes in new tables of organization and equipment published in December 1944. The new tables provided for two parachute and one glider infantry regiments in the division. They added a third battalion to the glider regiment, a third platoon to the glider infantry company, and a third rifle squad to the parachute infantry platoon. They modified artillery and engineer units to conform to the new infantry arrangement, authorized a reconnaissance company and a parachute maintenance company, and enlarged the general staff (principally in the addition of air advisers and air-ground liaison officers) and the military police platoon.[37] The new table of organization and equipment was published as a tentative table,[38] but the airborne divisions in the European theater reorganized under the tables in March 1945.[39] In the Pacific the Eleventh Airborne Division remained on the old table, but accomplished some of the same objectives by organizing its glider regiments as para-glider regiments, capable of going into combat either by glider or by parachute.[40]*

The First Allied Airborne Army

After the Normandy invasion, airborne operations in Europe came under the direction of the First Allied Airborne Army. Activated on 2 August 1944 under the command of Lt. Gen. Lewis H. Brereton, previously commanding general of the Ninth Air Force, the new organization brought under centralized operational control Allied troop carrier units as well as airborne units in the European theater.

Several weeks before the cross-channel operation in 1944, SHAEF was considering an organization to control the airborne troops in the European theater after the completion of that mission. As early as 20 May the Airborne Sub-Section of SHAEF G-3 Division drew up recommendations for such control. Recalling that "Airborne and troop carrier units are theater of operations forces," and that "plans for their combined employment must be prepared by the agency having authority to direct the necessary coordinated action of all land, sea, and air forces in the area involved," the plan proposed to unify control of American and British airborne troops under an "airborne forces." Directly responsible to SHAEF, the new headquarters would be on the level of army groups and the Allied Expeditionary Air Force. Troop carrier units would continue to operate under the control of Allied Expeditionary Air Force. The Airborne Sub-Section of SHAEF G-3 Division itself proposed to take over the functions of a planning staff for the new headquarters. Thus in the beginning the proposal for a combined airborne headquarters had as its object the joining of British and American airborne troops into a single

* Early in 1945 General Arnold suggested that future organization should contemplate *parachute divisions* and the airlanding of standard units. *The Brereton Diaries*, p. 391.

striking force rather than the unification of command over troop carrier and airborne forces. The other principal object was to keep control of airborne forces directly under the supreme commander instead of delegating it to the army groups.[41]

After approval of SHAEF G-3, this proposal went out to First U.S. Army Group, Twenty-first Army Group, and Allied Expeditionary Air Force for comment.[42] In the absence of General Bradley from First U.S. Army Group, the Chief of Staff, Maj. Gen. Leven C. Allen, recommended that a U.S. airborne command be formed to assume control over all American airborne troops, but that no combined U.S.-British airborne headquarters be attempted. He saw a need for an "airborne command" to supervise training, supply, reorganization and administration, and to coordinate air lifts. But he thought that the large number of American airborne troops present or to arrive in the theater, their probable use in another theater later, the difference in equipment and staff functioning between American and British units, and the fact that the aircraft available in the theater could lift no more than the equivalent of the American troops anyway made necessary an American, but not a combined, airborne headquarters. He suggested that SHAEF could control airborne forces through separate American and British commands as effectively as through a single command.[43] The reply from Twenty-first Army Group expressed full agreement with the proposal, except that it should not become effective until the supreme commander assumed direct operational control of the army groups on the Continent.[44] Comments from Allied Expeditionary Air Force indicated agreement with the plan, and suggested only a few minor changes – generally aimed at defining more clearly the need of collaboration with AEAF in the planning of airborne operations and of the duties of the proposed airborne commander.[45]

Incorporating most of the proposed changes, Maj. Gen. H. R. Bull, SHAEF G-3, on 17 June recommended that the combined airborne troops headquarters be established. Noting that the supreme commander had approved the organization of an American airborne corps, he suggested that this should meet the major objections of First U.S. Army Group. His proposed organization chart still showed troop carrier units under the Allied Expeditionary Air Force.[46] General Eisenhower, however, apparently had been thinking in terms of an organization which would bring troop carrier and airborne forces under a unified command. His intention was that this should be organized as a modified corps headquarters, and would be "commanded by a General Officer of the U.S. Army Air Corps, presumably with the rank of Lieutenant General."[47] Here the position of the Royal Air Force in Great Britain as an independent establishment complicated matters. After consulting the views of Lt. Gen. F.A.M. Browning, commander of British Airborne

Troops, and other British airborne officers, a staff officer noted that British troop carrier and transport units – Thirty-eighth and Forty-sixth Groups, RAF – and the U.S. IX Troop Carrier Command should be placed under the new Airborne Headquarters. "If this were so," he wrote, "it would not be necessary to consult AEAF on airborne planning except for Air Support. If this were not so then there is no necessity for this proposed headquarters as it would simply do the same thing as Airborne H.Q., British Airborne Troops do now, i.e., have to take the Army plan to the Air Commander who always has different views."[48] But British airborne leaders were somewhat apprehensive about having an Air Force officer command soldiers, lest one day the RAF should take this as a precedent for insisting that an RAF officer should command British Airborne Troops.[49] Officers of Allied Expeditionary Air Force pointed to the administrative difficulties involved in assigning RAF units to the proposed combined headquarters, and objected to the assignment of troop carrier units to the new command.[50] Air Chief Marshal T. Leigh-Mallory, air commander-in-chief, Allied Expeditionary Air Force, reiterated these objections, and urged that the organization should be as originally proposed: formation of a corps headquarters for the American airborne divisions and then unification under one commander of British and American airborne (but not troop carrier) forces. He maintained that the air support for and the air movement of airborne forces "form one indivisible air operation and must be welded into one plan from the outset. . . . From time (of) take-off to landing, an airborne operation being a purely air operation – must be the responsibility of the Air C.-in-C., who must retain the power of veto."[51] Replying for General Eisenhower, General W. Bedell Smith, his chief of staff, wrote: "The Supreme Commander has personally studied alternative plans of organization for more than one and one-half years, and is determined to test thoroughly the one now set up."[52]

General Eisenhower remained convinced of the need for a unified troop carrier-airborne command. He outlined the proposal in messages to General Marshall and General Arnold and asked the assignment of an Air Corps officer as commander. But Marshall asked further clarification of the duties of the proposed commander. It had not been made clear whether he was to function as a corps commander of airborne divisions; whether he would command all troops, air and ground, participating in an operation, including the ground action of the airborne divisions after landing, or whether another officer, as a corps commander, would command the airborne divisions on the ground, and whether he would be responsible to an army group commander or to the combined airborne commander.[53] General Arnold discussed the subject further with Marshall, and the chief of staff accepted in principle the procedure that an Air

Forces commander should control an airborne task force until the situation on the ground permitted normal logistic support, when control should revert to the ground commander in the normal theater chain of command.[54] Eisenhower felt that experience had proved the need for an agency under the high command to assume responsibility for joint training, development of operational projects, and logistic support by air. A single agency also would simplify the necessary coordination with ground and naval forces. In addition the agency would have the responsibility of getting the types and quantities of technical equipment needed. The proposed over-all commander would not, in Eisenhower's view, command troops actually fighting on the ground, but he would be responsible for providing their logistic support until lines of communication could be established on the ground. Thus in an airborne attack by two or three divisions a temporary corps commander would be designated to command the ground action after landing, and as soon as his forces joined up with the nearest army, the ground army commander would take over both operational and logistic responsibility.[55]

Lt. Gen. Lewis H. Brereton, right, commander of the First Allied Airborne Army, talks with Col. Howard Johnson before the invasion of Holland.

An important problem arising from plans to create an airborne corps headquarters and a Combined Airborne Headquarters was that of finding qualified officers to staff the organization. One possible source was the Airborne Center at Camp Mackall. Now that the center was nearing the completion of its major task of training airborne divisions, Colonel Dalbey, the commander, was entertaining hopes that the whole organization might move to the United Kingdom to continue its functions in the development of airborne doctrine, tactics, and techniques.[56] Actually that move did not take place, but the War Department did indicate that some of the experienced airborne officers at the Airborne Center would be available for the new headquarters.[57] In addition, Headquarters and Headquarters Company, Second Airborne Brigade, then in the United Kingdom, would be disbanded and its personnel assigned to the new Combined Headquarters; the U.S. Strategic Air Forces in Europe would furnish Air Force grades and ratings not to exceed ten officers and fifty enlisted men; Headquarters and Headquarters Company, XVIII Corps, scheduled for arrival in the theater in August, would be redesignated "airborne" for the American airborne corps, and excess personnel would be available for Combined Headquarters.[58]

After consideration of several possible commanders, and an exchange of messages with Marshall and Arnold, Eisenhower decided that the commander of the Combined Airborne Headquarters should be Lt. Gen. Lewis H. Brereton, then commander of the Ninth Air Force. Maj. Gen. Matthew B. Ridgway, then commander of the Eighty-second Airborne Division, would become commanding general of the XVIII Corps (Airborne). Brig. Gen. Floyd L. Parks, Army Ground Forces G-3, was appointed chief of staff for Combined Airborne Headquarters.[59]

General Brereton first learned of his new assignment on 16 July in a conference with General Carl Spaatz, commanding general, U.S. Strategic Air Forces in Europe. The next day Eisenhower explained more fully what he had in mind. Brereton wrote in his diary: "In parting, I told General Eisenhower that if he wanted plans with daring and imagination he would get them, but that I did not think his staff or the ground commanders would like it."[60] Brereton himself was not yet convinced on the proposed organization for a Combined Airborne Headquarters, and he suggested that the American airborne corps be placed under the Ninth Air Force.[61] This would bring American airborne troops and the troop carriers, as well as tactical air commands, under the unified command of the Ninth Air Force, but it would not achieve that unity over British forces, though he suggested that they too could be brought under operational control of Ninth Air Force when needed. General Brereton's conviction "that direct command of the air and ground forces concerned in such an operation must be vested in a single commander"[62] would have made it more logical to suggest that all airborne troops be placed under command of the Allied Expeditionary Air Force which already existed as a combined headquarters over British and American tactical air forces. This is a suggestion which undoubtedly would have won the favor of Air Chief Marshall Leigh-Mallory who had objected so strongly to the taking of the troop carrier units from his command, but probably the greatest objection to such a suggestion was that it would bring the whole thing under British command.

During the period that new airborne headquarters were being organized, American airborne troops in the United Kingdom were under command of the Ninth Army. But even before the proposed XVIII Corps (Airborne) had been organized, Lt. Gen. W. H. Simpson, commander of the Ninth Army, directed General Ridgway as the designated corps commander, to assume responsibility for directing and supervising all training of airborne troops and for allocating and coordinating their training areas and facilities.[63]

Before it had begun to function, General Brereton recommended that Combined Airborne Forces be redesignated, "First Allied Airborne Army."[64] General Bull, SHAEF G-3, commented: "The Headquarters is organized as a planning and coordinating headquarters only, and has no facilities for functioning as an army headquarters in the field. An army is a flexible combat force capable of independent operations. No intention exists to use the forces concerned as an army."[65] He therefore disapproved the recommendation, but the chief of staff overruled that disapproval, and Eisenhower approved the new designation. The change was announced on 16 August.[66]

Assigned operational control over the IX Troop Carrier Command, the XVIII Corps (Airborne) (including the Eighty-second, 101st, and Seventeenth Airborne Divisions plus certain independent airborne units), British Airborne Troops, and such Royal Air Force troop carrier formations as might be allocated from time to time, the commanding general, First Allied Airborne Army, was directly responsible to the supreme commander for the following functions: (1) supervision of training and allocation of facilities; (2) study and recommendations for improvements in airborne equipment; (3) coordination of supply; (4) consultation with Allied naval commander, Expeditionary Force, concerning naval requirements and routine of airborne formations over the sea; (5) consultation with the air commander-in-chief, Allied Expeditionary Air Force, concerning tactical air requirements; (6) the assembly of troops, equipment, and supplies at designated air bases; (7) the preparation and examination, in conjunction with the SHAEF planning staff, of the outline plan for the employment of airborne troops, and preparation of detailed plans in conjunction with air and ground commanders; (8) direction and control of the execution of such plans, until the ground force commander should take command of units on the ground; (9) determination of resupply requirements, arrangements for delivery to departure air bases, and supervision of resupply; (10) arrangements for the return of airborne units to their home bases on their release by ground commanders; (11) the reconstitution of airborne forces.[67] The Combined Air Transport Operations Room (CATOR) – the agency for coordinating the hauling of freight and personnel within the theater, including supply by air for the ground armies – also came under control of the First Allied Airborne Army.[68]

Originally the Combined Airborne Headquarters had been conceived as a small planning and coordinating agency. Supply and administration would be through the channels previously operating, and corps and troop carrier headquarters would perform the operational functions. Almost at once, however, the responsibilities and activities of First Allied Airborne Army began to grow, and Brereton repeatedly asked for additional personnel in order to carry out his directive. The original authorized strength for the Combined Headquarters – British and American – was 58 officers and 265 enlisted men. By 4 October the number actually on duty with the headquarters had grown to 188 officers and 1,197 enlisted men. Because of the provisional nature of the organization, all American personnel had to be assigned, "on paper," to the Second Airborne Brigade. This was an unsatisfactory administrative arrangement, and later Brereton recommended that the War Department approve new tables of organization and equipment to cover the American elements assigned to Headquarters and Headquarters Company, First Allied Airborne Army and the special units operating under the headquarters. Compensations in the troop basis could be made by disbanding the First Airborne Task Force, which was assigned to First Allied Airborne Army after the Dragoon operation in Southern France.[69] Subsequently the War Department published tables of organization and equipment for a headquarters, headquarters company, and signal battalion of an airborne army[70] and on 29 January 1945 Headquarters First Airborne Army and Headquarters Company First Airborne Army were activated for the assignment of American personnel of the First Allied Airborne Army.[71]

Chapter IV

The Machines: Quality and Quantity

The Troop Carrier Command of 1942 was supposed to include over 600 transport aircraft and over 2,000 gliders, as well as the necessary air echelon and parachute equipment, and both ground and airborne communication equipment to perform its intended mission effectively.[1] It began its activities with fifty-six cargo airplanes, basic materiel sufficient for equipping four squadrons, and miscellaneous and incomplete equipment for twenty-seven squadrons. It opened its headquarters at Stout Field, Indianapolis, Indiana, with the promise that there would be forthcoming, between April and December 1942, 597 additional aircraft.[2] The airfields to be used for operational training of troop carrier units were at Sedalia, Missouri; Ardmore, Oklahoma; and Alliance, Nebraska. A new field was constructed in 1942 at Laurinburg, North Carolina, known as the Laurinburg-Maxton Army Air Base, specifically to serve the training program with the Airborne Command. Prior to its completion, and afterwards as an additional base, Pope Field, at Fort Bragg, based troop carrier units. Other units were kept at Lawson Field, Fort Benning, to meet training needs of the Parachute School and units stationed there.[3]

An innovation of the scope of the airborne program could be expected to create problems of the first magnitude. With each of the three major commands of the Army, upon which it depended, it found itself a minor competitor, to receive attention after more urgent and well-established activities had been cared for.

Development of Transport Aircraft

Throughout the war, the C-47 – "workhorse of the AAF" – served as the principal troop carrier airplane. Since 1931 the commercial predecessor of this troop transport, the familiar Douglas DC-3, had been building up confidence for itself on airlines of the United States. Because it was the most satisfactory transport plane already in production, it became the vehicle for the inauguration of the parachute training program. Its airworthiness had been proved; it could operate at the slow speeds necessary for parachute and glider operations, and it could operate out of relatively small airfields. Some twenty-eight modifications went into the fifty planes obtained from the commercial airlines for the initial equipment of the Troop Carrier Command (then Air Transport Command), but by mid-1943 most of the necessary modifications had been introduced in the factory production lines. The C-47 "Skytrain," however, never was a completely satisfactory troop carrier airplane. Soon it became evident that airborne operations on a big scale should have the use of aircraft with a greater capacity than the payload of 5,000 to 6,000 pounds.[4] A slight modification of the C-47 – principally in doors – was known as the C-53, "Skytrooper."

In a test in September 1944, a C-47 equipped with a conveyor system flew from the Laurinburg-Maxton Army Air Base with a cargo of approximately 6,000 pounds packed in aerial delivery containers. The plane dropped twenty-four containers, with 3,300 pounds of supplies, in five seconds. This distributed the supplies in a line about 250 yards long. The plane made a second run to drop the remainder of its load. Further tests in November 1944 demonstrated the relative effectiveness of various types of containers, and confirmed the practicability of the conveyors.[5]

A bigger plane, designed as a heavy cargo transport originally, appeared in June 1942. Although this aircraft – the C-46 – subsequently proved capable of carrying a payload of approximately 10,500 pounds, with a range of 1,000 miles, it was found not to surpass the C-47 in other characteristics.[6] Tests conducted in the airborne area in December 1942 demonstrated that, while the plane could take artillery pieces of 75-mm. and 105-mm. types, there was difficulty in loading. The high doors made it necessary to build ramps and to use winches to get the howitzers aboard.[7] More desirable for such loadings would be an airplane with a belly door which would serve as a ramp. The C-46 "Commando" was not yet the answer to troop carrier requirements, and there were a number of questionable features about it, but the simple fact of its carrying capacity ultimately overruled other considerations. Production difficulties arose, however, and there were other demands – practically all of the 1943 production was taken by the Air Transport Command – so that the C-46 did not become available to the Troop Carrier Command until the summer of 1944.

In August 1944 conversion to the C-46 in I Troop Carrier Command began. From that time replacement crews as well as tactical units received training with the C-46. The aircraft performed very satisfactorily in tests

A C-47 transport plane pulls CG 4A gliders in double tow (over Wesel, Germany, in March 1945).

A C-46 cargo plane (at a base in Anselm, India).

A C-54 "Skymaster"

with parachute dummies and paratroopers in November 1944, though it was more difficult to fly than the C-47. It had the advantage of two doors as well as greater capacity. Paratroopers used both doors simultaneously in a jump in February 1945.[8]

The C-46 first appeared in combat as a troop carrier in the operation across the Rhine in March 1945, and the report of General Dalbey, concurred in by the commanding generals of the First Allied Airborne Army, IX Troop Carrier Command, XVIII Corps (Airborne), and Seventeenth Airborne Division, was: "The airplane is eminently suitable for airborne use, and should be advocated for future operations."[9] But at the same time Brig. Gen. W. D. Old, now commanding I Troop Carrier Command, was preparing a report which recommended that "production of C-46 type aircraft be halted and that plans for its use as a Troop Carrier aircraft be discontinued."[10] Maintenance difficulties growing out of continuing modification and use of numbers of different models of the airplanes, and a series of accidents with the plane between 28 January and 20 March 1945 led to that conclusion.

A four-engine commercial plane, the Douglas DC-4, came into military service as the C-54 (Skymaster), and it probably would have made a satisfactory troop carrier. In August 1943 the Airborne Command found that it could be used satisfactorily for the transportation of field artillery equipment. But these planes went to the Air Transport Command, and there never were enough of them for use by the Troop Carrier Command.[11] The I Troop Carrier Command received one four-engine transport plane of the C-54 type in 1944 for experimental purposes, and redeployment plans in 1945 anticipated the conversion of five B-24 bombardment groups to C-54 troop carrier units for long range operations. No troop carrier groups had been equipped with the C-54, however, when hostilities ceased.[12]

Another plane, still in the experimental stage, had been designed specifically for airborne operations. It was the Fairchild C-82. A representative of the Troop Carrier Command went to the factory at Hagerstown, Maryland, in September 1942 to inspect a mock-up of the new transport, and he came away favorably impressed. It represented a radical departure from the familiar commercial planes, but it met requirements for which airborne planners had been looking. It was to carry a payload of 15,000 pounds, and have a range of 1,000 miles. A high wing twin-engined monoplane, the C-82 had a huge (2,312 cubic feet) box-like central cabin suspended between twin tail booms. This "flying boxcar"had a loading platform only four feet off the ground, and ramp doors at each end. Its cruising speed was 170 miles per hour, and it was designed to fly at a slow speed of 90 to 95 miles per hour. As with any new model, there had to be modifications and tests, and there were further production delays. Production ultimately was supposed to begin in June or July 1944 – at a rate of seven a month.[13] But only one hand-tooled model was flying by that time.

It was of little satisfaction that a demonstration of the airplane at the Washington National Airport in November 1944 won the plaudits of the officers who saw it. Here was a plane which could carry a 2½-ton truck, or a 155-mm. howitzer, or a bulldozer. In August 1944 a study was made of the suitability of the C-47, C-46, and C-82 for carrying fifty items of equipment authorized for airborne and infantry divisions. Of the fifty items, fourteen could be transported in the C-47, twenty-six in the C-46, and forty-nine in the C-82. But suitability was of little consequence if no such planes were to be had. Production did not meet even the modest goals set up.

The Air Forces, by June 1945, had plans for the complete conversion of troop carrier units from the C-46 to the C-82. But these were plans which would have no effect on operations in World War II. In November 1945 the number of C-82's available was approximately five.[14]

Meanwhile experiments continued with other aircraft. One which held some promise was the B-24 heavy bomber (Liberator). It received consideration as early as June 1942. Its tricycle landing gear and high wings, which permitted low cabin suspension, made for ease of loading and unloading on the ground, and its range of 3,800 miles was a desirable feature from the Air Forces point of view, but its capacity for its size was limited.[15]

A C-82 drops paratroopers on a training flight.

A howitzer and a tractor stowed inside a B-17 Flying Fortress (over Australia in 1942).

However, considerations of radius of operation, armament, self-sealing gasoline tanks, and quantity of production recommended the B-24 for possible use in airborne operations in the Pacific. The B-24 – or C-87 as the modified transport model was designated – could not operate in formation at a speed of less than 150 miles per hour, and when paratroopers jumped at that speed they suffered considerable shock and painful strap burns. The plane would carry only sixteen paratroopers and their equipment, but it would take all airborne equipment except jeeps and large artillery pieces. It was estimated that one hundred hours of transition training would be necessary to qualify pilots to handle the B-24 as a troop carrier, and modifications in the plane would require considerable time – it took two months for the first airplane used for test purposes in May 1944.[16]

Tests by the Sixtieth Troop Carrier Wing and the Airborne Center in September 1944 demonstrated the B-17 "Flying Fortress" to be a "very satisfactory airplane for the transportation of personnel and supplies." In one test a B-17 made an eight-hour flight, of two legs, carrying sixty fully-equipped airborne soldiers and fifty five-gallon water cans. A tactically-equipped B-17G carried sixty-four passengers and a crew of five in a test flight.[17] For long-range airlanding missions, the B-17 was a promising carrier.

Some thought was given also to the use of aircraft other than transport as tow planes for gliders. The Swing Board recommended that tests be conducted in using a P-38 (Lightning) fighter unit and a B-17 (Flying Fortress) bomber unit, "or other suitable combat units" in a glider operation to test their feasibility for such use,[18] but no great shift toward the use of those planes ever developed.

For purposes of planning, ground forces officers thought of an airborne operation as including three phases – seizure of landing areas; reinforcement of the parachute and glider troops and establishment of an airhead; and the transportation of heavy equipment, including corps equipment, into the area. This was a return to the original airborne concept, but it was one which never had been followed in World War II. But here appeared a difference, with respect to aircraft, between AGF and AAF. The air officers were thinking in terms of developing one all-purpose troop carrier plane which would carry the maximum load required by ground units. Ground officers, on the other hand, saw a need for a different type of airplane for each of the three phases to which they referred. A maneuverable plane that could fly through flak and deliver parachutists and gliders accurately was needed for the first phase. For the second phase a plane capable of carrying all division equipment, excepting the very heaviest, would be desirable. For the third phase a plane that could carry a medium tank was desired. The result, for the time being, was a compromise looking toward the development of two planes – one to cover the first and second phases, and a bigger one for the third phase of airborne operations. Capacity was based on the 2½-ton truck for the first (net weight of the 2½-ton truck was more than 10,000 pounds; loaded it would weigh over 15,000 pounds), and the medium tank (the Sherman, M-4, weighed more than 60,000 pounds) for the second. In general it was agreed that both planes should have radius of range of 750 miles, that they should be capable of dropping heavy loads and of disembarking all personnel, regardless of number, in ten seconds, and that they should have "straight-away" loading facilities which would permit vehicles to be driven aboard quickly.[19]

The Shortage of Aircraft for Training

A serious and persistent obstacle to adequate airborne training was a chronic shortage of aircraft. The availability of transport aircraft throughout 1942-1943 and early 1944 can be described in no other terms than "too little and too late." To this statement, many airborne commanders and thousands of enlisted men would undoubtedly add, "and with crews not sufficiently trained."[20]

It was to be expected that a shortage of transport aircraft would greet the initiation of the airborne program, but here was a problem which gave little indication of subsiding with time. It was a problem which had been recognized in 1941,[21] and it was a matter of concern to Army Ground Forces early in 1942.[22]

This does not mean that the shortage of aircraft was the only impediment to training. When General Lee said that the greatest training obstacle for the Airborne Command in April 1942 was "lack of equipment,"[23] he was referring principally to such items as rifles, pistols, machine guns, mortars, helmets, and communications equipment. He reported that enough transport planes were available at that time for regularly scheduled novice jumping at the Infantry School and for some small unit jumps.

For training in airborne operations, Airborne Command needed at least one airplane every day, and it asked for up to 147 planes for periods of three consecutive days. At least thirty-nine aircraft were required for routine training only, exclusive of any special missions, and in addition the troop carrier units needed another thirty-nine planes for their own combined training at Alliance, Nebraska. Trying to make the most of a difficult situation, the Airborne Command and Troop Carrier Command agreed upon a precise division of training time for both Fort Bragg and Fort Benning; airborne units were to have exclusive use of troop carrier aircraft from 0800 to 1200 daily; all airborne missions were to be consecutive, without waiting time, or even stopping of engines, between flights; any time that airborne missions were completed early, and always after 1200, aircraft were to revert automatically to the troop carrier units for their own unit training. It was evident that some other arrangements would have to be made before any satisfactory joint maneuvers could be held. During the summer of 1942 a number of troop carrier groups departed for overseas stations without having participated in any program of joint training with airborne troops.[24]

It should be noted that the Commanding General of Army Ground Forces, Lt. Gen. Lesley J. McNair, was not one to push extravagant requests for aircraft. Always interested above all in perfecting ground combat training, he believed that a large share of the training of an airborne division could be accomplished with only one previous trip in a plane or glider. He believed that necessary training commitments could be met with a considerable reduction in the number of planes and gliders previously requested.[25]

The position of the Troop Carrier Command with respect to airborne training seemed to be another case in which "the spirit was willing, but the flesh was weak."

From its point of view, three factors contributed largely to its inability to meet the needs for airborne training. The first was the advanced date for overseas shipment of troop carrier units; a second was the requirement for attaching two groups to the Flying Training Command (mainly for use as tow ships in the training of glider pilots), and finally, there had been a "recent tie-up in aircraft production."[26]

Even when additional troop carrier units were organized and their crews trained for airborne operations, that did not mean necessarily that they would be available for training or operations with airborne troops. The "inherent flexibility" emphasized so frequently as one of the unique advantages of air power was a distinct handicap for the airborne program, because crews and planes intended for airborne training and operations could easily be diverted to other uses. One transport (troop carrier) group – the Sixtieth – had been assigned to the Eighth Air Force, and in June it moved with that organization to the United Kingdom. During the weeks immediately preceding its overseas movement, the Sixtieth Group had been used in moving men and supplies into the air bases being built along the North Atlantic ferry route in Newfoundland, Labrador, Greenland, and Iceland.[27] In August the Sixty-fourth Troop Carrier Group joined the Eighth Air Force in England; thus by the end of that month two troop carrier groups and 103 C-47 aircraft had crossed the Atlantic.[28] Obviously this number was far greater than was needed for the one parachute battalion then in the United Kingdom – it took only thirty-nine planes to carry that battalion to North Africa. Presumably the transports were being used in cargo carrying operations for the Eighth Air Force as well as in training and activities with the British. By November the Sixty-second Troop Carrier Group had joined the Twelfth Air Force in North Africa,[29] and the 316th Troop Carrier Group, which had been standing by in the United States to join a proposed British-American air task force to operate from the Caucasus, had arrived in the Middle East under control of the Ninth Air Force.[30] Again, these dispositions hardly could have been regarded as aimed toward support of the airborne effort, for no American airborne troops, other than the battalion which had flown from England, were in the Mediterranean theater at that time. Rather the arrivals of the C-47's were calculated to improve desert mobility at a time when the British were very short of cargo planes.[31] The principal task of the 316th Group was to carry supplies – mainly 200 drums of gasoline a day – for the American and British air units supporting the British Eighth Army.[32]

Carrying supplies for striking air units turned out to be the major mission for troop carrier units in the Pacific.[33] "As tenders serve naval vessels, so the C-47's served the striking air arms with the greater speed and mobility inherent in air movement."[34] In the spring of 1942, Japanese threats to Alaska resulted in the emergency mobilization of commercial airlines to carry men and equipment to that area,[35] and forty-three military transport planes were delivered to the Alaska Command.[36] The critical situation in the Pacific, from Japanese threats to Midway to the battles for Guadalcanal, and the tremendous distances involved, created urgent demands for more of the transport planes. During the year, 148 transport planes of all types arrived in the Pacific Ocean areas and the Far East.[37]

In addition to meeting demands of the theaters for transport aircraft, the United States undertook to furnish a number of planes for Allied powers. In a conference in May 1942 with Air Chief Marshall Sir Charles Portal, chief of air staff of the Royal Air Force, General Arnold had agreed that the Americans, in line with an earlier decision dividing aircraft production responsibilities between the United States and Great Britain, would undertake to provide a major share of the air transport, even for the training of British airborne divisions.[38] Deliveries of aircraft overseas in 1942 included 197 transport planes, all types, to the British Empire, and thirty-one to China.[39]

While crises in the Middle East, in the Soviet Union, and in the Pacific during 1942 added to the demands placed upon transport aircraft and troop carrier units, another consideration which operated against plans for larger troop carrier forces, or for their use for airborne troops, was the commitment of the Air Forces to a policy of reducing Germany by strategic bombardment. "Fulfillment of the ambitious plans of the AAF for its bomber offensive would mean a top priority, possibly even an overriding priority, for the production of airplanes, especially of heavy bombers,"[40] in the total American war production program. "The requirements of the bomber offensive . . . became the critical item in the aircraft production program which, when it had taken account of the minimum needs of other theaters and of training projects, had reached a startling figure."[41] It could be expected, under those assumptions, that many of the transport planes which were produced were built to serve as auxiliaries in the bomber offensive, and the airborne program was not to be a matter of major concern to the Air Forces. Aircraft acceptances of the Army Air Forces in 1942 included a total of 12,634 bombers, heavy, medium, and light; 10,780 fighters, and 1,985 transport planes of all types. Acceptances for the following year included 28,362 bombers, 24,005 fighters (the principal mission of most of the fighters was to protect the bombers), and 7,013 transports.[42] In addition, other resources went into 17,632 trainers in 1942, and 19,942 the next year for the training of crews – mostly for the bomber offensive. At the beginning of a war it could be expected that many military items would be in short supply; it has been noted that weapons were lacking at first. Whether or not early deficiencies would be overcome would depend upon the nature and demands of competing programs, and upon basic long-term planning on the bases of policies accepted for the conduct of the war.

The year 1942 came to a close with a gloomy outlook for the training program of the Airborne Command. General Chapman said that the shortage of aircraft for airborne training had become so acute that the timely completion of training programs of the two airborne divisions was being "seriously jeopardized."[43] He attributed the shortage, in large part, to a number of activities which were being given a priority for troop carrier aircraft over and above airborne training missions. He pointed out that, although the "paramount mission" of the Troop Carrier Command was "to furnish planes for airborne training," records of Airborne Command indicated that "less than 50 percent of the planes organically assigned to the Troop Carrier Command" were available for training elements of the Airborne Command.

War Department Allocation

The Airborne Command and the I Troop Carrier Command were grappling with insurmountable discrepancies between missions and facilities in their training programs. That is to say they were insurmountable so far as finding solutions within their own organizations was concerned, for both the missions and the assignment of facilities came from above. It was not enough for them to appeal respectively to Army Ground Forces and

Army Air Forces. That merely carried the same problems – with the same need for coordination – to a higher level. Each of those major commands had a multitude of other problems, often other matters held a greater interest for them, and neither of them was the planning agency wherein airborne requirements originated. This was a question requiring the attention of the War Department. Not only did it need to play the role of arbiter between its subordinate agencies, but it needed to coordinate its own plans. If the Air Forces failed to provide enough air transport for adequate training, perhaps the reason was to be found in the heavy demands which were being made in other commitments.

The General Staff failed to anticipate the problems which would arise inevitably as a result of its own plans and directives. It entered the picture, during this period, only after the problems had come to a head and appeals had been made for its decision.[44] Recognizing the continuing discrepancy between commitments and capabilities in the use of troop carrier aircraft, G-3 (General Edwards) suggested in October 1942 that the programs for troop carrier units and airborne divisions might be better coordinated in three ways: "(1) Increase the output of Troop Carrier Groups; (2) decrease the commitments of Troop Carrier Groups, such as to UK and Panama; (3) delay the activation of additional Airborne Divisions until the availability of essential training facilities can be foreseen."[45]

G-3 had taken steps toward the activation of four additional troop carrier groups, and on the basis of the memorandum referred to above, the Operations Division, on 7 November, undertook to set up a new priority for troop carrier units. In doing so, however, it made up a vertical list which showed the Airborne Command below the major combat theaters and in sixth place. The result, G-3 felt, was to nullify largely the effect of the activation of the four new groups and was to reduce the troop carrier units available for airborne training "almost to zero."[46] The whole theory of priorities became an absurdity in this situation. To say that a certain activity may have certain supplies if there are any left after all demands of a number of other activities have been satisfied is to suggest that that activity is regarded as relatively unimportant. If the essential materials are very short in that case, such a decision amounts to eliminating that activity. If the high command decision was that there should be airborne troops as well as air cargo units and bomber units, it was imperative that available materials be divided according to the needs of the various activities – their needs always with respect to the use which the high command intended to make of them. Of course there hardly could be any airborne program at all if the five agencies listed above the Airborne Command took all available troop carrier groups. Reaction of G-3 was to recommend the establishment of new priorities for all air support and troop carrier units by one of two methods:

a. *Preferred Method.* (1) Determine the number of each type unit required for each essential purpose.

(2) Convert the number of such units required for each purpose to the percent it represents of the total essential requirements for that type of unit.

(3) Apply this percent in each case to the total number of such units which can be organized, equipped, trained and made available for assignment. The result shows the actual number of units which can be made available for each purpose.

(4) As units become available, assign them to each approved project in rotation (as cards are dealt) until requirements are met. This is similar to the "repeating block system" of distribution which the Joint Chiefs of Staff consider to be the only practicable system for the distribution of airplanes (paragraph *j* of JCS 184, dates January 1, 1943).

b. *Alternate Method.* (1) Establish the essential minimum requirements for training purposes in first priority. This included pilot, glider pilot, O.T.U., R.T.U. and combined air-ground training. Unless these requirements are placed in first priority, full advantage cannot be taken of aircraft production nor can Air Force and Airborne Units be produced at the maximum rate for future requirements and commitment by the Operations Division.

(2) By placing only the relatively small proportion required for training in first priority, the bulk of these units will be available for assignment to theaters by any method chosen by the Operations Division.[47]

General Edwards laid responsibility for the inability of troop carrier and airborne units to complete joint training directly to the lack of coordination in planning. Operations Division (OPD) requested, 25 January 1943, that G-3 take steps to insure that one airborne division would complete its training by 15 April, for high-level planning then in progress was assuming the use of such a division in the invasion of Sicily. General Edwards replied immediately, "No airborne division is now available nor will be available by April 15 unless the troops carrier units required for the training of such a division be given the highest priority for this purpose."[48] He pointed out that this would require adequately trained troop carrier groups at full table of organization (T/O) strength in aircraft and personnel—and that one such group should be made available for the period 1 March to 15 April, for the exclusive purpose of training with that division. He recalled that previous directives on combined troop carrier-airborne training issued by his division had been "ineffective due to overseas commitments of troop carrier units." His action brought prompt results. Four days later OPD informed G-3 that the commanding general, Army Air Forces, had authorized, and the deputy chief of staff had approved, the employment of the 313th Troop Carrier Group, 1 February to 15 April, and the Sixty-first and 314th Groups, 1 March to 15 April, exclusively for the training of the Eighty-second Airborne Division, "The bringing of these units up to full T/O strength in aircraft and personnel and the allocation of these units to the Airborne Command for the training of the 82d Airborne Division during the periods indicated takes precedence over any other commitment or assignment."[49]

Continuing Shortages

Caught between demands for early preparation of airborne troops for overseas and the lack of means for training them, the Army Ground Forces staff decided early in 1943 that another appeal would have to be made to the War Department. Preparation of a memorandum for War Department G-3 went through at least three drafts. The second perhaps described the sentiments of AGF more accurately – if more bluntly – than the final one:

> Troop Carrier units are being sent overseas to serve as cargo carriers for air supply. The necessity of this procedure is not questioned by this headquarters. It is desired to point out that the continuation of this procedure will result in assembling sufficient air transport facilities for airborne operations of considerable magnitude in the theaters of operation while airborne troops in the United States will be only partially trained.
>
> If a reasonable amount of air transportation cannot be made available, it would appear sensible to suspend activation of subsequent airborne units immediately in order to avoid accumulation of personnel and units until adequate air training facilities can be made available. Such action, however, will necessitate cessation of all special procurement of parachute volunteers and the immobilization of a rather elaborate procurement and training system. It will require about four months lag to resume normal functioning of this system once it has been stopped.[50]

In the memorandum which he finally used, General McNair toned down that part of the earlier draft, but he offered a clear statement of the case. He referred to seven previous letters and memoranda on the subject, and then pointed out that in addition to the Eighty-second and 101st Airborne Divisions, activated since 15 August 1942, there was provision in the 1943 troop basis for four more such divisions to be activated at bi-monthly intervals beginning 15 February. The War Department, Army Air Forces, and Army Ground Forces, he reiterated, had agreed in July 1942 that "208 transport planes and 500 gliders were the minimum air transport requirements for the essential training of one airborne division."[51] Both the Eighty-second and the 101st Airborne Divisions were ready to proceed with glider unit and combined training, but only one combat team of the 101st Division had been able to complete glider unit training at Laurinburg. General McNair concluded that if requirements could not be met "in a reasonable degree" it would be "in order to suspend activation of new airborne units," though such a step "would have the disadvantage of interrupting the . . . rather elaborate procurement and ground training system."[52]

In spite of complaints and efforts at correction, the aircraft shortage – a shortage always relative to the size of the airborne program being attempted – hardly could be described as a case of passing from crisis to crisis; more exactly it seemed to maintain itself upon a plateau of continuing difficulty. An inspection of the 101st Airborne Division in January 1943 only corroborated what already was known – that the lack of airplanes had reduced airborne training to that of small unit training only.[53] At the same time, however, Army Ground Forces was receiving an inquiry from Operations Division as to how soon an airborne division could be made available for movement overseas. The answer depended mostly upon the availability of aircraft. The 101st Airborne Division (at that time it was planned that the 101st should be the first airborne division to move overseas) could "complete its combined training by March 27th, provided 50 transport planes and 100 gliders are made available each training day until March 20th, and 150 transport planes and 300 gliders made available from March 20th to March 27th."[54] In addition the division should have no less than two weeks, "and preferably one month," of maneuvers, which required 150 planes and 300 gliders for that period.

Now it appeared training plans could be supported. But the new schedule did not hold up even for the first month. Some delay in the training program resulted from the substitution of the Eighty-second for the 101st Airborne Division as the first airborne division ear-marked for overseas movement.[55] Then, in spite of categorical statements that the bringing of the troop carrier groups assigned to this training mission would take "precedence over any other commitment or assignment," overseas demands superseded the training requirement to the extent of reducing the total number of aircraft available to those groups from the T/O allowance of 156 to 103.[56] A conference between General Ridgway and General Arnold on 1 March resulted in an increase of this allotment to 135 airplanes.[57]

Still hopeful, Army Ground Forces mapped out a program for airborne training for the remainder of 1943. The program outlined five periods: First would be the completion of airborne training of the 101st Airborne Division, with the 506th Parachute Infantry attached, and already three groups had been made available for this for the period 1 May to 1 June. From 6 June to 20 June the 101st Division would participate in Tennessee maneuvers, and for this three groups would be available only until 15 June, after which one group would remain for completion of the period. June, August, and September would be for the airborne training of the First Airborne Infantry Brigade at Alliance, Nebraska, and Fort Meade, South Dakota, and for this two groups – with 104 airplanes and 104 gliders – would be the minimum requirement. The brigade would participate in maneuvers during September to the extent that aircraft were available. Activation of additional airborne divisions only magnified the training problem. During October and November the Eleventh Airborne Division would undergo training similar to that of the 101st, with a minimum requirement of 156 airplanes and 156 gliders, and during November and December the Seventeenth Airborne Division was scheduled for a similar program.[58]

Even the requirements for this moderate program could not be met. On 31 May staff officers drew up a revised schedule which was specific – it named particular groups for participation in defined areas on specific dates – but it was disappointing for Army Ground Forces. Only two groups, in separate areas (Fort Bragg-Camp Mackall area and Alliance, Nebraska, area) would be available from July to September; two groups would be concentrated in the Fort Bragg-Camp Mackall area during September and October, and three groups would be available in November and December. And the Air Forces warned that "it should not be assumed that over 47 of the 52 airplanes allocated to each group will be available for any particular action."[59] War Department G-3 finding, at that time, the acquisition of additional troop carrier planes unlikely and the alteration of other troop carrier commitments unfeasible, reluctantly approved the plans.[60] Very soon the revised program, as had been anticipated, proved to be inadequate.

Meanwhile further aircraft restrictions had appeared. Seeking to provide as many planes as possible for use in airborne training activities, the I Troop Carrier Command had made available, when possible, additional units not regularly assigned to that duty; now because of demands of a replacement training program of its own, the Fifth Troop Carrier Squadron, at Lawson Field working with the Parachute School, no longer would be available for use in regular parachute training.[61]

Army Ground Forces recommended, as the only immediately practicable solution to the continuing shortages, that overseas commitment dates of four troop carrier groups (the 436th, 437th, 438th and 439th) be deferred thirty days. Only two groups would be available for November, but this would make possible three groups for the maneuvers of the Eleventh Airborne Division in December, and three groups for January

1944.[62] Brig. Gen. Ray E. Porter, War Department G-3, notified AGF and AAF in August that since all troop carrier groups had commitment dates, while neither the Eleventh nor the Seventeenth Airborne Divisions had yet been committed, first priority in combined training and maneuvers would be to the troop carrier units.[63] Maj. Gen. Joseph M. Swing, new commanding general of the Airborne Command, countered with the observation that "unless the commitment dates for Troop Carrier Groups . . . are postponed neither the Groups nor the Airborne Divisions will be able to attain a satisfactory standard of efficiency."[64] In September, fortunately for the airborne training program, commitment dates for the four troop carrier groups were deferred.[65]

Projecting, on the basis of current plans, troop carrier requirements and schedules a year ahead, the Swing Board found that the aircraft shortage would be worse a year hence than at present. (See Appendix IV.) The discrepancy could be overcome only by reducing the commitments for troop carrier units or by activating and equipping a greater number of such units. The board suggested that a reduction in commitments might be made by one or all of three ways: by reducing aircraft commitments to theaters in which there were no airborne units; by reducing commitments to lift other than American airborne divisions; by reducing the number of American airborne divisions. On the other hand, it stated: "Availabilities can be increased only by the activation of additional Troop Carrier units which will not appear on this chart as ready for combined training until at least five months after activation. If the present activation rate is continued, the eleven groups necessary to balance the shortage shown above will not be available until February 1945."[66] Further efforts toward coordination led to the definition of plans for the movement of

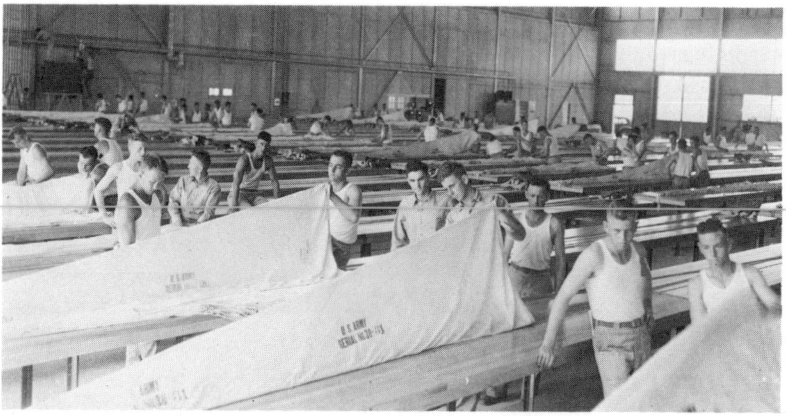

Parachutes are folded in a shed at Fort Benning.

troop carrier units. Operations Division, with the concurrence of Army Air Forces, notified the commanding general, European theater of operations, in September 1943, that ten troop carrier groups would be shipped to that theater during the period through June 1944 as follows: one group each in September, October, December, and January; two groups in February, two and one-half in March, one-half in April, and one group in June.[67] The troop carrier schedule became more definite when G-3 issued a schedule showing for each of the ten groups the date it would be available for joint training and maneuvers, when it would enter the staging area, and the date it would be available for shipment. No changes were to be made in this schedule without approval in each instance of G-3.[68]

In another memorandum on 28 October 1943, War Department G-3 laid down these instructions for the Army Air Forces:

> It is desired that each troop carrier unit be at full Table of Organization strength in personnel, airplanes, gliders, and equipment throughout the total training period of five months.
>
> No withdrawals below Table of Organization strength in personnel, airplanes, gliders, and equipment will be made from these units during their five month training period, without prior approval in each instance of the Assistant Chief of Staff, G-3.
>
> It is desired that the necessary maintenance facilities for gliders be established to insure that each troop carrier unit will have its full Table of Organization complement of flyable gliders during its five month training period.[69]

As the war approached its climax in 1944, demands for troop carrier aircraft for training subsided somewhat, but major problems of coordination remained, and difficulties persisted in meeting even the lesser requirements for aircraft. These requirements varied in detail.

After May 1944 the 349th Troop Carrier Group – last tactical units to be trained under I Troop Carrier Command – received the assignment to remain indefinitely in the Camp Mackall-Fort Bragg area to be available for airborne training. To augment the few other troop carrier tactical units remaining in the United States in the summer of 1944 it became necessary, while they were participating in airborne training, to attach combat replacement crews during the latters' final month of training.[70]

Parachutes

Obviously the first requirement for the training of parachute troops was a sufficient quantity of parachutes, and here, in this very first neccssity, handicaps began to appear at once. True, it was possible to begin preliminary training without a full quota of parachutes, and the Parachute

School could make use of such devices as suspended harness, airplane mock-up, landing trainer, jumping platforms, parachute tower, and dummy parachutes.[71] But after all of this, a man could not become a parachutist until he had completed some jump training with a parachute. Moreover the American procedure of providing each man with a second, emergency, 'chute served to double the total number required.

The Air Corps was the supply agency for parachutes, but the previous interest of the Air Corps in those items had been confined mainly to their procurement as safety devices for air crews. Any sudden increase in demand for a completely different purpose could only create an immediate shortage. The shortage of parachutes, and the consequent impediment to training, continued throughout 1941 and much of 1942. Even contract commitments which were undertaken were not kept. Although the Switlick Parachute Company had promised 3,750 packs, T-5, by July 1941, and the Irving Air Chute Company had contracted to produce 200 parachutes by 8 September 1941 and 100 per week thereafter, on 15 October 1941 neither company had delivered, nor was ready to deliver, any parachutes.[72] With total stocks down to 208 parachutes, the Provisional Parachute Group resorted to open market

A 12-foot web strap is attached to the parachute pack and snapped onto a steel cable inside the plane for automatically opening the parachute.

purchases while its leaders sought any opportunity to encourage fulfillment of commitments on the part of manufacturers. Fortunately the Air Corps was able to divert some of its own parachute appropriations to help meet the immediate needs.[73]

On the basis of two 'chutes per man, the three parachute regiments training at Fort Benning in May 1942 needed a total of 8,654 parachutes,[74] and the early activation of three additional regiments, as contemplated, would double that requirement. Still, these plans seemed to

The quick-release harness was operated by twisting the center disk to cock a spring mechanism, then slapping the disk, releasing the fasteners.

be reasonable enough, for the Air Force was preparing to procure parachutes at a rate of 8,500 per month after 1 June 1942 – a number regarded as sufficient to train all six parachute regiments as well as the replacement pool.[75] A difference yet remained, however, between promise and performance. Further delay in production developed when sub-contractors failed to deliver a new type of metal snap on schedule. Then great expectations of parachute production arose when Field Services of Air Service Command, Wright Field, announced that delivery of the metal snaps was expected to begin early in June, and that no less than 20,000 complete parachutes could be expected to be delivered by 24 July, and 20,000 per month thereafter.[76]

Nevertheless the Airborne Command reported on 1 July that so far only 300 parachutes had become available on the contracts referred to, and it had information from its liaison officer at Wright Field that only 1,000 type T-5 parachutes per week could be expected for the next two months; evidently the figure of 20,000 per month had included all types of 'chutes.[77] Beyond that date, perhaps there could be real hope that this particular difficulty could be overcome.

A kindred question of some importance in the supply of parachutes was that of issuing 'chutes to airborne troops who were to be landed by glider or airplane. Pointing out that neither the British nor the Germans provided parachutes for airborne troops, and emphasizing the need for conservation of cargo space for other equipment, AAF questioned the desirability of the practice. AGF held that in training, all troops transported by air, whether by airplane or glider, should be provided with parachutes, and suggested that in theaters of operations parachutes should be provided on the basis of approximately one-half of the troop carrying capacity of transport planes and gliders.[78]

A serious deficiency in the T-5 parachute harness, from the point of view of airborne troops, was its lack of a quick-release device. Once on the ground, it was a matter of vital importance that a parachutist be able to free himself quickly from his harness so that he would not be delayed in getting his weapon into action. This need had been foreseen, and the Parachute School had tested various quick-release devices as early as 1941, but they were rejected because of the safety factor. The danger was in the possibility of accidental release. Initial airborne operations brought stronger demands for such a device. In April 1943 Colonel Edson D. Raff, commander of the 509th Parachute Infantry Battalion, then in North Africa, obtained a German quick-release device. Upon examination by the Airborne Command, the German device was found to be similar to one developed in 1941 by the Irving Parachute Company, but it had the addition of a safety fork to prevent premature release. The Airborne Command and the Air Forces Materiel Command recommended that the

Irving quick-release device, modified to include the safety fork similar to that in the German design, be accepted and that the new T-7 parachute assembly replace the T-5. The decision to make the change came in December 1943, but several months were to pass before airborne divisions would be equipped with the T-7 parachute.

After preliminary delays had been overcome, the Air Forces, ironically, diverted initial production to Air Forces units for use as personnel escape parachutes. Parachutes of the T-5 type already in supply were being converted by attaching the new harness assembly, but this too lagged behind schedule. Not until early in 1945 could all of the parachute units in the European theater be equipped with the new parachute.[79]

Another use of parachutes which continued to develop was for the delivery of supplies and equipment. In general use in 1944 was a twenty-four-foot cargo parachute, suitable for a load of 200 pounds, and five types of delivery units and a cargo net for use with this parachute.[80] Experiments looked to broadening the scope of uses. In 1944 parachute delivery of certain types of engineer demolition equipment was found to be practicable.[81]

Gliders

The standard glider for airborne operations in the U.S. Army was the Waco CG-4A. It would carry a payload of 3,750 pounds – fifteen men or one jeep.[82] The British were using the plywood Horsa, of considerably larger size (payload: 6,900 pounds) as a troop carrier, and the big Hamilcar (payload: 16,000 pounds) for heavy cargo. Concluding that all three types were tactically sound and usable, and noting the need for a limited number of the big Hamilcars, General Lee and Lt. Col. Silas R. Richards (Air Corps) suggested in April 1943 that the British gliders be provided for American airborne units which were to be stationed in the United Kingdom, and that American gliders be provided for British airborne units in other theaters. This, they thought, would simplify the cooperation between the two airborne forces, and would permit a more efficient use of shipping facilities.[83] Actually American troops continued to use the CG-4A almost exclusively until they began training for the Normandy operation when they did use a considerable number of the Horsas.

The question of shipping space was a vital one. One crated CG-4A weighed 20,000 pounds, and this very consideration became dominant in a recommendation for reducing the ratio of glider troops in an airborne division.[84]

A proposed "40-place flying wing glider" was under consideration at the time. General Chapman had been impressed by an inspection of the design and a two-place flying model of the glider. Believing it to be

"Exceptionally well suited to the requirements of airborne troops," he had recommended the building and testing of a full scale glider.[85]

Another idea which was receiving some attention was the proposed development of an assault glider. Maj. Lewin B. Barringer, a glider specialist,[86] on the staff of AAF, presented blueprints for such a glider in the summer of 1942. Encountering opposition from AAF's Materiel Division, he asked AGF to indicate officially its position on the subject.[87] This was a project which Army Ground Forces could encourage; "in fact, the idea was originally presented by the Airborne Command."[88] AGF promptly stated its position in a letter to the commanding general, Army Air Forces:

> In the development of airborne tactics there is need for a glider which could be used by air landing infantry on fields which have not been secured by parachute troops.
>
> Such a glider, equipped with .50-caliber and .30-caliber machine guns should be capable of being towed by combat airplanes and should have a carrying capacity of five or six fully equipped infantrymen. Some protective armament might well be provided.[89]

Subsequently, Christopher Aircraft and Timm went to work on the proposed craft, designated AG-1, and a year later a mock-up was presented for examination.[90] The assault glider was seen as a kind of "flying pillbox" which would land immediately preceding initial landings of cargo gliders and/or parachute troops. With two .50-caliber and two .30-caliber machine guns mounted separately behind armor plates, the assault glider would cover the landing and reorganization of the other airborne troops. Personnel would include a pilot, co-pilot, and four gunners. In addition to the machine guns and individual weapons there would be two rocket launchers. The glider should be capable of being towed at high speed by fighters or bombers.[91]

Many suggestions arose for more extensive and varied use of gliders. They were tested satisfactorily in landing on packed snow and on water in mountain operations.[92] It was suggested that gliders could be used for routine supply "to fixed and mobile ground and air force units of all types with weapons, ammunition, food, and personnel."[93] It was pointed out that this type of supply would be especially useful for armored units. Another suggestion was that an airborne repair depot might be dropped wherever mechanized ground force equipment or ordnance needed repair. Airborne field hospitals might be moved from one location to another by glider, and wounded might be evacuated. Gliders might be used as carriers for raiding parties, and ground force elements which had become isolated might be rescued. They might be used to move ground echelons of air force units, and they would permit the routine use of airborne engineers for emergency maintenance and repair.

Many of these suggestions, which at first might have sounded far beyond the scope of glider capabilities, were made feasible by the improvement of a pick-up device which enabled a flying tow plane to whisk away a loaded glider resting in a field. In July 1943 Maj. L. B. Magic, Jr., Air Corps glider officer on the staff of the Airborne Command, reported his participating in tests of the pick-up device: "The C-47 picked up the glider while flying at 140 mph and within 3 and 3/5 seconds from the time they made contact with my tow rope, I was in the air and flying at 120 mph."[94] He reported less strain on the airplane motors than in a conventional take-off. That pick-up unit, designed to pick up an 8,000-pound load, had picked up a fully loaded CG-4A without difficulty. It picked up another which was resting on skids on a sod surface. A much larger glider was being developed at that time, and it was still in the experimental stage (XCG-13); one of those was loaded lightly to a gross weight of 9,000 pounds, and the C-47 demonstrated similar success in taking it into the air. Another pick-up unit, capable of taking a fully loaded 30-place glider (16,000 pounds) was being developed.

After tests at Camp Mackall it became commonplace for C-47's to take gliders in double tow. This had an advantage of decreasing the required air space, delivering troops in better mass, and doubling the glider capacity of the airplanes. In September 1943 these tests included parachute jumps from gliders in double tow. The results were more successful than had been expected, and in October Lt. Col. W. S. Ryan recommended that gliders be modified for the use of parachute troops. This use of gliders, however, would be to abandon their most desirable features. The advantage of gliderborne troops was that tactical units, with greater loads of ammunition and equipment than parachutists, were landed in compact groups organized for immediate action. As an expedient when sufficient transport airplanes were not available, gliders might be used, but in general the procedure was not adopted for normal tactical operations.[95]

Glider improvements followed two general lines of thought. One was for a heavy cargo glider which could bring in vehicles and medium artillery, and the other was for an improved assault glider.

By March 1944 a bigger glider, the CG-13, was in production, and another, the CG-16, was undergoing tests.[96] Its capacity more than double that of the CG-4A, the CG-13 could carry forty-two men or a cargo of 8,500 to (in an emergency) 9,700 pounds. As on the earlier glider, the nose opened upward to form the cargo door.[97] It could carry a 105-mm. howitzer (M2) together with a 3/4-ton truck prime mover without disassembly or modification, or it could carry a 1½-ton 6 x 6 cargo truck.[98]

Another glider which soon appeared was a "clipped wing" version of the CG-4A. Designated the CG-15A, it was found to be more stable in the air, and had some desirable modifications, but its carrying capacity and construction were about the same as those of the CG-4A.[99] Attention then turned to the CG-10A, a big plywood glider comparable to the British Hamilcar.[100]

In January 1945 an Army Ground Forces statement re-emphasized the importance of the glider: "A careful analysis of observer reports, film reports, operational reports, captured enemy documents, and the comments of Ground Force Commanders on the assault type CG-4 glider show conclusively that its general military characteristics, including cargo space capabilities, design, and construction, are needs of the ground arm."[101] After considering all current types of gliders, the Air Force proposed the development of two all-metal types adaptable for power installation. One would be designed to carry a 6,000 pound load, and the other a 16,000 pound load.[102] The catch, of course, was in the time it would take to make such gliders available.

Army Ground Forces, therefore, recommended in May 1945 the procurement of 139 CG-10A gliders (the Hamilcar type) – a planning figure based on the number necessary for moving an airborne division in a

A C-47 snatches the line of a CG 4A glider at rest by means of a special pick-up device during practice in England, March 1944.

The tail section is removed from the British Horsa glider for the fastest method of unloading equipment.

The newer CG-13 gliders were bigger than previous models.

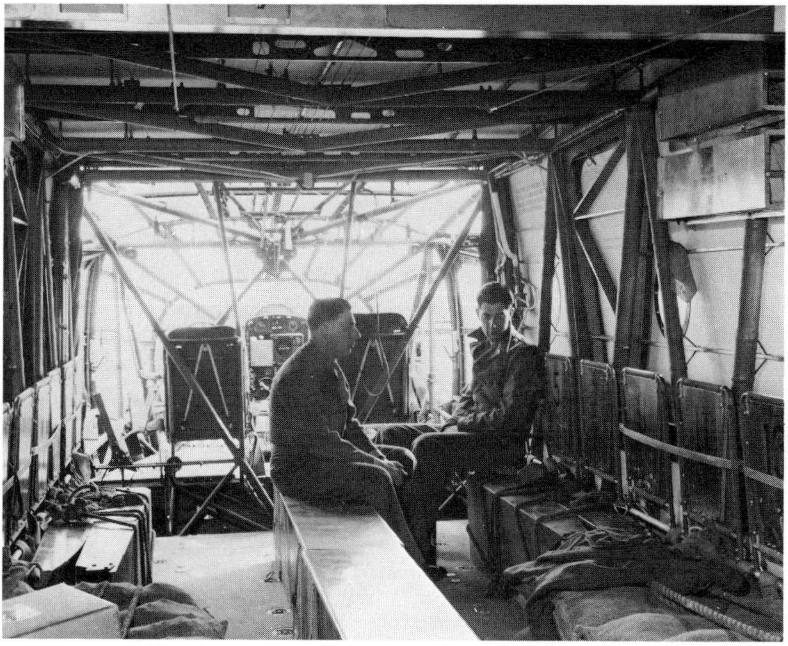

The interior of a CG-13.

single lift. The War Department approved this figure, but upon the cessation of hostilities against Japan the Air Forces, in compliance with instructions from the War Department, terminated the contracts at a run-out quantity of ten gliders. Army Ground Forces, even then, urged the renewal of the contract, for plans for the post-war establishment included the retention of an airborne division in strategic reserve, and although the proposed all-metal power gliders would be highly desirable, they were not available. It was pointed out that Ground Forces' objective of achieving air transportability of the standard infantry division could be achieved – aside from the medium tank – with the C-82 airplane and the CG-10A glider. The glider could be used for the landing of heavy equipment prior to the construction of landing strips in any operation, and the C-82 for landings thereafter. Nevertheless the War Department returned the request "not favorably considered."[103]

Shortage of Gliders for Training

> Back in 1942 the only person that could fly a glider back of an airplane was some "darn fool" out on the West Coast, who won a little extra money for a demonstration.

> After the invasion of Crete, where gliders were used more or less successfully, the Flying Training Command suddenly came afire with the development of a glider training program.[104]

Not only the shortage of transport aircraft, but the inability to obtain sufficient gliders as well hampered the early months of the glider training program. Once again it was a story of conflict between training requirements and overseas and other commitments.

Delivery of a small nine-place glider was scheduled to begin in April or May 1942,[105] but there was little promise that either that model or the fifteen-place CG-4A, which became the standard, would be available in sufficient numbers for the satisfactory training of glider units when they were ready for such training. To make matter worse, gliders were to be shipped overseas before they could be used for training. AGF had recommended consistently that no major airborne unit be shipped overseas without first having participated in a tactical exercise, conducted under simulated combat conditions, in this country – an exercise which would involve the whole unit in an airborne maneuver. By August 1942 no glider training had been conducted, and the logistics for moving a large airborne force had not been worked out. The time was at hand for activation of two airborne divisions, and it was expected that their major elements would be gliderborne. Yet only 165 gliders – hardly enough for a regimental combat team – had been allotted to the airborne training program. "Just why foreign requirements make it necessary to ship gliders overseas before the troops that are to use them is not known by this section."[106] (Late in 1942 some gliders arrived in Panama, where neither air nor ground commanders exhibited any interest in their use; glider activities there never went beyond a few experimental flights.)[107] AAF plans called for a total of 255 gliders to be made available for training – 165 would be for airborne training and 90 would be for glider pilot training; above that total, gliders, as they were produced, would be crated and shipped overseas. Army Ground Forces urged that, at least for the period 1 November to 31 December 1942, the number of gliders allotted to airborne training be increased from 165 to 500 to permit the tactical training of a division.[108] Air Force plans anticipated the assignment of thirty-nine gliders as well as thirty-nine airplanes to Laurinburg for airborne training for the period 15-30 November, and fifty-two thereafter.[109]

There were insufficient numbers of gliders at best, and the shortage became more critical with the additional difficulties which developed in handling the gliders on the ground and the necessity for grounding numbers of the craft for the changing of parts in compliance with Air Force technical orders.[110] The inauguration of the glider program presented another example of having immediate plans which were too big for available resources and long range plans which were inadequate for the approved airborne program – and too little coordination for the whole of it. With the adoption of the Waco-design CG-4A as the standard tactical glider, orders were placed with fifteen factories for a total of 5,290 of them to be delivered by June 1943. Production was to begin 1 June 1942. But by April it had become evident that the gliders would not be coming off the production lines before August or September 1943, and there appeared to be little hope of speeding up glider deliveries. Even then an enlargement of the program was being planned.[111]

Plans for the activation of four more airborne divisions during 1943 meant that there would be six airborne divisions plus a GHQ Glider Infantry Regiment with a total of approximately 36,400 glider troops.[112] Plans for the rotation of the troops through four glider tactical training bases had to be abandoned because of the lack of aircraft. It took about five weeks to give one division glider training at one base (Laurinburg-Maxton).[113]

Though glider production did give some hope that that shortage might be eased during 1943, other difficulties appeared. One was the call upon troop carrier units for duty in ferrying gliders. This meant the diversion of tow planes and glider pilots away from the airborne training program in order to accomplish the movement of gliders from factories to bases, or to ports, or from one base to another. When such assignments came for squadrons participating in airborne training, the result, of course, was to require complete revision of previously-made plans and commitments with the Airborne Command.[114] From this type of duty the I Troop Carrier Command tried to escape. It urged that the Air Transport Command or the Flying Training Command be given the assignment. The latter had crews and tow planes, and Troop Carrier Command would, if necessary, do without additional glider pilots for sixty days to permit use of training facilities for that purpose. After several months of such diversion, the Troop Carrier Command was relieved from ferrying gliders to bases of other commands. For the ferrying duties which still remained for serving its own bases, it organized, in February 1943, a Provisional Tow Detachment at Stout Field in order to protect the squadrons from further interference with training activities.[115]

Meanwhile the general shortage continued to affect the glider program as well as other airborne activities. By April 1943, CG-4A production was improving. The earlier goal of 5,290 by June hardly was being approached, but production schedules still called for delivery of 6,006 by the end of the year. Of the gliders produced up to that time, 677 had been shipped, or were awaiting shipment overseas. At the same time the British had been advised to proceed with the construction of 600 Horsa and 100 of the big Hamilcar gliders during 1943, and 900 Horsas by June 1944, and 100 more Hamilcars that year. It was estimated that the monthly production rate of the CG-4A gliders (which so far had not met its schedules) could be increased 25 percent within thirty days by raising the priority.[116]

The Airborne Command estimated that 1,000 gliders of all types would be needed for training purposes during 1943, and 2,000 would be needed for 1944. It found that 823 CG-4A gliders were required to transport an airborne division on a tactical mission. Satisfactory training, however, could be accomplished by using 150 flyable gliders in three echelons. Training losses were amounting to three to six gliders a day – some reparable, some total losses – and it suggested that a 25 percent surplus should be sufficient to cover this loss.[117]

Although General Arnold seemed to be highly enthusiastic about war use of the glider, such enthusiasm failed to spread throughout the Air Forces. His instructions, in July 1943, were to make every effort to speed up the development and the maximum use of the motorless aircraft, but in I Troop Carrier Command there was a feeling that it had "lost the ball on this performance because of procrastination."[118] No program had been developed as a result of experiments which the Troop Carrier Command had conducted, there had been no definite policy formed with respect to equipment and training for glider pilots, nor any demonstration of what could be accomplished with gliders during unit training periods.

The rather sudden announcement of a 1,000 glider pilot program on 22 June 1943 – 800 to 1,000 were to be ready for shipment by early September[119] – inevitably had repercussions for airborne training. But more serious was the further evidence of the low priority which I Troop Carrier Command enjoyed in the Air Forces in the low quality of many of the glider pilots which it then was receiving.[120]

For its part, the I Troop Carrier Command concluded later that its greatest training problem had been "to get the required personnel and equipment on schedule."[121]

Here was another area requiring the attention of higher authority. When AGF G-3 asked the Airborne Command to estimate its glider needs for 1943 and 1944, the reply was one of helplessness for want of a master plan or intelligible information. It stated the difficulty in these words:

> It is the opinion of this headquarters, however, that the War Department Operations Section is the only source which can give even an approximation of the requirements for 1943 and 1944. This headquarters has no definite information as to commitments abroad, no definite information on activation of airborne units in the future, and therefore has no basis upon which a logical time factor can be computed.[122]

Development of Special Equipment

It did not take very many airborne operations to make clear the necessity for navigational aids. At first commanders tried to overcome the difficulties by more intensive training of pilots. But radar offered a more promising solution. Heavy and medium bomber units projected special "pathfinder" groups during the summer of 1943, and in October experimentation began with pathfinder equipment for troop carrier operations. As a matter of fact its feasibility already had been proved in combat. After the navigational difficulties of the Sicilian operation, a pathfinder unit was organized for the reinforcement of the Salerno beachhead in September 1943. Three pathfinder aircraft preceded the main force to locate the drop zone and to drop a parachute pathfinder team from the Eighty-second Airborne Division. The pathfinder team then set up portable lightweight navigational aids to guide the succeeding serials of airplanes to the drop zones. In the autumn of 1943, the Eighty-second Division and the North African Air Force Troop Carrier Command continued their development of pathfinder units and techniques.[123]

Lt. General Lewis H. Brereton, when preparing to go to Europe to take command of the Ninth Air Force – which would include the IX Troop Carrier Command – was convinced that "this radar equipment, which provides a reliable means of position-finding, is absolutely necessary for large-scale airborne operations," and he asked that every effort be made to install the Rebecca, Eureka, and ITF radar equipment on the C-47's before their departure for the European theater.[124]

The pathfinder development emphasized the need for communication between airborne units, after they had jumped or landed, and troop carrier formations. It was reported in November 1943 that a special two-channel Very High Frequency radio had been developed for the purpose, and in January 1944 the Troop Carrier Command requested eight of the units (An-TRC-7) for use at Pope Field.[125]

Concentration of effort against the Japanese in 1945 raised the question of using carrier-borne naval aircraft for pathfinder operations. Army Ground Forces and the War Department approved a proposal of the Airborne Board for such a project in May 1945. Tests completed early in August indicated that a modified "Avenger" torpedo bomber could be used for dropping pathfinder personnel and equipment. The primary advantage of using carrier-borne aircraft for dropping pathfinder teams was the deception which would be gained by using the same type of plane which would operate in any carrier strike.[126]

Another new development in 1945 was the introduction of the infrared direction finder. In experiments in May, forty-five pathfinder crews of the IX Troop Carrier Command in Europe were able to obtain positive identification at a distance of seven nautical miles with the new type of equipment. It promised to be a useful supplement to the Rebecca-Eureka equipment and the radio compass beacon. The same principle was used in tests with airborne troops with a view to its use for night assembly of units. It was promising, but its cost – approximately $150 per man – might have been prohibitive.[127]

Poverty of equipment prevented the execution of a comprehensive pathfinder training program in the United States. An AGF request in November 1944 for the shipment of radar equipment to the Parachute School and for C-47 airplanes with radar equipment to be included in the planes being furnished for parachute training at Fort Benning could not be met. Availability dates for the equipment were so remote that Army Air Forces suggested that the request be resubmitted about 1 April 1945.[128]

This was the story, in a way, of all special equipment so badly needed for training in order to make effective its priority assignment to combat.

Chapter V

The Men: Morale and Training

> It goes without saying that the high demands made on the air arm in an operation by airborne troops are only within the capacity of a support air fleet which in organization and tactical employment is most carefully coordinated with the ground forces. It must, therefore, be conceded that an air arm constructed purely for long-range bombing is hardly in a position to cooperate successfully in a major operation by airborne troops. The bombardment of towns...requires from the air staff, flying personnel and signalling service, in respect of organization and training, desiderata which are in principle simpler than those required in close cooperative action with ground forces. One might say, indeed, that for the latter type of work a higher grade of tactical handling is required; and if this be so, it will be a difficult matter to advance from a lower to a higher function.*

The first major airborne training exercise in the United States Army – the maneuver of the 550th Infantry Airborne Battalion, with Company C, 501st Parachute Infantry Battalion attached, in Panama in August 1941 (using B-18 and C-39 airplanes) – pointed up the nature of problems which should have been apparent at the outset. That exercise demonstrated the requirement for complete staff coordination between Air Corps and airborne forces; it brought out the need for the development of aircraft designed to transport ground combat troops and their equipment.[1]

* F. O. Miksche, *Paratroops* (New York: Random House, 1943), p. 185.

Policy and the Troops

A serious problem which could have wrecked the entire airborne program was the morale of the troops involved. There was reason to believe that I Troop Carrier Command, though itself completely cooperative with the Airborne Command, was little more than an unattended stepchild in the over-all structure of the Army Air Forces. In comparison to the more attractive activities of the bomber and long-range fighter programs, the troop carriers apparently had a very low priority in the Air Forces. When a serious shortage of communications men developed early in 1943, Army Air Forces offered hope of an increased flow of such men in view of "reduced physical requirements for air crews serving on non-combat type aircraft, such as those used by I Troop Carrier Command."[2] Troop carrier units used transport aircraft, without benefit of armament or armor, but they had to fly them into combat, and they would not be flying at 300 miles an hour at 20,000 feet; they were called upon to deliver soldiers while flying through flak at 120 miles an hour at an altitude of a few hundred feet. Naturally the Troop Carrier Command resented its classification as "noncombat," and replied that some misunderstanding surely existed concerning the nature of troop carrier missions. In an endorsement to AAF, the troop carrier commander said: "In order to preclude publication of any regulation which refers to Troop Carrier units as noncombat organizations, it is believed that the Assistant Chief of Air Staff, Personnel, should be officially advised of the missions of Troop Carrier units."[3] Nevertheless, AAF Regulation No. 50-12, 10 September 1943, set up physical standards for crew members of "AAF Troop Carrier Command...and air crews of noncombat airplanes in other commands."[4] This was on the ground that physical requirements for pilots of planes operating at low altitudes and slow speeds did not have to be as rigorous as for those flying high-performance aircraft.

The quality of pilots being assigned the Troop Carrier Command became a matter of concern as well:

> The receipt of pilot trainees indicates that this Command has a low priority as regards the quality of pilot trainees received...Our pilot training is unique in its difficulty due to the importance of the load we carry, the necessity for hitting our target and the nature of the navigational mission. It is firmly believed that Troop Carrier Pilots have as tough a job as any pilot in the Air Corps, because in addition to all of the capabilities normally required of a military pilot he must in addition be proficient in extremely low altitude navigation at night with multiple gliders in tow and likewise be proficient in the aerial pick-up of loaded tactical gliders, this last being an operation involving the utmost skill and coordination. It would seem, therefore, that the pilot material for such a job should

> be of the highest caliber. At Troop Carrier Command Transition School, there is a sizeable percentage of below average eliminees of 4-engine school and a disturbing percentage are service pilots rated in another Command and sent to this Command for training and utilization. In view of the fact that Troop Carrier Command has no requirements for service pilots, this is, indeed, short-sighted planning.[5]

The very nature of troop carrier work magnified the ordinary problems of morale which could be expected in any military organization. First of all, most men "would rather lay an egg or shoot a gun than fly a truck or tractor."[6] Beyond that, flying day and night in unarmed and unarmored aircraft, at low altitude and low speed, in formations prohibiting evasive action, over enemy-held territory required courage of the highest order. Moreover the manner in which troop carriers were diverted to carrying cargo made it necessary frequently to rebuild *esprit de corps* as well as technical proficiency.

The low priority of the Troop Carrier Command for scarce materials created a special morale problem throughout the war. That was in the lack of self-sealing gasoline tanks in troop carrier aircraft. A hit in the gasoline tank area of a wing was likely to cause fire. If the bullet were incendiary, fire would break out immediately; more often gasoline would flow out of the trailing edge of the wing and become ignited near the engine exhaust. If the plane did not catch fire the loss of gasoline was likely to force a landing. Fire in the wing section caused the wing to collapse within four or five minutes, and because of the low altitude they flew, crews had little time to jump to safety. Crews might face the threat of being shot down or having a forced landing, but it was another matter for them to have to face a likelihood greater than for other airmen of crashing in flames.[7]

Although General McNair was opposed in general to preferential treatment in matters of personnel within the ground forces, the one exception which he did permit in 1942 was the clearing out of Class IV and V men in excess of the Army average in airborne divisions.[8] This doubtless provided a much needed boost in launching the new program. If nothing else came of it, here was an opportunity to build some superior infantry divisions. At least in personnel policies, airborne divisions, in contrast with troop carrier units, enjoyed a favored position.

A closely related problem involved another matter of preferential treatment, or equality of treatment – depending upon whether the comparison were being made with other ground forces troops or with flying crews of the Air Forces. That was the matter of extra pay. From the beginning of parachute troop activity, flying pay was authorized for those participating, and the whole question was clarified for all parachutists when Congress authorized parachute pay ($100 for officers and $50 a month for enlisted men) in 1942.[9] This, however, made no provision for extra pay for glider troops, and the apparent discrimination could hardly have been expected to have a healthy morale effect in airborne divisions – which included both glider and parachute units. It did not help the situation when glider pilots were granted flight pay.[10] The situation then was that the pilots, who took the gliders into the landing zone and then had no further specified ground combat role, received extra pay for their part, while the soldiers whom they carried through the same hazards, and who would have to attack the enemy positions, received no additional consideration. Worse, members of the crew of the transport plane who went through the same air spaces and flak as the gliders, and then, after the gliders had cast off, returned to comfortable bases in rear areas, drew extra pay for that part, while the glidermen who rode their motorless craft down behind enemy lines for life and death combat enjoyed no such favored financial status.

Furthermore, the hazard was present in training as well as in combat. In the period of tactical training from May 1943 to 19 February 1944 there were 162 injuries among glidermen and 17 deaths in glider accidents.[11] The condition found expression in a celebrated poster which appeared at the Laurinburg-Maxton Army Air Base. It presented a group of five photographs showing gliders in various stages of twisted wreckage, with captions that screamed in large letters: "JOIN THE GLIDER TROOPS! No Flight Pay; No Jump Pay; BUT – Never a Dull Moment!"[12] It was not until 1 July 1944 that extra glider pay became effective for all glider personnel.[13] Until that difference was eliminated, it was next to impossible to overcome the friction between glider and parachute troops or to build a closely-knit team in the airborne division. Differences in uniform – especially in the paratrooper's highly prized jump boots – added to the resentment of glider troops and increased the difficulty of achieving cooperation between the two elements.[14] Apparent discrimination or favor for one group of men over another engaged in similar activities, particularly when they had to work together as a team, was bound to have unfortunate consequences.

The personal interest which General McNair and his staff displayed during a visit to the Eighty-second Airborne Division at Fort Bragg in February 1943 was calculated to make an effective contribution to the morale of the glider troops. Maj. Gen. Matthew B. Ridgway, division commander, wrote in a personal letter to Brig. Gen. John M. Lentz:

> You earned an enduring place with the men of the 82d Division in your voluntary pick-up ride in the glider. When we asked the men who were with you, themselves all volunteers, what their reactions were, we found that the thing they enjoyed most was that they had a colonel for a pilot and a brigadier general for a co-pilot. To have

> had you in one glider and Gen. McNair in another was a magnificent thing . . . .
>
> The entire division got a tremendous inspiration and incentive to increased effort from Gen. McNair's personality and dominant leadership during his visit.[15]

Troop Carrier Training

Participation of troop carrier units in airborne operations demanded more than simply furnishing so many planes and so many pilots. It involved special training of the air crews and long practice in cooperation between air and ground forces.

A four-months' training program announced by the Air Transport Command (later I Troop Carrier Command) in May 1942 for the training of troop carrier units provided for five weeks of joint training with airborne troops.[16] This included one week for air crews in supplying airplane time for the Parachute School at Lawson Field, two weeks of glider practice, with dead and live loads, and two weeks in joint maneuvers. The first two wings scheduled for overseas shipment could follow the prescribed program only in part, but subsequent wings were supposed to follow it in full. After initial commitments had been met, one transport group and one hundred replacement crews, "all of whom will have had special instructions in [Troop Carrier] Command type of flight and work together as a unit in cooperative operations with the Airborne Command," were to be turned out each month.[17]

In order to condition troop carrier crews to face antiaircraft fire, I Troop Carrier Command worked out a plan along the principles of the ground force combat course. It was planned to have each troop carrier unit make a night low-level formation flight of 300 miles, which would include a leg from St. Joseph, Michigan, across Lake Michigan to Great Lakes Naval Training Station (Great Lakes being chosen because it was the only place where substantial amounts of all types of antiaircraft weapons could be found in place). Each formation, on approaching the naval station, was to pass between two walls of antiaircraft fire. Although winning both Army and Navy approval, the plan was never carried out, apparently because of the objections of the local naval commander, who feared damage to his installation by falling aircraft.[18]

A special contribution of the Airborne Command (Center) to the joint training of troop carrier crews was the assignment of airborne jumpmaster teams to troop carrier training bases. Three such teams were made available in January and February 1944, and a fourth was added the following December. The airborne teams used dummy parachutists for the training exercises, and they cooperated in orientation of troop carrier crews in airborne operations and in defining training procedures. The teams first assisted in the training of pilots of the Sixty-first Troop Carrier Wing and the Sixty-third Troop Carrier Group in the aerial delivery of personnel, equipment, and supplies.

In February training began with the 443d and 349th Troop Carrier Groups at the Alliance Army Air Base. There airborne and troop carrier officers worked out a standard operating procedure to govern the training. The basic formation for parachute operations was to be a flight of three planes, flying in V formation. All planes were to fly at the same altitude. The altitude during the approach for a parachute drop – in contour flying – was to be 250 feet above the ground. For the actual parachute drop the airplanes were to fly at a speed of 110 miles per hour, without using wheels or flaps for speed reduction. The jump altitude (in this case the altitude from which the dummy parachutists would be dropped) was set at 450 feet, and the altitude for the dropping of aerial delivery containers was to be 150 feet.[19]

After those troop carrier groups had completed their prescribed joint training, the airborne teams were retained for the training of troop carrier replacement crews.[20]

Glider Pilots

Glider pilot training, obviously, was closely related to the airborne training program. Glider pilots had to be made available before any gliders could be used, and the demands for aircraft and gliders for the glider pilot training meant less of the same, at the particular time, for the training of airborne troops.

Glider pilots, after basic training by the Flying Training Command, were assigned to the Troop Carrier Command for operational training. This involved training with airborne troops. The pilots were assigned to tactical groups which were based at locations near, and operated with, airborne glider units. Ninety days after activation, troop carrier groups were scheduled to begin a two months' period of unit training, and during this period it was possible to work with glider infantry and artillery in conducting familiarization flights and in loading and unloading the gliders. "Normal procedure" was for troop carrier groups, after completion of unit training, to go to Pope Field, the Laurinburg-Maxton Air Base, or Lawson Field to carry on concentrated training in gliderborne (and parachute) operations and to participate in field problems and maneuvers.[21]

The problems became further complicated when Army Air Forces requested ground forces to assist in infantry training for glider pilots. Actually the question did not grow principally out of a desire to insure that Air Force glider pilots would be able to play an effective role in ground combat after landing. Its more direct origin lay in the search for a solution to a morale problem which was developing among idle glider pilots who, having completed basic glider training, were awaiting assignment to advanced training schools. A pool of 2,754 such glider candidates, in December 1942, was awaiting assignment to four schools in Texas and Arkansas whose total capacity was 600 students a month. This meant that, even if no more students completed basic training, some of those in the pool would have to wait as long as five months in that bottleneck. The director of glider training hoped that an active ground training program would alleviate the state of low morale and discontent which was the natural consequence of such a stalemate.

Willing to see what could be done, Army Ground Forces directed the Airborne Command to furnish the necessary instructors and to work out the details with the Flying Training Command. General Chapman sent Lt. Col. M. A. Quinto of the Eighty-eighth Glider Infantry to the Flying Training Command headquarters to get further information. His report was to the effect that obstacles were practically insurmountable. The program would require an estimated 30 officers and 150 enlisted men as instructors, but worst of all, they would have no training aids with which to work – no ranges, no bayonet or grenade courses, not even any infantry weapons. The Airborne Command felt that the program exceeded its scope and capabilities. In any case the nature of the training was not peculiar to airborne and might well fall within the province of the Replacement and School Command. Moreover, current doctrine did not contemplate the active employment of glider pilots with airborne troops in tactical operations following landings in hostile territory. Finally General Chapman suggested that the Airborne Command could very well undertake the ground training of glider pilots at glider tactical stations, where instructors and equipment might be obtained from glider infantry units, but it would be difficult for his command to conduct such training at other installations. General Lentz, AGF G-3, concluded that, if an interim ground training program were to be held necessary, it might be possible to work out a system of attaching glider students to nearby ground units who were undergoing basic training. This became the attitude of AGF.[22]

Joint Training for Airborne Units

Immediately the desirability of close liaison became apparent. "It was felt, in this union of air and ground forces, each staff could do well to have representatives of the other arm on which it was depending."[23] Although never realized in practice, "the ideal situation would have been to have each new Troop Carrier unit activated and trained in its elementary phases right alongside the airborne outfit with which it would ultimately function which would provide a maximum of teaming, understanding, and liaison."[24] Actually the advantages of such an arrangement were more apparent than real, because trained crews were needed to work with untrained paratroops.

The Airborne Command and the Troop Carrier Command began the exchange of liaison officers in May 1942. The primary purpose was to keep "each command informed as to the needs, programs and problems of the other, insofar as they may affect the other, to result in the eventual perfection of technique and procedures covering the various types of joint operations, which may be required of the two Commands."[25]

Both commands demonstrated a willingness to cooperate. Expressing a conviction that complete understanding of "joint objectives and each other's problems" was essential, Col. Fred C. Borum, air transport commander, invited General Lee and his staff of the Airborne Command to visit the troop carrier headquarters – "in order that we may sit down over a table with our sleeves rolled up and our cards spread out above the board, to determine the most practicable and expeditious manner in which we can weld our raw material into a smoothly running tool with which our country may carve out victory."[26] Arrangements were made during that same month for troop carrier staff officers to visit Fort Bragg to discuss problems of joint operations.[27] In the absence of any unified command for training purposes, it was necessary for the Airborne Command and the I Troop Carrier Command, operating on directives and plans submitted by separate higher headquarters, to function through numerous special committees and boards as well as with regular liaison officers.[28]

The training of airborne divisions was to include instruction in loading and unloading men and equipment in transport aircraft and gliders; orientation flights; command post exercises involving staffs of the airborne divisions, troop carrier unit, and supporting fighter aviation; unit and combined training in airborne operations, and airborne task force maneuvers, "to include the simultaneous movement of the entire division by air under simulated combat conditions."[29] The training of an airborne division was divided into three phases: (1) individual training, thirteen weeks; (2) unit training, thirteen weeks, and (3) combined training, twelve weeks.[30]

Probably nothing during 1943 had a greater impact on the training program than the airborne operation in Sicily. General Arnold's reaction was that "Troop Carrier and Airborne Units in the Sicilian operation had not given deserved emphasis to night operations,"[31] and he promised that thereafter "first emphasis in Troop Carrier training" would be night operations. Beyond that, reports of that operation were largely instrumental in bringing the War Department into the picture with a broad training directive.[32]

A draft training directive attached to the report of the special board headed by Maj. Gen. Joseph M. Swing called for a minimum of twelve weeks of joint training. It suggested a small unit training period of six weeks, a four weeks' large unit training period, and a two-week period for divisional training.[33]

As a result of various conferences, special studies, and recommendations, the War Department issued, on 9 October 1943, a new directive on airborne training. (See Appendix VIII.) It provided additional impetus to the more positive role which the War Department now was playing in directing the airborne program. No less cooperation between the Army Ground Forces and the Army Air Forces was necessary, but here was an agency over both which could make coordination effective. Now their airborne activities would be conducted on the basis of law rather than upon the basis of gentlemen's agreements. This is not to suggest an imposition from above; action still was based upon recommendations of the major commands as well as those of the general staff, but when there was a demand for resolving differences, an arbiter was at hand to settle those which persisted, and there was authority behind a decision once given. The directive held out three principal objectives for the training program. The first was to insure that airborne and troop carrier staffs could plan and supervise efficiently their joint operations. For airborne troops the aim was to develop an ability to participate in orderly and efficient air movements, and to assemble rapidly after landing for attack by combined arms, day or night. For troop carrier units the aim was to develop skill in transporting airborne troops and supplies properly, and in providing evacuation and resupply by air.[34]

Based largely upon the recommendations of the Swing Board, the War Department directive outlined a joint training program. Its chief variation from the Swing proposals was in a reduction of the time allotted to this training from a total of twelve weeks to eight weeks. But its substance was similar. It laid down that there should be three phases – a small unit training period of four weeks, a large unit training period of three weeks, and a divisional training period of one week. During the first period emphasis would be on loading, landing, assembly, and entry into combat by company or battery (parachute and glider units were to employ tugs and gliders on the same flight, and the troop carrier units would carry on complementary operations by squadrons). Training in the second period would be by battalion combat teams and troop carrier groups, and the final phase would be a maneuver by division and wing (moving in two lifts). One troop carrier group was to participate in the joint training during the first period, two groups and one wing headquarters in the second, and four groups and wing headquarters in the last. It laid down specific instructions for the maneuver:

> 12. Before troop carrier and airborne units are considered capable of performing their primary mission in a combat theater, each airborne division and complementing troop carrier wing must satisfactorily engage in a combined maneuver of the following scope . . .
>
> *a.* Duration – approximately 5 days.
>
> *b.* Employ at least four departure air bases.
>
> *c.* Objective area to be reached by a circuitous route of approximately 300 miles.
>
> *d.* At least one-half of the landings and assembly of units to be made at night.
>
> *e.* No contact to be made with friendly ground forces prior to D plus 4.
>
> *f.* Resupply and evacuation by air and/or air landing during period D to D plus four.

It was directed that the commanding generals, Army Ground Forces and Army Air Forces, prescribe tests to determine the ability of airborne and troop carrier forces to operate efficiently as a team in each of the phases of the joint training program.

In commenting on the training directive, General Lentz noted, "Par 12 is a honey. Hope it is practicable."[35]

General McNair's comment was, "I agree that this concept is idealistic and trust that the era of perfection has arrived at last."[36]

Following up the new training directive, the War Department G-3, at the request of the deputy chief of staff, brought together a summary of the Swing Board's recommendations, the reaction of each agency concerned, and the steps being taken in each instance to carry out the recommendations.[37] (See Appendix V.)

It was the completely logical, though perhaps tardy, recommendation of the Operations Division that G-3, in collaboration with OPD, take steps to insure that future troop bases containing provision for additional airborne divisions also include troop carrier groups in the ratio of four to one airborne division. It was suggested further that the training schedules of airborne and troop carrier units should be so coordinated that units would be available for concurrent training and for commitment in that ratio.[38] In accordance with the wishes of the deputy chief of staff, G-3 requested Operations Division to inform G-3 of any contemplated employment of additional airborne units "in ample time to insure the provision of necessary troop carrier and airborne units and the separate and combined training of these units!"[39] The memorandum stated further:

> If the Operations Division will inform this Division as to the contemplated employment of the 13th Airborne Division and any additional airborne units, the training of such units on a current basis to permit their simultaneous commitments to overseas theaters will be accomplished. The 13th Airborne Division can be trained without increasing the current troop carrier program, provided the temporary diversion of replacement training units is feasible as indicated above. This Division can also be employed overseas, provided one of the five existing airborne divisions is sent to the South or Southwest Pacific Theater and the remaining four to UK or Africa. Any other distribution of these divisions will require the shifting of troop carrier units between theaters or the activation of additional troop carrier units. In the event that the decision is made to employ the 13th Airborne Division, it is recommended that the Troop Basis be increased by one Troop Carrier Wing consisting of four troop carrier groups.[40]

This received the prompt assurance the OPD would "advise the Assistant Chief of Staff, G-3, of the requirements for additional airborne units at the earliest date possible, should it become apparent that additional units of this type will be required."[41] The criterion for assigning training priorities was the planned employment of the units involved. Accordingly when the question came up of diverting three troop carrier groups temporarily from replacement training to joint training with the Thirteenth Airborne

Ground and air forces work together in an airborne training maneuver at Fort Bragg, North Carolina.

Division, the decision was deferred because there was then no definite commitment of that division.[42] Now Operations Division requested of G-3 that no more airborne divisions be activated until strategic planning should indicate a need for them; further it asked that if any additional airborne divisions were set up in the troop basis that additional troop carrier groups also be set up in a ratio of four to one, and that joint training of the Thirteenth Airborne Division be confined to that which could be given without interfering with the troop carrier replacement training program. Of the five airborne divisions then included in the 1943 Troop Basis, OPD found requirements for only four overseas. As of 2 November 1943, the planned deployment of airborne divisions was as follows: Eighty-second, 101st, and Seventeenth Airborne Divisions for the European theater; the Eleventh Airborne Division for strategic reserve in the United States.[43]

Special Projects in Joint Training

Early airborne operations demonstrated the desirability of employing mechanical navigational aids to assure greater accuracy in delivery of airborne units. Development of the pathfinder technique was a two-sided accomplishment. It involved special training for selected troop carrier crews in navigation and use of radar equipment and it entailed the organization and training of special pathfinder teams among the airborne troops in setting up aids to guide the airborne columns to their drop zones. Two considerations encouraged such procedures. In the first place specially trained troop carrier crews would be more likely to find the designated drop zone, and in the second place, even if the leading plane did err, succeeding troop carriers, guiding on the signals from the pathfinder team on the ground, would be more likely to drop the parachute units in concentrated patterns. In most cases airborne commanders doubtless would prefer to have concentrated units, even though dropped in the wrong place, than to have widely scattered units dropped around the correct zone.

Details of pathfinder procedure were expected to vary according to local conditions and the situation obtaining for a given operation. Equipment might include radar, radio, light, colored smoke, or any combination of these. Pathfinder teams might be dropped from high flying night bombers several days in advance of the planned operation, or they might be dropped from low flying transport planes in which case it would be desirable to to drop them on the selected drop zone only long enough in advance of the main serials to get equipment into operation.[44]

Both the Airborne Center and I Troop Carrier Command were fully aware of the desirability of joint pathfinder training, but no satisfactory program for such training seems ever to have come into being. The I Troop Carrier Command established a Pathfinder School on 1 September 1944 for the training of its selected air crews in pathfinder techniques. A month later Army Air Forces raised the question of moving the Troop Carrier Pathfinder Training Unit from Stout Field (Indianapolis, Indiana) to the North Carolina area in order to facilitate joint training with the airborne units at Camp Mackall. This fitted into the views of airborne officers. They cooperated with the Troop Carrier Command in the preparation of training directives and drew up plans for a program of joint training. It was the proposal of the Airborne Center that joint training begin on 8 January 1945 for twenty-five parachute pathfinder teams. The Pathfinder Division of the I Troop Carrier Command submitted a similar proposal for one month of joint training at the Airborne Center, but it expressed a preference for joint training to be conducted at the Parachute School. A directive for joint training at the Airborne Center still was being prepared at the end of the month, and a week later the Troop Carrier Command received notice that pathfinder training was going to be discontinued.[45]

Introduction of the use of radar on troop carriers brought up the question of whether the radar operator, guiding on Eureka equipment set up by parachute pathfinders, might be better able to give the parachute jump signal than the pilot. Tests at Pope Field in April 1944 indicated that the jump would be more accurate, in most cases, when given by the pilot. Under night conditions, with poor visibility and no visual aids, the radar operator was found to be as accurate as the pilot in locating the drop zone. Recommended procedure was that, except under those conditions, the Rebecca-Eureka should be relied on to assist the pilot in arriving at the correct drop zone, but then the pilot should decide the exact moment and give the signal for the jump.[46]

Early in the development of the airborne program it became evident that two different kinds of engineer units would be desirable. There would be the regular parachute or glider engineer units which would be parts of airborne combat teams and would perform the normal functions of divisional combat engineers, but in addition, it was agreed that there should be airborne engineers (aviation). These would be Air Forces troops. Brig. Gen. S. C. Godfrey, commanding general of the Engineer Section, AAF Directorate of Base Services, raised the question in May 1942. In a letter to the chief of engineers he pointed to the likely need of airborne aviation engineers for rapid repair of airdromes and preparation of airstrips in airborne operations.[47] The suggestion won the concurrence of other interested agencies, and the War Department authorized direct communication among those concerned – including the Airborne Command, Army Air Forces, and the Engineer Board – to work out the technical details in the development of organization and equipment.[48] A conference held on

8 June concluded that doctrine on employment and training of such troops should be correlated with the Airborne Command, the Chief of Engineers, and the Ground-Air Support Directorate. An informal committee, including, in addition to representatives from those three agencies, representatives from the Engineer Board, Air Transport (later Troop Carrier) Command, AAF Materiel Command, and aviation engineers, was set up to coordinate the activities.[49]

The training program for airborne aviation engineers was another three-phase plan. The first would cover basic military training; the second, initial and basic engineer, and the third, operational and tactical training. During the last phase the units were to participate in airborne tactical training with the Airborne Command.[50] In September 1942 the Troop Carrier Command sent four C-47's to Westover Field, Massachusetts, to begin airborne training for the new units, and during the first thirty days each plane flew 120 hours in training missions with the 871st Airborne Engineer (Aviation) Battalion.[51] Originally established at Westover Field on 1 April 1943, the First Airborne Engineer Aviation Unit Training Center moved to Richmond Army Air Base, Virginia, on 1 December 1943. After battalions had completed unit training at the center, they were to go to troop carrier bases for the last six weeks of their eighteen-week training program. It became the policy of I Troop Carrier Command to have the aviation engineer battalions participate in joint maneuvers of Troop Carrier Command and Airborne Command whenever practicable.[52] In undertaking these additional duties, the Troop Carrier Command announced that the prescribed training would be accomplished "insofar as possible without interference with individual and unit training in Troop Carrier Groups and without compromising commitments made with the Airborne Command."[53]

One of the principal concerns of airborne commanders was the lack of armor to support their units as long as they were out of contact with other ground units. Armored force officers at Fort Knox, Kentucky, sought a partial answer to this need in developing an airborne tank organization. Planning in this direction had progressed to the point by January 1944 that tables of organization and equipment were published for an airborne tank battalion, its headquarters and headquarters and service company, and its airborne tank companies. The airborne tank battalion was to have fifty-six light tanks, T9E1 (airborne), as well as thirty-eight ¼-ton trucks and thirteen ¾-ton trucks.[54] Carrying one caliber .30 machine gun and a 37-mm. gun, the airborne tank was considerably smaller than other tanks. Its weight of 16,000 pounds was only half that of most other light models. Its width was about the same as others (over seven feet), but its height (68½ inches) was two feet less and it was nearly two feet shorter (length:

12 feet 11 inches) than standard models.* Even so, of aircraft then available, only the C-46 (and then only under emergency conditions) the C-54 (if some cargo door alterations were made or the turret of the tank removed), and the British Hamilcar glider would have been able to carry the airborne tank.

Nevertheless the Twenty-eighth Airborne Tank Company was organized at Fort Knox, and by the end of April it was nearing completion of its tank training and was expecting to enter airborne training soon – and its commander was raising the question of parachute pay for his men. Already the unit had been alerted for movement overseas.[55]

Further tests sought an improved airborne tank – or one more easily transported by air. A model was constructed in the summer of 1944, but there was difficulty in obtaining an aviation engine for it so that it could be tested. There even was some thought given to the possibility of carrying the tank on a plane externally, and launching it while the plane was still in the air, but the Army Air Forces recommended that no further consideration be given those proposals.[56]

After tests conducted in cooperation with the Chemical Warfare Board in March 1945 demonstrated the practicability of landing the 4.2-inch chemical mortar by parachute, the Airborne Center recommended the activation of three airborne mortar battalions. Each battalion would be made up of two parachute companies and one glider company. Army Ground Forces G-3 concurred in that recommendation. It was expected that the airborne mortar battalions would be included on the redeployment troop basis. That troop basis contemplated three airborne divisions, and the activation of three airborne mortar battalions would permit the employment of one such battalion with each of the airborne divisions. Army Service Forces recommended that activation be on the basis of the five actual airborne divisions then existing. In April AGF directed the Airborne Center to draw up tables of organization and equipment for the 4.2-inch Chemical Mortar Battalion, Airborne. Again, however, the conclusion of hostilities made unnecessary the calling of the new units into action.[57]

There were a number of other special activities in joint training. In September 1942 airborne and troop carrier elements participated in desert maneuvers in California.[58] Then there was the matter in the spring of

* Tm 9-724, Light Tank T9E1, 17 Nov 43, par 4. Actually the weight of the tank was given as 14,600 pounds without fuel, accessories, or crews, or 16,400 pounds with its crew of three and fuel and accessories. It was assumed that the tank could be transported by air by carrying it without disassembly, "or by removing the complete turret from the hull and stowing it separately in the fuselage while the hull . . . is suspended below" (par 3d).

1943 of providing a thirty-day course in parachute training at Fort Benning for a team of one officer and eighteen enlisted men of the 660th Signal Aircraft Warning Company so that they could be used in mobile air defense tests at the AAF School of Applied Tactics, Orlando, Florida.[59] In September 1943, the Airborne Command, at the request of Army Air Forces, set up a short course of instruction on airborne tactics and techniques for AAF staff officers who had just completed the course at the Command and General Staff School, Fort Leavenworth; four classes received such instruction during 1943.[60]

A number of special activities in 1944 called for joint participation of airborne and troop carrier units. In April 1944 a flight of three C-47's went to DeRitter, Louisiana, to fly parachute training missions for the Eleventh Airborne Division for a period of five days. The Seventeenth Airborne Division, at Camp Forrest, Tennessee, in June 1944, undertook the parachute training of about half of its glider personnel. In two weeks six troop carrier aircraft at Tullahoma, Tennessee, flew missions for 2,800 men to make five parachute jumps each.[61]

Other projects in which airborne and troop carrier units participated included demonstrations for the Army Air Forces School of Applied Tactics and airborne training in safe loading for AAF glider pilots.[62]

A series of training tests and joint training missions conducted at Camp Mackall, North Carolina, in February 1944 brought out weaknesses as well as strong points. A double tow glider test of the 441st Troop Carrier group on 15 February resulted in ragged formations and difficulties in returning to bases after the 300-mile flight in which the lead plane – the only plane carrying radar equipment – crashed. A parachute drop on the night of 16 February was no more satisfactory. A pathfinder team preceded the main column of twenty-nine airplanes (of the 442d Group), but the radar equipment failed to function properly. The troop carriers made two passes in unsuccessful attempts to locate the drop zone, and then dropped the paratroopers anyway. None landed in the designated area, and most of them went into a woods, and some into a small lake near the area. An observer concluded that mechanical aid could not be relied upon altogether for navigation and that more training was needed in double glider towing. A second parachute mission of the 442d Group obtained much more satisfactory results. On the night of 24 February a formation of forty airplanes flew a 317-mile triangular course and arrived over the designated drop zone only about twenty seconds off schedule. Dummy parachutists were dropped this time. The next day forty airplanes towed eighty gliders (of the same group) carrying airborne infantry over a 300-mile course in a very satisfactory manner.

For the joint training of the airborne troops at Camp Mackall, the Second Provisional Troop Carrier Group was flying the necessary missions at this time. Battalion drops of the 541st Parachute Infantry were among the most successful that had been executed for the Airborne Command. One of the three drops was a night mission – the first one for the Second Provisional Group – and airborne officers rated it "superior." It appeared that a provisional group, organized for the purpose of assisting in the training of airborne troops, was doing a better job than tactical units. The answer undoubtedly was to be found in the greater amount of training which the provisional group pilots had had; perhaps more important than the amount of training time was the greater amount of *joint training* which their assignment provided.[63]

Air Transport Training of Infantry Divisions

In July 1944 Army Ground Forces announced plans for renewing the program of air transport training for infantry divisions. According to those plans six divisions – the 84th, 103d, 100th, 78th, 76th, and 66th – would receive that training during the period between 31 July and 7 October 1944. The Airborne Center organized and trained five instruction teams. Division schedules overlapped, so that the teams could carry on instruction in three divisions concurrently. Of Army Air Forces AGF requested three C-47 aircraft and three CG-4A gliders, 1,800 parachute packs and harnesses, 1,200 safety belts, 30 plywood airplane ramps for each division, and 3,000 lengths of rope for lashing. In addition a troop carrier squadron would be needed for the transportation of the instruction teams. Of Army Service Forces AGF requested the construction of sixty C-47 airplane mock-ups and sixty CG-4A glider mock-ups at Camp Clairborne, Louisiana, (for the 84th Division) by 27 July; a similar number of mock-ups to be constructed at Camp Howze, Texas, (for the 103d Division) by 3 August, and a third set to be built at Camp Pickett, Virginia, (for the 78th Division) by 10 August. Then mock-ups would be moved from Camp Mackall to Fort Bragg (for the 100th Division), from Camp Clairborne to Camp McCoy, Wisconsin (for the 76th Division), and from Camp Howze to Camp Rucker, Alabama (for the 66th Division). The Airborne Center needed six 57-mm. guns, six 105-mm. howitzers, and six 75-mm. howitzers at Camp Mackall.[64]

Actually the new training program was being undertaken after War Department approval of a suggestion from the European theater, but this addition was not going to change the scheduled completion of training dates for the divisions concerned. Representatives of Operations Division, AGF, ASF, and AAF, agreed upon the schedule, and OPD directed that the required training aids be made available. After agreement on the schedule, however, the plans for the training of the 100th, 78th, 76th, and 66th Divisions were put on a tentative basis.[65]

An immediate problem was the organization and training of the required instruction teams. Each team was to include 25 officers and 130 enlisted men – a requirement which could be expected to tax the personnel resources of the Airborne Center. The first two teams would have to come from the Thirteenth Airborne Division. AGF directed that 50 officers and 260 enlisted men from that division be assigned to the Airborne Center for temporary duty until 1 September. Again, this assignment was not to affect the shipment date of the Thirteenth Airborne Division. The Airborne Center could find enough enlisted men for the other three teams, but there were only fifty-three officers in all the units then assigned to its command. Therefore it was necessary to request the assignment of twenty-five additional officers to complete the organization of those teams – and they had to be trained as airborne loading and lashing instructors by 1 September.[66]

Training plans contemplated no actual air movement of the infantry divisions or of their units as had been done in the training of the Second Division. Instruction would be confined to the use of mock-ups – wooden models of the aircraft – in each case. During the period of approximately three weeks in which the selected divisions would be participating in air transport training, that type of training would have priority over all other division training.[67] Concurrently with the air transport training of the division, airborne officers gave a special nine-hour course for all staff officers – division to battalion. This course covered orientation, theory and problems in safe loading of aircraft, airborne organization, and doctrine including transported units and aerial supply.[68]

On 1 August Operations Division cancelled the air transport training scheduled for the 100th, 78th, 76th, and 66th Divisions,[69] but the program for the other two divisions went through to completion. Lt. Col F. E. Ross, the officer in AGF G-3 Section most directly concerned with the air transport training program, found preparations highly satisfactory when he visited Camp Clairborne and Camp Howze immediately before instruction was scheduled to begin. Construction of mock-ups had been completed in good time, instruction teams had arrived with preliminary training completed and prepared to go to work, and the divisions were cooperating well with the teams from the Airborne Center.[70]

Air transport training was intended to be general, so that the divisions might be prepared to move – as a division or by combat teams – as required for any specific operation. No attempt was made to reorganize the divisions for air transport, nor was there any effort to substitute equipment for that divisional equipment which was not air transportable. But it was intended that the loading and lashing instruction would prepare the men to load any equipment which might be substituted in a particular operation. Gun crews of the 155-mm. howitzer battalions were trained to load the quarter-ton truck and trailer. In the process of giving this training the Airborne Center was able to develop more complete reference data, loading plans and planning procedures for air transportation.[71]

On conclusion of the special training program, each of the two divisions was considered "capable of conducting a safe, orderly and expeditious movement of air utilizing transport airplanes and gliders." On the basis of interest, complete participation, actual accomplishment – and the quality of instruction given by the teams from the Airborne Center – the Eighty-fourth Division received a rating of excellent and the 103d Division a rating of superior.[72]

Airborne Maneuvers

Culmination of efforts in joint training was the staging of large-scale maneuvers. There was only one extensive exercise during 1942 – the airlanding maneuver of the Second Infantry Division, spearheaded by parachute troops, in Texas. Basically, the Second Division maneuver represented "a series of logistical exercises to establish facts and figures on what proportion of a triangular infantry division could be transported by air and how much of a troop carrier force would be required for its transportation."[73] Preparatory to the actual airlanding exercises, instruction teams from the Airborne Command went to Fort Sam Houston to conduct training in loading procedures in airplane mock-ups, to organize the units into air-transportable combat teams, to supervise staff work in the detailed planning for air movement, and to effect the necessary coordination with Air Forces troop carrier units.[74] After a number of preliminary problems to establish fundamentals, there was a flying command post exercise. Finally came the air-movement, by combat team, of the division. The problem involved the seizure of three airfields at Bracketville, Eagle Pass, and Del Rio, Texas. First came the participating parachute troops to clear the fields. Then the air-transported infantry landed with heavy weapons, jeeps and trailers, motorcycles, and supplies. Troop carrier planes then returned for additional loads. On the second day, gliders landed with more troops and equipment, and aircraft flew resupply missions. Then they began the fourth phase of the operation – evacuating the "casualties" and later evacuating the whole force.[75] Available aircraft could lift only a combat team at a time, but 104 planes flew a total of 10,635 hours in the exercises.[76] The C-47's and C-53's delivered 1,100 tons of equipment and supplies.[77] The maneuver pointed up the essential need for cooperation in every phase of planning and execution. It indicated the desirability of having a single task force commander for unified control.[78]

A colorful demonstration by the Eighty-second and 101st Airborne Divisions and their troop carriers, supported by combat aviation and heavy artillery units – using live ammunition – in March 1943, left observers favorably impressed. After the visitors – including Foreign Secretary Anthony Eden and Sir John Dill of Great Britain, and General George C. Marshall, U. S. chief of staff – had seen the parachute drops, the glider landings, the aggressive ground attack, and "capture" of Pope Field as a base of landing of air-transported infantry, they "highly praised this evidence of cooperation and close coordination between the airborne and Air Force elements participating, and also expressed the opinion that the airborne units were approaching the stage of readiness for combat."[79] Closer examination, however, revealed much to be desired in training proficiency. Only three days after the big demonstration, a command inspection revealed that the Eighty-second Airborne Division had "had insufficient combined training in the field" and required "maneuver experience" before it could be "considered fully prepared for combat duty."[80]

In planning for the overseas shipment of an airborne division, the War Department General Staff had agreed that the ratio of parachute to glider regiments should be changed so that there would be two parachute regiments and one glider regiment in the division. The reason for the modification was more the result of consideration of shipping requirements for gliders than it was of any change in tactical concept.[81] Consequently the 326th Glider Infantry was withdrawn from the Eighty-second Airborne Division and the 505th Parachute Infantry was attached. In order to have balanced combat teams, then, the 456th Parachute Field Artillery Battalion was added, and one glider engineer company was converted into a parachute engineer company.[82]

Aside from the demonstration mentioned above, the only joint maneuvers in which the units of the Eighty-second Airborne Division were able to participate before their departure overseas in April 1943 were a regimental jump by the 505th Parachute Infantry at Camden, South Carolina, and one by the 504th Parachute Infantry at Myrtle Beach, South Carolina.[83]

In May 1943 a maneuver was scheduled in the Carolina area which would be the "first large-scale maneuver in which air and ground have worked together to utilize the characteristics of an airborne division."[84] The maneuver was to go through five phases: (1) establishment of an airhead by a parachute combat team in a night landing; (2) reinforcement of the airhead secured in Phase I with the parachute landing of another regiment and the glider landing of a composite battalion of artillery, antiaircraft and antitank units at dawn; (3) seizure of an airfield by a parachute combat team and glider troops, and a regimental "vertical envelopment" of "enemy" position; (4) seizure of an airfield by an attacking force and reinforcement by the remainder of the division brought in by air transport and glider shuttle; (5) a coordinated attack by the division.[85] At the conclusion of the exercises, most observers agreed upon the need for more of the same. Both the training of the pilots and the ground training of the airborne troops left something to be desired. One conclusion was that the "maneuvers which involved the 101st Airborne Division . . . demonstrated for the first time in this country the tactical use of an Airborne division. . . . The greenness of the pilots flying the planes which towed the gliders and carried the paratroopers was the biggest flaw in the maneuver. Several elements of the units participating did not reach the proper area because of the pilots' inability to locate it from the air."[86] General McNair felt that technical training peculiar to airborne units had been emphasized to the detriment of training in ground combat.

Security measures and organization and control immediately after landing had not been satisfactory, but on the other hand, it could be said that the battalions compared favorably with those of an infantry division on first maneuvers, and it was concluded: "Considering that this was the first effort of a large airborne unit moving tactically, it was highly successful. The 101st Airborne Division moved over 7000 troops 120 miles by air in 32 hours."[87]

Hardly had the Carolina maneuvers been concluded when plans were being completed for participation of the 101st Airborne Division in Tennessee maneuvers during June and July. This time there were three problems, but exercises were not of the magnitude of the earlier operations in Carolina. Now only two groups of troop carriers were on hand instead of the three as before, and one of those, because of its state of training and shortage of aircraft, was available only for limited use. The Troop Carrier Command turned down a request of the Airborne Command for use of this partially trained group through July in maneuvers, and in troop carrier headquarters the thought was expressed that "as long as the Airborne Command has an outfit in this country awaiting shipment, they will want at least one group to play with, whether its training has been completed or not."[88]

Deficiencies which had appeared in the earlier maneuvers were not entirely absent in Tennessee. In glider operations particularly, poor control indicated inadequate air discipline and training. A new development in technique grew out of the maneuvers – "area" dropping of parachute troops, though apparently the practice was not used offensively in combat operations. This procedure substituted the selection of alternate fields within a given area for the earlier practice of specifying a particular field as the drop zone. Consideration had been given to this since the Carolina maneuvers, and unfavorable weather conditions in Tennessee made its use almost mandatory. On the whole the new method showed promise.[89]

One thing in particular which General McNair did not like to see was a suggestion that units had neglected ground combat training. When he received a report later that the 101st Airborne Division was not up to training standards, he wrote: "I am not surprised about the 101st Airborne Division. These trick outfits practically without exception emphasize their tricks to the exclusion of sound basic and other training for everyday fighting. More power to you in correcting such deficiencies."[90]

Four troop carrier groups of the Fifty-third Wing joined the Eleventh Airborne Division and its attached units in December 1943 for the most ambitious airborne maneuver attempted thus far. Planning for such an exercise had begun in the summer with the hope of staging it by fall. However, the aircraft and units could not be brought together until in October it could be assumed that arrangements could be completed for December. A provisional combined headquarters set up at Camp Mackall would make preparations, and then serve as task force headquarters for the operation itself. As director of the maneuver, Brig. Gen. F. W. Evans, commanding general of I Troop Carrier Command, would preside over the unified command with the commanding general of the Airborne Command, General Donovan, as co-director. The maneuver was scheduled to cover only five days, but the initial commitment of forces was to be on a big scale. Preparations through November included extensive practice sessions with gliders in double tow at night.

Troops and aircraft were divided among four airfields in the Carolina area for the operation. Taking to the air on the night of 7 December, serials of airplanes and gliders, making use of various navigational aids, including radar and the pathfinder techniques, found their ways to thirteen designated areas, and dropped 85 percent of their personnel on the target. Two groups carried paratroopers, and the other two – moving in separate serials – towed 100 gliders in double tow. They dropped, or landed by glider, 4,800 troops in the first wave. The spear-heading airborne units then prior to daylight seized an airport and covered the airlanding of the remainder of the division. All together the troop carriers–using 200 C-47 aircraft and 234 CG-4A gliders – delivered 10,282 men into the "combat area" within a period of 39 hours. Of these, 4,679 were dropped by parachute, 1,869 went in by glider, and 3,734 were airlanded by transport aircraft. Subsequent operations consisted of a coordinated ground attack by the division and the attached parachute regiment against a reinforced infantry regiment, and aerial resupply and evacuation missions. A total of 1,612 tons of equipment and supplies were landed. This included 108 jeeps and 23 trailers landed by glider, and 187 jeeps and

251 trailers landed by transport planes.[91] Participation of the 874th Airborne Engineer Battalion (Aviation) demonstrated the value of that type of unit in an operation requiring the use of a captured airport.[92]

Appraisals of the maneuver generally agreed that it was a considerable improvement over its predecessors. Principal criticism was reserved for the delays in loading for airlanding and resupply missions. Loading teams, furnished by the Airborne Command, were undermanned and insufficiently trained, on the one hand, and air crews interfered with their activities on the other. However, the War Department had directed that resupply was an Air Force function, and it was expected that activation and training of units by the Air Service Command for that specific function would go far toward correcting the situation.[93] The Airborne Command recommended to the Air Service Command "that one or more officers responsible for the organization and training of units . . . to perform aerial supply to ground forces, and such enlisted personnel as . . . desired, be placed on special duty with Combined Airborne-Troop Carrier Maneuver Headquarters – to remain until the completion of these maneuvers" (another was scheduled for January 1944).[94]

General McNair, who observed the maneuver with Secretary of War Stimson, was "very pleased." Compared with the maneuver in May, he thought that "great progress" had been made. The Airborne Command had only praise for General Evans of the Troop Carrier Command.[95]

The December maneuver demonstrated that the double glider tow "can now be accepted as routine,"[96] and that mass glider landings at night, when conducted "under fairly favorable conditions are feasible."[97] Other results were a demonstration of the practicability of jumping paratroopers from tow planes which had released gliders in double tow, and the desirability of maximum use of radar and other navigational aids.[98]

Shortly after completion of the large scale joint maneuver of the Eleventh Airborne Division and Fifty-third Troop Carrier Wing in December 1943, plans were completed for another in the same Carolina area to be held early in January 1944. Facing the growing hazards of winter operations in this maneuver were the Seventeenth Airborne Division and the Sixtieth Troop Carrier Wing (with operational control over the 438th, 439th, and 441st Groups). The Airborne-Troop Carrier Headquarters which had been organized to supervise the December maneuver continued for the January exercise, but this time the commanders changed positions, so that Brig. Gen. Leo Donovan of the Airborne Command was maneuver director, and Brig. Gen. F. W. Evans of the I Troop Carrier Command was co-director.[99]

Once again emphasis was upon night operations. After bad weather forced a 24-hour postponement, the first phase of the operation began on the night of 6 January. Four pathfinder planes dropped parachute pathfinder teams well in advance of the main serials, and then two groups, one with 50 gliders in single tow, and the other with 100 gliders in double tow – and paratroopers in the tow planes – flew a 300-mile course to the landing area and 300 miles return. Landing under blackout conditions on eleven unprepared fields, most of the gliders arrived on the designated landing zones. During an eight hour period, 4,417 paratroopers and glider-borne troops landed. The next morning a serial of 50 aircraft dropped its paratroopers about 1,200 yards beyond the designated drop zone, but they went into an area of second growth pine in a well bunched formation. Additional elements of the division were airlanded, and then as the troops began ground operations, troop carriers turned to resupply missions. All together, 208 C-47 aircraft and 250 CG-4A gliders, using four bases, transported 7,536 troops and 1,428 tons of supplies and equipment.[100]

Observers at the maneuver questioned the advisability of dropping parachute troops from planes which were towing gliders as tending to make the arrival and assembly of the unit "prolonged and piecemeal."[101] There seemed to be some question again about the training of the glider pilots. One problem which never had been solved satisfactorily was the ground action of glider pilots after landing. In a major operation the number of glider pilots would be such as to demand some attention. Two hundred leaderless Air Force glider pilots in the midst of ground combat troops could lead to an embarrassing situation. In this maneuver announced plans for the employment of glider pilots as ground troops after landing were not carried out.*[102]

Generally, the cooperation between troop carrier and airborne staffs and commanders was found to be good,[103] and the conclusion was: "The Airborne be air transported during hours of darkness and can be landed in a predetermined tactical area . . . and after landing it can be assembled and developed for coordinated offensive or defensive action."[104]

* Immediately after this maneuver, I Troop Carrier Command recommended that the individual training of glider pilots be taken out of the hands of the Flying Training Command, and that the whole program of glider pilot training be assigned the I Troop Carrier Command. Not only would this put the training responsibility under the command to which the pilots would be assigned, but it would relieve the Troop Carrier Command of furnishing gliders and tow planes to the Flying Training Command. Finally, in November 1944 I Troop Carrier Command received that responsibility. AAF, I Troop Carrier Command, "The Glider Training Program," p. 16 Air Hist Off, 252-1, v 2.

The greatest value of such maneuvers was to be found in the training of the various staffs in mastering the details involved in achieving the coordination which was so essential. It made little difference to the individual paratrooper, or to the small unit commander, whether he was participating in a battalion exercise or in a corps maneuver; his own personal problems would be essentially the same. It would make some difference to air crews and commanders, for mass flights would increase their problems. But it would make a great deal of difference to higher commanders and staffs. The problems of handling two regimental combat teams would be considerably more than twice as complicated as handling one combat team. If one were seeking a formal statement it might be nearer the truth to say that the complexity of the problems increased in direct proportion to the square of the number of given units involved. Thus there might have been more total training if, in the general program, the idea of progressive training had applied not to the progress from small unit to large unit training but rather to progress from simple large unit training to more complex large unit training. This would have permitted continuous tactical training for higher commanders and staffs instead of reserving their tactical training to the last phase of the training period. But considerations of supervision and facilities would be important in any such case, and with airborne units there never would have been sufficient aircraft for such continuous employment. The few days of maneuvers, then, had to fill an important gap in the training of higher commanders and staffs to master the logistical intricacies characteristic of such operations.

Only one airborne division remained which had not participated in a joint maneuver. That was the Thirteenth Airborne Division, and it was scheduled for that training in July 1944. But demands for overseas replacements made it necessary to postpone the maneuver. This time it was the airborne unit rather than the troop carrier units which could not meet the schedule because of overseas demands. When the exercise was postponed in April, Army Ground Forces did not expect the division to be ready for maneuvers until November or December.[105] By the end of June it was possible to begin definite planning for the final joint maneuver. Army Ground Forces G-3 announced that the division would be ready for that phase of training during the week of 17 September.[106] Another postponement set 24 September as the date for the maneuver to begin.[107]

Similar in objectives and scope to the two preceding maneuvers, the September maneuver likewise took place in the area around Camp Mackall. Only two troop carrier groups remained in the United States at this time, and it was necessary to reinforce them with replacement crews and provisional groups. Tentative plans called for the participation of the First Provisional Troop Carrier Group and the Second Combat Cargo Group with the 349th Troop Carrier Group (again operating under the Sixtieth Troop Carrier Wing), but changes were necessary when Army Air Forces decided to convert the Second Combat Cargo Group from C-47 to C-46 aircraft, and one of the troop carrier squadrons received a special assignment with the Third Air Force. Air Force units taking part in the maneuver, then, were the 349th Troop Carrier Group (reinforced by the addition of twenty-eight replacement and combat cargo crews), the First Provisional Troop Carrier Group (reinforced by the addition of twenty-three crews from training stations), the First Air Cargo Resupply Squadron, and a detachment of ten B-17 bombers.[108]

Again the initial phase of the problem was a night tactical movement. Weather delayed the beginning until the night of 25 September, and then began the task of getting three battalions of paratroops to three designated drop zones for the opening assault. Difficulties of poor visibility – and lack of sufficient joint airborne training of many of the pilots – resulted in a wide dispersal of the paratroops. About 65 percent of the personnel and equipment landed on or near the first drop zone, and were available for action an hour and a half later. But at the second drop zone the men were so scattered that at 1000 the next morning the battalion commander had control over no more than 20 percent of his men. A number of paratroops missed the third drop zone, but they were fairly well massed. An airplane crash in which eight infantrymen and four airmen were killed marred the operation.[109] A serial of planes with twenty gliders in double tow followed the parachute operation to bring in jeeps and additional men. Succeeding glider operations had to be delayed two hours because of unfavorable weather, but then more than 200 CG-4A gliders in double tow, and four CG-13 gliders in single tow, proceeded to seven selected landing zones. Only four gliders missed the zones, and all landed within forty-four minutes, though, because of the delay, the operation was not completed until after dawn. In airlanding operations, the ten B-17's each brought in forty-five fully-equipped airborne troops. Air supply operations – including the supply of an isolated battalion by six airplanes – supported the ground action during the next three days.[110]

Glider operations showed a marked improvement over the previous maneuver,[111] but the training of the airplane pilots in night formation flying and navigation was not satisfactory.[112] Ground action of glider pilots was better. Assigned by sections to serve with particular units of the division after the landing, the glider pilots received instructions to report to specific rendezvous. General Chapman, commanding the Thirteenth Airborne Division, received the commendation of observers for his briefing of the glider pilots in which he "made them feel a part of the team."[113]

This maneuver raised some doubts on the confidence in night airborne operations which had been expressed after the January maneuver. Now it was recommended that night glider landings should be considered only as an operational emergency, and that the normal procedure should be for gliders to take off during darkness and arrive over the landing zones at dawn.[114] To the earlier conclusion, "An airborne division can be air transported during hours of darkness and can be landed in a predetermined tactical area," was added the qualification – "only if the light from a quarter moon or better is available, unless better navigational aid can be provided."[115]

Paratroop Replacement Training

With unit training of planned airborne units pretty well completed, and with combat operations mounting in scope and intensity, the training of parachutist replacements by 1944 was demanding more and more of the attention of the Parachute School at Fort Benning, Georgia. This is not to overlook the replacement training responsibilities of the Parachute School during the earlier period. Already in 1943 there had been some expression of dissatisfaction regarding the slowness of the established procedure in meeting parachute troop replacement needs. There was a suggestion in August of that year that the Airborne Training Center in North Africa be authorized to undertake the training of parachute replacements. That headquarters indicated that it could conduct such a training program on an eight-week basis for 100 parachute trainees a week.[116] But the suggestion received a cool reception in Army Ground Forces. The comment of the Special Projects Division was:

> It looks as though the airborne training center in the North African Theater was trying to make a job for itself. I feel that we are much better prepared in this country to do the training required than they are in either North Africa or the United Kingdom. The principal difficulty in furnishing parachutist replacements up to the present time has been the lack of an established replacement policy and the short time between the call for these men and the shipment date.[117]

Later the airborne divisions stationed in the United Kingdom began a program for training their own replacements so that staffs would have a more firm basis on which to plan for their operations.[118]

By May 1944 the replacement situation was one described as "very critical." The number of parachute volunteers could not nearly meet the demands of the large requisitions which then were being received. Army Ground Forces G-3 therefore recommended an intensive publicity and recruiting program aimed at gaining 2,515 volunteers from the Army at large, regardless of branch, and then an increase in the capacity of the Parachute School to take care of them.[119] Contributing to this shortage of replacements was the almost universal practice, contrary to the doctrine announced in Training Circular 113, 9 October 1943, of keeping parachute units in continuous action as straight infantry after their initial commitment.[120]

A preliminary recruiting program in replacement training centers proved to be insufficient to meet the needs. Thereupon AGF appealed to the War Department. Two basic problems had to be met. The first was that the capacity of the Parachute School was not enough to provide the necessary replacements, and the other was that sufficient volunteers could not be obtained from the replacement training centers – which suggested that there should be recruiting from the units, but that would leave the units below strength without replacements readily available for them. Again it was a matter of policy which required the decision of higher headquarters – "The War Department should advise us what is more important in the war effort – to keep the Parachute School filled, or to prevent inroads on personnel of earmarked units."[121] In order to provide a firmer basis for a parachute replacement program the War Department queried the theater on the status of such replacements and the estimated requirements for the remainder of 1944,[122] and then called a conference to establish a program. Directly concerned with the proposed expansion of parachutist output would be the Army Air Forces, for not only was this likely to mean a requirement for additional troop carrier aircraft, but a program of intensive recruiting in the Army at large would touch upon AAF's personnel policies. Present at the meeting on 12 June were representatives of the War Department, Operations Division, Army Air Forces, Army Service Forces, and Army Ground Forces. It was agreed that parachutist replacements should be considered of the highest priority as replacements. The War Department approved the recruiting of volunteers from the Army at large, and AAF and ASF concurred. The War Department directed that volunteers for shipment during August and September would be obtained immediately through the Ground Forces, and the theaters would be directed to call for volunteers and to train parachutists to make up any shortages in shipments. Parachute units of the Thirteenth Airborne Division, the 541st Parachute Infantry Regiment and the 542d Parachute Infantry Battalion were authorized a 15 percent overstrength which would be used for the basic training of volunteers being converted to infantry. Authority was granted to increase the capacity of the Parachute School. Responsibility for the recruiting program and for training would remain with AGF.[123] Two weeks later a War Department memorandum stated that no further increase in the capacity of the Parachute School was necessary. The parachute pool there was authorized for 3,300 men. The flow through the jump course was not considered beyond capacity.[124]

Jumping from platforms at the Parachute School at Fort Benning.

Parachutists learn manual techniques for manipulating their 'chutes during descent.

The incline rail and trolley help trainees learn to land with the correct forward momentum.

Parachute towers for practice jumps.

Yet, little more than half the paratroops required in July 1944 were available for shipment. The requirement had been stated as 224 officers and 3,434 enlisted men, but there were available only 150 officers and 1,700 enlisted men. Shortages for July had to be disregarded, but there was hope that there would be no such discrepancy in the future. Within two weeks after the new program had been laid down, the recruiting program began. The first week's efforts resulted in 1,500 volunteers. It was estimated that the Parachute School would graduate 1,080 parachutists in July, and by September that figure would be up to 2,400 a month. Thus during the next five months it was expected that the Parachute School would turn out 12,840 replacements. In addition it was estimated that the theaters would train 3,000 parachute replacements during the same period. This total of 15,840 would cover the total estimated requirements for the theaters during that period, – 703 officers and 10,584 enlisted men for the European theater, 175 officers and 1,750 enlisted men for the North African theater, and 164 officers and 1,792 enlisted men for the Southwest Pacific. The Parachute School found that with the aircraft and other training aids available, and with a faculty to handle 700 casual students, it could train 500 additional students a week for limited periods if they were in units with their own officers and noncommissioned officers. In other words the Parachute School could handle 700 a week as casuals and 500 a week by units, or a total of 1,200 a week if necessary.[125]

Hardly had this increased program begun when a revision of requirements called for further expansion of facilities of the Parachute School. Now it was estimated that more than 4,000 parachute replacements would be needed in August, there would be a peak of 373 officers and 4,609 enlisted men for October, and then, it was thought, there would be need for only 40 officers and 455 enlisted men in December. As a result, the capacities of courses at the Parachute School were revised to permit 4,800 for the jump course, 125 for the riggers, 150 for the demolition, and 150 for the basic communication. This meant a total monthly capacity of 5,255.[126]

Although on paper it appeared that facilities of the Parachute School would be adequate to meet the demands for replacements during the remainder of 1944, the school pointed out that the number of volunteers received could not be taken as the number of parachutists that would be graduated, for allowance had to be made for training losses. It doubted that requirements could be met unless the recruiting drives were intensified.[127]

A War Department suggestion that the final phase of jump training be given at the four Troop Carrier Replacement Combat Training Bases seemed at first glance a reasonable suggestion. Such an arrangement would be to the advantage of both the troop carrier and parachute replacement training programs. Each program required the cooperation of the other. Parachutists had to jump from troop carrier planes, and troop carrier pilots, in their training, had to drop parachutists. It was not to be recommended, however, that the two cooperate at a common level of training. It was considered "an axiom of airborne training that inexperienced parachutists are always dropped by experienced pilots and the most experienced parachutists are required when pilots are inexperienced."[128]

To a suggestion of the War Department that there should be a replacement training program for glider troops, General Donovan replied that this would be a "needless complication." He referred to the concurrence of "all theaters" in the opinion that it was not necessary to ship glider replacements as such, but that they could be trained to travel by glider and aircraft in a short period of training after assignment to an airborne unit.

Organized to turn out approximately 3,500 replacements a month in November 1944, the Parachute School received new Operations Division estimates which indicated a monthly requirement of approximately 1,400 for the first half of 1945. Officers in AGF G-3 Section thought the new War Department figures unrealistic. Estimates were being made on the October 1943 level when now more than twice as many units would be needing replacements. It was pointed out that any cutback in capacity of training replacements would put AGF in a difficult position for any future expansion in the event that the new estimates proved to be incorrect. It was recommended that all applicants accepted thus far be trained, at least, and that the program be carried out which would provide a pool of approximately 8,000 replacements to be retained at the Parachute School in case the estimates were correct. But the thing which worked against this was the fact that the European theater already had requested 18,000 more infantry replacements than could possibly be shipped under the current troop basis. In any case, there was a deep-seated apprehension that there would be calls for parachute replacements by January which would be beyond the ability of the Parachute School to meet.[129]

Ironically, it was 15 December 1944 when the War Department issued its instructions for reducing the training of paratroop replacements. A memorandum on that date stated:

> Overseas losses of paratroops have been less than expected and overseas production of replacements greater than expected. This situation results in the present paratroop replacement training program being unbalanced.
>
> It is desired that input to the parachute school be reduced at once to 400 per month and maintained at that level until such time as the supply of qualified paratroop replacements under your

> control is reduced to 2,000 at which time further instructions will be requested of this office. No increase will be made without reference to this office.[130]

Even as this memorandum was being received, the great German counteroffensive was moving through the Ardennes which would call into intense ground combat all the airborne divisions in the European theater – the 82d, 101st, and 17th. It hardly need be added that increased calls for paratroop replacements cancelled any action on that memorandum.[131]

It has been suggested that the joint training of replacements for airborne operations was a two-way proposition. Not only were troop carrier airplanes and crews required for parachute training, but paratroop teams were needed for the training of troop carrier replacement crews. When the War Department, in August 1944, asked that a plan be submitted for providing airborne teams at the four troop carrier replacement training bases, such teams, of one officer and three enlisted men each, already were on duty at three of the bases, so that it was only necessary to furnish a similar team for the fourth.[132] According to War Department G-3, the minimum airborne elements required to provide joint training for troop carrier replacement crews were one parachute infantry battalion (separate), one parachute field artillery battery, and one parachute engineer company.[133] Responsibility for furnishing teams for the joint training of troop carrier replacement crews was transferred in December from the Parachute School to the Airborne Center. In addition to providing the four teams of one officer and three enlisted men each for the four troop carrier replacement training bases, the Airborne Center was directed to organize a composite parachute force of a rifle platoon, a howitzer gun section, and an engineer squad to be available during the final phase of training of each class at each base. The composite force was to demonstrate a parachute drop with typical door and rack loads.[134]

In January 1945 there was a call – a call which had not been anticipated – for 250 officers and 5,000 enlisted men, parachute replacements.[135] Operations Division was promising the European theater that 100 officers and 2,500 enlisted paratroopers a month would be procured and trained.[136] A new War Department memorandum set up an objective of making 2,847 paratroopers available for shipment by the 15th of each month during the period from April to September. Monthly input for the Parachute School – based upon a 40 percent loss rate in training – was set at 4,550.[137]

Redeployment

A cable of 27 October 1944 from the European theatre of operations requested the immediate assignment of the Thirteenth Airborne Division –

the only airborne division then remaining in the United States – to that theater. The division received a readiness date of 15 November. This meant that the only airborne unit of any kind, in training at full strength, in the United States would be the 464th Parachute Field Artillery. The 541st Parachute Infantry had been stripped to cadre strength for replacements, and the cadre was serving in a "housekeeper" capacity at the Parachute School, Fort Benning. Likewise the 542d Parachute Infantry Battalion had been stripped for replacements, but it had received new men to build to within about 90 percent of authorized strength; it was expected that this unit, if it were spared further calls for replacements, could be made ready for commitment between 15 March and 15 May. The 161st Airborne Engineer Battalion, less one company which had been shipped to the Southwest Pacific, was in the early stages of unit training. The 151st Airborne Tank Company was on the troop basis at 100 percent enlisted over-strength, and it had completed much of its training, but it never had had any airborne training with its tanks, nor even flown with them; its disposition or possible commitment was predicated upon the use of aircraft not then available. The 151st Antiaircraft Artillery Machine Gun Battery (Separate), Airborne, was scheduled to complete training 3 February 1945. In these circumstances, officers in Army Ground Forces G-3 Section recommended strongly that the 541st Parachute Infantry be relieved of its housekeeping assignment and be moved to Camp Mackall for rebuilding so that there would be available a trained parachute combat team in strategic reserve.[138] Apparently the recommendation did not receive immediate attention.

Meanwhile the training of the Thirteenth Airborne Division, interrupted earlier by calls to furnish replacements, could be resumed. When General Eisenhower in mid-December inquired of the training status of the reserve divisions earmarked for the European theater, he could be informed that deficiencies remained in the training of the nine infantry divisions, but the Thirteenth Airborne Division, as well as two armored divisions, would be qualified to perform its primary mission upon arrival.[139] The Thirteenth Airborne Division arrived in France in February 1945.

By the spring of 1945 strategic planning was turning to the problem of speeding up the war in the Pacific. Three airborne divisions and two separate parachute regiments were included in the redeployment troop basis. One airborne division and one parachute regiment would remain in the Pacific Ocean area, and two airborne divisions and one parachute regiment would be designated Pacific reserve.[140] Accordingly, the Thirteenth Airborne Division would return to Camp Mackall about 1 October to reorganize as a standard infantry division for redeployment to the Pacific. The Eighty-second Airborne Division and the 508th Parachute

Infantry were to remain, for the time being, in the European occupation forces. The 101st Airborne Division was scheduled to return to the United States in January as Pacific reserve. The Seventeenth Airborne Division and the 501st Parachute Infantry would return to the United States with high-point personnel, and be disbanded. Remaining in the Pacific would be the Eleventh Airborne Division and the 503rd Parachute Regimental Combat Team.[141]

The arrangement which left the 349th Troop Carrier Group to work with the Airborne Center in airborne training continued only until February 1945, when the troop carrier group was alerted for overseas movement. This left no tactical troop carrier units for airborne training requirements. I Troop Carrier Command had to concentrate surplus personnel in its organization at Pope Field to fill this need. A tentative organization, without official authorization, designated the Second Provisional Group, assumed the responsibility for furnishing aircraft for airborne training.[142] Army Air Forces was reluctant to increase troop carrier personnel unless Army Ground Forces expressed a definite need for aircraft during the interval between the departure of the 349th Troop Carrier Group for overseas, and the return of another group to the United States.[143] Army Ground Forces estimated that for the period 1 May 1945 to 31 December 1945, a minimum of three troop carrier squadrons would be required for the activities of the Airborne Center at Camp Mackall. This did not include aviation necessary to conduct redeployment training; in that case, a minimum of two troop carrier groups for each airborne division would be required.[144] It appeared of course now that redeployment training would be the biggest item on the schedule for 1945 and 1946, and Army Air Forces asked to be furnished a schedule of redeployment training as soon as possible in order to ascertain aircraft requirements. In July 1945 Army Ground Forces could report that one airborne division would arrive at Camp Mackall during December 1945, and one airborne division was scheduled to arrive at Fort Bragg during January 1946. It was expected that the level of airborne training would be very low in both divisions. One troop carrier wing, AGF noted, would be adequate for their training, and two troop carrier groups the absolute minimum.[145] The Second Provisional Group went out of existence on 20 June 1945, and the 316th Troop Carrier Group, returning from overseas, received the airborne training assignment.[146]

During June 1945 activities of the Airborne Center required an average of twelve transport aircraft a day. The scheduled arrival of a number of small units for possible redeployment during July increased that requirement to approximately twenty airplanes a day for that station. Estimated future requirements included one group of troop carriers for each of the airborne divisions upon their arrival.[147]

The Parachute School at Fort Benning would need an average of twelve C-47 aircraft, nine C-46's and fourteen CG-4 gliders five days a week, and one day a week twelve additional C-47 airplanes would be needed. As classes at the Parachute School increased, a total of thirty-one C-47 aircraft and twelve C-46's were assigned to Lawson Field, Fort Benning, to overcome attrition and maintenance losses.[148] Increasing activities at the Airborne Center during late summer would require twenty C-46 or C-47 airplanes and three CG-4 gliders twenty-four days a month, and four additional airplanes and three additional gliders two days a month. In addition the Thirteenth Airborne Division was at Camp Mackall, and even though no further airborne training was planned for the division it had to have ten airplanes and ten gliders three days a week during the period 15 October to 15 December so that 7,000 men could take non-tactical glider rides in order to retain their qualification for extra glider pay. A future requirement for the training of an airborne division, not yet designated, was expected for the period 15 February to 15 April 1946. Army Ground Forces promised to forward a summary of troop carrier requirements each month so that better coordination could be effected.[149]

Uncertainties of redeployment and the accompanying changes in personnel made it difficult to hold to definite schedules in training, but I Troop Carrier Command found that, in general, the resources at its disposal were sufficient to meet the airborne training requirements which Army Ground Forces had outlined. It recommended that a troop carrier group not scheduled for redeployment be brought to full strength and be stationed in the Camp Mackall area to meet the requirements of the Airborne Center. Victory against Japan, however, came before action on the recommendation, and then training plans turned to the requirements for a post-war establishment.

Chapter VI

Trial by Battle

Even when the organization and training of airborne units had little more than begun, plans already were underway to test them in battle at the first opportunity. They first saw action in North Africa and the Mediterranean.[1]

Paratroops in North Africa

First combat action of airborne troops of the U. S. Army in World War II was the landings of the Second Battalion, 503d Parachute Infantry Regiment (later redesignated 509th Parachute Infantry Regiment) in conjunction with the U.S.-British invasion of North Africa. The first mission was at Oran on 8 November 1942; the second was the drop on Youks-les-Bains airport on 16 November, and the third was a demolition mission of thirty men near El Djem, Tunisia, on 26 December 1942.[2]

The use of a parachute battalion in the North African invasion had not been added to General Eisenhower's plan until early October. The battalion was to be flown all the way from England to Algeria – a flight of some twelve hours – in unarmed transports which would have to land very shortly after dropping their loads.[3] After arriving in England in June 1942, the Second Battalion, 503d Parachute Infantry, had been attached for training to a British Airborne division under the command of Maj. Gen. F. A. M. Browning, D.S.O.[4] It would be available for the first American airborne mission.

Uncertain whether they faced a hostile and determined defense or an unopposed landing, the paratroops took off at 2130 hours on 7 November 1942, in thirty-nine C-47 transport planes of the Sixtieth Troop Carrier Group, from two airdromes in southern England. Their mission was to seize the Tafaraoui and La Senia airports near Oran, but whether they were to jump by parachute on a drop zone between the two airports, or were to ride the planes down to the fields for a peaceful welcome, they would not know until a signal was flashed from Gibralter – a signal which, three hours before take-off, indicated a peaceful reception. The parachutists had trained well for their first combat mission. All had become familiar with details of the plan. For six weeks they had studied maps, sketches and sandtable models of the ground. They had engaged in tactical exercises on terrain in England which was similar to that on which they would operate.[5] But on this night flight their fate was in the hands of men who had not shared that training. It was the first night formation flight for many of the pilots.[6] A number of the navigators had been assigned to the squadrons just before the operation. English flying restrictions, grounding of planes for modifications, requirements of other missions, and bad weather had denied to the airmen an opportunity to familiarize themselves with all details, to participate in rehearsals, or even to practice long-range instrument flying at night.[7] In a wedding of well-trained with inadequately-trained components of an airborne task force, the skill of the former cannot be expected to compensate for deficiencies of the latter. Rather, the poorest tends to impose its level on the effectiveness of the whole operation. A tactical flight of 1500 miles would have been a serious test for an experienced bomber unit; it was too much to expect of a hastily assembled, ill-trained troop carrier group.

After assembling in the air and beginning the flight toward Algeria, the planes maintained fairly good order until they approached Spain. Then the formation began to break up in the face of fog and the difficulties of night flying. By dawn there was no single formation of more than six planes, and most pilots had no idea of their location. Neither prearranged homing signals from a war vessel twenty-five miles off the coast nor from Allied agents in the vicinity of Tafaraoui were effective. (It turned out that the ship was sending the signals on the wrong frequency, and the operator at Tafaraoui, thinking the operation had been cancelled, turned off his radar at 0100.) The airplanes were scattered from Spanish Morocco to points east of Oran. Half a dozen planes, however, were able to fly directly to the objective, and eventually most of the others found their way to that area. Their first hint as to which plan – "war" or "peace" – actually was to be in operation came with their arrival over La Senia airport as it was being bombed. Three planes jumped their parachutists on high ground north of the Sebkra, a dry lake bed about thirty miles west of Tafaraoui, and others which had arrived, or arrived subsequently in the area, landed in the Sebkra. Later some six planes jumped their parachutists in order to help protect the others from an armored column – later found to be American. Three planes landed in Spanish Morocco, and were interned;

one landed at Gibraltar because of engine trouble; one landed southeast ot Oran, and two landed in French Morocco, were released and the next day arrived at La Senia airport. About 300 parachutists had assembled in the Sebkra by 0900. While the only three planes with sufficient gasoline took off with full loads of parachutists for Tafaraoui, the remainder of the troops set out for that objective on foot. An attack by six enemy fighters, however, forced all three planes down – with three parachutists and two airmen killed, and fifteen parachutists wounded. Survivors continued on foot and arrived at Tafaraoui airdrome at dawn the next morning to find it already in the hands of an American armored unit. A motor convoy then went out to meet the column marching from the Sebkra. The paratroopers took over defense of the airport.[8]

The next mission of the Second Battalion, 503d Parachute Infantry, came a week later. In this case even the airborne commanders and staff had no opportunity for advance planning. The battalion was not completely reassembled at Maison Blanche airport, Algiers, until the night of 14 November, and then it received orders to take off at dawn the next morning. Now its objective was the big Youks-les-Bains airport, with its important gasoline reserves, near Tebessa on the Tunisian border. There had been no adequate reconnaissance; there had been no terrain study; there were no photographs available; there were no detailed orders. Troop carrier pilots were assembled overnight, and their briefing was little more than instructions to "follow me." After taking off at 0800, thirty-three C-47's, with an escort of six fighters, arrived over the target at 1030. Even then it was not known whether the drop would be opposed. Orders were to hold fire unless fired upon. Some of the planes had to circle over the field several times in order to determine the correct drop zone. The paratroopers jumped directly onto the field, where an entrenched French battalion sat with machine guns sited to sweep the whole field, and armored cars were out to protect the road. Fortunately, neither side was willing to fire the first shot, and Col. Edson D. Raff, commander of the parachute battalion, was able to effect the seizure of the airport in a conference with the French commander.[9] Again it was doubtful whether the airborne attempt would have been successful in the face of a determined enemy.

The third parachute drop of American troops in the North African campaign was for the purpose of blowing up an important railroad bridge six miles north of El Djem, Tunisia. For this mission three C-47 transports, at 2220 on 26 December 1942, dropped a team consisting of one officer, two French soldiers who spoke Arabic, six demolition men, and twenty-one riflemen. Unfortunately, they were unable to find the bridge that night, and the next day, when they saw German patrols searching the countryside, they demolished what rails they could, and split up into small groups to try to find their way back to friendly lines – about seventy miles to the west. Only the lieutenant, the two French guides, and three other parachutists had been able to do so a month later.[10]

Airborne operations in North Africa demonstrated that sufficient time for detailed planning was imperative. Observers recommended that not less than five days be allowed for operations involving a battalion or less, and ten days for larger operations. Moreover, planning could not be satisfactory without well-organized standard operating procedures.[11] These were lessons which long since should have been established by maneuvers, but there had been insufficient airplanes to permit their use for training; they had to go directly to combat. It was only by good fortune that the lessons were not learned at a much greater cost. The observers reached these further conclusions:

> Troop carrier airplanes must be furnished in sufficient quantity to permit primary usage in airborne operations. The air force staffs could thus employ the airplanes for cargo missions, for economical usage, but the number available must be sufficient to prevent the interruption of essential supply functions in order to launch an airborne effort. It is necessary that the air staffs make provision for the rapid assembly of troop carrier airplanes without throwing freight schedules into disorder annd without, in each instance, having to overcome the objection of higher Air Headquarters. (In each of the operation plannings observed, the air forces fought the operation because routine schedules had to be interrupted.)
>
> Airborne and troop carrier units must train together before entering a combat operation. We should not permit transport pilots to carry well-trained American soldiers with the same nonchalance that routine cargo is flown on a freight line. Unless the parachutists and troop carrier personnel have an opportunity to work together and understand the other's problems the best planned operation may fail due to lack of good teamwork and cooperation.[12]

Sicily

The year 1943 was a year rich in airborne experience. It was the critical year for the airborne effort. It was the year which decided whether the airborne program should continue to expand, or whether it should be curtailed.

Thus far airborne doctrine, the organization of airborne troops, and the policies which were being followed had been growing without the benefit of direct combat experience other than those battalion drops in North Africa. During the last half of 1943, American airborne troops were put to a wide variety of uses. In Sicily troops of the Eighty-second Airborne Division were dropped to support an amphibious landing; in Italy they parachuted to reinforce a threatened beachhead, and in the Southwest Pacific the 503d Parachute Regimental Combat Team was dropped to seize an airfield far behind enemy lines.

Preparations

Sicily provided the greatest trial in 1943 for airborne operations. It was the first operation for any American airborne division (though the whole division was not committed), and it was the first major airborne attack at night.

Invasion plans called for the Seventh U.S. Army and the British Eighth Army to make a series of simultaneous seaborne assaults, assisted by American and British airborne landings, on the southeast coast of the island. With the British going in on the right, and the Americans on the left, the amphibious landings were to cover about one hundred miles of coastline from Cap Murro di Porco, just south of Syracuse, around the southeastern tip of Sicily, and westward to Licata. Immediate objectives were the ports of Syracuse and Licata and the airfields between those two ports which were within striking distance of the coast.[13] Originally it had been intended to use the airborne troops directly against the beach defenses, but their mission finally was to seize key points to block enemy reinforcements and to clear the way for advancing inland. Before midnight on D minus 1 a brigade of the British First Airborne Division was to land in the area immediately south of Syracuse to seize a vital bridge and key points commanding the city. Meanwhile a reinforced combat team of the U.S. Eighty-second Airborne Division was to drop behind Gela in order to block enemy attempts to reinforce that sector against the beachlandings, and to clear the way for the advance of the U.S. First Infantry Division on Ponte Olivo and its airfield.[14] Among other things, the timing for the operation depended upon reconciling airborne requirements for a light moon and naval demands for darkness. The Combined Chiefs of Staff had set the target date as the favorable period of the July moon. General Eisenhower and his staff interpreted this to mean the period of the second quarter of the moon, when there should be enough moonlight early in the night for airborne troops to drop and assemble, but complete darkness after midnight, when the moon had set, for the approach of the naval convoys. Thus D Day was determined almost automatically as 10 July.[15]

For the operation the Fifty-first and Fifty-second Troop Carrier Wings, together with two British squadrons, were brought together into the Northwest African Air Force Troop Carrier Command (Provisional) under the command of Brig. Gen. Paul L. Williams. The three groups (Sixtieth, Sixty-second, and Sixty-fourth) of the Fifty-first Troop Carrier Wing had been in Northwest Africa since the November invasion. One group was being used continuously, on a rotation basis, on detached

Paratroopers of the Eighty-second Airborne Division practice jump in French Morocco, June 1943.

service with the Northwest African Air Force Air Service Command. By the middle of May the three groups which made up the Fifty-second Wing (61st, 313th and 314th) had arrived. Later in the month the 315th Troop Carrier Group arrived, but it had only two of its four squadrons. One squadron had gone to the Pacific in answer to an emergency call in October 1942, and the other had gone to Alaska in November. The 315th was assigned to the Air Service Command to relieve the groups of the Fifty-first Wing of that duty. Later three squadrons of the 316th Troop Carrier Group, which had been working with the British Eighth Army in the Western Desert, joined the Fifty-second Wing. That group's other squadron remained in Egypt.[16] Units of the Fifty-first Wing concentrated in the Macara area of Algeria to train with the British First Airborne Division, and units of the Fifty-second Wing worked with the U.S. Eighty-second Airborne Division in the Oujda area of French Morocco,[17] where the Fifth Army Airborne Training Center had been established in March.[18]

One of the greatest difficulties in training for the Sicilian operation was in handling gliders. The 105 glider pilots of the Fifty-first Wing had had only four CG-4A's with which to train, and now those were found to be unsafe. New gliders, each packed in five cases, were being delivered at six different ports. Shortages of trained men and lack of truck and rail transportation delayed the assembly of the gliders. It took about 250 man-hours to put one together, and the best production that any one of the three depots working at the task could get was twelve gliders a day. Then aircraft had to tow the gliders to the training areas. Of 485 gliders received in North Africa during the spring, 375 were operational in the forward areas by June.[19]

In preparing for this, the first major night airborne attack in history, airborne and troop carrier commanders coordinated loading plans, memorized aerial photographs, made a night reconnaissance over the objective area just a month before D Day when the moonlight would be similar. Battalions rehearsed their ground attacks on replicas of the objectives set up in their Moroccan training areas, and troop carrier squadrons practiced runs over simulated drop zones. Yet there remained some doubts in the minds of airborne leaders about how effective the night assembly would be.[20]

Between 15 June and 2 July transport planes were busy moving the airborne and troop carrier units from Morocco and Algeria to their forward staging areas in Tunisia. The planes carried 18,000 troops and 3,650 tons of equipment in the movement.[21]

Attack

At dusk on 9 July the airborne forces began taking off from Tunisia for Sicily. The British brigade was going entirely by glider for the first Allied glider assault of the war, while the Americans would all jump by parachute. All but 28 of the 134 planes taking off with the British were American C-47's of the Fifty-first Wing, and all of the gliders except eight British Horsas were American-made CG-4A's manned by British glider pilots none of whom had had training in night releases over water. A high wind which had sprung up during the late afternoon and evening added to the difficulties of following the crooked course. As the widely scattered glider formations approached the Sicilian coast, some tug pilots exhibited an inclination to release the gliders quickly and head for the home base.[22] At least seventy gliders came down in the sea. Only about twelve landed near the selected landing zone. Nevertheless, a force of eight officers and sixty-five men did reach the canal bridge south of Syracuse which was their objective. They held it until late afternoon (9 July), and then were forced to withdraw. But forces attacking from the beaches arrived in time to retake the bridge intact.[23]

It took some 226 C-47's of the Fifty-second Troop Carrier Wing to carry the assault combat team from the U.S. Eighty-second Airborne Division – the 505th Parachute Infantry Regiment; Third Battalion, 504th Parachute Infantry; 456th Parachute Field Artillery Battalion; Company B, 307th Airborne Engineer Battalion; and signal, medical, air support, and naval support detachments – a total of 3,405 paratroopers.[24] The planes took off on schedule on the evening of 9 July from their bases in Tunisia, but that was the last of the schedule. Their course lay eastward from Tunisia to a point off Malta, thence generally northward to the coast of

Sicily, westward to a point opposite Gela, northward to the drop zones, and then back southwestward via Pantelleria to Tunisia.[25] The desire to follow certain check points, and at the same time to meet the demands of Allied naval commanders for avoiding their formations, made necessary such a circuitous route. The flight would have been difficult enough for inexperienced troop-carrier crews as a nontactical daytime maneuver, but at night, in a high wind, as a part of a great invasion, and at an altitude of only 500 feet to avoid radar detection, it was next to impossible.

The principal check point en route was Malta, but the planes failed to come within sight of it. As they came over the coast of Sicily leaders looked in vain for the landmarks which they had memorized from photographs and which they had seen so clearly in the moonlight a month before. Pre-invasion bombing had stirred up a haze over the ground, and the planes, fighting a thirty-five-mile-an-hour wind, became scattered. Some antiaircraft fire came up, and evasive action brought further scattering. But orders were to drop every parachutist and piece of equipment somewhere in Sicily, even if the correct drop zone could not be found; and drop they did.

They dropped as far apart as fifty and sixty miles, from Cap Moto to Licata. While only about one-eighth of the force landed in front of the First Division, as planned, others landed in front of the Forty-fifth Division, in front of the Canadians and in front of the British. Nevertheless, most assigned missions were accomplished, and much unplanned assistance was given along a wide frontage. Indeed, it is possible that the importance of the airborne operations in disrupting the enemy was greater than it would have been had landings been made according to plan. Scattered groups of paratroops collected all across the front and fell upon enemy strong points wherever they found them. The Third Battalion of the 505th Parachute Infantry seized high ground near Vittoria, well to the east of Gela, and held it against a German battalion equipped with Tiger tanks until American reinforcements could arrive from the beach. Troops of the Second Battalion dropped beyond the easternmost point of intended American landings, near Cap Scaramia. They destroyed road blocks and strong points along the highway to Marina di Raqusa, captured that town, and made contact with the U.S. Forty-fifth Division on D plus 1. Italian prisoners estimated the number of American paratroops at between 20,000 and 30,000.[26]

Tragic Reinforcement

The plan had been to drop the 504th Regimental Combat Team, less the battalion which dropped earlier, on the night of D Day to reinforce troops of Eighty-second Airborne Division in the Gela area, but the confusion in the situation led to postponement until the following night.

The time was too short to warn all the ships off the southeastern shore of Sicily of the change,[27] but such a warning should not have been necessary. A message had gone out to ground commanders on 6 July instructing them to warn their commands that they should expect flights of friendly troop carrier planes on each of the nights of D plus 1 to D plus 6. They were to advise the respective naval commanders.[28]

There was no previous experience upon which to draw for an operation of this kind, but Maj. Gen. Matthew B. Ridgway, commander of the Eighty-second Airborne Division, sensed in the situation a serious danger of encountering fire from friendly surface forces. Troubled by misgivings, he had moved energetically to forestall such an eventuality. During the planning for the Sicily invasion, Ridgway repeatedly had sought assurances that naval vessels would recognize an air corridor through which the troop carriers could fly with a guarantee that Allied vessels would not fire on them. After several failures to get such a promise, on 7 July he had received an assurance from the naval commanders that if the troop carriers flew close to the designated route, making sure to arrive over Sicily at Sampieri, at the extreme right (east) flank of the Seventh Army zone, and then turn northwest and fly at an altitude of 1,000 feet through a two-mile-wide corridor thirty miles to the Gela-Farello landing zones, freedom from the fire of friendly naval forces could be guaranteed. Landing with the seaborne follow-up shortly after dawn on D Day, Ridgway had continued to worry about the reinforcing elements of his division scheduled to parachute in the following night. A check of six antiaircraft artillery crews in the area of the First Division on the afternoon of 11 July revealed that five of the six had been warned to expect a parachute jump on the Gela-Farello field that night. He then had obtained assurances from the antiaircraft battalion commander that all crews would be warned that afternoon.[29]

The 144 air transports carrying approximately 2,000 men on the night of 11 July had to follow about the same dog-leg route as before, though they were to turn inland thirty miles east of Gela in order to avoid invasion convoys, and now would have to pass over about thirty-five miles of battle front. The airborne force chanced to be approaching the battle area just after an enemy bombing attack. The sounds of bombs and guns had died away by the time the leading elements of the troop carrier formations reached the coast, and began their turns. All remained quiet as the leading flight arrived over the drop zone, and the first paratroopers jumped. Then, as the second flight approached the final checkpoint before the drop zone, and the first flights of the second serial were beginning their turns into the overland aerial corridor, while the third serial was following over the sea, all hell broke loose. Within minutes it seemed that every gun in the vicinity, on land and sea, was turned on the low-flying,

The leader of the assault combat team of the Eighty-second Airborne Division in Sicily, Col. James M. Gavin (right), talks with Jack Thompson, war correspondent for the *Chicago Tribune* (11 July 1943). Gavin later became assistant division commander and then commanding general of the Eighty-second.

Matthew B. Rigdway, commanding general of the Eighty-second, confers with Master Sergeant Frank Morang. Ridgway later became commanding general of XVIII Corps (Airborne).

slow C-47's. The display of amber belly lights for recognition made no impression on the gunners. Clinging to an enemy-held coast in black night, and edgy from heavy enemy bombing attacks which had just preceded, surface forces responded to the opening of fire with a contagion which became worse as additional flights arrived. And their fire was remarkably more effective against the transport planes than it had been against the German bombers. Twenty-three of the troop carriers, six with paratroopers still on board, were shot down, and thirty-seven were badly damaged. As parachutists jumped, they too came under fire, and some were fired upon even after they were on the ground. As pilots took evasive action, and lost track of landmarks, the formations became widely scattered. As on the initial assault, paratroopers were scattered all the way from Gela to the east coast. Several of the planes turned back to North Africa without jumping their parachutists; one arrived back at its base with 1,000 holes in its wings and fuselage. On the battlefield confusion reigned. Even the First Division, in whose area the paratroopers were supposed to drop, listed the 504th Parachute Infantry in its G-2 report as an unidentified German parachute regiment. Out of this action the 504th Combat Team reported 81 killed, 132 wounded, and 16 missing, and the Fifty-second Troop Carrier Wing reported 7 killed, 30 wounded, and 53 missing.[30]

Headquarters personnel of the Eighty-second Airborne Division flew into the area on D plus 6 (16 July) in fifty-one planes, with fighter escort, in a daylight movement without serious incident.

Meanwhile on the night of 13-14 July another British airborne force took off. Once more the troop carriers came under friendly fire, with a loss of eleven planes and damage to fifty others, but the results were less disastrous and a much larger percentage of the British paratroops reached their objective south of Catania.[31] Unwittingly, the British may have made a contribution to airborne doctrine in their jump. Unknown to them, German parachutists who had been brought in by air to serve as reinforcements had jumped into the same area just ahead of the British. Reports differ greatly as to the results, but it probably was the only operation of the war in which paratroops of one side jumped onto paratroops who had just arrived from the other. Some airborne specialists contended that that was the best way to neutralize an enemy airhead – to launch a counterjump into it.[32] This might be a kind of present-day counterpart to the practice in early naval battles of boarding an enemy's ship.

Results and Appraisals

Sicily was a bitter disappointment for men who had put great faith in airborne operations. How could it happen in this age of modern communications that "friendly" fire from vessels and from ground troops should become the greatest menace to an airborne reinforcement? Surely a part of the problem was in having friendly planes flying over at night. Perhaps the men on the ground and on the sea had grown accustomed to expect American planes only by day, and German planes by night. Even while he was trying to find his scattered paratroopers, and with impressions of the operation still burning freshly, General Ridgway took time out to set down these "principles":

13 July 1943

PRINCIPLES

1. Night operations offer chance of greater surprise, but with far greater dispersion upon dropping, and greater loss from fire of own forces, both ground and sea. If employed, training under one commander must be intensified, and no operation attempted unless results of training indicate desired probability of success.

2. Routes over enemy territory should be selected based on best obtainable intelligence, so as to pass over or near the minimum of antiaircraft ground defenses. If these defenses are at all strong, they must be neutralized or that route abandoned.

3. Daylight operations, without ruinous losses, will be practicable only with adequate air support against both hostile ground and air resistance.

4. Under limitations as to types and quantities of available aircraft, the employment of airborne divisions in airborne operations is not warranted, since it results in their piecemeal use against minor objectives.

5. A limited number of these divisions, properly trained, should be available against their need in such time as the strategic situation in the European Theater opens up sufficiently to justify their use as divisions in support of the effort of other forces against larger objectives, or in the final exploitation stage, as Axis opposition crumbles.

6. Until that time, the airborne divisions should be organized, equipped, and trained to operate as light infantry divisions, and should be used in combat for short periods in order to give them essential battle experience. Following this, except for such brief repetitions as may be necessary, they should be held out of action, awaiting airborne employment as divisions.

Ridgway

Maj. Gen. Joseph M. Swing, American airborne adviser on the Allied staff, attributed the unsatisfactory results to five principal reasons: (1) insufficient prior planning in coordinating routes with all forces several weeks earlier; (2) the inability of the troop carrier formations to follow the routes given – partly because of the state of training of the pilots, and partly because of the complicated route; (3) the rigid policy of naval forces to fire at all aircraft at night coming within range – regardless of their efforts to identify themselves; (4) the unfortunate circumstance of an enemy bombing raid's coinciding with the arrival of the airborne force; (5) the failure of some ground commanders to warn the men manning antiaircraft weapons of the expected arrival of the troop carrier formations.[33] Maj. Gen. F. A. M. Browning, British airborne expert and adviser on the staff of Allied Force Headquarters, was sharp in his criticism of the aerial navigation:

> In spite of the clear weather, suitable moon, the existence of MALTA as a check point only 70 miles from SICILY and the latter's very obvious and easily recognizable coast line, the navigation by the troop carrier aircrews was bad.
>
> The troops comprising both British and American Airborne Divisions are of a very high quality and their training takes time and is expensive. They are given important tasks which may acutely affect the operations as a whole. It is essential both from the operational and moral point of view that energetic steps be taken to improve greatly on the aircrews' performance up to date.
>
> Intensive training in low flying navigation by night, especially over coast lines, must be organized and carried oncontinuously.This must form part of the aircrews' training before they reach a theater of war and the standard set must be very high.[34]

Ridgway stated weeks later that "both the 82d Airborne Division and the North African Air Force Troop Carrier Command are today at airborne training levels below combat requirements."[35] He emphasized that airborne and troop carrier units were "unprepared to conduct with reasonable chances of success night operations either glider or parachute, employing forces the size of Regimental Combat Teams."

A report on the Sicilian airborne operations prepared by Headquarters, Fifth Army Airborne Training Center, was more blunt:

> The (82d) Division was in superb physical condition, well qualified in the use of infantry arms, in combined ground operations, and in individual jumping. It was extremely deficient in its air operations. The (52d) Troop Carrier Wing did not cooperate well. Training was, in general, inadequate. Combat efficiency for night glider operations was practically zero. The combined force of (82d) Airborne Division and troop carrier units was extremely deficient.[36]

This ran contrary to General McNair's fears about "trick outfits'" tendency to emphasize their "tricks" at the expense of basic combat training. In this case, it was in the "tricks" that marked deficiencies appeared.

General Browning saw a need for a central authority to supervise the planning for airborne operations:

> It is not realized yet that the planning, staffwork and control

> during operations must be centralized to a very great extent. The experiences in HUSKY are quoted as a typical example and it has borne out views expressed repeatedly in the past.
>
> It has been abundantly proved that, although Airborne Divisions may be used sub-allotted to formations, centralized planning and control of all airborne matters, apart from the detailed ground planning between formations with whom they will be working after landing, are an essential.[37]

Yet, in spite of all the difficulties and shortcomings which appeared in the operation, there was, too, achievement. The fact that such small fractions of the planned force were able to accomplish missions assigned to whole reinforced battalions indicated the merits of the airborne approach. There was "little doubt that the action of the American airborne troops speeded up the landing and advance inland at least 48 hours."[38] General Patton, commanding the Seventh Army, affirmed that "his swift and successful landings followed by a rapid advance inland would not have been achieved at such a light cost or at such a speed without the action of his Airborne Division."[39]

Field Marshal Kesselring, German commander in chief for the area, reported shortly after the invasion that the paratroops had imposed unusual delays in the movement of German reserves.[40] In a postwar interrogation, General Kurt Student, commander of German parachute troops (and, of course, an airborne enthusiast) expressed in strong terms his appraisal of the effectiveness of the operation. He described the operation as successful in spite of the scattering of troops which was to be expected in darkness. He stated that in his opinion the Hermann Goering Division would have hurled the initial seaborne units back to the sea if airborne troops had not blocked it. The German parachute officer attributed the entire success of the operation to the delaying of German reserves until the amphibious forces had built up enough strength to resist counter-attacks.[41]

It is possible, however, that the Allied airborne operation could have been a far greater factor in the conquest of Sicily had the airborne troops been dropped, not between the reserves and the beach defenses, but *en masse* on the central plateau, where they could have assembled with little interference and then struck aggressively at the enemy rear.[42]

In some respects the Allied airborne operations in Sicily bore certain similarities to the German airborne invasion of Crete. In each case the attacker considered the operation a disappointment, while the defender considered the operation a more or less spectacular success. Each operation was something of a turning point for the airborne effort in the respective military establishments. For the Germans, Crete was the end of major airborne operations. For the Allies, Sicily was only the beginning of airborne operations on an even larger scale.

Members of the Eighty-second Airborne Division advance through the Sicilian countryside after a night jump.

Scattered paratroopers move through Vittoria, Sicily, on the morning of 13 July.

Still, a great deal of disillusionment followed the airborne effort in the Sicilian operation, and a number of responsible officers became convinced that the airborne division never would be able to operate tactically as a division. The Ground Forces staff could see no immediate requirement for the airborne strength which had been assembled, and it seemed that three airborne divisions, plus additional parachute regiments, faced the prospect of an indefinite period of waiting in the United States. AGF, therefore, was willing to abandon the idea of special airborne divisions. It suggested that airborne divisions be reorganized as light divisions. Parachute units would be removed, and the light divisions would be given a variety of basic training. Whenever an airborne operation was contemplated then, the light division could be trained, preferably in the theater, for that specific operation. Parachute units would be organized into separate battalions, after the fashion of the armored infantry battalions, and then would be grouped as necessary for training and tactical employment.[43]

At the same time General Eisenhower was writing from North Africa in this manner:

> To digress for a moment I do not believe in the airborne division. I believe that airborne troops should be organized in self-contained units, comprising infantry, artillery, and special services, all of about the strength of a regimental combat team. Even if one had all the air transport he could possibly use the fact is at any given time and in any given spot only a reasonable number of air transports can be operated because of technical difficulties. To employ at any time and place a whole division would require a dropping over such an extended area, that I seriously doubt that a division commander could regain control and operate the scattered forces as one unit. In any event, if these troops were organized in smaller, self-contained units, a senior commander, with a small staff and radio communications, could always be dropped in the area to insure necessary coordination.[44]

Earlier another observer in Allied Force Headquarters, Maj. Gen. J. P. Lucas, had expressed the same sentiments. He was convinced, "from the experience of this campaign and from numerous conversations with participants in airborne operations therein, that the organization of Airborne troops into divisions is unsound." He did not believe that a unit the size of a division could be landed in an area where a headquarters could exercise control over its subsequent action.[45]

Standing against this trend was General Swing who had left as an airborne adviser in the Mediterranean to become commander of the Airborne Command. He protested that these views were based upon a campaign where there had been certain adverse conditions which were remediable. He stated that in that operation the troop carrier convoy had been required by naval restrictions to fly too circuitous a route, that troop carrier elements had had insufficient training in night operations, that there had been insufficient time for reconnaissance and briefing by subordinate flight leaders, and that weather conditions had been severe. General Swing maintained that conditions which resulted in the commitment of one-half of the division piecemeal by combat team while the other half remained in Africa – "certainly an abortive effort from a division standpoint" – could not be accepted as general. He pointed to the Nadzab (Markham Valley) airborne operation in New Guinea as an example of what could be done with proper planning and training. His conclusion was: "Airborne divisions are tactically sound. Successful employment requires careful and exact planning and coordination with the major ground effort," and he repeated an earlier recommendation that an airborne staff section, headed by a general officer, be established in each theater, "in order that the theater commander may take full advantage of the capabilities of airborne troops."[46] These also represented the views of another commanding general of the Airborne Command, Maj. Gen. Elbridge G. Chapman. In their study of the subject the Combined Staff Planners saw no combat experience, either British or American, which indicated that the division was not the proper organization for airborne troops. Taking cognizance of the expressed views of Generals Eisenhower, Swing, and Chapman, and of continuing plans for joint maneuvers in the United States, they recommended that no change be made in the policy until further experience indicated the need for a change.[47]

Airborne Assistance in Italy

Several plans came under consideration for the use of airborne forces in connection with the Fifth Army's invasion of the Italian mainland in September 1943. After rejection of other possibilities, including a plan to seize the mountain passes in Sorrento, most prominent was a plan for a combat team of the Eighty-second Airborne Division to drop along the Volturno River, twenty miles northwest of Naples – and some forty miles from the nearest beach landings at Salerno. Its mission would be to destroy all crossings of the Volturno from Triflisco to the sea and the defense of the river line against enemy efforts to send reinforcements. General Ridgway hoped to strengthen the airhead by sending a glider regiment to land by sea at the river mouth and then fight its way inland. Supply would have to be made by nightly parachute drops, by bombers if necessary, until ground forces had made contact. In view of the supply difficulty, the proposed force was reduced by one battalion on 1 September.

The tactical value of blocking enemy reinforcements at the Volturno was very great, but the plan had to be given up when sandbars were discovered at the mouth of the river, and an even more ambitious plan superseded it – the plan to drop forces around Rome and seize the airfields there. This grew out of negotiations for Italy's surrender, and was intended to save the Italian capital from German occupation. The attempt was to be timed with the Salerno invasion – the night of 8-9 September. However, after pathfinder planes already were warmed up and loaded, the mission was postponed twenty-four hours. Then it was called off altogether. Brig. Gen. Maxwell D. Taylor, chief of artillery of the Eighty-second Airborne Division, had gone on a secret mission to Rome to confer with Italian officials on the feasibility of the operation, and his message came back negative. As a result, there was no airborne action of any kind in conjunction with the Fifth Army's invasion.[48]

Later, however, an urgent call came for airborne troops to reinforce the Salerno beachhead. German counterattacks on 12 September threatened to drive a wedge all the way to the beaches. General Clark the next day sent an air courier to Sicily to call upon the Eighty-second Airborne Division. One regimental combat team was to drop, not behind the enemy lines, but inside the beachhead, that same night, and a second combat team was to drop there the next night. In addition a parachute battalion was to carry out a separate mission on the mountain village of Avellino, far behind the German lines, on the night of 15 September. Eight hours later (2130) thirty-five C-47's were taking to the air with the 504th Parachute Infantry, with Company C, 307th Airborne Engineers, attached. At the insistence of Ridgway, Clark ordered all antiaircraft guns in the Salerno area to remain silent from 2100 hours on 13 September until further notice, and he sent staff officers to the gun positions in the beachhead to make sure that the order had been received and understood. This time pilots found their course well. Without mishap they arrived over the drop zone near Paestum – guided by pathfinders. The lighting of a prearranged signal on the ground – gasoline-soaked sand in the form of the letter "T" – shortly after the first jumps began reassured them that they had found their target. Jumping from an altitude of 800 feet, most of the troops hit the ground within 200 yards of the drop zone, and virtually none came down more than 1,500 yards away. Another serial of forty-five planes, delayed by mechanical trouble, arrived several hours later, and one of the companies landed eight to ten miles off target. Another fourteen planes dropped parachutists on or near the drop zone a little later still. All together about 1,300 parachute troops in ninety planes had arrived in the beachhead within fifteen hours after Clark's original request. By dawn the regiment was in the lines, ready to attack. The next night the 505th Parachute Infantry, with Company B, 307th Airborne Engineer Battalion, attached, landed in the same drop zone with equal facility, and again was ready for a dawn attack.[49]

Unquestionably, the attacks of the parachute infantry were highly effective, and they made a real contribution to the holding and the extension of the beachhead,[50] but airborne officers questioned the use of airborne troops to reinforce positions which already were held. Regimental commanders felt that their units could have completely demoralized the German forces by dropping in their rear north of Naples and then undertaking widespread harrassing attacks and demolitions.[51] Highlight of the operation had been the successful use of the pathfinder technique. Routing and antiaircraft restrictions had been such that there was no repetition of the tragedy of friendly surface fire as at Sicily. It had been no mean achievement to make the shifts in plans and dispositions dictated by the urgent orders and the dispersion of the troops and planes over nine airfields in Sicily, and then to arrive at the beachhead with the reinforcements on schedule. But troop carrier units were still unable to function in a wholly satisfactory way as troop carriers. Demands upon them for carrying freight and passengers had been at the expense of maintaining the aircraft in first class condition. Many had as much as 500 hours on their engines, and some were unable to take off,[52] in spite of the fact that an airborne operation had been assumed for weeks.

There had been some hope of making the battalion drop on Avellino as early as the night of 12-13 September, but it could not be done until the night of 14-15 September. The Second Battalion, 509th Parachute Infantry – the same unit which had made the first jump in North Africa – received the assignment. It was to make a night drop in that mountainous area some twenty miles north of Salerno, with a demolition section attached, and block all roads going through that important mountain pass. The town was a center of activity for German service units, and it was on the route over which reinforcements would move toward the Salerno beachhead. Unit commanders had only two hours to study their maps and they had no opportunity for even a short meeting with their leaders. Taking to the air from Sicily in planes of the Sixty-fourth Troop Carrier Group, the battalion faced a most risky enterprise. The men were overburdened with five days' rations and ammunition, and they had no reliable radio communication with Fifth Army. They were supposed to harass the Germans for five days, and then, if ground troops had not yet made contact, they were to withdraw by infiltration to Allied lines. Once again the misfortune of dispersion overtook the flight. The 640 paratroopers were scattered over 100 square miles of the mountainous, enemy-held territory. Some of them formed into small parties and proceeded to lay mines, ambush small columns, shoot lone messengers, and filter toward the beaches. Eventually about 510 of them got back.[53]

Chapter VII

Invasion of France

Having survived the trials of Sicily and Italy in the Mediterranean and of Nadzab in the Southwest Pacific, the American airborne effort during 1944 attracted an ever-increasing interest and attention. In the critical Allied campaigns planned for this year, airborne warfare was being scheduled for more and more impressive roles. Whether it ever should win a leading part remained a moot question. But for the cross-channel invasion of Europe, nearly everyone considered airborne support in one form or another as essential.

Plans and Preparations for Overlord

One of the major questions to be settled in the planning for the Normandy invasion was the manner and scope of the employment of airborne troops. Upon that decision would depend much of the allotment of resources and the development of subsidiary tactical plans. The decision at SHAEF came in February 1944, and, contrary to the hopes of General Marshall, it was one which called for the initial airborne role to be a tactical one with the primary purpose of facilitating the establishment of the beachhead. It would be the greatest airborne operation of the war up to that time, but it would not be one conducted according to the pattern which had become almost traditional in thought and maneuvers if not in combat. That is, its objectives would not be concerned with the seizure of airfields, the consolidation of an airhead and subsequent build-up by airlanding operations. Had the command of the forces in the European theater devolved upon General Marshall, as it almost did, it is likely that the airborne phase of the operation, for better or worse, would have been quite different. It probably would have followed more closely the concept of a deep vertical envelopment and the build-up of an airhead. Actually, Marshall urged such a course upon Eisenhower, and sent Brig. Gen. Frederick W. Evans, commanding general of the I Troop Carrier Command, and Col. Bruce W. Bidwell of the War Department Operations Division, to London to sell the idea to the supreme Allied commander and his staff.[1] (See Appendix XII.)

This idea was not a new one upon which the chief of staff had suddenly seized to spring upon the supreme Allied commander. As early as August 1943 the plan was being seriously considered. When Gen. Sir Frederick Morgan, then chief of staff to the Supreme Allied Command (designate)(COSSAC), was in Washington for conferences at that time, he was "subjected to an intense course of indoctrination" at the hands of General Arnold and General Marshall.[2] They had explained to the British officer what had been done in the way of air transportation of troops in the Southwest Pacific, and had impressed him with photographs and charts showing how elements of an Australian division had been transported by air over the Owen-Stanley Mountains in New Guinea. Pointing to the difficulties which were being met in trying to obtain enough landing craft for the amphibious attack then contemplated, they had raised the question of doing the same sort of thing in Europe. "Why not switch the whole thing round so as to make the main effort by airborne and air-landed troops, with the subsidiary operation by sea?"[3] General Morgan then had summoned Air Marshal Sir Trafford Leigh-Mallory, the RAF officer designated to command the Allied Expeditionary Air Force, but the air marshal was dubious about such an ambitious airborne undertaking. Apparently the plan had remained more or less dormant thereafter until now hopefully revived.

Evans and Bidwell presented their plan to Eisenhower, alone, on 16 February. The supreme commander's first reaction was an expression of concern about the mobility of the troops landed at the proposed airhead. He feared that lack of mobility would make them incapable of effective offensive action, but he said that he would reserve final judgment until General Montgomery and Lt. Gen. Omar Bradley (then commander of the U.S. First Army) had had a chance to comment on the proposal. The next day the visiting officers presented the plan to members of General Eisenhower's staff. Present were Lt. Gen. Walter B. Smith, chief of staff; Lt. Gen. Sir F. E. Morgan, deputy chief of staff; Maj. Gen. H. R. Bull, G-3, and Maj. Gen. J. F. M. Whitely, deputy G-3; General Hull of War Department Operations Division also was there. The staff officers had been instructed not to comment on the plan during the meeting, but from their questions Evans and Bidwell concluded that they were very interested, but were concerned about how such an operation would weaken the effort against the beaches and delay the capture of Cherbourg. On 18 February

General Montgomery, General Bradley, and General Ridgway listened to the plan. Montgomery asked Bradley his opinion, and the latter stated that he did not favor it, because he felt that nothing should be allowed to deflect from the capture of Cherbourg at the earliest time possible. General Ridgway agreed with that view, and then General Montgomery, likewise agreeing, summed up his views on airborne forces. He said that Allied airborne potential should be developed to the maximum, and that an agreement should be reached on what would constitute the maximum practical program. He stated then that a decision should be made on where to use that airborne effort, later on as well as initially, and that initially it should be used only to win the main battle – the beach landing. It was obvious that the decision was going against the proposal. General Smith confirmed this on 21 February, but he suggested that it might be desirable to execute a vertical envelopment *en masse* later, and he asked that the plans and data be left with him.[4]

Eisenhower went to some length to explain his position to General Marshall. Reflecting the views of his commanders and staff, the supreme Allied commander ruled against this Marshall plan. He was concerned first of all with getting a port. Secondly, he doubted that Allied air power really could isolate the battlefield sufficiently to protect an airborne airhead, relatively weak in antitank defense, against a strong armored counterattack. Eisenhower was worried most of all about the German coastal defenses – he still could not think of the attack by sea as being secondary to the airborne – and he wanted airborne forces to help make secure a lodgement on the beaches. Finally, the priority in air support would go to tactical and strategic bombing, and this would limit air support for an airborne operation.[5] (See Appendix XII.)

General Arnold made clear his reaction to this decision in a memorandum for Marshall: "I am afraid we have failed to put over to General Eisenhower the point that massed airborne forces are capable of being employed in an immediate strategic or long-range tactical role in addition to the immediate tactical role."[6] He expressed the conviction that, with the capture of the airfields, which had been planned, the airborne forces could be made tactically mobile. Bidwell prepared a draft letter for Marshall to send in reply to the letter of Eisenhower. The chief of staff made some revision on the draft, and then did not send it. He forwarded a copy of Arnold's memorandum without any covering letter.[7]

While agreeing with Arnold's contention on the capabilities of airborne troops in strategic or long-range tactical employment, Bidwell believed that Eisenhower did realize those strategic capabilities, but felt that airborne troops were essential for the early capture of Cherbourg. Bidwell suggested that Arnold neglected, in his discussion, the problem not only of seizing landing fields, but of maintaining security and holding them during ferrying operations. This was a problem that was of greatest weight in the thinking of Eisenhower, Bradley, and Montgomery. They doubted the ability of an airborne force defending an airhead to hold out against determined armored attack long enough to permit the build-up of an effective striking force.[8] The threat of armored counterattack was a matter of major concern in any airborne operation. It was in the minds of members of the airborne divisions as they planned for even the relatively limited employment of their units in Normandy. Brig. Gen. James M. Gavin, assistant division commander of the Eighty-second Airborne Division, said in a report, "Give us anything that will stop the German Tiger Tank as a counterattack by them is the first thing that will hit us after we jump."[9]

From the beginning of planning for a cross-channel invasion of Europe, use of airborne troops had been contemplated. While exact composition of the airborne force was not clear in the early planning, nor its tactical role well defined, the assumption was there that it was necessary to have a force which could hurdle the Atlantic Wall and operate in rear of the enemy's coastal defenses. As planning progressed from the abandonment of the Roundup and Sledgehammer plans for 1943 to Overlord and Neptune for 1944, the airborne phase of the plan grew as well. Finally it became clear that the airborne assault, a night operation which would precede the D Day beach landings by several hours, would be a key factor in the success of the whole invasion effort. Eisenhower attached major importance to the cutting of the Cotentin Peninsula and the rapid capture of the port of Cherbourg. He felt the airborne role an essential one. Indeed, he held to the plan for use of airborne troops against the Cotentin in the face of estimates of Air Chief Marshal Leigh-Mallory that landing losses to aircraft and personnel would run as high as 75 to 80 percent.[10]

In the late summer and autumn of 1943, Maj. Gen. William C. Lee and his 101st Airborne Division arrived in Great Britain to begin preparations for the airborne invasion of France tentatively scheduled for the next spring. On paper, the division included two glider infantry regiments, the 327th and the 401st, and one parachute regiment, the 502d. However, the 506th Parachute Infantry had been attached since June 1943, and then in January 1944 a third parachute regiment, the 501st, arrived in the United Kingdom, to be attached to the "Screaming Eagles."[11]

After completion of its combat missions in Italy, the Eighty-second Airborne Division arrived at Belfast, Northern Ireland, in December 1943,[12] and the 507th Parachute Infantry was attached to it there. In January the 508th Parachute Infantry arrived at Belfast from the United States and was also attached to the Eighty-second Airborne Division.[13]

(The 504th Parachute Infantry, the regiment which was the victim of the friendly fire in Sicily, had been committed at Anzio, and would not participate in the Normandy operation.) Men from the 505th Parachute Infantry, veterans of the jumps in Sicily and Italy, lived with each company of the 508th for about a week so that the newcomers could have some of the benefit of their experience in the small unit training which followed.[14]

Troop carrier units likewise were moving into the United Kingdom. With a cadre of six officers from the I Troop Carrier Command, the IX Troop Carrier Command was organized under the Ninth Air Force with Brig. Gen. Benjamin F. Giles of the North Atlantic Wing, Air Transport Command, in charge. By the end of February 1944, three wings – Fiftieth, Fifty-second, and Fifty-third – had been assigned to the new command. Then Brig. Gen. Paul R. Williams, who had commanded the XII Troop Carrier Command (Provisional) in the Mediterranean, was shifted to England to take over the IX Troop Carrier Command. A survey on 22 May showed 1,176 transport planes (though only 1,004 crews) on hand.[15]

Yet it was seldom possible to get enough planes together for a training exercise involving a regiment or larger unit before March. Demands on aircraft for other missions and requirements of troop carriers for their own air training accounted for much of the difficulty. In addition, the tactical air forces were reluctant to divert fighters from bomber escort missions to the protection of troop carrier training formations over Great Britain, and it was necessary to obtain permission from British authorities to use land for training at a distance from bases. Moreover the divisions were scattered in many stations without motor trucks to assemble their men or move their bulky equipment about.[16]

Units did make several company and battalion parachute jumps, as well as continue almost uninterrupted ground combat training. Soon after arrival the divisions had set up parachute schools, and in May the two airborne division commanding generals received authority to rate as parachutists members of glider units who completed the jump course.[17] Now there was opportunity for regimental drops, but commanders, concerned about casualties, and anxious to perfect ground training, preferred not to accept all the joint exercises now proposed.

During the spring, troop carrier units trained with the British First and Sixth Airborne Divisions as well as with the Eighty-second (which had moved to England from Northern Ireland in March) and 101st Divisions. Between 15 March and 27 March the various units participated in thirty-eight joint exercises at the troop carrier wing-airborne regimental combat team level. But it took a great deal of training for troop carrier pilots, after becoming used to flying freight, to recover the skills of formation flying, day and night, with and without gliders in tow. The

315th Group with two squadrons returning from North Africa to join two others in the United Kingdom in mid-March had little time to develop effective teamwork. Its original squadrons had experienced crews, but they had spent the last ten months on routine transport duty, and had had little training for airborne operations. The 442d Group, newly arrived from the United States, had had almost no night formation flying nor practice in dropping paratroops. Other units of the IX Troop Carrier Command in England had had considerable experience, and were "old hands" in airborne operations. In general the Fifty-second Wing worked with the Eighty-second Airborne Division, and thee Fifth-third Wing with the 101st Division. Later the Fiftieth Wing also worked mostly with the 101st.[18]

Training continued until time for troops to move to the marshalling areas for the Normandy invasion. For many, exercises began with jumps from moving trucks to simulate parachute jumps.[19]

Instructions were given in March 1944 that each airborne division would organize eighteen parachute pathfinder teams – each including one officer and nine men as the technical party – and train them to mark glider landing zones as well as parachute drop zones. The IX Troop Carrier Command would organize and train six pathfinder crews for each troop carrier group, and it would have three airplanes in each group equipped with the special navigational aids. (In addition, the Thirty-eighth Group of the Royal Air Force would have 75 percent of its aircraft specially equipped, and would have all its crews trained for pathfinder operations.) Pathfinder teams were to precede the first serial of the main effort by thirty minutes, or as agreed by air and airborne commanders. Parachutists of the first serial would drop as scheduled even though the pathfinders might have been neutralized, and would be prepared in necessary to reestablish pathfinder aids for succeeding groups. The specially trained crew of the initial pathfinder aircraft was to find the designated zone by accurate dead reckoning and map reading, with close checking by radar aids, and the use of special drop zone maps. Main serials would be led to the area by dead reckoning and radar aids, and then to the drop zones and landing zones by use of Rebecca/Eureka (radar) equipment. The standard marking for drop zones was a series of five lights placed to form a "T," and a Eureka installation at the head of the "T." The jump signal was to be given when the leader of the group was over the head of the "T." For marking a glider landing zone a line of seven lights in the order, going downwind, one red, five amber, one green was to be set up. The lights were to be placed through the main axis of the landing area, and a Eureka installation was to be set up off the down-wind end of the light.[20]

Near the end of April the entire 101st Airborne Division, with the Fiftieth and Fifty-third Troop Carrier Wings, was scheduled to participate in a great rehearsal, Exercise Eagle, for the Normandy operation. In

Members of the First Airborne Task Force pause for mass under the wing of a glider on a rainy night before taking off on a mission.

keeping with the evolving plans for use of the airborne forces, the Eighty-second Division and Fifty-second Wing were added to the exercise, though at the late date of inclusion, the Eighty-second was able to assemble only a token force of paratroops for participation. The date was set for the night of 11 May. Seven pathfinder teams led off. All did well in finding the assigned drop zones and getting equipment into operation except one which became lost in a haze, and did not reach the drop zone in time to be of any assistance. Half an hour behind the pathfinders, over 6,000 paratroopers of the 101st Division followed in 432 aircraft, half each from the Fiftieth and Fifty-third Wings, in ten serials. Flying over an open-square course of 264 miles, the planes arrived in good formation over their target areas, and the paratroops made generally accurate jumps. For the nine serials of the Fifty-second Wing, the Eighty-second Airborne Division had only two jumpers per plane. These were less successful. One group broke up on the way, and only sixteen of its forty-five aircraft reached the vicinity of the drop zone where they dropped their troops ten miles off target; the other, lost in the haze, returned to the base to try again at dawn. Another group had almost the same experience, and a third returned without making any drop at all. Two glider serials arrived just before dawn, and their landings were good.

Except for failures on the part of the inexperienced groups, the exercise supported the hope of those who put a great deal of faith in this kind of airborne operation, and they looked forward with confidence to the real test in Normandy.[21] General Brereton, then commanding the Ninth Air Force of which the troop carrier wings were a part, commented:

> The dress rehearsal indicated to my satisfaction that the plan of employment is practicable from a flight and navigational point of view, and that we have reached an effective state of readiness to carry out the plan. I have no illusions as to the extreme difficulty of this operation. We have, however, the best Troop Carrier Command in the world, and its morale could not be higher.[22]

For the Normandy operation the American airborne divisions were to remain directly under the control of First Army until landing, when they would come under VII Corps (Maj. Gen. J. Lawton Collins). The mission of the VII Corps was to land at Utah Beach near the base of the Cotentin Peninsula, and then capture Cherbourg. The airborne troops were to block the movement of enemy reinforcements into the peninsula. According to the original plan, the 101st Airborne Division, after landing southeast of Ste. Mère-Église, was to destroy the bridges near Carentan and seize the crossing over the Douve River at Pont l'Abbe and Beuzeville-la Bastille in order to protect the southern flank of the beachhead and block enemy movements into the east half of the peninsula. The Eighty-second Airborne Division was to land west of St. Sauveur-le Vicomte where it could block off the western half of the Cotentin.[23] However, intelligence reports near the end of May indicated that the German Ninety-first Division had moved into the Carentan-St. Sauveur-le Vicomte-Valognes area. This development made necessary some last-minute changes in the airborne plans. After some study the decision was to have the Eighty-second Airborne Division drop astride the Merderet River – one parachute regiment to the east and two to the west of the river. The mission of the Eighty-second now was to capture Ste. Mère-Église and to establish bridgeheads over the Merderet on the two main roads running westward from Ste. Mère-Église in order to protect the beachhead from the west and to clear the way for a drive toward St. Sauveur-le Vicomte. The 101st Airborne Division was to protect the flanks, seize four roads which served as westward exits from the beach across an inundated area, and secure crossing of the Douve River to the south for a later drive toward Carentan.[24]*

* A heart attack in February had forced General Lee to give up his command of the 101st Airborne Division on the eve of seeing a dream come true which he had entertained since he began drawing up plans on airborne warfare for the chief of infantry back in 1940.

Brig. Gen. Maxwell D. Taylor, previously artillery commander of the Eighty-second Airborne Division, succeeded Lee as commander of the 101st.

Prime Minister Winston Churchill and General Dwight Eisenhower were among the crowd watching a mass training jump in England, March 1944.

Aerial view of Utah Beach, taken on the morning of 6 June 1944.

Pvt. Clarence C. Ware of San Pedro, Calif., (left) and Pvt. Charles R. Plaudo of Minneapolis applied Indian war paint for the invasion of Normandy.

Loaded with equipment, a paratrooper climbs aboard a plane headed for Normandy on 6 June.

In their first planning conference troop carrier and airborne officers could agree on tentative drop zones, on a tentative allotment of airplanes and gliders, and schedules for training exercises. The selection of landing zones for gliders presented a more difficult problem. Trees in the hedgerows surrounding the small meadows of Normandy limited the number of gliders that could come into a given field. After studying aerial photographs to estimate the height of trees, and applying the minimum gliding angle for gliders to clear those obstacles, troop carrier planners found that the landing zones which had been tentatively chosen could receive only one-third the number of gliders intended. After the routes had been determined, staffs restudied the ground, enemy dispositions, and the results of training. Another joint conference settled upon new drop zones and landing zones, air movement tables, and plans for marshalling, briefing, loading, and communications. Minor changes continued throughout the training phase in response to improvements in techniques, the shifting of units of the air movement table, and to changes in the over-all enemy or friendly situation.[25]

Early in the planning stages, Allied planners were startled to discover a book in circulation, written by a Czechoslovak officer attached to the French Army in England, which carried a map on which the author had anticipated almost precisely the areas in Normandy chosen for the airborne landings.[26] After some investigation to establish that the publication was not the result of any leak in security, this was allowed to pass without public notice. Then, just before the invasion, a series of recent aerial photographs of the landing area showed that stakes and poles suddenly had appeared on some of the very drop zones and landing zones which had been selected for D Day. This made some last-minute readjustment necessary in plans for landing and for approaching certain of the local objectives.[27]

Normandy

The eyes of the world were on the paratroopers and the glidermen of the Eighty-second and 101st Airborne Divisions – and their counterparts in the British Sixth Airborne Division – when they dropped from the skies over Normandy, in the hours of darkness early on 6 June 1944, to become the vanguard of the great Allied invasion of France. They were participating in no simple experiment. They were being committed in force with the full expectation that their success would make possible the early seizure of port and beach facilities and the rapid consolidation of a permanent beachhead. Upon their achievement might very well depend the success of the whole invasion effort.

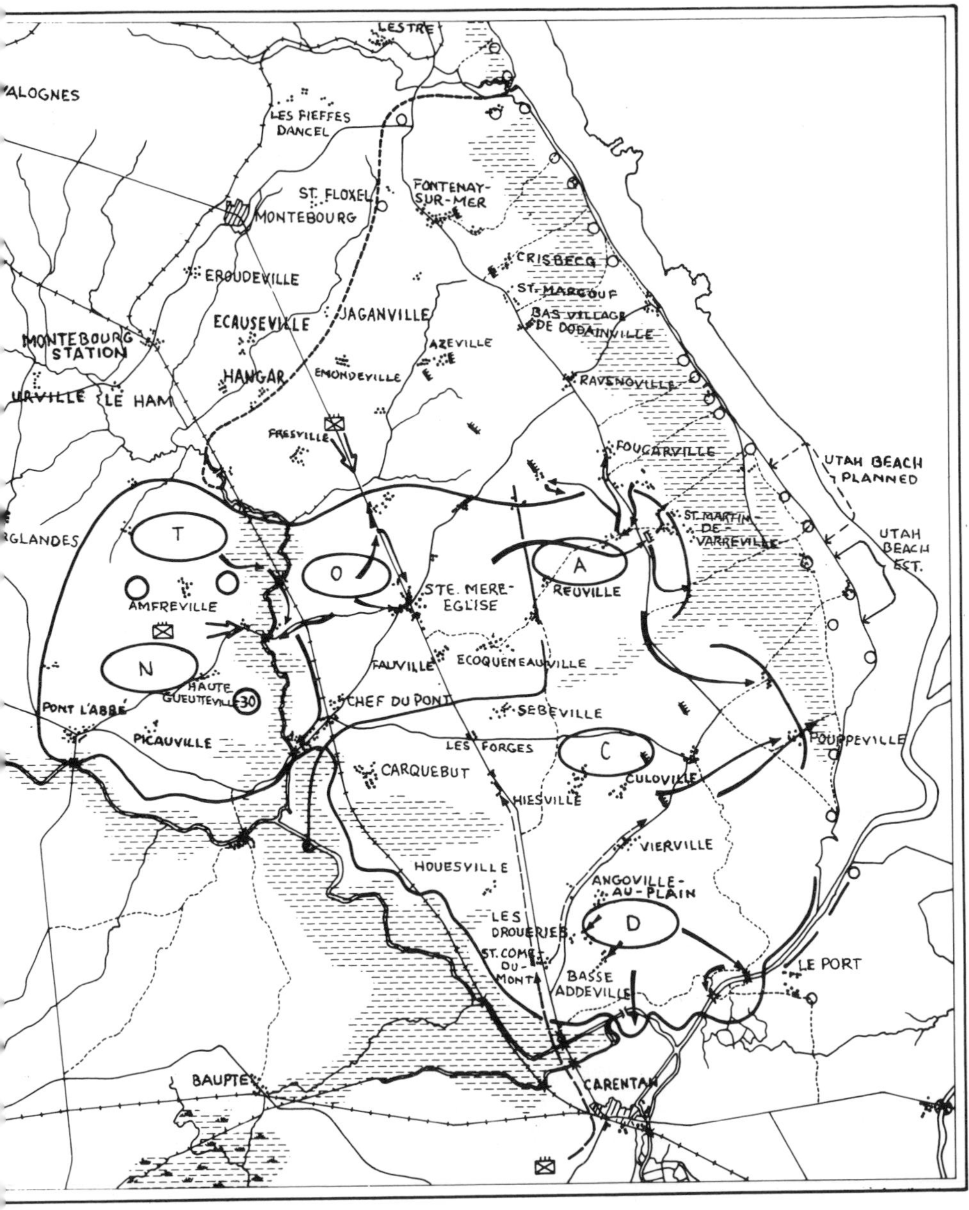

DROP ZONE

AIRBORNE DIVISIONS' OBJECTIVE LINE

INUNDATED AREA

AXIS OF GERMAN COUNTERATTACK

RESISTANCE NEST

BATTERY, 4 152MM HOWITZERS

UNOCCUPIED BATTERY POSITION

e airborne assault, 6 June 1944.

That any such success would attend those efforts was anything but certain during the first hours of the operation. Things began to go wrong almost as soon as the formations arrived over the French coast. About half of the serials unexpectedly ran into a cloudbank off the coast, and became dispersed. Bursts of antiaircraft fire brought a natural response, though it was contrary to instructions, on the part of inexperienced pilots – evasive action; other formations began to loosen up and scatter, until "all semblance of formation had been lost. . . . One or two pilots slammed the doors of their compartments and circled back for England."[28] Only four or five serials were able to arrive at their drop zones in a tight and orderly formation.

Such scattering of air formations could only result in a wide dispersal of the troops on the ground. Parachutists of the 101st Airborne Division began dropping in a wide area southeast of Ste. Mère-Église about 0130. Glider landings began at 0400 with little more promise of success. Additional elements of the division which could not be included in the initial lift went in by glider between 2000 and 2100 in the evening; but again there were numerous crash landings and landings in enemy dominated areas.[29] Methodical assembly of the units was almost out of the question. Commanders simply gathered up what men they could find in the vicinity, regardless of unit, and proceeded toward their objectives. Elements of the Fourth Infantry Division, driving inland from the beach, contacted the Third Battalion, 501st Parachute Infantry (101st Airborne Division) at 1215, but the airborne divisions were yet far from being under unified control. As of 2400 that night approximately 50 percent of the airborne echelon of the 101st Division Headquarters had been accounted for; there had been no word from the 501st Parachute Infantry other than from the Third Battalion, and it had assembled only 120 officers and men; the 502d Parachute Infantry was holding a series of strong points generally north of St. Germain de Varreville with approximately 500 men; the 506th Parachute Infantry had some 240 men at Culeville, with no word from its Third Battalion; some 85 men of the 377th Parachute Field Artillery Battalion, with one gun, were with the 502d Infantry.[30] Some of these units had had fairly good drops, but were out of communication. Eleven of the twelve 75-mm. pack howitzers – together with their crews – of the 377th Battalion were lost completely. Brig. Gen. A. C. McAuliffe, division artillery commander, attributed that loss mainly to evasive flying tactics on the part of some of the pilots, and the failure of pilots to reduce their speed to the required 110 miles per hour.[31]

In spite of the scattered landings, the 101st was able to take its objectives, including St. Martin de Varreville and Pouppeville, relatively quickly. Most important, it had been able to secure the vital exits from the beaches which would permit the troops landing by sea to move inland.

The situation with the Eighty-second Airborne Division was more precarious. Its dispersion had been so broad that two days later, on the morning of 8 June, it was reported that the division had only 2,100 effectives under unified control. Contact had been established with only one battalion of the 508th Parachute Infantry and half a battalion of the 507th which had dropped west of the Merderet River.[32] Men of the 508th and 507th had come down at or close to the assembly position of the German Ninety-first Division. A number of the heavily-laden paratroopers[33] dropped into the Merderet Creek or the nearby marshes. By a cruel distortion of maps and aerial photographs, the marshes along the Merderet showed up as innocent meadows, and this has been blamed for the grief of paratroopers who found themselves fighting the deep water and mud which lay beneath the tall grass.[34] But the map and reconnaissance error really did not matter so very much, for those who dropped into the marsh were victims of another error, an error in missing the intended drop zones. They had no more intention of landing there than if they had *known* it to be marsh. Anyway, it was the Germans, not the map-makers, who had flooded the marshes late in May.

In contrast to its sister regiments of the Eighty-second Airborne Division, the 505th Parachute Infantry probably had the best drop in the whole operation. Its troop carrier planes too had been scattered, but many of them were able to circle back (itself a dangerous undertaking when serials were following closely and formations had become broken) and find the drop zone which pathfinders had clearly marked. Unfortunately for the others, enemy troops on four of six designated drop zones made it impossible for pathfinders to display their visual signals. Under orders to use only knives, bayonets, and grenades so that enemy fire could be spotted in the darkness, about a quarter of the men of the Third Battalion collected and moved in to capture Ste. Mère-Église before dawn. Other members of the regiment reinforced the holders of the town during the morning. It was the only one of the Eighty-second Division's initial missions which had gone according to plan.

Other D Day missions assigned the Eighty-second Airborne Division had included the securing of crossings of the Merderet Creek near la Fiere and Chef du Pont. Here the flooded marshlands were especially troublesome. Small bands of paratroopers were able to establish bridgeheads both at la Fiere and Chef du Pont, but both had to yield to stronger German forces. At the end of D Day the situation of the Eighty-second around Ste. Mère-Église remained obscure and tenuous. It was not until the next afternoon, 7 June, that forces coming in from Utah Beach were able to link up effectively with airborne forces at Ste. Mère-Église. General Ridgway was able to get word to the corps commander that a German armored force appeared to be building up, and General Collins immediately ordered a task force from the 704th Tank Battalion to move directly to Ste. Mère. The tanks rolled into the town early in the afternoon amidst wild cheers of local inhabitants.

Some gliders had landed in the morning shortly after the parachute drops, and other glider serials were scheduled for the evening of D Day, though the main glider elements were to come in the next morning. Glider landings, too, were somewhat scattered, but the small fields enclosed by hedgerows and enemy fire were their principal hazards. Late in the afternoon of D Day, Col. E. D. Raff arrived by sea with a company of tanks and ninety riflemen of the 325th Glider Infantry for the Eighty-second Airborne Division. Colonel Raff found the glider landing zones in German hands, and he tried to get them cleared before the glider serial, scheduled for 2100, arrived. The gliders arrived on schedule, while Germans yet held the landing zones. Coming under intense fire, many of the gliders crashed with heavy casualties; some came down in enemy-held territory, and others drifted farther south. But the next morning most of the 325th Glider Infantry was able to land and assemble. Glider serials also had arrived for the 101st Airborne Division at 0400 and 2100 on D Day and with somewhat similar results. (The 327th Glider Infantry arrived by sea on D Day and D plus 1.) One of the casualties in the early morning glider landings was Brig. Gen. Don F. Pratt, assistant division commander of the 101st, who was killed. Damage to the bigger British-type Horsa gliders which came in the evening was greater than for the Waco CG-4A's because of their greater landing speed and size in the small landing fields.[35]

In a way the widespread landings may have actually contributed to airborne successes. German patrols dispatched to liquidate the invaders became involved in fighting in every direction. There were no battalion concentrations against which an effective counterattack might be launched. All this confusion did not fit into the plans for defense; it had no place in German antiairborne doctrine. Small groups of paratroopers and glidermen fought as they worked toward assembly areas – one group, for example, was reported to have dropped twenty miles beyond its objective, but the men worked their way back and destroyed two light tanks en route. The effect of all this action was a very real contribution to the rapid reduction of Utah Beach defenses and the establishment of a deep beachhead line.[36] Meanwhile troops of the British Sixth Airborne, using gliders in the assault wave, had had relatively good landings in the Caen area, and had taken their objectives beyond the River Orne. General Student, in discussing airborne operations in postwar interrogations, did not assign the same decisiveness to the Normandy operation that he did to the Sicily parachute drop, but he did consider it highly successful in speeding up consolidation of the beachhead.[37] In a period of five days

Follow-up serials of C-47's and gliders cross the coast of England on June 7, flying over landing craft in a harbor.

An American glider is dismantled for unloading in Normandy.

approximately 17,400 paratroopers and gliderborne troops had been landed in Normandy; C-47 transport aircraft had flown 1,672 sorties, with a loss of 43 airplanes, and a total of 517 gliders participated in the effort, and by D plus 6, approximately 90 percent of the glider pilots involved had been returned to Great Britain or had been reported safe elsewhere.[38] Landing losses to aircraft and personnel amounted to less than 10 percent rather than the 75 to 80 percent which Leigh-Mallory had predicted.

Airborne forces fought continuously for thirty-three days in a ground role until they were relieved on 8 July.

For the skeptical perhaps the Normandy operation was a convincing demonstration that the employment of airborne troops on a large scale was a feasible undertaking. But for airborne enthusiasts it doubtless was a disappointment. True, the airborne units had taken their major objectives, but divisions had not been able to function as such before twenty-four to forty-eight hours after landing. Leaders could see a need for more effective joint training and planning. Colonel Bidwell, who participated in the operation as an official War Department observer, reported:

> In accordance with decision made in March, 1944, all airborne troops were used during this operation directly to assist the inland progress of the beach landing assault troops. To accomplish this, the airborne troops were called upon to land in the midst of a well-organized defensive position. Transports and gliders were under practically continuous fire and broke formation. Airborne units were badly scattered and intermingled on landing. The majority of the men had no opportunity to secure their heavy arms and equipment. In spite of all this, the operation was a success. It succeeded, however, only because the airborne troops slugged it out with the defenders and had no thought other than to achieve eventual victory. Two reinforced U.S. airborne divisions (82d and 101st), reorganized for this particular operation, and one reinforced British airborne division (6th) were committed.[39]

On the basis of this operation Colonel Bidwell recommended that the airborne division be retained as a special organization, but that the table of organization be revised to provide for two parachute regiments and one glider regiment in each case until a division should be earmarked for a theater, when it should be reorganized according to the wishes of the theater commander. A shortcoming in the operation had been the lack of direct support combat aviation. Communications for air support requests had not been effective, and this was a particularly serious matter for airborne divisions inasmuch as they could not depend upon mass artillery support during the first hours of an operation. He urged that a study be made of direct air support. Again recommendations were for troop carrier aircraft to be equipped with self-sealing gasoline tanks and some light armor, and that "highest priority be assigned the development of quick-release parachute harness."[40]

Commanders of both the divisions which had taken part in the Normandy operation recommended that the organization of the airborne division be modified to bring it into line with practice. The two-battalion glider infantry regiment, the two-platoon glider infantry company, and to a less extent, the two-rifle-squad, one 66-mm. mortar squad platoon had forced commanders to improvise new units or new tactics. Training directives and infantry doctrine were based upon a triangular organization. Moreover, the lack of communications, reconnaissance, and administrative men and the lack of transportation, far from "streamlining" the airborne division, had more nearly immobilized it. By juggling figures and using replacements received before combat, commanders organized additional rifle squads, reconnaissance detachments, and military police platoons and thus built what they considered a sound organization.[41]

The Eighty-second and 101st Airborne Divisions had overcome the handicaps of the two-battalion glider organization by attaching one of the battalions of the 401st Glider infantry to the Eighty-second Airborne Division to act as a third battalion with the 325th Glider Infantry, while the battalion that remained with the 101st Division then acted as a third battalion for the 327th Glider Infantry. The attachment of additional parachute regiments had had the effect of providing each division with a three parachute to one glider infantry regiment for the Normandy assault.

Both General Ridgway and General Taylor urged that the organization of the airborne division be changed by the addition of a third battalion to the glider infantry regiment, the addition of a third rifle squad to the parachute platoon, and the substitution of a standard infantry division signal company for the current airborne signal company. General Taylor recommended that the arrangement of having two additional parachute regiments attached, and one glider regiment eliminated, for each division be made permanent for the European theater. Other changes which he considered essential included the addition of a third platoon in each glider infantry company, the addition of a second parachute engineer company, and the addition of a fourth battalion of 105-mm. field artillery.[42] Of his own recommendation, General Ridgway wrote:

> Thirty-three days' front line participation by this Division in operations on the continent of EUROPE demonstrate once more, and with increasing emphasis, the need for (these) changes in the organization of the airborne division. . . .
>
> These changes are fundamental and of primary importance. Recommendation for their adoption has followed participation of this Division in its preceding campaigns in SICILY and ITALY.

> To date these recommendations have been disapproved, largely if not entirely on the basis of inadequate manpower. In my opinion there are means available to the War Department for surmounting this obstacle. In my opinion it is far better to have a smaller number of airborne divisions soundly organized than to have a larger number basically defective in organization.[43]

It still would be several months before the War Department would get around to revising tables of organization in any far-reaching way. Meanwhile airborne commanders would continue to improvise.

Dragoon: Invasion of Southern France

When a second invasion hit France on 15 August 1944 – this time it was along the Mediterranean coast – airborne troops once again were in the vanguard. Planning for the airborne phase of this operation – known as Dragoon – had begun in the staff of the Seventh Army in February 1944. But at that time a great deal of doubt remained regarding what airborne and troop carrier units would be available. Having to await the organization of available forces, final planning could not begin until less than a month before the operation. Organization took the form of a provisional airborne division, under the command of Maj. Gen. Robert T. Frederick, later designated the First Airborne Task Force, and a provisional troop carrier air division, under the command of Brig. Gen. Paul L. Williams. All available U.S. airborne units, together with the British Second Parachute Brigade Group and special units activated for the mission came together in the airborne task force. A special request to the War Department brought thirty-six airborne staff officers in mid-July for General Frederick's headquarters. Most of them had come from the Thirteenth Airborne Division, and a few had come from the Airborne Center.

Parachute units attached to the First Airborne Task Force included the 517th Combat Team, the 509th Battalion, the First Battalion of the 551st Parachute Infantry, and the 463d Parachute Field Artillery Battalion. One glider infantry battalion, the 550th, and a number of special units made up the remainder. These independent units were able to operate without very much supervision, and most of the major combat units already were well trained. Time was too short to permit the joint training with the troop carrier units which was desirable. More urgent was the task of training the newly organized glider units – field artillery, antitank, engineers, signal, chemical mortar, ordnance, medical. During July the units assembled at the Airborne Training Center which had been moved to Rome. Here pathfinder units were able to complete a period of

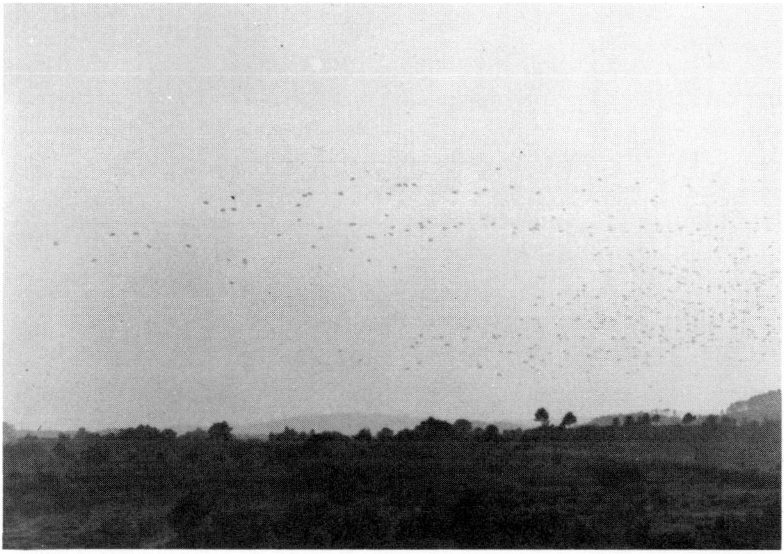

Parachute drop joins the First Airborne Task Force on D Day (15 August) in southern France.

Glider troops prepare for attack after landing near La Motte in southern France on 15 August.

Gliders of the 550th Airborne Infantry Battalion land in southern France.

Pvt. Winifred D. Eason of Atlanta talks with leaders of the French Forces of the Interior in southern France. M. Marc Rainaut (left) saved the soldier's life, and Mlle. Nicola Celebonovitch, with a .45 secured by her belt, led the paratroopers to a German hideout.

joint training, and all troop carrier serial leaders flew a practice flight over a course set up to resemble the one to be used for the operation. Cooperating naval vessels, carrying navigational aids, marked the route below as they would on D Day. Time did not permit a final dress rehearsal, but combat teams perfected plans and learned to work together, and individual parachute units made skeleton jumps of two or three men at a time from planes which they would use later.[44] By the time of the invasion, the task force had become a fairly cohesive organization.

A diversionary mission preceded the main assault early on 15 August. About two hours before parachute troops were to begin jumping, six airplanes, dropping "window" (masses of aluminum foil strips) en route to create the impression on enemy radar of a mass flight, dropped 600 parachute dummies and rifle similators and other battle noise effects on a false drop zone north and west of Toulon. According to German radio reports, the ruse was a success.[45]

From ten airfields, extending along 150 miles of the Italian peninsula, the main parachute lift of 396 aircraft in nine serials took off about 0330. Preceding the main column by about three hours were the three pathfinder teams. The pathfinders were jumping into southern France as the main column formed into its V of V's formation and set out through the clear night over the Mediterranean. Only one of the pathfinder teams jumped onto its assigned drop zone. One jumped prematurely east of Le Muy, and found its way to the drop zone only in time to help guide in one afternoon glider serial. The other became completely lost and jumped between ten and fifteen miles away from its designated place. However, the troop carriers of the main body, preserving formation, flew their course of 500 miles in darkness without accident. Guiding on navigation aids set up at departure bases, on naval vessels, on North Corsica and Elba, the planes arrived over the French coast without fire either from the enemy or from friendly naval vessels. A thick haze cut down visibility over the coast, and over the drop zones the pilots were flying blind. They had to depend upon the Eureka-Rebecca radar equipment, which did not always function satisfactorily, and on radio compass homing devices (MF beacons) which the pathfinders had set up in addition to their Eureka sets. But the results were the most accurate mass combat drop to date. Approximately 60 percent of the paratroopers landed on the three assigned drop zones or in the immediate vicinity of them. About 120 airplanes missed the drop zones altogether. Some parachutists dropped as far as twenty miles from the selected zone. In one serial paratroopers from twenty planes jumped prematurely on the red signal. But those widely separated groups took decisive action on the ground, cooperating with the French Forces of the Interior in seizing towns, undertaking local missions, or finding their way back to their units.[46]

Glider landings began at 0900, after heavy overcast delayed the first serial for an hour. Nine gliders were released prematurely, and four of them made water landings, but prompt action on the part of the Navy rescued most of the men. The skill of the glider pilots was described as "highly satisfactory." Hazardous both to parachute and glider landings were anti-airborne obstacles, in the form of poles, which had been set up on the drop zones and landing zones, but they proved to be no real barrier to the operation. Troop carriers flew a resupply mission on the morning of D plus 1, and another that night with the use of pathfinder aids. In both cases the drops were made from altitudes of over 2,000 feet, and this led to considerable scattering and confusion in getting supplies to the correct units. Altogether the troop carriers flew 987 sorties and brought in 407 gliders. They carried 9,000 troops and 221 jeeps and 213 artillery pieces.[47] In some parachute resupply missions for ground troops on Cap Negre and near Vidauban, the A-20 airplane was used with greater success than the C-47.[48]

Once on the ground the airborne troops almost immediately came into contact with the enemy, but opposition was limited mostly to rifle fire, and was generally light. By 1800 on D Day the command post of the airborne task force was in operation. By the end of the day the airborne units had captured the villages of La Mitan, La Motte, Castron, and Les Serres. They had cut the roads which linked the invasion coast with the interior, and thus were in a position to block the arrival of enemy reserves. Late in the afternoon of D plus 1, they made contact with the Forty-fifth Division which had attacked from the sea.

The Third Division, as it approached St. Tropez, one of its objectives, found that airborne troops already were in the area, and had captured one antiaircraft battery, two coastal batteries, and a garrison of 240 Germans – the airborne troops were those who had jumped on the wrong signal.[49]

During the next ten days the Allied forces consolidated their Mediterranean beachhead from Nice to Marseilles and Toulon. Units of the U.S. Seventh Army and the French First Army moved rapidly up the Rhone valley to make contact with the Third Army of General Eisenhower's forces northwest of Dijon on 11 September.

Chapter VIII

Follow-Up in Europe

Training in the United Kingdom

Upon their return to the United Kingdom, American airborne troops who had participated in the Normandy operation resumed rigorous training programs. This training, however, could not include large-scale airborne exercises. One difficulty was the dispersion of the troops in their locations in England, another was the question of obtaining suitable training areas, but most important was the question of coordinating with troop carrier units. Additional demands on the IX Troop Carrier Command during August made it impossible for units of that command to participate in large-scale joint training exercises. Two troop carrier wings had gone to participate in the invasion of Southern France, and others were diverted to the carrying of supplies to the ground armies then speeding across France.

These multiple demands upon troop carriers created shortages of aircraft for airborne training in the theaters, just as it did in the United States. General Eisenhower explained:

> The withdrawing of the planes caused considerable embarrassment to the Airborne Army's commander, Lieut. Gen. L. H. Brereton, whose program of training was thereby interrupted. He justly pointed out that there was risk that continued cargo carrying would render the troop carrier commands unfit for a successful airborne operation. Since the procedure and training required for the two functions were in many respects diametrically opposed, combined exercises by airborne troops and the air transport personnel were of the utmost importance. I consider, however, that my decision to use the planes for ground resupply purposes was justified by the fact that thereby the speed of our armies' advances was maintained, and as a consequence of this the projected airborne operations in France were rendered unnecessary.[1]

Nevertheless training programs, even by the IX Troop Carrier Command, did continue, and they showed good results. When their supply responsibilities permitted, troop carrier crews practiced day and night formation flying, dual glider tow, and glider pick-ups. They participated in exercises with the First Polish Parachute Brigade on 14 July and the night of 1-2 August, and then began a program with the Eighty-second and 101st Airborne Divisions covering aircraft and glider loadings, simulated airlandings, and glider flights.[2] Glider units participated in practice tactical flights, and some of the parachute units had practice drops, while others scheduled had to be cancelled when the aircraft were diverted to other missions.[3] Commanders and staffs of all units, meanwhile, were getting a great deal of experience in planning as one operation after another was planned and then cancelled as speeding ground armies occupied the proposed target areas or other conditions made the operations unfeasible.

Plans and Cancellations

Planning for an airborne operation, known as Transfigure, to close the line of German retreat through the Paris-Orleans gap had begun in July 1944 at Headquarters, British Airborne Troops. This became the first project for the newly-organized First Allied Airborne Army. The U.S. 101st Airborne Division, the British First Airborne Division, the First Polish Parachute Brigade, and the British Fifty-second (Lowland) Division (Airportable) would make up the task force under command of Lt. Gen. F. A. M. Browning, deputy commander of the First Allied Airborne Army and commander of British Airborne Troops. The tentative date for the operation was 20 August. After the planning section had brought plans to their final stage, the Airborne Army chief of staff on 11 August visited General Bradley, commander of the Twelfth Army Group, in whose area the operation was to take place. Bradley expressed some doubts, but asked that preparations continue. Eisenhower, moreover, was harboring doubts because of the supply situation. Two days later the troops moved to the departure airfields, and prepared to take off on short notice. Seaborne echelons of the units involved moved to France. Now 17 August was the date given on which the operation could be launched. Then on 15 August, the same day that formal orders were issued, a message from the Twelfth Army Group indicated that Transfigure would not be wanted on 17 August and that thirty-six hours' warning would be given on the final decision. On the morning of 17 August the operation was postponed twenty-four hours, and then at 1600 that day General Bull, SHAEF G-3, called to say that Montgomery and Bradley had discussed the operation, and had agreed to cancel it. The troops returned to their billets, and the seaborne tail of the 101st Airborne Division returned to England.[4]

Even as preparation proceeded for Transfigure, alternative plans were being developed. Bradley thought that airborne troops would be more useful in securing crossings of the Seine than in the gap between the Seine and the Loire. By 17 August Outline Plan No. 1, "Airborne Operation West and Southwest of the River Seine," was ready. It anticipated the use of the same forces scheduled for Transfigure to seize the areas around Rambouillet, Noudan, St. Andre, Evreux, and Neubourg. The next day a staff officer from the Twenty-first Army Group arrived at Headquarters, First Allied Airborne Army, to ask for an airborne operation to secure a bridgehead east of Louviers. Outline Plan No. 2, 19 August, incorporated this objective as a mission for the British First Airborne Division and the First Polish Parachute Brigade; at the same time Outline Plan No. 3 assigned to the 101st Airborne Division the tentative mission of seizing a bridgehead near Melun. Then, the same day, 19 August, the whole thing was cancelled.[5]

In a conference at Headquarters, First Allied Airborne Army, on 17 August, Air Chief Marshal Sir Arthur Tedder suggested an airborne landing in the Pas de Calais area behind Boulogne, and General Brereton directed the plans section to go to work on it. On 22 August the plans section submitted an estimate of the situation which suggested that an airborne force committed to that area would be in a position to (1) capture Boulogne; (2) operate in a south or southeasterly direction against the right flank and rear of the enemy; (3) attack the area from which the flying bombs were launched, and (4) draw off the enemy forces from the main front by creating a diversion in the Boulogne area. Two days later SHAEF G-3 reported that Operation Boxer, as it was called, was first priority for the First Allied Airborne Army, and the SHAEF chief of staff called to say that Boxer was "on in a big way."[6] However, when Brereton conferred with the chief of staff of the Twenty-first Army Group, they agreed that an operation more directly on the enemy's main line of retreat and the army group's axis of advance would be preferable, and Boxer was cancelled.[7]

That preferable operation received the code name "Linnet." Brereton outlined the mission at a staff meeting on 27 August. The plan was for a task force essentially the same as that contemplated for Transfigure, but enlarged to include the U.S. Eighty-second Airborne Division, to seize an area near Tournai, to secure and hold a bridgehead over the Escaut River, and to obtain control of the roads leading northeast through Tournai, Lille, and Courtai.[8] It was planned to use two air lifts each on D Day (tentatively set for 3 September) and D plus 1. The first lift, to begin arriving at the drop zone at 0824, was to include 1,055 parachute aircraft, 120 aircraft towing two gliders each, and 358 tug aircraft with one glider each. Total length of the column would be two hours and one minute. The second lift, to begin arriving at 1830, was to include 126 parachute aircraft, 880 tug aircraft with double glider tow, and 307 aircraft with single glider tow. A lift of 114 parachute aircraft and 75 tugs with two gliders each was scheduled for the morning of D plus 1, and 436 parachute aircraft were to fly a resupply lift that afternoon. On D plus 2 the British Fifty-second (Lowland) Division (Airportable) was to begin airlanding operations. Each hour, from H to H plus 11 hours, thirty-six aircraft were to land, unload, and depart at each of three airstrips. This operation was to be completed on D plus 3, and parachute resupply missions as well were to continue on D plus 1 and 2. Then on D plus 4, after movement of the Fifty-second Division had been completed, resupply by airlanding was to begin on the three airstrips and to continue as long as necessary.[9] On 31 August the airborne troops again moved to departure airfields. The next day was confusing. Two officers brought word to First Allied Airborne Army from the Twenty-first Army Group that the operation would not be required; but at noon General Browning said that a staff officer of that army group believed that the operation was desired. General Bull told General Parks that there was no reason to cancel Linnet, and at 2342 a message from army group said the operation should go on. Seaborne echelons again moved to France. When bad weather delayed the operation, Brereton recommended that it be cancelled. He pointed out that the British Second Army would overrun the target area before the airborne forces could land. He noted that an operation to seize Meuse River crossings between Liege and Maastricht could be mounted on thirty-six hours' notice, and this would be the last strategic objective within range of present bases.[10] That night the Airborne Army commander announced that operation Linnet had been cancelled because of the weather, but troops were to remain on alert at the airdromes; thirty-six hours' warning would be given for a new operation.[11]

Brereton already, on 1 September, had directed the planning staff to prepare plans for an operation in the Aachen-Maastricht gap as an alternative to Linnet. On 2 September he instructed the IX Troop Carrier Command to study the Liege area. As finally worked out, the plan for "Linnet II" was to use the same force as planned for Linnet to secure a firm base in the Liege-Maastricht area, to seize an airfield, and to effect a crossing of the Meuse River. Brereton went to SHAEF Forward Headquarters in France on 3 September to discuss the plan with Eisenhower, but the supreme commander said that the final decision on whether or not the operation was to be mounted would be left to Montgomery and Bradley. At 2125 a staff officer of the Twenty-first Army Group telephoned to say that Linnet II had been cancelled. The American airborne troops returned to their billets, and the British troops were told to stand by for another possible operation. The seaborne tails of the two American divisions returned to England.[12]

Brereton wrote in his diary (5 September):

> I feel that, inasmuch as the airborne army is a strategic general headquarters reserve, the planning should be held on the Supreme Commander's level. When the planning is below Army Group level, it represents time wasted, because in practically every case the operation is not feasible or has to be replanned. The conception of the employment of the Airborne Army as a strategic army is not understood.[13]

The same evening that Linnet II was cancelled, First Allied Airborne Army received a message from the Twenty-first Army Group asking for an operation to seize the Rhine bridges from Arnhem to Wesel in order to prepare for a ground advance to the north of the Ruhr. Later the plan, called Comet, was narrowed to he Nijmegen-Arnhem area. The British First Airborne Division, with the First Polish Parachute Brigade, was to seize and hold bridges over the Maas at Grave, over the Waal at Nijmegen, and over the Lower Rhine (Neder Rijn) at Arnhem. The U.S. 878th Airborne Engineer Battalion (Aviation) then was to prepare an airstrip for the airlanding of the British Fifty-second (Lowland) Division (Airportable). D Day was set for 8 September. Postponed once because of the weather, and twice because of the ground situation, Comet finally was cancelled on 10 September in favor of Operation Market which now was to take place not earlier than 14 September. British and Polish troops who had been at the airfields since 31 August, and the gliders which had been loaded since 2 September remained in readiness for the next scheduled operation.[14]

In addition to Operation Market and the cancelled plans which had preceded it, no less than eight other plans for possible future airborne operations were being considered at Headquarters, First Allied Airborne Army. Briefly these were: (1) Operation Infatuate, a landing on Walcheren Island to assist the Canadian Army in clearing the approaches to the port of Antwerp; (2) Naples I, an operation behind the Siegfried Line east of Aachen; (3) Naples II, to get a bridgehead over the Rhine near Cologne; (4) Milan I, to pierce the Siegfried Line at Trier; (5) Milan II, a crossing of the Rhine between Neuweid and Coblenz; (6) Choker I, to assist in breaking through the Siegfried Line at Saarbrucken; (7) Choker II, a crossing of the Rhine between Mainz and Mannheim; (8) Talisman, to seize airfields in the Berlin area, in the event of a German surrender, and to seize the German naval base at Kiel.[15]

On 5 September Eisenhower had directed that the First Allied Airborne Army should operate in support of the Twenty-first Army Group until after the Rhine had been crossed, and then should be prepared to operate on a large scale for the advance into Germany.[16] This meant of course that the plan for the air invasion of Holland – Operation Market – had first priority. Now it appeared at last that the operation actually would take place. Brereton wrote in his diary (16 September): "We were all glad to be getting into action. In the 40 days since the formation of the First Allied Airborne Army we have planned 18 different operations, some of which were scrubbed because our armies moved too fast and others because Troop Carriers were engaged in air supply."[17] (See Chapter I.)

Supply by Air

Continuous demands made upon troop carrier units to deliver supplies to the ground armies troubled airborne planners throughout the war in western Europe. That the use of troop carrier aircraft in the carrying of supplies became a major diversion is indicated by the figures: During the period between 11 June and 16 September, the IX Troop Carrier Command carried a total of 33,421 tons of freight and 48,767 passengers, and evacuated 42,139 patients.[18] "From the St. Lo breakthrough until the 3rd Army was stopped at Metz, the supply of all ground units by air was a major activity in the theater."[19] Some officers contended that if all the aircraft and supplies diverted to the First Allied Airborne Army had been used to supply General Patton's Third Army, the result very likely would have been a breakthrough across the Rhine into southern Germany.

But General Brereton saw in these supply activities the crippling of potentially decisive airborne operations. When formation of the Allied Airborne Army was being discussed, Brereton had noted in his diary (17 July 1944): "I foresaw the maximum amount of resistance from the ground commanders and from G-4 (Supply) who would insist on using C-47's for other purposes than transporting and supplying the airborne army."[20] Subsequently Brereton felt that his fears had been confirmed. Again he wrote (7 September 1944):

> The biggest obstacle to date in the employment of airborne forces in their proper role has been the refusal on the part of higher authority to employ the Troop Carrier Command in its primary mission of carrying troops for combat. The Troop Carriers will be used either to supply ground forces or for their proper mission of delivering airborne troops. They cannot do both. There has been practically solid opposition on the part of the ground commanders to releasing aircraft, intended primarily for tactical mission, from their secondary jobs of carrying supplies. Inability to take advantage of the chance of delivering a paralyzing blow by airborne action was due to the lack of Troop Carrier aircraft which could have been made immediately available for airborne operations had they not

> been used for resupply and evacuation. This decision must be a High Command function. It cannot be delegated to lower commands whose conception of their successful operations depends invariably on the supply situation.[21]

Actually the policy which Supreme Headquarters had laid down before the Normandy invasion apparently had conformed to War Department doctrine:

> First priority for the employment of all heavy transport and troop carrier aircraft controlled by Commanding General (CG) IX Troop Carrier Command and the Air Officers Commanding (AOC's) 46 and 38 Groups will normally be given to airborne operations. Should there be simultaneous demands for emergency movement of supplies or personnel by air which conflict with the requirements of airborne operations, the allocation of the aforementioned aircraft to meet these demands will only be made with the authority of the Supreme Commander.[22]

After the Normandy operation, procedures for resupplying airborne divisions had become fairly well established. For that operation the supply plan for the 101st Airborne Division had been set up on an "on-call basis." After air reconnaissance had reported panels requesting supplies, airplanes had taken off without any radio confirmation. It turned out that the commanding general had not requested the supplies, had not expected them, and had not prepared to receive them. Later the division had requested other missions for supplies which were on call, but the Troop Carrier Command had not received the requests. Subsequently, therefore, the standard procedure was to schedule all supply anticipated, and then to cancel a mission later should it not be needed. In preparing for an operation the airborne division G-4 would requisition supplies from the base section supply services, and turn them over to the air supply loading agency for packaging and loading on aircraft. Airborne troops packaged, fitted with parachutes, and loaded on aircraft the supplies which accompanied them, but for resupply missions other arrangements were necessary. An Air Forces responsibility, this work had to be done by service troops attached or assigned to the Provisional Service Wing of the IX Troop Carrier Command (earlier this had been a function of the Ninth Air Force Service Command).* The recommended procedure was to have

*The British had an Airborne Base organization to coordinate aircraft needs with the RAF, and an Air Dispatch Group from the Royal Army Service Corps to receive supplies, transport all containers and parachutes to the airfields, load them under the supervision of RAF crews, and send men with the aircraft to release the bundles over the drop zones. (British Airborne Corps) Allied Ops in Holland, Part I, Appendix A, Annexure 1, and Part II, Appendix C.

available in the departure areas five days' supplies for each division, packaged and packed in containers with parachute attached, and to have an additional three days' supplies unpacked, but with containers and parachutes available. The nature of the operations and the shortage of men to handle supplies on a day-to-day basis while an airborne operation was in progress would have been an uneconomical use of manpower. As a result the work of packaging and rigging crews was almost continuous. When special needs arose beyond those anticipated in plans for automatic supply, or conditions demanded modification, the division made requests directly to its rear headquarters. This headquarters then obtained supplies from the air supply center, or, if not in stock, it made arrangements with the base section for delivery of supplies to the depot, and arranged with the Troop Carrier Command for air delivery. Coordination of these activities became a function of Headquarters, XVIII Corps (Airborne.)[23]

The problem of developing an organization to package and load supplies on aircraft was one which required special attention. The 490th Quartermaster Depot Company had received training in packing and parachute rigging in the United States. In Europe it had been attached to the Ninth Air Force Service Command and then sent to the 101st Airborne Division for further training. Two additional quartermaster companies had been organized in the theater provisionally and attached to the Ninth Air Service Command to be trained by the 490th Quartermaster Depot Company. Training included loading and lashing in aircraft for airlanding operations as well as packaging and parachute rigging, and small teams were formed and trained to accompany the aircraft in flight to release bundles over the drop zones. Then the provisional quartermaster companies, all Army Service Forces units, had disbanded and the men transferred to the Air Forces and organized into the First, Second, and Third Air Cargo Resupply Squadrons. Together with the 490th Quartermaster Depot Company, still an ASF unit, they had been grouped into the Second Quartermaster Battalion Mobile (provisional) and attached to the IX Troop Carrier Command. In September the battalion had come under control of the Troop Carrier Command's Service Wing (Provisional). These were the units, reinforced from time to time by men from service and tactical groups, which performed the work of packaging and loading supplies on aircraft both for airborne and airlanding operations.[24]

For the airlanding of supplies, special packaging and handling were unnecessary. The trucks of the supply agency concerned usually brought the supplies to the airfield where men of the Second Quartermaster Battalion Mobile (Provisional) loaded them directly to the aircraft. Here one of the greatest difficulties was in coordinating the arrival of trucks and airplanes at the airdromes and of finding enough men at the right time to handle the supplies. Truck companies and labor troops of Communications

One hundred-twenty five-gallon cans of gasoline are tied down aboard a C-47 plane before transport to Lt. Gen. George S. Patton's Third Army.

Zone (or in the case of the British, from the Royal Army Service Corps) ordinarily unloaded the supplies at the delivery airfield.[25] How unloading of aircraft should be handled in maintaining an isolated airborne division under tactical conditions had not been well established. American organization had no equivalent for the British Airborne Forward Delivery Airfield Group.[26] And the only time that that organization ever flew into a forward airfield to function in receiving supplies for airborne divisions was in the Holland operation when it had to give up the airfield near Grave to the tactical air forces.

Procedures for handling supplies by air for the ground armies continued to follow the instructions which Supreme Headquarters had issued in April 1944.[27] All requests for scheduled or emergency supply by air were to be submitted to a combined Air Transport Operations Room (CATOR). Organized originally under Headquarters, Allied Expeditionary Air Force, CATOR came under the control of First Allied Airborne Army on the formation of that headquarters.[28] It was CATOR's responsibility to arrange for scheduled air and routine carrier services, and for all aircraft to meet emergency demands; to arrange with Allied Expeditionary Air Force for fighter escort when necessary, and to notify supply organizations of the location of airfields and the time when supplies were to be delivered to them.[29] Army groups forwarded requests for supply by air through their respective tactical air forces. CATOR, on receiving the requests, processed them and assigned the task to the most appropriate air transport agency.[30] Should demands for supply by air exceed the capacity of available aircraft, the matter was to be referred to SHAEF for a decision on priorities.[31]

Allied air transport units in the European theater included the IX Troop Carrier Command, the Thirty-first Transport Group of the Ninth Air Service Command, the Twenty-seventh Transport Group of the Eighth Air Service Command, the Forty-sixth Group (RAF), and the Thirty-eighth Group (RAF). In the RAF, the Forty-sixth Group was the equivalent of a transport command, and the Thirty-eighth Group was the troop carrier unit; aircraft of the latter were to be used only for airborne operations. After a decision then, that the two service command transport groups (of the Eighth and Ninth Air Forces) should be used only in work for their own air forces (aside from certain scheduled passenger and freight services), the only aircraft available to CATOR to meet demands for air supply were those of the Forty-sixth Group and the IX Troop Carrier Command.

A number of failures in coordination had appeared during the early weeks of carrying supplies by air to ground units. Requests often were duplicated. A supply agency would announce the availability of supplies and the time for their arrival at airfields without checking the availability of trucks to deliver them. Delays arose when supplies were found to be located in depots far removed from the airfield, and delays multiplied when bad weather set in before the supplies could be delivered to the fields. Sometimes air crews were kept on the alert for twenty-four hours while they waited for supplies to arrive.

With Allied armies streaming rapidly across France and Belgium during the summer of 1944, demands for supplies soon were far exceeding all available air lift capacity. Troop carrier units could not keep pace with the growing demands for air supply, and at the same time, prepare for other airborne operations. It was for the supreme commander to decide whether airborne training should be suspended in favor of air supply. Then a Priorities Board was set up at SHAEF to allocate the lift which was made available. In August B-24 bombers of the Eighth Force were pressed into service for the supply lift. Between 29 August and 17 September the bombers, landing only at fields where there were suitable concrete runways, delivered 1,383 tons of food, 434 tons of gasoline, and 105 tons of medical supplies.[32]

Aside from the conflicting requirements for airborne operations, several other factors imposed serious restrictions on the extent to which supplies could be delivered to ground armies by air. One of the most important considerations was the availability of airfields, for the announced policy was that tactical air forces would occupy all suitable fields on the Continent, and these fields should be used for air supply only in special cases. Another question was the degree of air superiority which had been achieved and whether fighter escorts would be available when needed. The special equipment and handling required limited the dropping of supplies. And operations always would be dependent on the weather.[33]

Actually the lack of airfields often was a more important restriction than any shortage of aircraft, and this is a factor which must be weighed in any speculation on what the Third Army might have done if troop carrier aircraft had been used for supplying it instead of in an airborne operation in Holland. Ground commanders sometimes requested supplies when they knew that enough aircraft were available for all requirements, but they failed to take into account the limitations of landing strips. A strip 3,600 feet long, with good approaches and at least one perimeter taxi strip connecting each end could accommodate seventy-two C-47's an hour if trucks and unloading crews were available. The B-24's required a 4,000-foot hard-surfaced runway and taxi and unloading areas. About thirty of them could be handled in an hour. The Air Forces had ruled that tactical fields should not be used for airlanding supplies, because such use might interfere with tactical operations. Supply operations consequently were limited to fields not yet occupied by tactical units, or fields abandoned by them, or those unsuitable for tactical use.[34] Urgently-needed supplies airlanded during the Market-Garden operation had to be landed at Brussels and forwarded by truck more than one hundred miles, because the only closer airdromes, at Eindhoven and Grave, were loaded to capacity with fighters and fighter-bombers. During the battle for Aachen the closest that supplies could be landed was at Maubouge, 120 miles from the front. The nearest that tank fuel and ammunition could be landed for the Third Army after the fall of Paris was Orleans, more than eighty miles from the area where they were needed, and unloading at Orleans lasted for only the short time until a tactical air unit was ready to move in. A landing strip for C-47's could be constructed more easily and more quickly than a strip for fighters and bombers, and if planning had included a provision for cargo aircraft landing strips in addition to those for tactical air forces, the whole program might have been much more effective than it was. A landing strip seventy-five miles closer to the front would have meant only another half-hour's flying time for the airplanes, but that distance meant many man-hours and added hauls for busy trucks over congested highways. Advance planning might have included provisions for the additional sites, engineers, and materials necessary for large-scale supply by air activities.[35]

To a considerable extent, supply by air was being carried out on a make-shift, field expedient basis. General Carl Spaatz, commander of U.S. Strategic Air Forces in Europe, held that use of troop carrier units primarily for freight was uneconomical, because their organization was designed for airborne operations. He felt that the air transport wing of the tactical air forces, or some similar organization, should have been made responsible for hauling freight. He suggested that troop carrier aircraft, when not employed in training or in their primary mission of carrying airborne troops, should report to the tactical air forces for assignment of freight missions with the air transport wing. The latter should do all the planning and be responsible for landing fields and departure areas. The theater, then, should call for supplies by type and tonnage rather than by number of aircraft. This, Spaatz maintained, would permit the hauling of supplies to be organized for the theater as a whole, and it could be put on a much more efficient basis.

> There is universal recognition that the hauling of supplies by air is a tremendous advantage to ground units particularly during a breakthrough and pursuit. It was pointed out, however, that there is a tendency to use aircraft for supply purposes to overcome the lack of planning of ground force staffs and that close scrutiny should be given to the necessity of much hauling. In properly planned operations much of the supplies being carried by air would normally be hauled amphibiously or overland.[36]

Supplies for Bastogne

When the German counteroffensive broke through the Ardennes in mid-December 1944, the strategic reserve available to the supreme commander consisted mainly of the airborne divisions. The Eighty-second and 101st Airborne Divisions were in the Reims area, in France, where they had gone a few weeks earlier following their release from operations in Holland. The Seventeenth Airborne Division still was in the United Kingdom. Quickly the 101st Airborne Division moved to Bastogne, while the Eighty-second moved toward St. Vith. Soon thereafter the Seventeenth Airborne Division began moving by air to the Reims area. Very soon it became evident that many American units in the path of the attack were in critical circumstances.

During the night of 17-18 December the IX Troop Carrier Command received a message from CATOR saying that two regiments of the 106th Division had been cut off in the St. Vith area and needed resupply by air. Initially the request was for forty loads. Troop carrier leaders decided that the planes should load and take off from fields near Greenham Common, England, land at a continental field for briefing and to pick up a fighter escort, and fly the mission from there. The items needed, mainly ammunition and medical supplies, were not packed, and bad flying weather prevailed, but the next morning twenty-three aircraft were able to get away. But when they arrived over the continental field, they were not permitted to land. The flight leader did land, but he found that no one seemed to know anything about the situation, and had no information, such as coordinator for the drop and rendezvous with the fighter escort, needed for briefing. The planes went on to land at a base of the Fiftieth Troop Carrier Wing, also on the Continent. When additional requests brought the number of aircraft to 138, General Williams decided that it would be best to carry out the operation directly from the United Kingdom, and he asked that all information be sent there. After several delays, then, the mission was cancelled on 22 December when General Patton asked that the 101st Airborne Division be granted first priority on all air resupply.[37]

When German tank columns had completed the encirclement of the Bastogne garrison during the night of 20-21 December the only means for immediate resupply was by air. By 22 December the supply situation had become critical. Requisitions of local stocks had replenished the food supply somewhat, but the shortage of artillery ammunition particularly was becoming serious. A check-up revealed that, except for one battalion which was using short-range 105-mm. ammunition and had several hundred rounds on hand, the batteries were down to less than ten rounds per gun.[38]

The division requested 104 airplane loads of ammunition and rations. At first the troop carrier arrangements were for the airplanes to load in England and proceed to a continental field where a Third Army officer would brief the crews, and a fighter group of the Ninth Air Force would join them. Then it became evident that by the time supplies could be located and packed into parachute containers that it would be too late in the day to fly the mission. Troop carrier leaders determined, however, to drop two pathfinder teams of the 101st Airborne Division and fly the mission at night, or whenever loaded, on the pathfinder aids. When it was decided that the situation did not yet require that urgency the mission was scheduled for the next day. In a meeting that same day (22 December) representatives of interested organizations laid plans to meet future requests. They hoped to maintain a stockpile in the United Kingdom sufficient for two days' needs for one regimental combat team, one armored regimental combat team, one tank battalion, and one infantry battalion. In addition they hoped to maintain one day's supply for one regimental combat team, together with 60,000 gallons of gasoline in 1,200 cans, at a base of the Fiftieth Troop Carrier Wing in France for any emergency when the weather might close in over England and yet permit flying over the Continent. Shortage of trained packing crews seemed to preclude any extensive operations from France.[39]

Ordinarily arrangements for the collection of bundles on the ground were the responsibility of the quartermaster and ordnance companies who set up dumps for the various classes of supplies under division control. But those companies had failed to get into Bastogne after coming under enemy fire,[40] and Lt. Col. Carl W. Kohls, Division G-4, therefore instructed the S-4's of the 501st and the 506th Parachute Infantry Regiments to organize make-shift recovery details. Each regiment was to send at least five jeeps to the drop zone to haul the supplies directly to unit dumps. Units were to report what supplies they had recovered, and then distribute them according to instructions from G-4. Crews and vehicles had been ready and waiting all day on the 22d. At 1700 the division rear base had radioed that sixty C-47's would drop supplies on the first flyable day.

Shortly after dawn the next morning two pathfinder aircraft of the IX Troop Carrier Command dropped two pathfinder teams of the 101st Airborne Division into an open field northwest of Bastogne. They had jumped in the area of the Second Battalion, 327th Glider Infantry, and the glidermen quickly rounded them up. The pathfinder leader soon was on a telephone to tell Division G-4 that the supply planes should be arriving in about ninety minutes. Soon the navigation aids were operating, and the supply planes had little difficulty in finding the drop zone.

Again the regimental supply men were alerted and identification panels were displayed on the field. It was 1150 when men all along the front cheered the troop carriers coming in with their supplies. First to arrive were twenty-one planes which had been standing by at a continental field with loads originally intended for the 106th Division near St. Vith. Almost at the same time 239 aircraft from the United Kingdom began to arrive.

The recovery parties, each assigned a specific zone, were waiting on the field. All afternoon they worked while jeeps shuttled back and forth between the drop zone and unit dumps. The artillery already was firing some of the newly arrived ammunition before the drop zone had been completely cleared. It developed, however, that the ammunition dropped did not always correspond in type and quantity to the needs. More than enough caliber .50 machine gun ammunition had arrived, but not enough 76-mm. and 75-mm. ammunition. Shortages continued, but it was reassuring to know that some supplies had arrived, and that more would be coming. All together the 260 cargo planes dropped 334 tons of supplies by parachute, while 95 P-47's flew escort. Flak brought down eight of the transports.[41]

On that same day another body of troops isolated in the town of Marcoury had requested about fifty loads of supplies by air. Here it seemed impractical to drop a pathfinder because friendly troops held only the town, and it appeared likely that a pathfinder team and its equipment would either fall into enemy hands or be seriously injured on buildings and wires in the town. Thirty planes took off on the missions, and pilots tried to drop by map coordinates, but the supplies fell into enemy hands.[42]

As requests for air supply mounted, it soon became evident that they all could not be filled without interfering with the air movement of the Seventeenth Airborne Division to the Continent. It was necessary for the SHAEF Air Staff to clarify priorities. Most of one mission for the 101st was cancelled, but after that requests for emergency supplies were to take priority over movement of the Seventeenth Airborne Division.[43]

The weather remained generally good on 24 December, and 160 aircraft of the IX Troop Carrier Command dropped 159 tons of supplies to the 101st Airborne Division, as well as 24 tons to other ground units, and the air shuttle operation with the Seventeenth continued. Aware of the heavy burden then on American troop carriers, the British offered the assistance of the Thirty-eighth Group, RAF, in carrying either supplies or troops. Different containers were necessary for British aircraft, however, and no supplies had been packed in British containers. It was decided, therefore, to use airplanes of the Thirty-eighth Group in the Seventeenth Airborne Division movement, thus releasing more American aircraft for supply missions, and to begin packing some supplies in British containers for future use if necessary.[44]

On Christmas Day the weather turned so bad that the mission of 116 aircraft scheduled to carry supplies to Bastogne had to be cancelled. The only troop carrier planes that took off the whole day were fourteen for the Seventeenth Airborne Division, and these encountered icing so serious that only five were able to complete their missions. Meanwhile German tanks were attacking the defenses around Bastogne, and artillery and antitank ammunition, as well as gasoline, were running critically short. Other supplies too were now a full day behind schedule. A message from Supreme Headquarters that evening stated that resupply for the 101st Airborne Division the next day was most urgent. But the weather report stated that there would be no flying weather over the United Kingdom the next day. It might be possible for planes to take off from fields in France, but there were not enough parachute containers there, and a parapacking unit which had been alerted to move to the Continent was itself held up by the weather. Moreover the item most needed, artillery ammunition, could not be packed very efficiently in parachute containers.[45] The G-4 of the 101st Airborne Division suggested a solution: gliders.[46] Gliders salvaged from the Normandy and Holland operations had been collected in France. They could carry artillery ammunition as efficiently as anything else, and they did not require special packaging. The first glider to land on

C-47 airplanes arrived over Bastogne with supplies.

Badly-needed medical supplies and ammunition were dropped through falling snow on Christmas Day to the 101st Airborne Division, then under German seige.

Men of the 101st recovered supplies dropped in the snow near Bastogne.

A C-47 crash-landed safely after dropping supplies near Bastogne.

the morning of 26 December carried a surgical team and medical supplies. Ten more, loaded mainly with artillery ammunition, landed in the afternoon. But this glider effort was not beginning to meet the needs of a situation rapidly growing more serious. Aircraft at bases in England were loaded and standing by, but the weather gave no indication of any improvement. "Finally, with mist sweeping across the runways and cold fog blanketing vision, 301 aircraft took off on instruments carrying 320 tons of material to the 101st Airborne Division."[47] After completing the mission a number of the planes had to land at fields in France to wait for better weather for returning to their bases in England.

The next day thirty-five more gliders landed. After the gliders had cut loose, the tow planes ran into heavy flak, and seventeen of them were shot down. Heavy fog continued over the United Kingdom, and of 238 planes scheduled to carry supplies by parachute, 188 took off. They dropped 162 tons without loss, but they too had to land at continental bases for the night. By now supplies had been loaded in British containers so that planes of the Thirty-eighth and Forty-sixth Groups could be used. But that evening all further resupply missions to Bastogne were cancelled; trucks were now getting through the corridor which the Fourth Armored Division had established to Bastogne from Arlon.[48]

During those five days, the IX Troop Carrier Command had dropped and landed by glider 1,112.1 tons of supplies, and it was reported that 1,046 tons – over 94 percent – went successfully into the division area. And during this same period the Troop Carrier Command was carrying 13,000 troops and 1,800 tons of equipment and supplies of the Seventeenth Airborne Division, and was evacuating 4,264 casualties. The supplies dropped successfully by parachute (about 96 percent of parachute supplies dispatched) included 656 tons of ammunition, 98 tons of rations, 87 tons of mines and explosives, 26 tons of medical supplies, 19 tons of signal equipment, 319 mortars and howitzers, and 4,840 gallons of gasoline. Supplies arriving successfully by glider (approximately 61 percent of those dispatched) included 53 tons of artillery ammunition and 2,975 gallons of gasoline.[49]

Although the 101st Airborne Division had on this occasion moved overland to the combat zone, the fact that it was an airborne division contributed a great deal to its survival at Bastogne. To fight in a situation where it was surrounded by the enemy was normal for it. It had had training and experience in working with the IX Troop Carrier Command on resupply by air. It had a rear base organization outside the encircled area which could help coordinate the resupply missions. It had its own pathfinder teams, experienced in working with the division and the troop carriers, which were able to drop into the area of Bastogne and set up radar aids to assure the arrival of the supply planes. Its staff and its soldiers were trained and experienced in recovering supplies dropped by parachute.

The actions of the airborne divisions in the Battle of the Bulge – and particularly the air movement of the Seventeenth Airborne Division to the Continent and the stand of the 101st Airborne Division which had been made possible by emergency air supply – demonstrated the value of airborne divisions as strategic reserve.

Varsity: The Jump Across the Rhine

If any doubts had crept into plans for granting to airborne operations an important place in the big efforts to achieve final military victory, they had been dispelled by the actions of airborne divisions in Normandy and of the First Allied Airborne Army in Holland. Now the assumption was that the airborne effort should play a major role not only in Europe, but in the Pacific and China-Burma as well. It was time for the big build-up to pay off.

Final airborne operation of the war in Europe was another effort launched in cooperation with Field Marshal Bernard L. Montgomery's Northern Group of Armies. It was the crossing of the Rhine. After the

Paratroopers of the Seventeenth Airborne Division jump from a new two-door C-46 "Commando" east of the Rhine, March 1944.

Lined up on an airfield near Orleans, France, C-47's and CG 4A gliders are prepared to take off for the Rhine.

The Seventeenth Airborne Division made the greatest single-lift airborne operation of the war, jumping across the Rhine near Wesel, 24 March 1945. (The B-17 from which this picture was taken was shot down only a few minutes later.)

operation in Holland, the staff of the First Allied Airborne Army again turned to planning for possible further airborne assaults. Plans for six operations preceded the planning for Operation Varsity. But there was no lack of time for planning this operation. The first planning staff study was completed on 7 November, and the XVIII Corps (Airborne) began detailed planning. The decision to make the attack on 24 March 1945 was made about ten days before that date. Participating in the attack would be the Seventeenth Airborne Division, under command of Maj. Gen. William M. Miley and the British Sixth Airborne Division. Both would operate under General Ridgway's XVIII Corps. Maj. Gen. Paul L. Williams, commander of the IX Troop Carrier Command, would exercise over-all troop carrier command. Originally it was planned that airborne and ground (amphibious) attacks should be launched simultaneously to seize a bridgehead across the Rhine in the Emmerich-Wesel area. But General Sir Milos C. Dempsey, commanding the British Second Army, urged that the airborne phase come after the ground attack had been launched, and this variation was accepted. The mission of the airborne forces remained the same – to seize and hold the high ground five miles north of Wesel in order to assist the ground action in establishing a bridgehead. Only three to five miles east of the Rhine, the whole area was within Allied artillery range. Other departures from previous operations appeared. Most striking was the fact that the entire airborne force would be flown in one lift. The double tow of gliders would be used in combat in Europe for the first time. The C-46 airplane would make its first battle appearance as a troop carrier.[50]

During the month preceding D Day on the Rhine, bombardment aircraft carried through a tremendous air attack program in the area north of the Ruhr where the main effort was to be made. On the night of 23-24 March, then, British Commandos and assault troops of the British Second Army and the U.S. Ninth Army, in Operation Plunder, crossed the Rhine against surprisingly light opposition. At 0600 on 24 March the greatest aerial armada of the war began taking off. From eleven airfields in East Anglia, the column of 699 airplanes and 429 gliders carrying the British airborne division converged south of Brussels with the stream of 903 airplanes and 897 gliders which were taking off with the Seventeenth Airborne Division from twelve fields in northern France and Belgium. While 1,253 fighters of the Eighth Air Force patrolled east of the Rhine and provided cover for a diversionary bombing attack by the Fifteenth Air Force on Berlin, 900 fighters of the British Second Tactical Air Force flew cover over the target area. Another 213 fighters of the RAF escorted the northern column (the British Sixth Airborne) to the Rhine, and 676 fighters of the Ninth Air Force escorted the southern column. Fewer than one hundred German fighters appeared over all of northwestern Germany, and none molested the troop carriers. Flak defense in the Ruhr area was

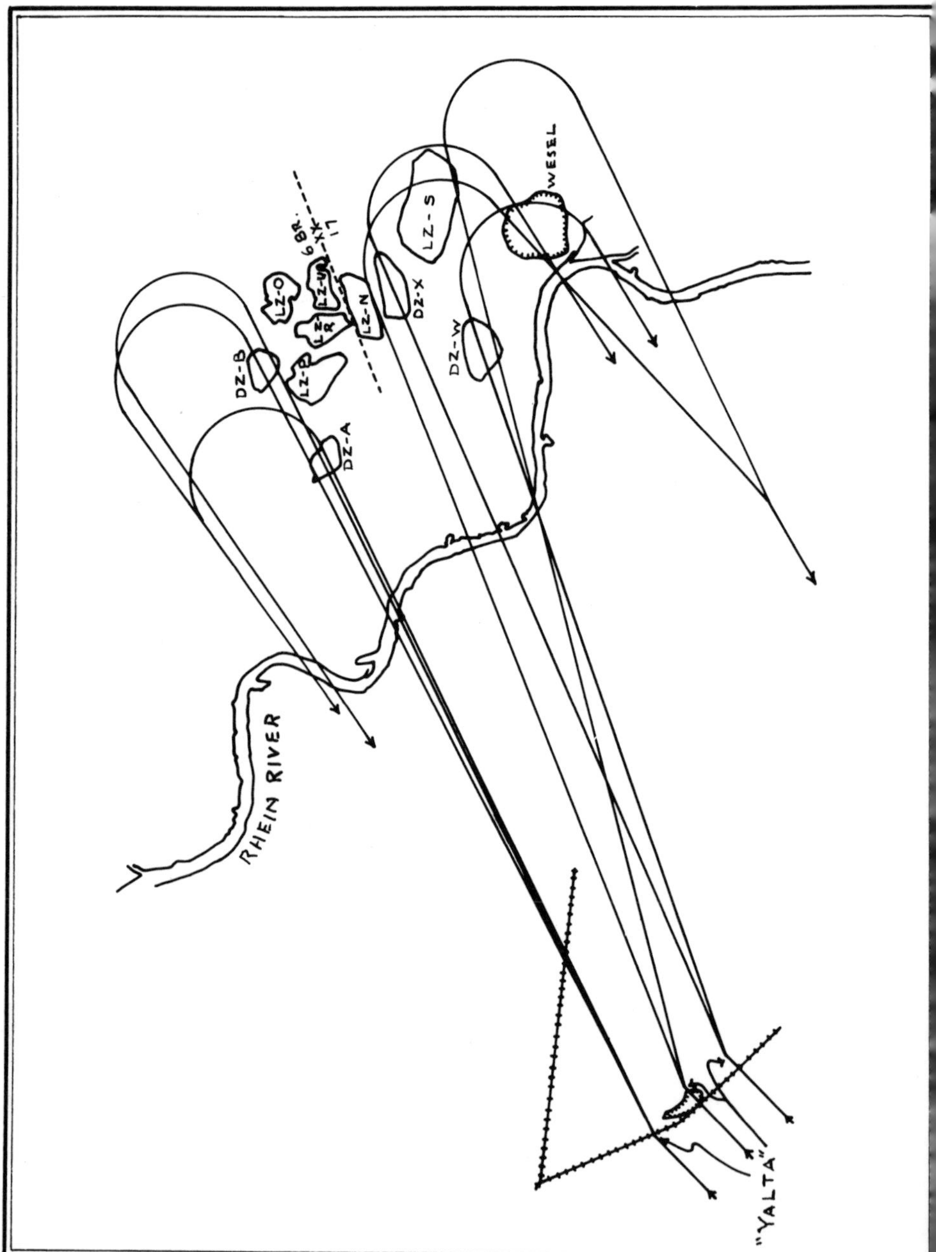

Flight routes for Operation Varsity, 24 March 1945.

known to be very extensive, and many antiaircraft guns were able to get into action; some 440 troop carrier aircraft were damaged seriously and 53 were destroyed. Landing casualties, however, were considerably less than had been expected. Parachute drops and glider landings were, for the most part, very accurate.

There were, however, a few interesting exceptions to this general accuracy. In one case a serial of American paratroopers dropped on the zone designated for the command post of the British Sixth Airborne Division. It was an area well covered by flak guns, light and heavy, and doubtless the unscheduled drop and quick action of the American parachutists saved the British headquarters considerable embarrassment when it arrived a few minutes later.

Parachute and glider landings continued from shortly before 1000 to shortly after 1300. Following the troop carriers, 240 heavy bombers of the Eighth Air Force brought in 582 tons of supplies. Airborne units on the ground assembled rapidly, and by mid-afternoon the two airborne divisions were in contact with each other. Contact then having been established with the ground forces advancing from the Rhine, the airborne phase of the operation may be considered to have ended by nightfall on D Day. An air supply mission scheduled for the next day was cancelled.

Operation Varsity was called "the most successful airborne operation carried out to date,"[51] and "the highest state of development attained by troop-carrier and airborne units."[52]

There was no question but that the complexities of getting the massive aerial fleet into the air at the proper time and of delivering parachutists, gliders, and supplies to the correct drop and landing zones on schedule required coordination, planning, and skill of execution of the highest order. But the operation did not settle the question of deep penetration in a strategic vertical envelopment. Some would question the real value of the airborne contribution in establishing the bridgehead across the Rhine at all. In view of the relatively little opposition to the assault boat crossings and the rapid advances of the ground forces, it does not appear that the airborne phase was essential to the success of the river crossing operation. Indeed, had the same resources been employed on the ground, it is conceivable that the advance to the east might have been even more rapid than it was.

The labor and materials that went into the preparation of airfields in northern France and Belgium for the operation was immense. During the thirty-four days that preparation went on, men of the British Army contributed 150,000 man hours and French civilians another 99,880 in addition to the 469,750 man hours furnished by men of the U.S. Army. Materials that went into the improvements included the following: 13,719 tons of pierced steel planking, 7,050 tons of Tarnax surfacing material,

2,500 tons of rock, 100 tons of stone chip screenings, 18,000 gallons of bitumen seal coat, 5,310 rolls of square mesh track, 51,070 rolls of Hessian mat, 53,000 cubic yards of hardcore, 55,686 bales of straw, and 300 barrels of tar.[53]

On the basis of the Varsity operation First Allied Airborne Army once more testified to the soundness of the doctrine stated in War Department Training Circular 113, 9 October 1943, but it suggested republication with certain modifications. The Airborne Army Headquarters pointed to the advantages of carrying an airborne division in one lift and of gliders' avoiding areas of heavy flak or ground weapons. Most important was a recommendation which hardly could have been the result of the Varsity experience, but more likely was expressed with an eye to the future. Contrary to the conclusions after the operation in Holland, the suggestion was that the reference to support or relief of airborne forces within a period of three days should be changed to extend this period. On organization, the First Allied Airborne Army recommended that it assume the administrative and supply responsibilities equivalent to those of a field army. It recommended the retention of the airborne corps, with some additions to its staff and corps troops, as a permanent organization. The new division organization was held to be generally sound. A new standard operating procedure for the employment of glider pilots on the ground had been agreed to, and now the training and equipment of glider pilots was reported satisfactory. Until a specially designed airplane could be had, the C-46 was considered a satisfactory troop carrier with the advantages over the C-47 of greater capacity – it carried thirty-six paratroops – double exits, and less propeller blast for the jumpers. However, fires had resulted from damage to the hydraulic system. Once more a plea was made for self-sealing gasoline tanks on all troop carrier aircraft.[54]

Arena: A Strategic Envelopment that Might Have Been

The fundamental question of whether airborne troops could maintain themselves in prolonged action from an airhead independent of connections with ground troops never was answered in World War II. A few officers like General Marshall and General Arnold held to the affirmative view consistently; others remained doubtful; still others shifted from one position to another. After the Holland operation General Brereton had fallen back to the stated doctrine that airborne troops should not operate without relief by ground troops for longer than three days. Early in 1945, however, he and his staff were becoming anxious to prove the feasibility of an independent airhead, and they did push planning for such an operation to an advanced stage.

Briefly the plan was to land six to ten divisions by parachute, glider, and airplane into a strategic airhead in the Kassel area of Germany. The purpose would be to establish a "fortress" area from which a decisive offensive could be launched at the east end of the Ruhr, to seize the high ground east of Paderborn in order to deny to the enemy this defensive position, and to provide an airhead toward which the Southern Group of Armies could advance. The operation would be conducted in four phases which, on a much bigger scale, would conform in a way to the phases which had been followed repeatedly in airborne maneuvers. First, four to six airborne divisions would go in by parachute and glider to seize airfields and airstrip sites and to set up defenses for the "fortress" area. It was estimated that this would take three to six days. Secondly, up to four infantry divisions would be airlanded, on the airfields and strips which had been prepared, in order to build up a force for offensive action. The third phase would be the launching of an offensive to the northwest to seize the high ground east of Paderborn and to cut lines of communication east and southeast of the Ruhr. The preliminary plan suggested the use of the following troops: Headquarters and Special Troops, First Allied Airborne Army; Headquarters and Special Troops, XVIII U.S. Corps (Airborne); Headquarters and Special Troops, I British Airborne Corps; one additional U.S. corps headquarters and special troops; the 13th, 17th, 82d, and 101st U.S. Airborne Divisions; the 1st and the 6th British Airborne Divisions; three U.S. airborne aviation engineer battalions; the 2d, 84th and 103d U.S. Infantry Divisions, and one additional U.S. infantry division. Supply plans were based on the assumption of providing 300 tons per division per day.* It was planned that each division should carry with it three days' initial supply. Troop carriers would fly two sorties on each flyable day. On D Day two airborne divisions and aviation engineers would go in and the same would follow on D plus 1. Thereafter one infantry division would go in each day until all had been delivered, and resupply missions would be flown during those same days. Then all aircraft would be devoted to resupply and evacuation. It was assumed that bombers would have to fly an important share of the resupply missions.[55]

General Eisenhower's reactions appeared to be favorable. He said that he "would dearly love to have one big airborne operation before the war ended" and "it would really be fun to do."[56] Whether or not the operation would be ordered hinged on "finding the divisions."[57]

* For Operation Varsity a U.S. airborne divisional day of air resupply was figured at 270.54 tons. FAAA Rpt on opn VARSITY, Appendix 9.

General Ridgway, commander of XVIII Corps (Airborne) commented at some length on the plan and raised several objections,* but he concluded, "I believe this plan, sound as I think it is in strategic and tactical concept, will stand or fall upon the hard facts of the ability and willingness of SHAEF to provide the aircraft and air fields in the quantities and for the periods of time which represent minimum essential needs; . . . and on other equally essential logistical factors."**

Planning went forward rapidly and on 15 March the target date was announced as 1 May.[58] SHAEF G-3 submitted a study on 26 March which suggested that the air power to accomplish the mission did exist, "but only at extreme expense to other air efforts, particularly as regards strategic air forces in their overall role. . . . The cost of launching the operation is a large one – chiefly in weakening the air support of the main operation, and diversion of strategic bombing." Finally, it concluded: "In view of the probably rapid progress of operations, it is considered that there will now be no need for an airborne operation in the KASSEL area."[59] Operation Arena was cancelled the same day.[60] Curiously the emphasis on strategic bombing remained right up to the end, even though it generally was agreed that strategic bombing could have little effect on military operations until weeks or months after the attack, while the effects of a large-scale airborne attack might be immediate.

* One objection was that no motor vehicle larger than a ¾-ton truck, and few of them, could be flown into the airhead, and consequently the problem of unloading and transporting supplies might prove insurmountable. A marginal comment replied, however, that a CG-13 glider could carry a 1½-ton truck, a British Hamilcar could carry a 2½-ton truck with certain adjustments, and that a C-47 could carry a 2½-ton in parts. See letter from Maj Gen M.B. Ridgway to CG FAAA, 7 Mar 45, sub: Opr ARENA, carbon copy and marginal notation thereon. In FAAA (ARENA)

** *Ibid.* A suggestion that the task might better be performed by a single corps with four divisions rather than two or three corps with eight to ten divisions under Airborne Army was interpreted in Headquarters, First Allied Airborne Army, as intimation that this should be a job for XVIII Corps. See marginal comments on original and carbon copies of letter cited above.

Chapter IX

Meanwhile, In the Pacific and Far East

The first large-scale airborne troop movement of American forces in any theater was in the Southwest Pacific. It began in September 1942 with the movement of an infantry battalion of the Thirty-second Division by air shuttle from Brisbane, Australia, to Port Moresby, New Guinea. Others followed from Townsville. To accomplish that mission, Lt. Gen. George C. Kenney, commander of the Allied Air Forces in the Southwest Pacific, pressed into service Australian civil transport planes, newly arrived B-17's – some with civilian crews – and some old German-built Dutch planes, as well as the few C-47's at his disposal. The B-17's ferried a four-gun battery of 105-mm. howitzers. Successive air shuttles in October and November carried perhaps 15,000 Americans and Australians across the Owen-Stanley Mountains for the campaign against Buna and Gona. After delivery of the troops, the air units were called upon to carry supplies to the forward positions. About twenty C-47's, with bombers reinforcing them from time to time, carried a weekly average of two million pounds of supplies to various points in Papua. Ground troops, under supervision of air officers, packaged the supplies, wrapped them in excelsior, and sewed burlap sacks around them so that they could be tossed from doors or dropped from bomb-bays for free falls at a time when parachutes were scarce. Other supplies were landed at advanced strips.[1]

Nadzab: First Parachute Operation in the Pacific

Airborne operations in the Pacific and Far East were not as extensive as those in the European and Mediterranean theaters. Tactical drops were on a scale of not more than a regimental combat team in any one operation. More often than not aerial supply became the principal mission of troop carrier aircraft, and in many cases supply by air was the major support for ground actions.

Preparatory to further penetrations of Japanese positions in New Guinea, an advance air base was set up in the summer of 1943 at Marilinen. Again the airlift played a prominent role. C-47's took in an Australian battalion which set up the initial perimeter defense, and then brought in engineers and equipment and other troops for construction work and defense. The air transports even performed the impossible feat of delivering 2½-ton trucks. They did it by cutting the frames in half with acetylene torches.[2]

The next step then was the first tactical employment of airborne troops in the Pacific theater. At 0825 on 5 September 1943 the 503d Parachute Infantry took off from Port Moresby in ninety-six C-47 transport planes. An Australian parachute artillery battery (25-pounders) reinforced the regiment. To assist a three-pronged Australian drive for the important Japanese-held port of Lae, the paratroopers were to seize an airstrip at Nadzab, some twenty miles inland. There had been weeks of detailed planning, and a dress rehearsal for this operation. The air formations included 302 planes: A-20's laid smoke screens to hide the drop zones from enemy observers; B-25's bombed and strafed the landing area; B-17's, especially prepared for the purpose, carried in each bomb bay a "basket" of twelve bundles of equipment, a parachute on each bundle, and the ammunition, heavy machine guns, and supplies, would be dropped according to signals from the ground wherever needed; squadrons of P-38 fighters flew cover above, and P-39's guarded the flanks; heavy bombers carried bomb loads to drop on enemy positions at the nearby Heath Plantation. It was about 1000 hours when the transport planes arrived over the drop zones. The three parachute infantry battalions dropped simultaneously in a cloverleaf pattern. The drop was completed within 2½ minutes while the planes flew in at minimum altitudes. The paratroopers found little resistance on the ground (three deaths and a number of fractures occurred in the jump), and they quickly organized a perimeter defense. An Australian pioneer battalion which had set out on foot six days earlier joined them, and work proceeded on the air strip. Shuttling by air of the Seventh Australian Division from Marilinen to Nadzab (an operation which required several weeks) began thirty-six hours later. Now the Japanese at Lae were caught in a squeeze and the way was open to the Markham Valley. The airborne operation was termed "completely successful." In an area where distances were great and means were meager, it had been demonstrated that airborne operations could make an important contribution to a major campaign.[3]

No gliders were used in the Nadzab operation though eleven, loaded with Australian men and equipment, were waiting to take off at Port

Moresby on 5 September when their mission was cancelled. Ostensibly the use of the gliders was cancelled because the outstanding success of the parachute drop made them unnecessary, but a contributing factor was the concern for the safety of the men they would carry. All the gliders were showing signs of deterioration. On the flight from Brisbane, where they were being assembled for the operation, one glider had lost its tail assembly in midair and the crew had been killed in the resulting crash.[4] The first glider contingent, thirty-five pilots and thirty-five mechanics for the Southwest Pacific, had arrived in Australia in February 1943, and, in April, another twenty-six pilots and twenty-six mechanics had joined them. Their crated gliders – twenty-seven of them – had arrived shortly afterwards. Actually none of these gliders ever was used in tactical operations. Some of the pilots and mechanics later were assigned to various other duties among widely separated troop carrier units, and others were returned to the United States.[5]

Airlandings in Burma

One of the most dramatic episodes in airborne support of operations was that for Wingate's Raiders and Merrill's Marauders in Burma by Col. Philip G. Cochran's first Air Commando Force and the troop carriers under Brig. Gen. W. D. Old. The British and Indian troops of Maj. Gen. Orde C. Wingate had invaded northern Burma in March 1943, and the success of their operations in rear of the Japanese positions led to an expansion of the effort. In the spring of 1944 the Air Commando Force, using C-47 transport, L-4 and L-5 liaison planes, gliders, fighters, and medium bombers, undertook the support of operations designed to disrupt the Japanese rear in the Chin Hills and northern Burma. The planes provided the only means of outside supply for Wingate's long-range penetration columns. Supplies were parachuted daily to designated areas, and airlanding operations brought in engineer equipment, animals, and reinforcements. Light planes and transports had to be depended upon for the evacuation of wounded and sick.

On the night of 5-6 March 1944 a fleet of twenty-six C-47's, with gliders in double tow, took off from India's tea garden valley of Silcher, climbed 8,000 feet over the Chin Hills, and released their gliders 250 miles to the east, 100 miles behind Japanese lines. The plan was to fly two brigades of Wingate's Third Indian Division while a third brigade marched in from the north. It had been intended to use two landing zones, dubbed "Broadway" and "Piccadily," for the D Day gliders, and then to prepare landing strips there for later airlanding operations. Acting on a hunch, Colonel Cochrane had ordered a special photo reconnaissance on the afternoon of D Day. Enlarged air photographs arrived just fifteen minutes before take-off time. They showed "Piccadily" so obstructed with tree trunks and other obstacles that the entire force had to be ordered, at the last minute, to use "Broadway." Two hours later gliders of the first wave began landing. Most of them were damaged on landing, and a second wave with the exception of one plane, was recalled soon after taking off. Three bulldozers were landed, however, and two of them could be put to use so that landings could continue the next day as no enemy opposition developed. Of the fifty-four gliders dispatched (and not recalled), thirty-seven arrived at "Broadway," eight landed west of the Chindwin river in friendly territory, and nine went down east of the Chindwin in enemy territory. In the landings, thirty men were killed and thirty-three were injured. According to figures prepared at Wingate's headquarters, 539 men, 3 mules, and 29,972 pounds of supplies had been delivered that first night. The 900th Airborne Engineer Company, and all other men not needed for other duties, quickly went to work clearing the field and filling ditches in preparation for the next night's operation. A secondary field, called "Chowringless" was added the next night. British and American squadrons, equipped with C-47's, of the Troop Carrier Command reinforced the Air Commandos for the fly-in which continued through the next six days. By the end of D plus 6 a total of 9,052 men, 175 ponies, 1,183 mules, and 509,083 pounds of stores had been landed. Some special glider missions were flown later, and squadrons of L-1 and L-5 light liaison planes dropped food and evacuated casualties for the marching columns.[6]

At this same time Chinese and American troops under Lt. Gen. Joseph W. Stilwell were pushing southward toward the general area where Wingate's columns were operating. Spearheading this drive was the special American force known as Merrill's Marauders. Again troop carriers were the principal means of supply. For the Marauders the Second Troop Carrier Squadron, and later the First Troop Carrier Squadron, carried the supplies from their base near Dinjan (thirty-two miles west of Ledo) to the forward drop zones. They dropped engineering equipment, ammunition, medical supplies, and rations by parachute from an altitude of about 200 feet. They dropped clothing and grain from 150 feet without parachutes. Flying seventeen missions, averaging six to seven planes, during March alone, the C-47's delivered 376 tons of supplies to the Marauders. When no open space or paddy field could be found in the area, ground troops had to prepare a field, but usually the line of march and supply requirements could be coordinated to take advantage of flat open ground. This not only relieved the troops of the hard work of clearing ground, but it also permitted the pilots to identify their drop zones from maps and aerial photographs. If the situation permitted, requests were radioed to the Dinjan base in the evening for supplies to be dropped the next afternoon.

Emergency requests would receive prompt attention. Once, on 6 May, a C-47 reached the drop zone, 128 miles from Dinjan, just two hours and twenty-two minutes after the message had been received. A rear echelon organization of the Marauders, consisting of 250 to 300 men, operated the warehouses, packed parachutes, loaded the planes, and furnished unloading details for kicking the supplies from the planes over the drop zones.[7]

By May Chinese and American troops were pushing toward Myitkyina, main Japanese supply base for the defense of Burma from the north and principal objective for the campaign. Columns of the Third Indian Division already had cut the single railway eighty miles to the south of Myitkyina, and were continuing to harrass the Japanese rear areas. Stealing through paddy fields and jungle, H Force of Merrill's Marauders arrived undetected at the Myitkyina airstrip on 17 May. While other elements struck at the nearby village of Pamati and its ferry, the Chinese 150th Regiment launched a surprise attack against the airstrip. By noon the field was in Allied hands. Immediately Col. Charles N. Hunter, commander of H Force, requested reinforcements and supplies in order to build up a defense before the Japanese could counterattack in strength. A battalion of the Eighty-ninth Regiment arrived by air from Ledo in the late afternoon, and C-47's could begin landing equipment and supplies too heavy or bulky for parachute dropping. At 1600 the 706 AAA Machine Gun Battery (Airborne) received a radio message to move to the Myitkyina airstrip immediately. All planes were loaded by 1600 and they began taking off at 1740. They arrived at the field an hour later, and all guns were in action by 0100. As it turned out the Japanese were able to build up a strong counterattack, and the battle for Myitkyina turned into a

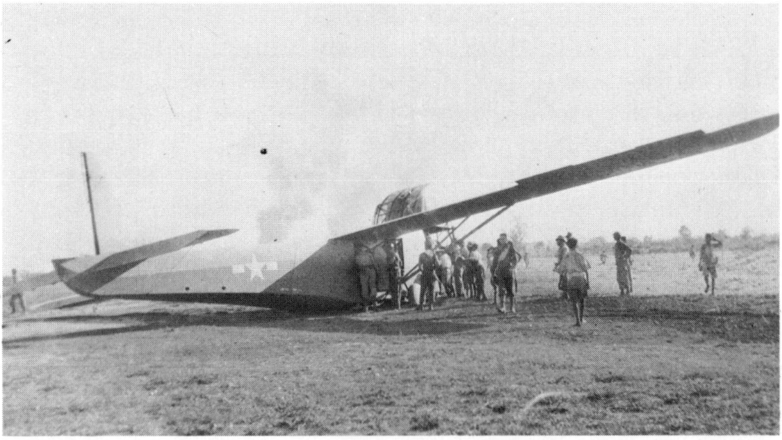

Local natives flocked into the Myitkyina Airfield to help the Americans unload the gliders during an invasion of the airfield. Japanese shells are bursting in the background, 17 May 1944.

struggle to hold the vital airfield where reinforcements and supplies could be brought in. Not until 3 August did Myitkyina itself fall.[8]

Operations in Burma had demonstrated the effectiveness of long-range airborne invasion and of airborne support for ground actions. However, the reaction of one observer was that some lessons, particularly in glider operations, were being learned the hard way when they already should have been known:

> As seems to be happening in all reports from operations, the people in the theaters must learn under fire what we already know from our maneuvers. Therefore, many of the things that are pointed out are not actually lessons as far as we are concerned, but are lessons to the theaters. It seems unfortunate that this situation is true since I know informally that certain organizations are being built up, in the Air Force particularly, based on the Burma Operations, and it seems rather discouraging that these things could not be done here with the knowledge that we already have.[9]

Noemfoor

The only parachute operation in the Pacific areas during 1944 was the drop of the 503d Parachute Infantry on Noemfoor Island off the northwest coast of New Guinea on 3 and 4 July to reinforce the ground attack of the 158th Regimental Combat Team. Although plans for several

Men of the 503rd Parachute Infantry made a muddy descent on Kamiri airstrip, Noemfoor Island, 4 July 1944.

other airborne operations had reached advanced stages, but had been discarded for various reasons, troop carrier units had been so busy with supply missions that they had had no training for such operations since the Markham Valley operation in September 1943. Skill in formation flying had been all but forgotten.[10] Supply of bomber and fighter units with gasoline, ammunition, and food had taken precedence over support for ground troops in the spring of 1944.[11]

A smoke screen over the Noemfoor drop zones added to the difficulties of pilots already hard pressed to find their way, and the parachute drop was widely scattered. Actually the paratroops encountered no enemy resistance, and engineers already were working on the airfield where they landed. But the force of 1,418 paratroops suffered 114 jump casualties. A number of them were due to landings on engineer equipment which already had arrived by sea![12]

To reestablish the skill of troop carrier crews in airborne operations, a training program was set up at Dobodura. But demands for air delivery of supplies were so great that only one squadron at a time could be spared for training. Paratroops made 6,400 practice jumps during that month.[13]

Return to the Rock

Airborne operations in the Pacific continued to be on a smaller scale than those common to the European theater. Troop carrier units were being kept busy on nearly every other kind of task – in transporting striking air units and guiding them from one base to another as advances continued from island to island, supplying air and ground units, carrying passengers, evacuating casualties, and even spraying swamps with DDT.[14] Some airborne activity returned, however, in the reconquest of the Philippines.

In its next mission, the 503d Parachute Combat Team spearheaded the American "return to the rock" when it descended on Corregidor on 16 February 1945. If the attack were to be effective in silencing the Japanese gun positions in the cliff, it would be necessary for the paratroops to land on the heights above them. The only areas which could be used for drop zones in that location were two small fields. One, previously a golf course, was an area of about 300 yards by 150 yards, and it was covered with debris and bomb craters. The other had been a parade ground, and it was even smaller. It was a situation which called for an approach completely different from that used in earlier airborne engagements. The airborne attack – it would have to be a daylight operation – was to precede by two hours a seaborne assault by the Thirty-fourth Infantry. Planners estimated that a minimum of 850 Japanese defenders waited in caves, pillboxes, and entrenchments. Later they revised that figure to nearly 6,000.[15]

A signal lineman released a member of the 503rd Parachute Infantry who landed in a tree on Noemfoor Island.

Members of the 503rd jump in a field on Corregidor, 6 February 1945.

The Corregidor Island terrain was bomb-battered before the landing of the 503rd.

Paratroops were divided into three battalion combat teams, each to go in a separate serial. The first serial was to land at 0830, the second at 1200, and the third at 0830 on D plus 1. A resupply lift of twelve C-47's was to follow the third serial. The parachute drops on the tiny drop zones called for a maximum of coordination. The plan was for each serial of troop carriers to form into two columns of single planes in trail, one for each drop zone. While an observer in a control plane high over the area gave instructions and corrections to pilot and jumpmasters by radio in the clear, the right column would circle to the right over its drop zone, and the left column would circle to the left. It was expected that each plane could drop about six to eight paratroops on each pass over the target. All participants studied oblique and vertical air photos of the area, and all battalion and company commanders made reconnaissance over the area in bombers. Meanwhile the Third Battalion, Thirty-fourth Infantry, prepared its closely coordinated amphibious attack, and naval and air bombardment prepared for their support.

At 0715 on 16 February fifty-one C-47 airplanes of the 317th Troop Carrier Group took off from Mindoro with the first echelon. It arrived over the target on schedule and parachutists began jumping. In contrast with other operations in which parachute units were delivered in a matter of a few minutes, it required more than an hour for the infantry battalion, artillery battery and supporting detachments to complete the first drop. Mainly because of the rough terrain and the 15- to 20-mile-an-hour winds, the first echelon of paratroops suffered landing losses of about 15 percent, but the attack had caught the defenders by surprise and active resistance was light. The units assembled quickly and went about consolidating their positions. Shortly after noon the second serial arrived, and the paratroops jumped according to plan. The amphibious attack, striking at 1040, likewise went well, and by 1100 the Thirty-fourth Infantry had gained Malinta Hill near the middle of the island – and the parachutists were lending 75-mm. artillery and .50 caliber machine gun support. During the afternoon the elements of the 503d Combat Team which had arrived extended their perimeter and made contact with the amphibious forces. Inasmuch as additional supplies and troops could be brought in by sea, the airborne lifts scheduled for the second day were cancelled. Ground action and mopping up continued for two weeks, but the surprise and tactical advantage gained in the initial assault had been decisive. Enemy dead reported by 2 March totalled 4,506.[16]

The Eleventh Airborne Division in the Philippines

One American airborne division – the Eleventh, under the command of Maj. Gen. Joseph M. Swing – was in the Pacific, but it was committed to action more frequently as an infantry division than by air. The division had a ground role in the battle on Leyte, but air supply – from L-5 and a few C-47 airplanes – had helped make it possible for it to fight its way across that island,[17] and a battery of field artillery was dropped in the Leyte mountains. Particularly impressive during this operation was the medical activity. The division surgeon persuaded medical personnel to organize two portable (parachute) surgical hospitals. Dropping from liaison planes, they operated for more than six weeks in a location "completely inaccessible from Base Camp except by jeep plane and hand-over-hand trail."[18]

The Eleventh Airborne Division had taken steps to introduce a greater flexibility into its organization than was possible with the official organization of one parachute regiment and two glider regiments. The glider elements of the division were formed into "para-glider" units as most of the glidermen became qualified parachutists. Thus a standard operating procedure (SOP) could be worked out which called for a distribution of gliders among all three regiments in a manner best suited for the operation. In this way all regiments had parachute personnel and all had the benefit of glider-borne equipment.[19] The division worked out SOP's with the Fifty-fourth Troop Carrier Wing which were based on War Department Training Circular 113, 9 October 1943, and which followed generally SOP's which had been developed in the United States and in the European theatre.*

Elements of the Eleventh Airborne Division executed three airborne operations during 1945 on Luzon.

After landing, on 31 January, on the coast of Batangas province near Nasugbu, about fifty miles southwest of Manila, the Eleventh Airborne Division advanced rapidly toward Tagaytay. By 2 February the American troops were able to begin their attack against the lower slopes of Tagaytay Ridge. An airborne operation was planned to assist in taking the main defense along the ridge, and it was scheduled for 3 February. That morning forty-six C-47 airplanes flew to that objective with the first echelon of the 511th Parachute Infantry (Eleventh Airborne Division). The accidental dropping of a supply parachute from one of the planes became a signal for the premature jump of a large proportion of the paratroops, and they landed about six miles northeast of the designated

* One difference was in the formation of troop carrier planes: for a parachute jump they were to fly in diamonds of V's rather than in V's of V's. Another departure was the rule that pathfinders should land at the pre-selected drop zones in the hours of darkness twelve to twenty-four hours preceding an operation. See Standing Operating Procedure, Joint Troop Carrier-Airborne Operation, 11th A/B Div-54th Tr Carrier Wing, n.d. Mimeo cy in C&GSC archives R-4780.

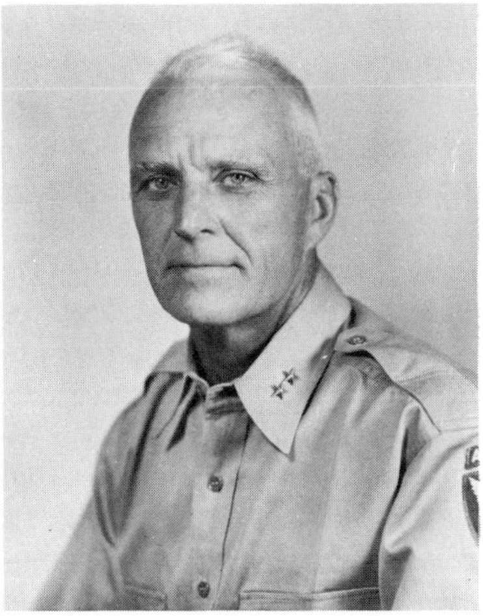

Maj. Gen. Joseph M. Swing, commanding general of the Eleventh Airborne Division, served earlier as War Department observer during the Sicily operation, as chairman of the special Board of Airborne Operations appointed in Washington to study airborne doctrine and training requirements, and as commanding general of the Airborne Command.

drop zone. When jumpmasters of the second flight of fifty-one C-47's saw the parachutes on the ground, most of the paratroopers again jumped in the wrong place. No opposition appeared on the ground, however, and units were able to assemble and make their way to the objective without difficulty. By 1300 they had cleared the ridge and made contact with the 188th Glider Infantry, advancing on the ground. The next day the airborne troops began advancing along the highway toward Manila.[20]

After Manila had fallen, the Eleventh Airborne Division turned toward the Laguna de Bay area south and east of the city. An immediate objective became the release of some 2,147 Allied civilians who were interned in a camp at Los Banos. The plan provided for a closely coordinated attack by parachute (Company B, 511th Parachute Infantry reinforced by the Light Machine Gun Platoon), by sea (511th Parachute Infantry less Company B and the Machine Gun Platoon with the 672d Amphibious Tractor Battalion for evacuating the internees), and land (troops of the 188th Para-Glider Regimental Combat Team). The division's provisional reconnaissance platoon moved by water to a landing point east of Los Banos where it contacted groups of guerillas, marked the landing beach, secured the drop zone, and then moved to the camp where at H Hour it attacked the sentinels and blocked the other guards from leaving their quarters to get to their rifle racks. At 0700 on 23 February the paratroop force dropped on a rice paddy east of the camp, and assembled quickly. Less than twenty minutes later the paratroopers were mopping up at the camp where they set up a defense and began organizing the internees. At this point the amphibious tractors arrived and evacuation began. Meanwhile the ground attack had run into resistance, but it did not matter. The combined operation had killed 240 Japanese prison guards and had succeeded completely in freeing their prisoners. American losses had been two killed and three wounded.[21]

A final airborne operation was intended as something of a *coup de grace* against a battered and confused enemy in the Cagayan Valley of Luzon. On 23 June 1945 Gypsy Task Force (a reinforced battalion of the 511th Parachute Infantry, one battery of the 457th Parachute Field Artillery and supporting elements, totalling about 1,000 men) flew from the Lipa airstrip in southern Luzon to drop at Camalaniugan airfield near Appari, at the northern end of the island. For the first time in the Pacific, gliders were being used in a tactical operation.* Seven gliders – six CG-4A's and one CG-13 – carried six jeeps, one trailer, machine guns, ammunition, radio and medical supplies, and nineteen men. The pathfinders had gone forward two days before, contacted guerillas on the west bank of the Cagayan River, and then slipped across the river at night to mark the drop zone with colored smoke. Fighter-bombers laid smoke between the drop zone and the hills to the southeast. Encountering no Japanese resistance, the airborne force contacted guerillas on the ground, seized Appari, and then turned southward to meet the advancing Thirty-seventh Division. With that contact established on 26 June the Luzon campaign was virtually completed.[22]

Airborne to Tokyo

While the Eleventh Airborne Division continued an intensive training program back at Lipa in anticipation of future airborne operations on a larger scale than any thus far undertaken in the Pacific, events were moving rapidly toward an unexpectedly early termination of hostilities. On 15 August instructions went out from General MacArthur's headquarters which included the following: "The United States Army Forces Pacific – simultaneously and in conjunction with landing of Fleet Landing Forces will conduct an initial airborne occupation of selected areas in the Tokyo area to impose the terms of surrender."[23] But already the Eleventh Airborne Division had been caught in rapid movements to catch up with the situation. First warning of a move had come at 0530 on 11 August, but the date had been uncertain. Then at noon the same day the division had received word that planes would begin the flight to Okinawa – the first leg of the trip. Transport planes from other troop carrier units, as well as fifty B-24's, had supplemented the planes of the Fifty-fourth Troop Carrier

* On 17 October 1944 four gliders carried engineers and their equipment to Ifitamin in Central New Guinea for the construction of an emergency air strip. See Tactical Employment in the U.S. Army and Transport Aircraft and Gliders, II, 322.

Wing. Heavy rains had interfered with operations on the ground, and had so weakened the support for the steel matting at Lipa airfield that one B-24 had crashed on the take-off and others had been unable to use the runway. But in less than seventy-two hours, the Eleventh Airborne Division had flown from Lipa, Nielson, Nichols, and Clark fields to Okinawa.

Preparations began immediately for the more difficult problems of completing the movement – to include the Twenty-seventh Infantry Division as well as the Eleventh Airborne – to Japan as soon as surrender negotiations permitted. Lack of knowledge on the Atsugi airdrome made necessary multiple plans. Staffs drew no less than five flight and loading plans. Again the Fifty-fourth Troop Carrier Wing was charged with coordinating the air movement. A reconnaissance party and an advance operations party which arrived at the Atsugi airdrome on 28 August found that the field would not take B-24 bombers. However, 165 C-54's from the Air Transport Command as well as forty-eight C-46's were collected. Loading began on the afternoon of 29 August and at 0100 that night the first plane, carrying General Swing and members of his staff, took off. It arrived at 0600. By 0730 a command post had been established in one of the hangars and the flag of the United States was flying over it. Bad weather and deterioration of the Japanese airfield caused the air movement to be extended over fifteen days. Quickly trained in air transportation with the assistance of teams from the Eleventh Airborne Division, the Twenty-seventh Division followed the airborne troops to Japan. By 13 September 21,721 men of the two divisions and higher headquarters had been flown to the Tokyo area to begin their duties of military occupation.[24]

Chapter X

The Airborne Effort

From small beginnings the American airborne program grew into a major enterprise. It was a long way from a test platoon at Fort Benning in 1940 to the Airborne Command at Camp Mackall in 1943. It was a remarkable advance from the scattered drops of a parachute battalion in North Africa in 1942 to the massive airborne invasions of Holland in 1944 and across the Rhine in 1945. It had been a long, difficult course beset with the troubles of selling new ways of warfare and of competing for men and equipment against more firmly ensconced programs. Not the least remarkable achievement of the airborne effort was the extent to which the handicaps to training were overcome in building combat units which were uniformly successful and whose troops won universal respect as effective fighters. They were able to achieve an *esprit de corps* which was the envy of other units, and their reputation for individual and small-unit fierceness in combat won the admiration of their comrades and the fear of their enemies.

Conclusions

The airborne effort played a significant part in operations impressive in size and number, and often added effective strength to ground combat. It would be difficult, however, to describe the use of airborne troops as such in any operation as unquestionably decisive. The first parachute drops in North Africa had little to contribute but experience for future plans and training. Perhaps the airborne operation in Sicily, in spite of the misfortunes which accompanied it, was decisive for the holding of a particular segment of the beach at a particular time; but even if that were so, it would be difficult to conclude that the whole amphibious assault would have been a failure had no airborne operation supported it. On the contrary, the results might have been more impressive if all the resources committed to the airborne attack had been diverted to building up the amphibious force. Possibly the reinforcement of the Salerno beachhead by airborne troops was decisive in saving that situation. There the speed with which parachute troops could be committed was important in a crisis where forces needed immediate strengthening.

The parachute drop near Nadzab, New Guinea, was an outstanding success, but again it cannot be concluded with finality that those troops would not have been just as effective had they marched in overland as did the engineers who joined them shortly after the drop. It probably was a useful thing to have airborne troops drop behind the defenses of Utah Beach in Normandy, but it would be far-fetched to assume that the amphibious assault against that beach would have failed without airborne troops when it succeeded against the more formidable defenses of Omaha Beach without them. Neither is it likely that the invasion of Southern France would have failed without the airborne phase of that operation any more than did the scores of American amphibious assaults which invariably succeeded elsewhere without the use of airborne troops. On the other hand some of those amphibious operations might have been less costly if airborne troops had been used in conjunction with them.

Burma presented a somewhat different situation. The use of gliders to carry British and Indian troops deep behind Japanese positions was disappointing, but the use of airplanes to fly in reinforcements, as at Mitkyina, and to drop or land supplies, may well have been a decisive factor in the reconquest of Burma.

The air invasion of Holland came very close to winning a decisive crossing of the Lower Rhine, but it did not. Undoubtedly it made a valuable contribution in securing a corridor deep into Holland, and in securing bridges over the Maas and Waal intact; but again it is questionable whether the results justified the cost in men, resources, and time expended.[1]

The use of paratroops on Noemfoor Island, where they landed on engineer equipment already landed by sea, hardly was necessary. Neither can it be said conclusively that the spectacular airborne assault across the Rhine added materially to the speed or effectiveness of the ground advance north of the Ruhr. The advances south of the Ruhr, without airborne support, were as rapid and less costly in resources. It may be that the parachute drop on Corregidor was the factor contributing most to the relatively low ratio of American to Japanese casualties in the retaking of "The Rock." But the airborne training and equipment of the Eleventh Airborne Division appears to have been mostly wasted, for airborne operations contributed little to the reconquest of the Philippines, and that division generally was committed to combat as an ordinary infantry division. This was a costly practice, for specially-trained parachutists had to replace those of the parachute units who became casualties in such actions.

Airborne operations seemed too frequently to bear the appearance of an expensive luxury – of something which created an impressive display, but which really was not essential to the task at hand. But if that were so, maybe it was because higher commanders failed to approach the use of airborne troops in any other manner. When a commander would agree to airborne operations only after it had been made clear that they would not create demands for resources from ground or other air actions, and as long as a commander expressed a desire to launch a major strategic airborne operation, but never could spare the divisions, the airborne effort hardly could escape the appearance of a military luxury. A difference in emphasis which, on the other hand, would have regarded the use of airborne troops as essential might have made it so. An approach which would have insisted upon the resources necessary for strategic airborne operations even at the expense of supply by air for ground troops and for strategic air forces might have seized upon an instrument which would have been far more effective in achieving ultimate military victory.

An important contribution of airborne forces, beyond any actual use ever made of them, it must be noted, was the strategic threat and consequent strain on enemy dispositions which they created by their presence in a theater. In this regard they were more valuable when out of action than when in action – another consideration which should have weighed heavily against prolonged commitment in an ordinary ground role.

Airborne experience in World War II really was not broad enough to furnish final answers as to how important a role parachute and glider troops might play. While the decisive influence of airborne troops in any major operation may be seriously questioned, the distinct possibility remains that, used with more imagination, more boldness, and greater skill, airborne troops might have been completely decisive in bringing military victory sooner at less cost in manpower, time, resources, and casualties.

Airborne Doctrine

When the introduction of parachute troops into the U.S. Army first was being seriously discussed, a general supposition seemed to be that such troops would be used principally in small detachments for demolition work in enemy rear areas. That notion very soon gave way to a conception that parachute troops should be used as a spearhead to seize airfields for airlanding troops. Neither assumption ever became the basis for actual major operations in World War II.

Actual operations did follow rather closely, however, the statements of doctrine published in War Department Training Circular 113, 9 October 1943. At that time only the experiences of airborne landings in North Africa, Sicily, Italy, and New Guinea, together with the examples of German operations, were at hand to form the basis for those generalizations. Yet airborne commanders generally considered the principles then stated as basically sound throughout the war. But practice frequently was at variance with stated doctrine, and experience suggested certain modifications and extensions.

American airborne operations in World War II provided examples for over half of the suggested missions outlined in War Department Training Circular 113, and the missions of the operations might be interpreted as covering several of those suggested. Thus the air invasion of Holland put into practice on a large scale the first suggested mission, "To seize, hold or otherwise exploit important tactical localities in conjunction with or pending the arrival of other naval or military forces," when airborne troops seized vital bridges pending the arrival of the Guards Armored Division. The second stated mission was: "To attack the enemy rear and assist the break-through or landing by the main force" – and the airborne landings in Normandy and east of the Rhine applied that statement. A third mission stated for airborne troops was: "To block or delay enemy reserves by capturing and holding critical terrain features, thereby isolating the immediate battlefield"; something of this was in the Normandy operation, but the Sicilian and Southern France operations probably are the best examples. At Salerno paratroops fulfilled the suggested mission, "To reinforce threatened or surrounded units." For the mission, "To seize islands or areas which are not strongly held and which the enemy cannot easily reinforce," Corregidor was the best American example, though that operation was closely coordinated with a sea landing force.(The German invasion of Crete remained the classic example.) Finally, airborne troops doubtless were useful "As a constant threat by their mere presence in the theater of operations, thereby causing the enemy to disperse his forces over a wide area in order to protect his vital installations." General Student, the German parachute commander, stated after the war that the very existence of airborne units within the Allied armies was an important factor for German leaders to consider, for it compelled them to hold out large reserves on all fronts in order to cope with the anticipated use of those forces. This single factor, he said, figured greatly in destroying flexibility in committing German units.[2]

To suggest that airborne operations generally had missions following accepted statements of doctrine does not, of course, mean that those missions were necessarily the best use for airborne troops. Other missions stated in the same circular, but neglected in combat, might have been far more effective, and others not mentioned in the circular might have been equally useful. Missions stated for airborne troops in the training circular included five others: (1) to capture enemy airfields; (2) to capture or destroy vital enemy installations and thus paralyze the enemy's system of command, communication, and supply; (3) to create diversions; (4) to assist the tactical air forces in delaying retreating enemy forces until the main ground forces could destroy them, and (5) to create confusion and disorder among hostile military and civil personnel.

In spite of repeated statements and the almost invariable assumption in maneuvers that enemy airfields should be major objectives for airborne attack, it almost never was so in actual operations. After the Holland operation the aviation engineer officer set down his views that an airfield should be among the primary objectives in any airborne operation – "They should not be relegated to secondary priority behind bridges, cities, or any other priorities, because without an airfield it may not be possible to hold primary ground objectives until the link-up with ground troops."[3] Why others did not accept that view is not clear. Perhaps it was because airborne troops in Europe always were used in conjunction with a ground attack planned for an early link-up, as well as the likelihood of strong antiaircraft defenses around an airfield. However that may be, Mitkyina airfield in Burma, while not captured by air assault, proved its critical value in permitting reinforcement and resupply of ground troops by airlanding operations. The use of airborne troops to seize airfields ahead of the racing ground armies in western Europe might have made possible much greater use of supply by air to keep those armies going. Paratroops did seize an airfield at Nadzab, New Guinea.

About the only example in World War II where airborne troops were used to paralyze the enemy's system of command, communication, and supply, to create diversions, and to create confusion and disorder deep in enemy rear areas, was the glider landing of General Wingate's long-range penetration columns in Burma. In this case the troop carrier aircraft were mostly American but the troops were British and Indian. Similar objectives might have been appropriate to Europe and North Africa, but there was an important difference. Because of the jungle in Burma it was difficult for the enemy to move reinforcements into the area where troops were landed and the threat of armored counterattack was not great. Quite the contrary was true, of course, in Europe, but that disadvantage might have been overcome through the skillful use of tactical aviation to isolate the battlefield and to provide close ground support. The scattered drop near Avellino, in Italy, had little effect.

Though the opportunity certainly presented itself several times in Europe, airborne troops never were used to block retreating enemy forces until the main ground forces could destroy them. It is possible that the drop of two or three airborne divisions between Falaise and Argentan about 12 August 1944 could have closed the escape route of the Germans in the pocket there and so brought about their complete annihilation. The First Allied Airborne Army was in fact at that time planning operations with similar objectives in view. On 13 August airborne units moved to departure fields for Operation Transfigure whose object was to block the German retreat through the Paris-Orleans gap. Apparently General Eisenhower was reluctant to launch the airborne attack because of the heavy demands for ground transport which he feared would be increased thereby.[4] Then "the capture of Dreux rendered the projected airborne operation in the Paris-Orleans gap unnecessary."[5] If the seizure of a particular piece of ground was the primary objective of that offensive, then of course the airborne attack was not necessary. But if a battle of annihilation were being sought, then an airborne operation might have been the very instrument to bring it about. Successive airborne operations were planned and mounted almost to the point of take-off, and then cancelled because the ground troops had overrun the proposed objective. That could only have meant that objectives were not being selected deep enough in enemy-held territory, or that airborne operations were not being mounted swiftly enough. Truly enough, ground forces were overrunning proposed airborne objectives, but they were only extending their lines of communications; they were not destroying completely the enemy's forces, and enemy troops were escaping eastward where one day they would turn and fight bitterly along the Moselle River and in the Siegfried Line. In those circumstances, airborne troops held out as a "strategic threat" could have little real effect.

Though not included in Training Circular 113, but always in the background of airborne thought, was the possible use of airborne forces to win strategic objectives – to seize and maintain an airhead from which an offensive could be launched without immediate ground support. Something of that concept entered into most of the airborne maneuver problems – the seizure of an airfield by paratroops, the build-up by glider and airlanding, and the launching of a ground attack – though there it generally had been presumed that a link-up with ground troops should not be delayed longer than three days. The nearest that any operations ever came to that conception was the Nadzab-Markham Valley operation in New Guinea, but there reinforcements and heavy equipment could move in overland, and the operation was not on the scale which some officers visualized for Europe. The Burma operations implied something of this concept on a small scale. Leaders thinking in bigger terms, however, always were disappointed. General Arnold and General Marshall both were anxious to try such an operation at the time of the invasion of Normandy. General Arnold wrote:

> It was obvious that General Eisenhower's staff had no intention of using airborne troops except for tactical missions directly in rear of enemy lines. The Air Force wanted to use these troops strategically, i.e., take a mass – four or five divisions – drop them down in a specially selected transportation center, for example – an area where there were several aviation fields, a locality that would be astride the German lines of communication, a position, the holding of which would make it impossible for the German troops to advance reinforcements and supplies, but definitely an area some distance behind the actual battlefield and beyond the area in which reserves were normally located.[6]

General Marshall stated in his letter to General Eisenhower of 10 February 1944 that if he (Marshall) were in command of Operation Overlord, this is exactly the sort of thing he would do. The eyes of General Eisenhower and his staff, however, were fixed on the need to protect the landings on Utah Beach in order to get the port of Cherbourg as quickly as possible; moreover airborne commanders were apprehensive about an armored counterattack against an airhead. To the first objection it could be replied that a port would have been less necessary if supplies were going in by air. (As it actually turned out Cherbourg did not fall until 27 June 1944, two weeks behind schedule, and then it was so thoroughly wrecked that it took another three weeks to get it into operation.[7])

The threat of armored counterattack was a serious one; again, antitank defense would have depended upon effective tactical air support and upon antitank guns which could have been airlanded. But the immediate danger of counterattack might have been much less in such an operation, far behind enemy reserves, than it was in the actual operation which came down in the very midst of enemy reserves.

Whether the maintenance of such an airhead would have been sound logistically is another moot question. On a tonnage basis it probably could be shown that it was possible, but of course transportation by air is not simply a matter of total tonnage. The difficulty of moving heavy, bulky equipment must be taken into account. Solutions to some of those problems had been demonstrated in New Guinea where transport planes and heavy bombers had carried 2½-ton trucks, 105-mm. howitzers, and tractors. In the actual airborne operation in Normandy 17,400 troops landed. On D plus 1 about 250 tons of supplies were dropped to the Eighty-second Airborne Division.[8] Presumably this performance could have been repeated for several days, and certainly the resupply missions would have been much more effective had the material been landed at adequate airfields instead of parachuted. That sufficient airlift was available was evident in the report that British and American heavy bombers on D Day dropped no less than 10,395 tons of bombs.[9]* During the month of May 1944 bombers of the RAF and the AAF dropped approximately 190,000 tons of bombs.[10] In his reply to General Marshall (19 February 1944) General Eisenhower noted that a greatly increased force to support and maintain airborne operations would have been available if all-out strategic and tactical bombing were not being planned. It seems, then, that the establishment of an independent airhead in France might have been made logistically feasible by diverting available heavy bombers to its support. Had such an operation been assumed in the early planning for Overlord it might have had further assurance of success if: (1) the C-97 ("Stratocruiser") had been assigned as high a priority in production as its bomber equivalent, the B-29; (2) four-engined C-54's had been made available to the Troop Carrier Commands as well as to the Air Transport Command (in numbers equal to those, say, of the postwar Berlin airlift); (3) some of the materials and labor which went into the more than 5,000 ships plus 4,000 additional "ship-to-shore" craft used for the amphibious assault had gone into the production of more transport aircraft; (4) the heavy bombers had carried cargo tonnage equal to a large percentage of the bomb tonnage which they carried; (5) tactical air support had been perfected to the point where it could protect the airhead against counterattack and replace heavy artillery for the ground offensives.

The Market operation in Holland suggested some of the possibilities, and the plans for Operation Arena – the operation which would have established such an airhead east of the Ruhr – were based largely on that experience. (Arena assumed a daily requirement of 300 tons for each division.) In Operation Varsity, across the Rhine, aircraft and gliders in one

* During late August, September, and October 1944, the U.S. First and Third Armies were almost entirely dependent on supplies delivered by trucks of the Red Ball Express. On its peak day this truck service carried 12,000 tons. It averaged less than 6,000 tons a day during September and October when it was the principal means of delivering supplies. *Logistics in World War II*, p. 161.

When the "blockade" of Berlin was imposed in the summer of 1948, American forces in Germany had only 100 C-47 transport and troop carrier aircraft. Soon four-engined C-54's (used extensively in World War II by the Air Transport Command) replaced the C-47's; 160 of the larger craft were ear-marked for the Berlin airlift by late 1947, and in 1948 the total allocated was 224. But these planes, with some British support, were able to carry a daily average of 5,500 tons during the winter weather of January and February and in the spring they reached an average of 8,000 tons a day. Their record day's haul was 13,000 tons. Lucius D. Clay, *Decision in Germany* (Garden City, N.Y., 1950) pp. 365, 380-91.

day dropped 22,341 troops, 2,390 tons of supplies, 1,096 vehicles, 454 artillery weapons, and 390 gallons of gasoline. A board of officers convened by Army Ground Forces in 1945 to study the equipment of the postwar Army made its recommendations for airborne and troop carrier equipment on the premise that operations from an airhead as planned for Operation Arena would be normal procedure in the future. The board agreed that airborne operations of the future, when executed on a major scale, should consist of four phases as follows:

> Phase I – In this phase airborne troops should be utilized to seize and secure an airhead, and prepare it for Phase II of the operation . . . .
>
> Phase II – In this phase, the transporting of any divisions started in Phase I should be completed and in addition standard ground divisions should be landed by cargo plane and glider for the purpose of expanding and further developing the airhead and objectives secured in Phase I . . . .
>
> Phase III – In the final operational phase, corps and army units should be landed for the completion of the combat mission, final objectives secured, and the airborne phase of the operation closed out . . . .
>
> Phase IV – This is the supply phase of the operation and is continuous throughout the mission or until such time as adequate supply through more economical channels can be established and maintained.[11]

Airborne officers foresaw the development of aircraft which, together with the development of devastating explosives, would make possible the movement of airborne and air-transported troops to points far within enemy territory, behind his reserves and within his industrial districts.

> This will place airborne and air transported operations on a par with the amphibious operations of the present. Air transported troops will be moved from one protected "Air Harbor" to the equivalent of a beachhead within enemy territory – not in front of the enemy lines, but well behind them. In operations of this sort, the strictly airborne troops will enter the landing area by parachute and glider as a spearhead to prepare the way and secure the landing area for regular infantry divisions being transported to fields within the area by plane. As the Air Forces are now working on the development of planes capable of transporting tanks, the possibility of such operations is not far in the future.[12]

Whether those new transport planes would enjoy any higher production priority in competition with long-range bombers than had the C-82 or the C-54 in World War II was, of course, another question.

Another possible tactical use of airborne troops which later won official recognition though it never had been attempted in combat was to counter enemy airborne attacks by landing on top of the enemy airborne forces. British paratroops had landed on German parachute reinforcements which had just arrived in Sicily, but the results are obscure. Surely that kind of an operation on a big scale would lead to a wild melee, but perhaps it could disrupt an enemy airborne attack. German specialists in airborne tactics adhered to the theory, again without practical experience, that the best defense against an airlanding was a counterlanding into the enemy airhead.[13] It may be that just as it developed that the best defense against aircraft were other aircraft, or more slowly the recognition that the best defense against tanks were other tanks, so it will develop that the best defense against airborne operations are counter airborne operations in the same area. Serious objections must be noted, however: ordinarily an airborne attack was not launched without almost complete air superiority, and it would be very difficult to launch a counter-landing against an enemy who retained mastery of the air. Another difficulty would be the time necessary to plan, coordinate, and mount an airborne counterattack when, to be most effective, it should come immediately after enemy troops have landed.

This does, however, suggest another possible use of airborne troops: that is to counterattack against an enemy ground offensive. An airborne drop astride the enemy's communications when he is disposed to attack might foil his operation and turn the tide of battle. The action of the 101st Airborne Division at Bastogne, though the division had moved in overland, was similar to what it might have been had the division landed there by parachute and glider after the German offensive had passed well beyond Bastogne, That is, it was similar with this important difference: the tanks which supported the Bastogne garrison could not have gone in by air. Airborne commanders felt that the troops of the Eighty-second Airborne Division who dropped to reinforce the Salerno beachhead would have been much more effective had they dropped behind the enemy lines instead of within the friendly positions.

Experience brought a great many changes in the techniques of employing airborne troops. Early in the war in North Africa and Europe daylight operations were avoided. The presumption was that disastrous losses from antiaircraft fire could be avoided only at night. The unfortunate episode of Sicily demonstrated that sometimes friendly antiaircraft fire could not be avoided even then. The price paid for caution was widely scattered drops in North Africa, in Italy (Avellino), and in Normandy. Ironically, the disappointing Sicilian operation led to new emphasis on night operations in all the big joint maneuvers which followed it for the Eleventh, Seventeenth, and Thirteenth Airborne Divisions – and then not one of those units ever participated in a night combat jump. By the time of the air invasion of Holland, airborne officers had become persuaded that the advantages of daylight operations, at least in the situation then obtaining, would outweigh the disadvantages. If antiaircraft batteries were controlled by radar, darkness would offer little protection against them. On the other hand flights of friendly fighters and dive bombers probably would be more effective in beating down flak in daylight. At the same time the German night fighter force in northwest Europe in September 1944 posed more of a threat than did daylight interceptions. Again escorting fighters could be more effective in daylight. Above all the problems of navigation, of keeping troop carriers in formation, and of the troops' assembling on thee ground were far simpler in daylight than in darkness. The success of the landings in Holland, in sharp contrast to the scattering of earlier operations, was such a convincing demonstration that no further night operations were attempted. The Varsity operation east of the Rhine was another notable success in daylight.

American experience with glider troops was so disappointing that Army Ground Forces, in its study of airborne forces for the postwar military establishment prepared after consultation with airborne officers in all theaters, concluded that gliders should be used only for the transportation of cargo. This was a decided change from the earlier concept that the greater portion of an airborne division should be gliderborne. The change was based upon several factors: the vulnerability of gliders to antiaircraft and ground fire resulting in a higher percentage of casualties to glider troops than to parachute troops before and immediately after landing, the need for open fields for glider landings, the great amount of air space taken up by glider formations, and the expense of using gliders which could be used only once in most operations and not often recovered intact.[14] One reason that glider troops suffered heavier casualties than paratroops, in the cases where that was so, may have been in the fallacy of the American principle that paratroops should always precede glider troops by enough time to clear the landing zones for the gliders. Instead of preparing the way for easier glider landings, such parachute drops were likely to alert the enemy defenses in time to become effective against the gliders. In a successful airborne operation, the safest place in the column generally was near the head, where the first elements could jump with the benefit of surprise. Doubtless impressed by the German glider assaults at Fort Eben Emael, in Belgium, at Corinth, and particularly on Crete, the British liked to send glider serials in ahead of, or at the same time as, the parachute serials. But the British glider assault on Sicily fared no better than the American parachute drop, though it might have if airplane and glider pilots had been better trained. The advantage of gliders (aside from their use to deliver heavy equipment) was that they landed whole units in one place where they could open fire in a matter of seconds. Skilled glider pilots could guide their craft to a pin-point target with much greater precision than parachutists could influence their own descent. The advantage of parachute troops was that a much greater number could be delivered in a much shorter time. This would suggest a flexible rule: that in some situations gliders should be preferred, and in others parachute drops would be better.

The need for open fields for glider landing zones imposed another limitation on gliders. This difficulty had become evident in planning for the Normandy operation. The experiences of the Eighty-second Airborne Division in Normandy when the Raff Force was unable to clear the landing zone before the glider serials arrived on the evening of D Day, and in Holland where gliders landed while German forces had the landing zone under fire might have indicated the desirability of selecting alternate landing zones in advance. War Department Training Circular 113 had included this rule, and its observance might have made those unfortunate experiences unnecessary.

The matter of timing and coordination was most important in airborne operations contemplating an early link-up with a surface attack. In most operations of this kind in World War II the airborne attack preceded the amphibious landing or the ground attack by several hours. Presumably this was to engage the enemy reserves and thus facilitate the surface operation. German appraisals after the Holland operation suggested, however, that that attempt might have been completely successful if the ground attack had been launched in advance to draw reserves from the critical areas which were the airborne objectives. General Dempsey insisted upon this pattern for the crossing of the Rhine. There the airborne assault came several hours after the river crossing. The results were completely successful, but the situation there was such that any well-planned and well-executed airborne attack probably would have been successful regardless of the time at which it was launched, and there was not the same concern there for seizing bridges intact before the enemy had a chance to destroy them.

Pathfinders unquestionably proved their worth at Salerno, in Normandy, and in the daylight operations in Holland and across the Rhine as well. In the Corregidor operation drop control was exercised from an airplane flying above the drop zone and the troop carrier formations. This procedure, however, did not prove to be as effective as the pathfinder technique and control from the ground.[15]

Air supply procedures in early operations left much to be desired, and any operation such as that planned for Arena would have strained the supply organizations existing near the end of the war. Experience of the IX Troop Carrier Command through November 1944 recommended the following: Resupply missions for an airborne operation should not be left on an"on-call" basis, but should be planned and scheduled to meet the maximum requirements of the division. These supplies should be packed and distributed to departure fields before the operation, and a reserve of empacked supplies, parachutes, and containers should be available. An air supply depot should be established in each wing area to receive and package the supplies. Adequate loading teams would have to be organized to load the aircraft and to accompany the planes to eject the bundles. Close coordination with tactical air forces for the use of forward delivery airfields was necessary, and front line control for incoming aircraft was needed. Plans should include possible use of fighter-bombers for emergency deliveries. Other recommendations were for an allocations and priority organization under the supreme commander, for plans for airfields for non-tactical supply operations, and for improvements in the aircraft to carry greater loads.[16]

Yet undetermined was the kind of logistical organization which should handle supplies in a big-scale airhead. The United States had developed no equivalent of the British Airborne Forward Delivery Airfield Group, but even that organization could hardly have handled supplies for a large airhead. Something equivalent to port battalions and other communications zone organizations would have been needed for that kind of an operation.

Actually many questions on the principles to govern the employment of airborne troops had to be left only partially answered. In spite of an impressive listing of airborne operations in World War II, airborne experience was insufficient to give conclusive answers to many fundamental questions. Efforts to arrive at sound principles on the basis of one or two, or even *no* experiences, are bound to be strained. Frequent reference to such and such an operation as "proof" of a particular generalization more than likely reflected a preconceived notion seeking justification – which idea might have been sound enough in itself though the quality of its factual proof might be doubted. At the same time, many principles should have been so obvious as to make unnecessary learning the hard way. Flexibility usually seems a safer rule in military affairs than hard and fast principles. This becomes especially true when new means of warfare are being considered. Too firm attachment to previously stated concepts may lead to a dogmation which denies to the full exploitation of all possibilities in new methods. Getting the maximum force on the ground in a minimum of time was a well-established principle of airborne operations. Special conditions on Corregidor, however, made it necessary to violate that principle in having troop carriers make several passes over the target area so that paratroops could hit the tiny drop zone.

Even the hallowed Principles of War deserve fresh consideration from time to time. The principle of mass, for example, nearly always appeared in official statements of doctrine – airborne troops should be employed in mass. Yet the Sicilian and Normandy operations were successful even though the drops were scattered. In fact they may have been successful in part because they were scattered. When airborne troops were to be used against immediate defense areas it may have been better to have them scattered than concentrated where effective counterattacks might have sought them out. Or it is conceivable that an airborne division assigned the missions of destroying enemy communication and supply installations, or creating confusion and disorder in enemy rear areas might accomplish the task well by scattered drops. The loosing of 243 well-trained, skillfully-led squads as separate patrols over a widespread area to cut wires, destroy bridges, disrupt railways, destroy communication centers, and plunder supply depots, might create havoc in enemy rear areas before the troops should infiltrate back to friendly lines.

Another of the Principles of War is the principle of simplicity. Strict adherence to that maxim would rule out all major airborne operations. Their complexity is one of their distinguishing characteristics. If a commander is disposed to choose always the more simple over the more complex plan, he will nearly always choose a ground attack. But if he seeks decisive results, then the extra effort needed to overcome the complexities of mounting an airborne attack may be more than worthwhile.

It may be a violation of the principle of economy of force to have highly trained and expensively equipped troops, like those which make up airborne and troop carrier units, remain idle. Yet airborne forces filled two important functions even when they were idle. First of all they constituted a strategic threat. Unquestionably this weakened enemy troop dispositions.[17] Indeed the German commanders almost gave a "sigh of relief" when the airborne troops were committed in Holland – though then they were uneasy about the Seventeenth Airborne Division – and again in the Ardennes when they learned the Eighty-second, 101st, and Seventeenth Airborne Divisions were being committed on the ground. Secondly, airborne troops held out of action formed an effective strategic reserve to meet emergencies. The best kind of reserve was one made up of excellent troops and one which could be committed quickly to battle in any sector. Airborne divisions filled those requirements admirably. They could be training and preparing for future operations and yet be committed on short notice anywhere in the theater. Committed to action, they could have a decisive influence. The parachute reinforcement of the Salerno beachhead and the air movement of the Seventeenth Airborne Division to the Continent during the Battle of the Bulge indicated the advantages of airborne troops for such emergencies. The airborne divisions which were in SHAEF reserve at the time of the German counteroffensive in the

Ardennes had an important influence on the outcome of that operation. The question can be raised whether any effective theater reserve would have been available had not those units been airborne and thus had a special plea for release from continuous ground action.

Organization and Control

Organization of airborne units usually was based first upon the limitations of air transportation and secondly upon the ground roles which the units should be expected to fill. As organized originally the parachute infantry rifle platoon had only two rifle squads – each equipped with a light machine gun – and a 60-mm. mortar squad. No doubt the lack of a third rifle squad and the addition of the machine guns and mortars were due to an attempt to keep the platoon small for air transportation and yet provide it with its own weapons so that in a parachute drop it would not have to rely on the uncertain proximity of a separate weapons platoon. Later the organization of the glider infantry regiment had only two battalions.

The disregard of standard American tactical doctrine which was based upon a triangular organization in the small unit made it necessary for commanders either to improvise new tactics or new units. Army Ground Forces had insisted that airborne troops should fight as other infantry units – that air was simply another means of transportation to the battlefield. But this disparity in organization between airborne units and standard units, and the lack of consistency between parachute and glider organization made the application of any uniform tactical doctrine extremely difficult. It doubtless would have been better to have fewer parachute units and fewer glider units, but have them organized along standard triangular lines than to have many units with such apparently incomplete organization. This was the position of airborne commanders after combat experience. Shortcomings in organization surely were obvious from the start, but not until they had been "proved" repeatedly in combat were modifications forthcoming.

These same tendencies appeared in the organization of the airborne division. At first, airborne thinking included no place for the airborne division as such. On the contrary the assumption was that parachute regiments could be attached to standard infantry divisions in any airborne operations employing units of that size. Then noting the German organization of parachute divisions and the implications of the capture of Crete as well as British experience in the organization of airborne divisions which included both parachute and glider troops, Army Ground Forces accepted the idea of the airborne division as a distinct type of organization to be specially trained and equipped. Again the emphasis was upon keeping the size and equipment down in conformity with requirements for air transportation.

But General McNair's dictum that the airborne division "should be evolved with a stinginess in overhead and in transportation which has absolutely no counterpart thus far in our military organization"[18] imposed severe limitations on the activities of those divisions. The lack of transportation, for example, posed a continuous, irritating problem in moving troops to training areas and in meeting administrative problems. As of October 1943, the airborne division had a total of 415 motor vehicles – mostly jeeps. It had eighty-two 2½-ton trucks, and twenty-two 3¼-ton trucks. The standard infantry division, of course, was considerably larger (14,248 officers and men compared to 8,520 for the airborne division), but its proportion of motor vehicles, including 386 2½-ton trucks, 107 1½-ton trucks, and 22 4-ton trucks was much greater. Thus it was necessary for airborne units to borrow trucks, or for special truck units to be attached, in order to carry out their training missions, their administrative tasks, and support for combat action. The limitation on transportation apparently was based on the assumption that airborne divisions would be relieved from combat within three to five days after being committed. This never did prove to be the case. The consideration of air transportability was not necessarily a valid one in restricting so severely the assignment of 2½-ton trucks. More nearly adequate numbers of heavy trucks not only would have contributed much to making the best use of training time and to permit supply while in garrison or training areas, but such organic transportation might have been invaluable in moving supplies to airfields for resupply missions in airborne operations and for addition to the divisions' seaborne tails when units were committed to sustained ground action as standard infantry divisions. The normal attachment of additional parachute units to the Eighty-second and 101st Airborne Divisions meant an even greater strain on the authorized transportation of these divisions.

The lack of a reconnaissance platoon, of enough military police, of a satisfactory parachute maintenance organization, and signal facilities led division commanders to improvise more adequate organizations. The fact that actual organization bore little resemblance to the official table of organization was something of an indication of the inadequacies of the latter. Difficult enough in any military organization, the question of which overhead personnel really were essential was especially troublesome in the airborne division. Perhaps the "stinginess in overhead and transportation" was over-emphasized. Sometimes reduction in size of an organization is equated to "streamlining," and the illusion of a "streamlined division, trimmed down for high mobility but with tremendous fire power for hard-hitting action" attracts adherents seeking to show the greatest results for efforts applied. Actually streamlining carried to the point that it was in the airborne division may render the organization relatively ineffective. It may be better to have only three battalions, but have them under control through good communications, supplied with adequate transportation, and operating with the benefit of sufficient reconnaissance than to have nine battalions without control and without effective reconnaissance and support. On the other hand, it may have been General McNair's view that it would be much easier to add to an organization than to subtract from it, and that needs should be clearly demonstrated before granted – that the more prudent course would be to err on the side of thrift in the initial organization.

Why British practice was not followed in the parachute-glider ratio in the airborne division is not clear. Apparently the American organization was predicated on the concept of using parachute troops as an "arrowhead" to prepare the way for glider landings, and General McNair could find no reasoning behind the British organization (two parachute brigades and one glider brigade) to justify a change. But no American division ever went into combat with one-parachute, two-glider regiments organization. The change in ratio of parachute and glider units in the Eighty-second Airborne Division when it moved overseas apparently was due as much to the need for conserving shipping space as to any change in concept, for other divisions retained the old organization. The advantages of parachute troops over glider troops in getting a maximum number of men on the ground in a minimum of time and the smaller number of aircraft and the shorter troop carrier columns needed for parachute troops impressed airborne planners. The Eighty-second and 101st Airborne Divisions each had an organization amounting to three parachute regiments and one glider regiment for both the Normandy and the Holland operations. Recommendations for permanent reorganization were made after each operation, and in December 1944 the War Department authorized the two-parachute, one-glider unit structure for the divisions in the European theater. They reorganized in the spring of 1945. The Eleventh Airborne Division, in the Pacific, had approached the problem in a different way. It had trained some of its glider troops as parachutists and reorganized the units as para-glider units. This approach was recommended for the postwar organization. Replying to the War Department questionnaire on the postwar military establishment, Army Ground Forces recommended that all personnel in the airborne division be trained both in parachute jumping and glider operation.[19]

Serious doubts concerning the value of airborne divisions arose after the Sicilian operation. In the background the earlier concept of organizing special task forces around smaller airborne units for each operation persisted. In the Pacific no airborne operations involved the use of airborne units larger than a regimental combat team. The operation which most nearly fitted the concept of a special task force on a larger scale was the invasion of southern France when the First Airborne Task Force was organized for the mission out of a number of separate units. That force functioned well, but it faced problems of coordination greater than those which an airborne division usually encountered. Again, officers studying the problem for Army Ground Forces recommended that the airborne division be retained. Suggesting that experience had shown only a limited need for small airborne units, such as in the taking of Corregidor, and pointing to the experience of the Marine Corps in organizing small parachute units (which were disbanded without ever being used), Army Ground Forces concluded that task forces should be taken from airborne divisions for small-scale operations. Moreover separate units were considered administrative "orphans" which added unnecessary problems to airborne organization.[20]

A special problem of organization was that of the glider pilots. This was another question which received the repeated attention of airborne commanders. The commanders of the Eighty-second and 101st Airborne Divisions recommended, after the Holland operation, that glider pilots be assigned to the airborne divisions. British practice was to organize glider pilots as ground troops, but American organization left them to the Air Forces. If air training was more important than ground action for glider pilots, perhaps there was merit in leaving their training and their control an Air Forces responsibility. If their ground combat role was considered essential, perhaps it would have been well to assign them to the divisions.

Overall control of the airborne program was the subject of some rivalry from its inception. The chief of infantry, the chief of engineers, and the chief of the Air Corps each could find compelling reasons why his branch ought to control the new development. The infantry won the assignment, but soon it was apparent that other branches were going to be involved as well as the Air Corps which would have to furnish the air transport. The reorganization of the War Department in 1942 brought the program under the aegis of Army Ground Forces. Recognizing the need for a coordinating and directing agency, AGF then set up the Airborne Command to perform those functions. The Army Air Forces for its part organized a troop carrier command to cooperate with the Airborne Command in airborne training. Overall direction remained in the hands of the War Department.

Culmination of organization at the top level – at a level which would bring under a single command both airborne and troop carrier units – was the activation of the First Allied Airborne Army in August 1944. Originally conceived as much to bring various Allied units under a unified command, the inclusion of all troop carrier and airborne units made possible a coordination in planning and execution never before possible.

As the war drew to a close there were suggestions that this kind of organization should be set up within the United States. Some proposed that an airborne command be set up which would include troop carrier and airborne units; others suggested the creation of an independent airborne forces. On the one hand, some Air Forces officers, for example General Arnold and General Brereton, were thinking that airborne divisions should be made a part of the Air Forces, and, on the other hand, some Ground Forces officers were raising the possibility of including the Troop Carrier Command in Army Ground Forces.[21]

The concept of bringing together airborne and troop carrier forces under an airborne army in the European theater won almost universal approval, but no similar organization ever was effected to supervise airborne and troop carrier training activities within the United States. In his reply to the War Department questionnaire on the postwar military establishment, General Devers, then commanding general of Army Ground Forces, agreed that in wartime a unified command should be established under the theater commander for airborne operations; but "for peacetime training and operations, the Airborne forces should remain under Army Ground Forces control and the Troop Carrier Command under Army Air Forces control."[22]

If unity of command was a sound principle in a theater of operations, it ought also to be a sound principle in the Zone of the Interior. The position of Supreme Headquarters in Europe was analogous to that of the War Department in the United States. Supreme Headquarters found it useful to have an airborne army to exercise control over both airborne and trooper carrier units. The War Department might have found such an agency equally useful. But at the same time, all the shortcomings of War Department coordination could not have been overcome merely by the addition of another headquarters. Too much depended upon policy decisions and strategic planning which were functions of the War Department General Staff.

Inconsistencies in organization and control escape definitive explanation, but certain tendencies can be suggested. Any broad historical generalization is likely to be questioned on the ground of offering too simple an explanation for complex situations. But runnning like a thread through many developments affecting organization and control of the airborne effort is a tendency which undoubtedly governs much in human affairs. Often alluded to but seldom spelled out, it probably goes further to explain proposals and reactions on organization and control than all the studies ever made, all the boards which ever sat, or all the experience ever acquired. It is simply the propensity in men to seek importance. Would the proposal add responsibilities and personnel? Then this headquarters concurs with enthusiasm. Would the proposal curtail activities and personnel? Then this headquarters does not concur, and it marshals impressive data to prove the essentiality of its functions. It seems almost a characteristic of human nature for a person to attach exaggerated importance to things with which he is associated, whether it be his home town, his club, his school, or his branch of military service. Thus identified with something important he builds a secure feeling of self-importance. Even those most anxious to be open-minded are likely to favor policies which would result in greatest enhancement of their own branches or their own organizations. This is not to imply that all suggestions are selfishly made, nor even that those which are selfishly made are necessarily wrong. To some extent there must be a narrowness of viewpoint in all men, depending upon limitations in experience as well as in understanding. It is to be expected that an experienced airman will think primarily in terms of how air power can best contribute to the war effort, or that an infantryman may see only the indispensability of the infantry. The impartial, fair-minded man who is personally unaffected by a series of proposals and counter-proposals may demand something of a compromise. Compromise appeals to a sense of fair play and to the desirability of escaping controversy, but that does not necessarily make compromise the best solution. Indeed compromise in military affairs may be the worst possible course.

A quest for importance, then, seems to loom in the background of many developments in the organization and control of airborne forces as well as the merits of the case being considered. Infantrymen, engineers, and airmen could see reasons for control of parachute troops by their own branch, but few officers proposed that the program be assigned to some branch other than their own. Officers associated with the Airborne Command applauded its growth, but they were strongly opposed to its reduction to an airborne center and to the transfer of the Parachute School to the Replacement and School Command. When the question of a unified airborne command arose in Europe, officers of the Allied Expeditionary Air Force supported the move enthusiastically until they found that it was planned to transfer control of troop carrier aviation from AEAF to the new headquarters; the Ninth Air Force agreed that troop carrier and airborne units should be brought under unified command, but it went further: supporting tactical aviation also should be included – all under command of the Ninth Air Force; First U.S. Army Group (FUSAG) agreed that a higher airborne headquarters was necessary, but felt that it should be limited to the organization of U.S. Airborne Corps which would remain under FUSAG. Similar reactions greeted proposals for setting up a similar organization for the post-war establishment in the United States. A number of Ground Forces officers proposed that troop carrier aviation be made organic to the Ground Forces. Several Air Forces officers proposed that airborne troops be made organic to the Air Forces. Practically in no case did an Air Forces officer propose Ground Forces control or vice versa. Proposals for a separate airborne army or airborne forces directly under the War Department won the approval of some, but Army Ground Forces opposed any move which would take the airborne troops from its control, and Army Air Force opposed any move which would take troop carrier aviation from its control. The result was compromise and continuation of the general structure used during World War II in the continental United States.

Appeals for enlargement followed the setting up of almost every new organization from parachute brigades to airborne divisions, and from the Airborne Command to the First Allied Airborne Army. Those appeals undoubtedly were due in part to real inadequacies of organization, but one cannot escape the belief that they were also due in part to the quest for importance on the part of the persons immediately concerned. Indeed some of the organizational shortcomings may have been due to General McNair's recognition of that tendency. In 1943 the commander of Army Ground Forces had written:

> I know of no instance where a commander had recommended a reduction of the means at his disposal – either personnel or material – and of few cases where a commander was satisfied with what he had. Invariably commanders seek more and tend always to make their unit self-contained. It was such proclivities that brought about the present wasteful and unwieldy organization. Commanders do not consider the large picture.[23]

Matters of Policy

It is arguable that hostilities in World War II might have been concluded much sooner had they been conducted with any of several kinds of emphasis. Military victory might have been obtained more quickly by: (1) reducing the airborne effort and diverting its equipment, men, and supplies to the supplying of ground armies by air; or (2) curtailing the production and operation of all troop carrier aircraft to make even more abundant resources available to the bomber offensive. At the same time, it may also be true that total results would have been much better: (1) if commitments of troop carrier aircraft to the delivery of supplies to ground armies had been reduced in favor of greater emphasis on the airborne effort; or (2) if, in view of the disappointing results of strategic bombing,[24] the heavy bomber program had been cut to make available resources for enough transport aircraft to provide adequately for *both* a bigger airborne effort and supply by air to ground armies. Such questions defy conclusive answers, but they need to be considered in any evaluation of the conduct of the war.

Whatever the relative merits of various ways of warfare, the means chosen depended upon high policy decisions and basic assumptions of war leaders. American conduct of World War II apparently was based on the notion that a more or less "balanced force," which recognized several essential means of combat, was desirable. Airborne warfare was made a significant part of that over-all program. But inconsistencies in implementation appeared almost at once. Unless a nation maintains almost permanent mobilization, shortages of equipment are bound to result from the rapid expansion of armed forces to meet a new emergency. This was especially true of the U.S. Army in the early 1940's, and such shortages were bound to be even more evident in new programs, like the airborne, which required such special equipment as airplanes, gliders, and parachutes. At a time when mortars and antitank guns were in short supply, it could not be expected that aircraft and parachutes would be abundant. Moreover an important time lag had to be taken into account between orders and deliveries, and few leaders were thinking seriously in terms of a major airborne program two or three years ahead of its inauguration. Some of the early shortages which handicapped the airborne program, then, could have been expected.

More serious was the chronic persistence of the shortages of troop carrier aircraft. In warfare there is seldom any such thing as "enough" of anything. When priorities are established on the basis that agencies in third or fourth priority will receive their share only after those in first and second priorities have been satisfied, those in the less-favored categories may find little or none of the materials left for them. If policy had determined that certain activities are to play essential parts in the war effort, then the more reasonable course would be to assure to each of those activities the percentage of the equipment or personnel in question which it must have early enough to carry out the assignments planned for it. Some of the difficulty of coordinating troop carrier and airborne requirements was due to the lack of precision in long-range strategic planning. Some of it was the result of poor coordination between G-3 and Operations Division within the War Department General Staff itself. Some of it grew out of lack of coordination between the Army Ground Forces and the Army Air Forces as well as lack of enthusiasm for the new effort within those headquarters. Some of it arose from diverting troop carrier aircraft to other missions.

What might have appeared to be a satisfactory ratio in the activation of troop carrier and airborne units had little meaning in practice when troop carrier units were sent to theaters where no airborne troops were even present. The primary, not the secondary, mission of troop carrier squadrons throughout the Pacific was to haul cargo – to act as tenders for striking air units. Troop carriers were diverted to similar activities in the

Mediterranean and European theaters, but there a more pressing demand was that of supplying ground armies by air. Again it was a matter for major policy decisions on whether troop carrier aircraft should be used mainly for supply by air or for preparing and carrying out airborne operations. In Europe the decision usually was in favor of supply by air missions. The dogma of the "inherent flexibility" of air power was something of a handicap to the airborne effort in two ways: (1) troop carrier units were shifted to tasks for which they were not intended and away from airborne participation; (2) airborne forces never had, in any numbers, aircraft designed specially for airborne operations.

As long as the Army Air Forces was committed to a policy of "proving" the decisive capabilities of strategic bombing, attention to troop carrier needs could not have been more than secondary. General Arnold, truly enough, was an airborne enthusiast. But he was more of a strategic bombardment enthusiast. In his study of recommendations for the postwar establishment, Col. J. J. Ewell (who had commanded a regiment in the 101st Airborne Division) noted: "Troop carrier and airborne are inseparable. Each has many other commitments but in the actual combat operation they must cooperate perfectly. The relatively slow growth of our airborne potentialities in this war has been primarily due to Air Force indifference to troop carrier needs."[25] Whether or not the holding of sizeable troop carrier units out of other activities to be used only for preparing and training for airborne operations would really have been a violation of the principle of economy of force depends somewhat on the point of view. Certainly this would have been of no use when the airborne units remained committed to ground action. Such a policy might have had the appearance of inaction as far as combat was concerned. On the other hand, it might have been just as effective as a policy which massed impressive totals in bomber sorties, hours flown, and tonnage of bombs dropped but which, though carrying the appearance of violent activity, had relatively little effect on enemy war-making capacity until the last months of the war. In addition to contributing a consequential strategic threat, a policy of holding out troop carriers might have permitted a perfection in airborne training and technique which would have rendered airborne operations considerably more effective in breaking the enemy will to resist than were many heavy bomber missions in accomplishing that result.

Policies affecting the troops and their morale grew out of the assumptions adopted for the airborne program. Differences in pay initially between parachute troops and glider troops could only have resulted from overlooking the obvious implications for morale and *esprit de corps.* The low priority of the Troop Carrier Command in the Air Forces led to discrimination against it in the assignment of pilots and communications men and in the withholding of such equipment as self-sealing gasoline tanks for troop carrier aircraft. To fly heavily armed and armored bombers at 300 miles an hour to drop bombs from an altitude of 20,000 feet – that was combat; but to fly an unarmed and unarmored transport at 110 miles an hour to drop men into a battle zone from an altitude of 500 feet – that was not combat. Further morale problems for troop carrier units arose from the idleness of glider pilots caught in training bottlenecks or shipped to the Pacific with no glider missions to fly.

A considerable part of the misfortunes of airborne operations in North Africa, Sicily, Normandy, and Leyte can be attributed to faulty training. In some cases training in the United States may have been adequate, but its effects were lost when the troop carrier units were assigned to cargo-hauling missions for long periods of time. In other cases the shortage of aircraft and the lack of coordination in the United States had left training unsatisfactory when units were sent overseas. General McNair was more interested in seeing airborne divisions trained well for ground combat than in perfecting certain techniques peculiar to airborne operations at the expense of such training, and he had noted a tendency of "trick outfits to over emphasize their tricks." But General Ridgway's comments on the Sicilian operation pointed to deficiencies of the Eighty-second Airborne Division in *airborne training.*

The most important problems of individual training for airborne troops were those concerned with parachute training. All men assigned initially to parachute units received their basic parachute training at the Parachute School. In addition the Parachute School trained all parachute replacements in the Zone of the Interior.[26] In the theaters, however, airborne divisions or training centers set up their own parachute schools in order to qualify certain key personnel as parachutists and in order to overcome shortages in replacements being received from the Parachute School.

The airborne effort was an expensive undertaking. Whether its cost was justified depends upon the importance attached to the results obtained in comparison with the cost and results of such other programs as the strategic bombing offensive or the development of the armored divisions. The initial cost of equipping an airborne division was about the same as that for equipping the much larger infantry division. Added to its cost then were the airplanes and gliders[27] required, the extra resources and time for training, and the extra shipping space needed for overseas movement of airborne and troop carrier units. It took three months to train an airborne division after it had completed ground training, and it took five months, two of which had to be completed before joint training could begin, to train a troop carrier group. Needs for paratroop replacements imposed additional costly burdens on resources for their training. Whether or not the effect of airborne troops in specific operations and their effect on enemy dispositions as a force in being was worth that cost is a matter of judgment. In any case the airborne effort attracted important resources and it left a mark on World War II which cannot be ignored.

Memory usually is kind in dimming some of the most unpleasant recollections of experience, and unattractive accompaniments of war have a way of fading, with the benefit of time and distance, into obscurity. Airborne war thus becomes only the sheer beauty of graceful airliners gliding through the thin clouds of a still, moonlight night, or the glamor of hundreds of silken canopies drifting earthward from sunny, blue skies. But in the mind of a veteran trooper, the sound of roaring engines, the order to "stand up and hook up," the cry of "Geronimo!" or "Bill Lee!" or the feel of prop blast would set to racing through his consciousness deep-seated fears of jumping into the unknown, of facing heavy flak, or the depressing confusion of scattered drops in strange and hostile country, of the thrill of decisive action. And he would know that plans for the future would have to recall the fears and shortcomings as well as the spectacle and the achievement. So would it be for men charged with strategic planning and with the development of airborne doctrine, organization, and policies.

Appendixes

Appendix I

Memorandum of Maj. Gen. Lesley J. McNair, commanding general, Army Ground Forces, for chief of staff, AGF, 19 June 1942, on proposed organization of airborne divisions. (AGF M/S, CG for CofS, 320.2/3 (A/B))

1. I believe that Lee's analysis of the situation (his paragraph 3) is sound. Consequently, we should inaugurate studies without delay looking to the organization of whatever airborne divisions can be formed from one triangular division, plus the available parachute regiments.

2. The following comments are made simply as a result of these studies:

a. It seems that, based on Lee's conception, two glider and one parachute regiments are more logical than one glider and two parachute regiments. The fact we are in process of forming six parachute regiments is beside the point. We might use two or three of them in airborne divisions and the remainder in separate parachute brigades or groups. The airborne division is of the second phase, and comes into the picture after the first phase has been executed. It seems reasonable that the first phase would be executed by fewer troops than the second phase.

b. In my view – not a considered one – the division artillery should consist of a 75-mm. howitzer battalion for each glider infantry regiment, plus a composite battalion composed of a 75-mm. howitzer battery for each parachute regiment, a 37-mm. antitank company (battery), and an antiaircraft battery.

c. Yarborough's engineer battalion is preferred to Lee's company.

d. Yarborough's signal company is preferred, also his quartermaster.

e. I cannot go along with the chemical company or detachment (4.2 mortar). There are sufficient infantry mortars and artillery to handle whatever smoke is needed, to say nothing of the use of smoke candles and airplane smoke screens.

3. An airborne division should be evolved with a stinginess in overhead and in transportation which has absolutely no counterpart thus far in our military organization.

4. Please initiate studies looking toward a program of airborne divisions, along with the development and procurement of suitable equipment. The two phases of the work go hand-in-hand. The preliminary studies should be completed as soon as possible, and in rather general form, sufficient only to present the matter to the War Department sufficiently to secure approval of the necessary initial measures.

L.J.M.

Appendix II

Personal letter, Brig. Gen. Elbridge G. Chapman, commanding general, the Airborne Command, to Brig. Gen. Floyd H. Parks, chief of staff, Army Ground Forces, on reasons for shortages of aircraft for training, 30 December 1942. (excerpt AGF 452.1/11 (A/B))

1. Assignment of troop carrier units to theaters of operations, prior to the dates specified in previously arranged schedules.

2. Use of troop carrier planes required in effecting the movement of these units from training stations to staging areas.

3. The high percentage of airplanes available to Troop Carrier Command required for use by that Command in the training of transport and glider pilots at all of the respective stations.

4. Directives calling for the use of troop carrier planes in connection with other projects; i.e., Amphibious Command, Antiaircraft Command, Desert training Command, etc.

5. The continued employment of the same aircraft by successive units as they rotate through these training centers. Units departing for theaters of operation are furnished with new aircraft and the old aircraft is reassigned to newly activated units here. This results in a greater maintenance requirement and resultant larger number of planes on the "Dead Line," unable to operate, than is normal in the ordinary tactical command.

6. The assignment of Troop Carrier Command units to additional duty with the Army Air Force Flying Training Command at advance glider training stations. Two groups (6 squadrons) are presently assigned to this effort.

Appendix III

Draft memorandum, Army Ground Forces, on status of airborne training, 23 June 43 (excerpts). (CG AGF for CofS USA, sub: Maneuver, 101st A/B Div, 353/2 (101st A/B Div))

Recent experience in a controlled maneuver of the 101st Airborne Division with three troop carrier groups proved conclusively that combined airborne training to date is unsatisfactory. This condition exists due to the lack of sufficient airplanes being made available for airborne maneuvers over a period of time necessary to develop proper command and control measures, especially in the initial landings.

Improvement . . . cannot be obtained without practice on a sufficiently large scale to develop procedure and coordination. Availability of troop carrier groups as indicated in the attached memorandum dated 3 June 1943 from the Commanding General, Army Air Forces, will make this practice impossible for the balance of 1943.

This headquarters considers four groups as a minimum requirement for maneuver training of an airborne division. It has constantly requested that they be made available. The Army Air Forces program of activation and training of troop carrier groups has not been able to provide more than three to date.

Memorandum to headquarters, Army Air Forces, dated 18 May 1943, requested three groups as the minimum requirement in an attempt to reconcile available equipment with training requirements. Results of the Camden maneuver indicated that three groups are insufficient.

Appendix IV

Tabulation of Requirements for Troop Carrier Groups (each of 52 airplanes) – Swing Report, 6 September 1943

Required for:	Groups each month												
	1943				1944								
	S	O	N	D	J	F	M	A	M	J	J	A	S
U.S. Airborne Divs.	8	9	10	13	14	16	16	16	16	17	18	20	20
Other Commitments (e.g., for air cargo)	5	5	5	5	5	5	5	5	5	5	5	5	5
British Airborne Divs.	7	7	7	7	7	7	7	7	7	7	7	7	7
Troop Carrier Tng	2	2	2	2	2	2	2	2	2	2	2	2	2
Replacement Tng (T.C.)	3	3	3	4	4	4	4	4	4	4	4	4	4
Total Requirement	25	26	27	31	34	34	34	34	34	35	36	38	38
Present Schedule	17	20	22	23	25	25	26	27	27	27	27	27	27
Shortage	8	6	5	8	9	9	8	7	7	8	9	11	11

Appendix V

Implementation of Recommendations of Swing Board (AGF 353/17 (A/B))

TABLE II

Swing Board Recommendations:	G-3 Comment or Concurrence	Army Air Forces Comment or Concurrence	Army Ground Forces Comment or Concurrence.	Operations Division Comment and Concurrence	Action taken or Recommendation made
1. That current training doctrine operational procedures and appropriate manuals be amended to incorporate in effect lessons learned from recent Airborne-Troop Carrier operations.	1. Concur.	1. Concur.	1. Concur.	1. Concur and recommend G-3 implement.	1. A new training circular on the employment of Airborne and Troop Carrier Forces has been prepared and forwarded to The Adjutant General for publication WDGCT 300.5 Circular (11 Oct 43), Subject: Training Circular, dated 11 October 1943. Advanced copies have been sent to Army Air Forces and Army Ground Forces with instructions that they be immediately reproduced and distributed to Airborne and Troop Carrier units in the United States the size of a Company or larger. An advanced copy was also sent to each Theater Commander.
2. That Theater Commanders be informed of changes in doctrine indicated in 1 above.	2. Concur.	2. Concur.	2. Concur.	2. Concur and recommend G-3 implement.	2. Implemented in 1 above.
3. That strategical plans be based on maximum use of air transport.	3. Concur.	3. Concur.	3. Concur.	3. Concur and recommend Operations Division implement.	3. Implemented in 1 above.
4. That attached Training directive be issued to Army Air Forces and Army Ground Forces.	4. Concur as emphasized by G-3.	4. Concur as modified by G-3.	4. Concur.	4. Concur and recommend G-3 implement.	4. Training directive issued without change except the addition of remarks emphasizing responsibilities of Army Ground Forces and Army Air Forces.
5. That the troop basis provide: a. 1 Troop Carrier Wing of 4 Troop Carrier groups for each Airborne Division. b. Additional Troop Carrier Units that may be committed to T/O's with other than Airborne Divisions. c. Additional Troop Carrier Units that may be committed to lifting other than American Airborne Divisions. d. Two Troop Carrier groups for Troop Carrier Training. e. 1 replacement training group for each 7½ Troop Carrier groups in Theaters.	5. a. Non-concur, when required, Troop Carrier groups could be flown in a Theater launching Airborne operations by borrowing from adjacent theaters. b. Non-concur. c. Non-concur. d. Non-concur. e. Non-concur.	5. Concur.	5. Believe Troop Carrier strength should be worked out according to specific operations contemplated.	5. Concur and recommend Operations Division implement.	5. a. There being enough Troop Carrier units to train the 11th and 17th Airborne Division, G-3 recommended to Chief of Staff 8 October 1943 that further plans for the employment of additional Airborne units (including the 13th Airborne Division) be so prepared as to permit the training periods necessary and to provide the Troop Carrier units necessary for the employment and training of Airborne units. b. See a above. c. See a above. d. The 10th and 63rd Troop Carrier Groups are now being used for replacement training centers training, and training provided in 4 above sufficient. e. Training being provided in 4 above plus further training received in theaters by Troop Carrier Groups makes this not necessary.

6. That shortages of Troop Carrier groups be corrected by one or more of the following means listed in order of preference: a. Increased activation of Troop Carrier units. b. Production of larger and better Troop Carrier airplanes and gliders. c. Production of commitments to theaters not having Airborne units. d. Reduction of commitments to lift other than Airborne Divisions. e. Reduction in number of Airborne Divisions.	6. a. Not necessary for Airborne Divisions now committed. b. Non-concur. c. Non-concur. d. Concur. e. Up to Operations Division.	6. Concur.	6. Concur	6. Concur and recommend Operations Division implement.	6. a. See 5 a above. b. Not considered possible in time to be used in this war. c. See 5 a above. d. See 5 a above. e. See 5 a above.
7. That 1 troop carrier wing of 4 groups be provided for training in the United States by withholding all troop carrier groups after the 435th group not yet committed.	7. Non-concur.	7. Concur.	7. Concur.	7. Recommend action on recommendation be withheld till views of CG, ETOUSA are obtained.	7. Not necessary in view of 4 and 5 above.
8. That future commitments be in accordance with attached table.	8. Concur as modified by G-3.	8. Concur as modified by G-3.	8. No comment.	8. Same as No. 7 above.	8. Schedule for troop carrier units was issued to Army Air Forces and Army Ground Forces on 24 September 1943 with minor changes approved by General Swing.
9. That Air Corps be responsible for navigational aids and that provision be made in troop carrier. T/O's for personnel to man Rebecca-Eureka.	9. Non-concur.	9. Non-concur.	9. Concur.	9. Concur and recommend Army Air Forces implement.	9. G-3 does not concur in the need of Rebecca-Eureka personnel in the T/O's of troop carrier units as the ground component is dropped with parachutists and simply requires being turned on.
10. That a general officer be assigned as airborne advisor to Commander in Chief of Theater having airborne operations.	10. Non-concur.	10. Concur, except qualified officer rather than general officer.	10. Concur in principle on airborne special staff section necessary in theater headquarters.	10. Concur and recommend Operations Division implement.	10. War Department Circular No. 113 dated 9 October 1943, Employment of Airborne and Troop Carrier Forces, states as a primary principle that plans for the combined employment of airborne and troop Carrier units must be prepared by the Commander in Chief or field Force Commander who controls all participating forces. Therefore this Division believes the Commander in Chief will designate an airborne advisor without any War Department action or recommendation being necessary.
11. That 1 depot Quartermaster Company supply be activated and trained by Airborne Command for each theater having airborne operations.	11. Handled by G-4.	11. Concur on G-4 solution.	11. Have agreed on another solution with G-4 and Army Air Forces.	11. Recommend refer to G-4 for comment.	11. G-4 with G-3, Army Ground Forces and Army Air Forces concurrence has directed Army Air Forces in memorandum dated 12 October 1943 to provide an organization to receive, package and load all classes of supplies to be delivered by air to ground force units, airborne or otherwise.
12. That a P-38 and B-17 unit or other suitable combat units participate in a glider operation to determine its feasibility.	12. Recommend obtaining Army Air Forces comment. Maximum allowable speed of a glider is about minimum speed of a combat plane. Greatest need for combat aircraft for combat will be during airborne operations.	12. Concur but doubt aircraft will be available as needed for support of airborne operations.	12. Concur.	12. Concur and recommend Army Air Forces implement.	12. Will be submitted to Army Air Forces for comment. Reproduced from chart incl (Tab A) with memo, G-3 WD for DCofS USA, 19 Oct 43, sub: A/B ops Board. In OPD 381 case 186.

Appendix VI

War Department Training Circular 113, 9 October 1943, Employment of Airborne and Troop Carrier Forces. Excerpts.

The following principles are so vital to the success of any airborne operation that they are repeated at the beginning of this publication.

Airborne and troop carrier units are theater of operations forces. Plans for their combined employment must be prepared by the agency having authority to direct the necessary coordinated action of all land, sea, and air forces in the areas involved. This responsibility should not be delegated to lower headquarters since positive coordination can be insured only by the one agency in control of all elements.

The coordinating directive must be issued in ample time to insure its receipt by all agencies concerned, including isolated antiaircraft units and individual naval and other vessels.

Routes, altitudes, time schedules, and means of identification, both while in the air and on the ground must be known in advance by all concerned. Procedures must be described which will insure that troop carrier aircraft which are on course, at proper altitudes and on the correct time schedules are not fired upon by friendly land, sea or air forces.

Plans should provide for the necessary preparation by troop carrier and airborne units to include training and practice operations and the concentration of these units in the departure areas.

Airborne units should remain under the direct control of the theater commander until they land in the ground combat area when control passes to the officer in command of that area.

* * *

(1) The primary mission of troop carrier units is to provide air transportation for airborne forces into combat; and to resupply such forces until they are withdrawn or can be supplied by other means.

(2) The secondary mission of troop carrier units within the combat theater is:

(a) Emergency supply and evacuation

(b) Ferrying of troops and supplies

(c) Routine transportation of personnel, supplies and mail.

(3) Troop carrier units must be diverted from secondary missions, by the highest headquarters in a theater, in ample time to allow complete preparation to accomplish primary missions.

* * *

The airborne operation should be an integral part of the basic plan. To superimpose an airborne operation on a major operation already planned will rarely, if ever, be successful.

The airborne and troop carrier commanders concerned will develop the detailed plans for the concentration of troops, the air movement, and the tactical operation at the objective. Troop Carrier-Airborne Standing Operating Procedure should be developed and followed for all airborne operations. During the planning phase, contacts by all commanders and staffs concerned with the operation should be authorized to communicate directly in all phases of operational training.

Appendix VII

Letter of Maj. Gen. Matthew B. Ridgway, commanding general, Eighty-second Airborne Division, to War Department Operations Division, on status of training, 5 November 1943. Excerpt. (AFTCC 353 (A/B Tng))

We are still below the airborne training level required to insure reasonable expectation under expected combat conditions that a reinforced parachute battalion combat team can be delivered on a pre-selected drop zone AT NIGHT. Night airborne operations are normally essential against our present enemy due to the vulnerability of the Troop Carrier C-47 aircraft. All five combat drops to date of the 82d Division Battalions behind enemy lines have been made at night, with resultant questionable success. Failure of these missions can be attributed to lack of training and the development of proper technique and facilities for location of dropping zones. Unit training, including the development of Pathfinder units, is now being conducted by this Division and the Troop Carrier Command. Opportunities for intensive combined night training must be made available to both units.

The Troop Carrier Command has attained a satisfactory training level for the delivery of reinforced parachute battalion combat teams in pre-selected fields in DAYLIGHT, but only UNDER TRAINING CONDITIONS. No such operation has been attempted in daylight under combat conditions, as the hazards have been too great . . . .

For NIGHT *glider* operations the deficiency in this Theater is even more pronounced than described . . . above. No night glider operations have been conducted in this Theater by American pilots. Up to the present, the Troop Carrier Command glider pilots have not had sufficient training to conduct a successful night glider operation. Several hundred well trained glider pilots will be required for an actual operation. If this requirement is to be met, it is most important that an intensive night glider pilot training program and combined training be pursued without interruption.

Appendix VIII

War Department Directive for Joint Training of Airborne and Troop Carrier Units, 9 October 1943. Excerpt. (WDGCT 353 (1 Oct 43) 353/199 (A/B))

1. Success in combined troop carrier-airborne operations requires that an essential minimum of such training be accomplished before units depart for combat theaters. The Commanding General, Army Ground Forces, is responsible for the training of airborne units and the Commanding General, Army Air Forces is responsible for the training of troop carrier units, prior to departure of these units for combat theaters.

2. Neither a troop carrier unit nor an airborne unit can obtain effective combined troop carrier-airborne training without joint participation. Combined troop carrier-airborne training is, therefore necessarily a joint responsibility of the Commanding Generals of the Army Air Forces and of the Army Ground Forces, which requires close coordination and cooperation. Difficulties beyond the authority of either commander to correct should be reported to the War Department in ample time to permit corrective action before training is affected.

3. The Commanding General, Army Ground Forces is responsible for the preparation of effective training plans, and the submission of requirements to the War Department sufficiently in advance to insure coordination with the Army Air Forces and the availability of the means required. He will designate airborne units in order of priority to receive combined troop carrier-airborne training. Units designated for overseas shipment will be placed in a higher priority than the others.

4. The Commanding General, Army Air Forces is responsible for the preparation of effective plans, made sufficiently in advance to insure coordination with the Airborne Training Program and to provide the necessary troop carrier units for this purpose. He will designate troop carrier units to receive combined troop carrier-airborne training in accordance with requirements established by the War Department. The current schedule of requirements is contained in War Department memorandum, subject: Schedule of Troop Carrier Units, dated 24 September, file WDGCT 350.01 (24 Sep 43). It is desired that the established training program be completed without interruption and that no changes be made in the schedule without prior approval of the War Department.

5. Direct correspondence on this subject is authorized between the Commanding Generals, Airborne Command and I Troop Carrier Command.

6. Exchange of necessary liaison officers is encouraged.

Appendix IX

Estimate of Aircraft Availability for Operation Husky, Sicily

DIVISION OF AIR FORCE EQUIPMENT FOR OPERATION HUSKY

ESTIMATED AVAILABILITY AIRCRAFT INCLUDING GLIDER AND TROOPS FOR OPERATION "HUSKY" BIGOT

DAY	U.S.A. Aircraft & Gliders	U.S.A. Troops	BRITISH Aircraft & Gliders	BRITISH Troops	SUPPLY
D-1/D	Five gps C47's 260 total Waco Gliders 200 total 61 gp 64 gp 313 gp 314 gp 316 gp	82 Airborne Div complete, of which one para regt plus one para Bn and para supporting arms are operating in the first assault. 2nd Bn 509 para regt also available	Two gps C47's 38 Wing RAF 137 Total Gliders HORSA 15 total Waco 200 total Plus 15 C47's from U.K. as replacement.	1 Airborne Div complete of which Airlanding Bde Gp is operating in first assault.	One Gp C47's 65 C47 total One Sqn C47's Waco gliders 50 total
D/D+1	Three gps C47's 120 total Waco Gliders 200 total Two of the original Five gps are switched over, one to supply and one (64) gp to 1 (Br) Airborne Division for D+2/D+3 operation	One Para Regt (less one Bn) One Airlanding Regt plus all glider-borne supporting arms and admn. Services 2nd Bn 509 para regt also available	Two gps C47's 103 total 38 Wing RAF Gliders HORSA 5 WACO 50	1 Airborne Div less 1 Airlanding Bde which is operating on night D/D+1	One gp C47's One Sqn C47's 100 (C47) total One gp C47's switched over from U.S. Airborne Div. Waco gliders 50 total
D+1/D+2	As for D/D+1 less losses sustained on any follow-up airborne operations ordered by Force 343.	As for D/D+1 depending on operations ordered	Two gps C47's 38 Wing RAF 64 Gp from U.S. Airborne Div 113 total Gliders HORSA Nil WACO 50	As for D/D+1	As for D/D+1 less losses sustained on any supply operations ordered.
D+2/D+3	As for D+1/D+2	As for D+1/D+2	As for D+1/D+2	As for D+1/D+2 less one para Bde operating on night D+2/D+3	As for D+1/D+2
D+3/D+4	As for D+2/D+3	As for D+2/D+3	Two gps C47's 38 Wing RAF 75 total 64 Gp C47's 64 Gp may be switched to supply after D+2/D+3 operation	One Para Bde (less one Bn) plus Lt Regt RA one A/TK Bty, lt AA Bty, Recon Sqn, one Fd sqn or Coy, i.e. one para bde gp plus airlanding supporting arms, adm and supply services (less one para Bn)	As for D+2/D+3, but if 64 Gp is switched to sup, total will be, allowing for losses, 120.
D+4/D+5	As for D+3/D+4 All or an unknown proportion of all Troop carrying aircraft may be switched over to either Airborne operations or supply or an unknown proportion to each according to the situation.	As for D+3/D+4	As for D+3/D+4	As for D+3/D+4 depending on operations ordered.	As for D+3/D+4
D+5/D+6	As for D+4/D+5	As for D+4/D+5	As for D+4/D+5	As for D+4/D+5	As for D+4/D+5
D+6/D+7	As for D+5/D+6	As for D+5/D+6	As for D+5/D+6	As for D+5/D+6	As for D+5/D+6

1. Unservicability and losses have been allowed for throughout in the totals given.
2. 20% Unservicability and losses must be allowed for in airborne operations and 10% in supply.

Appendix X

Messages relating to routing and warning to surface forces of flight of Eighty-second Airborne Division, Sicily.

RESTRICTED

FROM: FANTOX — 30 June 1030

TO : C IN C MED

ORIGINATOR'S NUMBER: HOW/109

BIGOT [redacted](.)

FROM AIRBORNE ADVISOR (.) ROUTING OF TROOP CARRIER AIRCRAFT FOR 82 (US) AIRBORNE DIVISION APPROX NUMBER 150 EARLY ON NIGHTS D/D/1 (,) D/1/D/2 AND PROBABLY D/2/D/3 URGENTLY REQUIRES DECISION (.) ROUTE WILL BE VIA HOBGOBLIN (.) A LANE BETWEEN FEDERAL AND SCOGLITTI IS REQUIRED TO BE KEPT CLEAR OF SHIPPING OR GUARANTEE THAT SHIPPING WILL NOT RPT NOT FIRE (.) EXACT TIMING WILL BE 2230 HRS TO 2330 HRS EACH NIGHT AND HEIGHT FOR ROUTE IN WILL BE 500 - 600 FEET (.) ROUTE HOME EITHER OVER SAME LANE AT OVER 1000 FEET OR OUT OVER COAST WEST OF FIBULA THE FORMER IS PREFERABLE(.) IT IS NOT RPT NOT PRACTICABLE FOR INCOMING AIRCRAFT TO PROCEED OVERLAND TO WESTWARD OF FIBULA OWING TO REQUIREMENTS OF HEIGHT FOR DROPPING PARACHUTE TROOPS AND INABILITY OF AIRCRAFT TO GAIN HEIGHT SUFFICIENTLY QUICKLY TO AVOID HIGH GROUND ON RETURN (.)

REQUEST URGENT DECISION BY C IN C MED (.) N L O HAS BEEN CONSULTED

IMMEDIATE.

S. 1320f. **NAVAL MESSAGE.**

For use in Cypher or Coding Office only.	

Originators Instructions: (Indication of Priority, AIDAC, NOTWT For Exercise).	INTERCEPT GROUP.

TO: COMNAVNAW (R) MAC DNIKF Force 343 NAAF AOC MALTA	FROM: C in C Med

Following is route agreed with Generals ~~SWING~~ BROWNING and SWING for 82nd Airborne Division night D-1/D day.

Pass close East of DELIMARA MALTA thence 024° to pass position 9 miles 225° from CAPE PASSERO between 2250 and 2330 thence 289° to position 3½ miles 200° from CAPE SCALAMBRI thence 333° for 12 miles thence due North to Dropping Zone

Book or Table to be used for		Initials of Cypherer or Coder.	Time of Receipt in Cypher or Coding Office.	Date.
Cyphering or Coding.	Recyphering or Recoding.			
Wt. 36005/D 8794. 150M Pads. 12/41.	J. D. & Co. Ltd. 51-1824.			9

S. 1320f.

NAVAL MESSAGE

For use in Cypher or Coding Office only.	

Originators Instructions: (Indication of Priority, AIDAC, NOTWT For Exercise).	INTERCEPT GROUP.
TO:	FROM:

Return westward to cross coast between GELA and LICATA thence to FANTELLAFIA ~~and~~ ~~[illegible] westward~~ keeping within 4 miles of coast until westward of longitude of LICATA

~~[illegible]~~ Red downward recognition lights will be shown during approach when in vicinity of convoys

2. Routes and times for BRITISH involving Operations D-1/D day remain unchanged lights will not be shown

Book or Table to be used for		Initials of Cypherer or Coder.	Time of Receipt in Cypher or Coding Office.	Date.
Cyphering or Coding.	Recyphering or Recoding.			
Wt. 36095/D 8794. 150M Pads. 12/41.	J.D. & Co. Ltd. 51-1824.			(9)

RADIO FROM CIN CMED[redacted]D CG F 141 CG F 343 CG 82D AB D[redacted] ACO MED

FOLLOWING ROUTE AGREED WITH GENERALS BROWNING AND SWING FOR EIGHTY SECOND

US AB DIV NIGHT D - 1 / D DAY

PASS CLOSE EAST OF DELIMARRA MALTA THENCE024 DEGREES TO PASS POSITION 9 MILES

225 DEGREES FROM CAPTE PASSERO BETWEEN 2250 AND 2330 THENCE 289 DEGREES TO

POSITION 3½ MILES 200 DEGREES FROM CAPE SCALAMBRI THENCE 333 DEGREES FOR

12 MILES THENCE DUE NORTH TO DROPPING ZONE STOP

RETURN WESTWARD TO CROSS COAST BETWEEN GELA AND LICATA THENCE TO PANTELLARIA

KEEPING WITHIN FOUR MILES OF COAST UNTIL WESTWARD OF LONGITUDE OF LICATA STOP

RED DOWNWARD RECOGNITION LIGHTS WILL BE SHOWN DURING APPROACH WHEN IN

VICINITY OF CONVOYS STOP

ROUTESAND TIMES FOR BRITISH AIRBORNE OPERATION D-1/D DAY REMAIN UNCHANGED

STOP LIGHTS WILL NOT BE SHOWN END

C IN C MED 5 July 43

RESTRICTED

To: Commanding General II Corps
" " 45th Inf. Div.
" " 1st Inf. Div.
" " 2nd Armored Div.
" " 3rd Inf. Div.

You will warn your command that on each of the nights of D/D plus 1 to D plus 6, all inclusive, they are to expect flights of friendly troop carrying TC transport planes, C-47 type, approaching coast vicinity SAMPIERI following northwesterly course, generally two to four miles inland at altitude below 1000 feet, leaving coast in vicinity LICATA. Flights will pass between 2230 and 2400 hours approximately. Length of flight approximately forty minutes. Flights will drop parachutists or release gliders. Advise respective Naval commanders.

Patton
Eisenhower

Appendix XI

General Swing's comments on night operation, Eighty-second Airborne Division (Sicily), 16 July 1943.

La Marsa Camp, Tunisia, N.A.
16 July, 1943

Memorandum:

Comments on Night Operation, 82d Airborne Division Night D plus 1/D plus 2.

1. On the night referred to above, 142 aircraft carrying elements of the 82nd Airborne Division endeavored to fly over a dropping zone in the vicinity of landing strip two miles east of Gela. Less than 50% dropped in the vicinity of the objective. Of the remainder, a small portion dropped as far west as the vicinity of Licata; the majority of one battalion of infantry and one battalion of artillery dropped between Vittorio and Scoglitti.

2. This dispersal covered a zone of approximately thirty miles from east to west. During and at the conclusion of the operation, 23 planes were lost. As to date, only eight have been counted on the island, it is presumed that the remainder were lost at sea before and after their approach to the island.

3. The following may be summed up as contributory causes:

a. Insufficient prior planning. Reluctance at Force 141 Headquarters to accept the plan of Force 343 with respect to successive lifts of the 82nd Airborne Division resulted in lack of coordination between Army, Air, and Navy. Routes of approach to the island and guarantees of immunity to anti-aircraft fire were not given until July 5th, were not disseminated to the Army until July 6th, and not broadcast to the Navy until 1100 hours on the day of the movement: July 11th. These directions could and should have been issued weeks previously.

b. Inability of some Troop Carrier elements to adhere closely to Routes given. This inability may be laid partly to the level of training of the pilots, and partly to the complicated route finally allocated.

c. The unalterable decision of Navy elements to fire at all aircraft at night coming within range of their weapons, whatever caliber, despite all efforts on the part of friendly aircraft to identify themselves.

d. The unfortunate circumstance of an enemy bombing raid coinciding exactly with the arrival of the Troop Carrier element.

e. The negligence on the part of some subordinate ground force commanders in communicating to the personnel immediately concerned with the operation of the ground anti-aircraft weapons, the time, course, and expected arrival of airborne formations.

J. M. SWING
Major General, U. S. A.

Appendix XII

Exchange of letters between Gen. George C. Marshall and Gen. Dwight D. Eisenhower on proposed airborne invasion of France, 1944. (OPD 381, Case 217)

OCS
GCM

10 February 1944

My dear Eisenhower:

Up to the present time I have not felt that we have properly exploited air power as regards its combination with ground troops. We have lacked planes, of course, in which to transport men and supplies, but our most serious deficiency I think has been a lack of conception. Our procedure has been a piecemeal proposition with each commander grabbing at a piece to assist his particular phase of the operation, very much as they did with tanks and as they tried to do with the airplane itself. It is my opinion that we now possess the means to give a proper application to this phase of air power in a combined operation.

I might say that it was my determination in the event I went to England to do this, even to the extent that should the British be in opposition I would carry it out exclusively with American troops. I am not mentioning this as pressure on you but merely to give you some idea of my own conclusions in the matter.

With the foregoing in mind and seeing the proposed plan for OVERLORD in Airborne troops, General Arnold had Brigadier General Fred Evans, Commanding General of the Troop Carrier Command, and Colonel Bruce Bidwell, the OPD Airborne Consultant, make a study of the proposition for OVERLORD.

They first presented to us Plan A, which utilizes the airborne troops in three major groups with mission to block the movement of hostile reserve divisions as now located. This was not acceptable to me. On paper it was fine; but on the ground it would be too few men at the critical points with almost the certainty that the Germans would circumvent them in vicious fighting. I saw exactly this happen in the great German offensives of March, 1918. In preparation for the attack the allies organized their forces in depth, the various points of resistance being staggered. On a map it was a perfect pin-ball setup to disrupt the enemy's effort. On the ground it was a series of quick collapses where small groups of lonely men were cut off and surrendered.

I then had them reconsider the plan more in accordance with my conception of the application of airborne troops on a large scale. This resulted in two plans.

Plan B – This establishes an air-head in the general Argentan area approximately thirty miles inland from Caen, with missions to seize two airfields, and restrict the movement of hostile reserves that threaten the beach landing area from the east and southeast.

This plan is not satisfactory to me because the airfields are small and not capable of rapid expansion and we could not take heavy planes in to provide quick build-up. Moreover, holding this particular locality would not pose a major strategic threat to the Germans.

Plan C – Establishes an air-head in keeping with my ideas on the subject, one that can be quickly established and developed to great strength in forty-eight hours. The area generally south of Evreux has been selected because of four excellent airfields.

This plan appeals to me because I feel that it is a true vertical envelopment and would create such a strategic threat to the Germans that it would call for a major revision of their defensive plans. It should be a complete surprise, an invaluable asset of any such plan. It would directly threaten the crossings of the Seine as well as the city of Paris. It should serve as a rallying point for considerable elements of the French underground.

In effect, we would be opening another front in France and your build-up would be tremendously increased in rapidity.

The trouble with this plan is that we have never done anything like this before, and frankly, that reaction makes me tired. Therefore I should like you to give these young men an opportunity to present the matter to you personally before your Staff tears it to ribbons. Please believe that, as usual, I do not want to embarrass you with undue pressure. I merely wish to be certain that you have viewed this possibility on a definite planning basis.

Faithfully yours,

G. C. Marshall

SHAEF

19 February 1944

Dear General:

This is a long letter, in tentative answer to yours of 10 February on the subject of Airborne operations. General Evans and Colonel Bidwell have presented their plan to me and are now working with others, pending opportunity to hold a meeting to be attended by Montgomery. If you are pushed for time I suggest that you have the Operations Division brief the following for your convenience.

You will recall that more than a year ago in Algiers, you talked to me on the idea that in the proper development of airborne operations lies one field in which we have a real opportunity and capability to get ahead of the enemy. Obviously, it is only by getting definitely ahead of him in some important method of operations that we can expect to accomplish his defeat. Since that time this has been one of my favorite subjects for contemplation.

My initial reaction to the specific proposal is that I agree thoroughly with the conception but disagree with the timing. Mass in vertical envelopments is sound – but since this kind of an enveloping force is *immobile on the ground* the collaborating force must be strategically and tactically mobile. So the time for the mass vertical envelopment is *after* the beach-head has been gained and a striking force built up! The reasons on which I base these conclusions are discussed below.

As I see it the first requisite is for the Expeditionary Force to gain a firm and solid footing on the Continent and to secure at least one really good sheltered harbor. All of our anxiety concerning Mulberries, Gooseberries, and other forms of artificial aids in landing supplies and troops for assault and build-up are merely an indication of the great concern that everyone feels toward this problem of establishing and maintaining ground forces on the Continent. This means that the initial crisis of the campaign will be the struggle to break through the beach defenses, exploit quickly to include a port and be solidly based for further operations. To meet this *first tactical crisis* I intend to devote everything that can be profitably used, including airborne troops.

The second consideration that enters my thinking on this problem is expressed in the very first sentence of your letter, in the phrase "air power as regards its *combination* with ground troops." Whatever the conditions in other Theaters of War, the one here that we must never forget is the enemy's highly efficient facilities for concentration of ground troops at any particular point. This is especially true in the whole of France and in the Low Countries. Our bombers will delay movement, but I cannot conceive of enough air power to prohibit movement on the network of roads throughout northwest France. For the past five days there has been good weather in Italy and our reports show an average of 1000 sorties per day. Yet with only two main roads and a railway on which to concentrate, our reports show a steady stream of traffic by night to the south and south east from Rome. We must arrange all our operations so that no significant part of our forces can be isolated and defeated in detail. There must exist either the definite capability of both forces to combine *tactically*, or the probability that each force can operate independently without danger of defeat.

The German has shown time and again that he does not particularly fear what we used to refer to as "strategic threat of envelopment." Any military man that might have been required to analyze, before the war, the situation that existed in Italy on about January 24, would have said that the only hope of the German was to begin the instant and rapid withdrawal of his troops in front of the Fifth Army. The situation was almost a model for the classical picture for initiating a battle of destruction. But the German decided that the thrust could not be immediately translated into *mobile tactical action*, and himself began attacking. The Nettuno landing, due to the incidence of bad weather, was really not much heavier in scale than an airborne landing would have been during those critical days when time was all-important. The force was *immobile* and could not carry out the promise that was implicit in the situation then existing. But from our standpoint the situation was saved by the fact that our complete command of the sea allowed us to continue to supply and maintain and reinforce the beachhead. I am convinced it will turn out all right in the end, but there will be *no* great destruction of German divisions as a result thereof. An airborne landing carried out at too great a distance from other forces which will also be immobile for some time, will result in a much worse situation.

The resistance to be expected by our landing forces at the beaches is far greater than anything we have yet encountered in the European War and I have felt that carefully planned airborne operations offer us an important means of increasing our chances in this regard. The American Division, which has first priority, dropping in the Cherbourg Peninsula, gives us a reasonable expectation of preventing reinforcement of that area and seizing exits from the great flooded area that separates, in that region, our only practicable landing beach from the interior of the Peninsula. Unless we throw a very strong force in this vicinity, the Division attempting to land there will be in a bad spot. The British Airborne Forces have the Caen area to seize. Subsequent airborne operations are planned to be as bold and in as large a mass as resources and the air situation then existing will permit. I do not agree with Bidwell that large-scale, mass use of airborne troops will thereafter be impracticable.

To a certain extent the conduct of airborne operations must be planned in accordance with technicians' ideas of feasibility. Even under the most favorable circumstances the air people anticipate quite large losses among troop carrier craft because of the high efficiency of hostile Radar coverage and the impossibility of preventing enemy fighters from getting into such formations. I hope soon to have here a man that Arnold is sending me from Kenny's command. Possibly he can show us wherein we may have been too conservative.

All of the above factors tend to compel the visualization of airborne operations as an immediate tactical rather than a long-range strategical adjunct of landing operations.

If we were not planning so definitely upon the bombardment effect of our bombers to help us both tactically and strategically, there would be available a greatly increased force to support and maintain airborne operations, but present plans call for an all-out effort on the part of both day and night bombers for a very considerable period both preceding and following D-Day.

I instinctively dislike ever to uphold the conservative as opposed to the bold. You may be sure that I will earnestly study the ideas presented by the two officers because on one point of your letter I am in almost fanatical agreement – I believe we can lick the Hun only by being ahead of him in ideas as well as in material resources.

Sincerely,

/s/ Dwight D. Eisenhower

Notes

Chapter I

"Out of the Blue Sky": A Case Study

1. Account by Erwin Kirchof, quoted in Milton Shulman, *Defeat in the West* (New York, 1948), p. 184.

2. Unless otherwise noted, this chapter is based on the following: (1) First Allied Airborne Army Rpt on Ops in Holland Sep-Nov 1944, 22 Dec 44 (Mimeo.) (2) XVIII Corps (Airborne) Opn MARKET, A/B phase, D to D plus 10, 4 Dec 44 (Mimeo.) (3) IX Troop Carrier Command Rpt on Opn MARKET, Air Invasion of Holland (Litho). All in SHAEF SGS 5364. (4) (Rpt of British Airborne Corps) Allied A/B Ops in Holland. (Litho.) In SHAEF SGS 381 (MARKET). (5) 21 Army Group, Opn MARKET-GARDEN 17-26 Sep 44 (Mimeo). (6) 82d A/B Div Graphic History Opn MARKET (Mimeo). (7) 101st A/B Div Rpt of A/B phase (17-27 Sep) Opn MARKET (Mimeo). (8) First Allied Airborne Army Narrative of Opn MARKET, 9 Oct 44 (Mimeo). (9) Rpt of Lt Col F. E. Ross on A/B in ETO, 6 Dec 44, Mimeo copy in OCMH files. (10) A/B Div British Rpt on Opn MARKET (Mimeo). In SHAEF SGS 381 (MARKET). (11) Combat Interviews 171, 82d A/B Div. (12) Combat Interviews 226, 101st A/B Div.

3. FAAA Rpt on Ops in Holland, pp. 16-17, IX Tr Carrier Cmd Rpt on Opn MARKET, p. 17 and Annex No. 5.

4. Parachute infantry battalions had only three letter companies instead of the normal four; hence the companies of the 1st Battalion in a regiment were A, B, C; those of the 2d, D, E, F, and those of the 3d G, H, I.

5. 1A/B Div Rpt on Opn MARKET, p. 4.

6. Msg. CG FAAA to SHAEF Fwd, Rear, 17 Sep 44. VX 25305. SHAEF Fwd 530/17. In SHAEF SGS 381 (MARKET).

7. Trans of postwar German study: Action in Belgium and Holland, Sep-Dec 1944. MS No. T-122, on file in Weapons System Evaluation Group.

8. Trans (excerpts) German Army Corps Special Orders (K.T.B.) OB West, 1-30 Sep 44, p. 69. On file in Wpns Sys Eval Gp.

9. Rpt Recd for OSS at Hq FAAA, 16 Dec 44, Trans of German Analysis of A/B Landings at Arnhem issued by Army Group B on 1 Oct 44. 461 (FAAB). In FAAA 322 (MARKET) (Microfilm roll No. 3).

10. Trans of postwar German study: Action in Belgium and Holland Sep-Dec 1944. MS No. T-122.

11. Trans, General Situation of Germany Army Group B (Sep 1944). MS No. T-122.

12. FAAA Rpt on Opns In Holland, p. 32.

13. German Army Corps Special Orders (K. T. B.) 17 Sep 44.

14. FAAA Rpt on Opns in Holland, p. 9.

15. (1)/Min of Meeting called by CG FAAA held at 1800, 10 Sep 44. FAAA 322 MARKET (Microfilm Roll 3). (2) Ltr, CG FAAA to Lt Gen F.A.M. Browning, 11 Sep 44, sub: Task Force for Opn MARKET (Mimeo). In SHAEF SGS 381 MARKET. (3) FAAA Rpt on Opns in Holland, p. 9.

16. Ltr, CG XVIII Corps (A./B.) to CG FAAA, 4 Dec 44, sub: Opn MARKET, A/B phase. 370 (CG). Incl in XVIII Corps (A/B) Rpt of A/B phase Opn MARKET.

17. FAAA Rpt on Opns in Holland, p. 9. Min of Meeting Called by CG FAAA held at 1800, 10 Sep 44. IX Tr Carrier Cmd Rpt on Opn MARKET, pp. 9-10.

18. Record of Tp Conversation, Gen Brereton – Gen Parkes, 1630, 11 Sep 44. FAAA GCT/24571/A.B. (Opn MARKET).

19. Notes on Conf, Gen Stearley and G-3 Staff, 1000, 13 Sep 44. FAAA 322 (MARKET) (Microfilm roll No. 3).

20. Ltr, Maj Gen Maxwell D. Taylor to Army Cmdr Second British Army, 14 Sep 44, sub: Eindhoven Mission of 101st A/B Div Annex I to ltr, same address, sub: Employment of 101st A/B Div Opn MARKET. In FAAA 322 (MARKET) (Microfilm roll No. 3).

21. Copy of msg recd in spl code, Personal for Eisenhower from Montgomery, 12 Sep 44. SHAEF Fwd M-197. In SHAEF SGS 381 (MARKET).

22. Memo, Col Campbell for Brig Gen Stearley, 12 Sep 44, sub: Notes on meeting of cmdrs and staffs at Moor Park. In FAAA 322 (MARKET) (Microfilm roll No. 3).

23. Minutes of Meeting called CG FAAA, held at 1800, 10 Sep 44. In FAAA 322 (MARKET) (Microfilm roll No. 3).

24. Memo, Col Campbell for Brig Gen Stearley, 12 Sep 44, sub: Notes on meeting of cmdrs and staffs at Moor Park. In FAAA 322 (MARKET) (Microfilm roll No. 3).

25. Draft ltr, CG FAAA to SCAEF, 13 Jan 45, sub: Lessons – Opn MARKET. 373.2 (FAAAC). In FAAA 322 (MARKET) (Microfilm roll No. 3).

26. Administrative Instruction No. 1, Opn MARKET, Hq A/B Trs, 12 Sep 44. HQ Air Tps/TS/4848/1/AQ. In SHAEF G-4 Central Files 381 (MARKET).

27. Administrative Instruction No. 1.

28. Notes on conf, Gen Stearley and G-3 staff, 1000, 13 Sep 44. Msg, CG FAAA/CGs IX Tr Carrier Cmd, British A/B Trs, US XVIII Corps (A/B), 16 Sep 44. VX 25282. Both in FAAA 322 MARKET (Microfilm roll No. 3).

29. Msg, G-4 FAAA sgd Brereton to (for action) SHAEF Fwd, 14 Sep 44. VX-25254 SHAEF Fwd 251/44. In SHAEF SGS 381 (MARKET).

30. Msg, SHAEF Fwd, sgnd SCAEF to 12th Army Group (Attn: Barriger, G-4 Div), 15 Sep 44. FS out 2502. Fwd-14940. In SHAEF SGS 381 (MARKET).

31. Deputy Director of Medical Services, British Airborne Corps, Rpt on A/B Medical Services, Opn MARKET. In FAAA 322 (MARKET) (Microfilm roll No 3).

32. Ltr, Maj J. D. Hancock to CG FAAA, 14 Oct 44, sub: Rpt of Activities in Opn MARKET. In FAAA 322 MARKET (Microfilm roll No. 3).

33. XVIII Corps (A/B), Opn MARKET, Preliminary Tactical Study of the Terrain. Counter Intelligence Dossier, Part II, Netherlands, 11 Sep 44. Both in FAAA 322 (MARKET) (Microfilm roll No. 3).

34. Tr Carrier Forces FO No. 4, 13 Sep 44, Annex No. 6 (Intelligence), p. 1. In SHAEF 381 MARKET.

35. 21 Army Group Rpt on Opn MARKET-GARDEN, p. 2.

36. Ltr, G-2 SHAEF to G-2 FAAA (Attn Lt Col A. G. Tasker), 4 Sep 44, sub: Defenses in Eastern Holland. GBI/OI-F/385.2-2. In FAAA 322 (MARKET) (Microfilm roll No. 3).

37. Tr Carrier Forces, FO No. 4, 13 Sep 44, Annex No. 6 (Intelligence), p. 6.

38. A/B Corps (British) Opn Instruction No. 1, 13 Sep 44. Reproduced in Allied Airborne Operations in Holland. In SHAEF SGS 381 (MARKET).

39. Notes, Maj T. J. Lowe, Hq FAAA, 12 Sep 44, sub: Flak Estimate, Opn MARKET, Arnhem-Nijmegen-Uden-Eindhoven. In FAAA 322 (MARKET) (Microfilm roll No. 3).

40. Ltr, Air Commodore L. C. Bouchier (RAF) to Hq Fighter Command, n.d., sub: Opn MARKET Anti-Flak Atk by Fighters, 11G/TS. 500/OPS. In FAAA 322 (MARKET) (Microfilm roll No. 3).

41. A/B Corps Opn Instructions No. 1.

42. 101st A/B Div FO No. 1, Sep 44. In FAAA 322 MARKET (Microfilm roll No. 3).

43. Maj Gen James M. Gavin, *Airborne Warfare* (Washington, 1947), p. 103.

44. 82d A/B Div FO No. 11, 13 Sep 44. In FAAA 322 MARKET (Microfilm roll No. 3).

45. 1 A/B Div Rpt on Opn MARKET, pp. 2-3. In SHAEF 381 (MARKET).

46. FAAA Rpt on Opns in Holland, p. 14.

47. Tr Carrier Forces, FO No. 4, Signal Annex; IX Tr Carrier Com'd Rpt on Opn MARKET, pp. 10-12; Notes on Meeting held at Main Hq, Second Army, 1530, 14 Sep, in FAAA 322 (MARKET) (Microfilm roll No. 3).

48. Tr Carrier Forces FO No. 4; IX Tr Carrier Cmd Rpt on Opn MARKET, p. 15.

49. Tr Carrier Forces FO No. 4; IX Tr Carrier Cmd Rpt on Opn MARKET, p. 13.

50. *Ibid.*

51. *Ibid.*, p. 12.

52. Tr Carrier Forces FO No. 4 Annex 1 A.

53. Tr Carrier Forces FO No. 4 Annex 1 B and 1 C.

54. Originally set at 1230, time was later changed to 1245, Amendment No. 2 to Field Order No. 4.

55. IX Tr Carrier Cmd. Rpt on Opn MARKET, pp. 15-16.

56. (1) Draft ltr, CG FAAA to SCAEF, 13 Jan 45, sub: Lessons – Opn MARKET. 373.2 (FAAAC). In FAAA 322 (MARKET) (Microfilm roll No. 3). (2) Memo, Lt Col Joseph B. Larocque, Jr., for G-3 FAAA, 12 Sep 44, sub: Meeting at Stanmore to discuss Air Effort for MARKET. In FAAA 322 (MARKET) (Microfilm roll No. 3). (3) FAAA Rpt on Opn in Holland, p. 13. (4) IX Tr Carrier Cmd Rpt on Opns in Holland, p. 16.

57. IX Tr Carrier Cmd, p. 9.

58. *Ibid.*, p. 16.

59. Msg, SHAEF to Army Groups, FAAA, AEAF, 14 Sep 44. 14794. In FAAA 322 (MARKET) (Microfilm roll No. 3).

60. John C. Warren, *Airborne Operations in World War II, European Theater* (Maxwell Air Force Base: Air University USAF Historical Division, 1956), p. 99.

61. Opn MARKET Weather Summary. In FAAA 322 MARKET (Microfilm roll No. 3).

62. FAAA Rpt on Opns in Holland, p. 14.

63. Ltr, Capt Frank L. Brown to CG XVIII Corps (A/B), 21 Oct 44, sub: Rpt of Pathfinder Mission, Opn MARKET, in FAAA 322 (MARKET) (Microfilm roll No. 3).

64. Ltr, 1 Lt G. W. Jaubert to CG XVIII Corps (A/B), 30 Nov 44, sub: Rpt of Pathfinder Mission, Opn MARKET. In FAAA 322 (MARKET). (Microfilm roll No. 3).

65. Ltr, Brig Gen J. M. Gavin to Maj Gen P. L. Williams, 25 Sep 44, Extracts reproduced in IX Tr Carrier Cmd, Rpt on Opn MARKET, pp. 72-76.

66. Ltr, Gen Gavin to Gen Williams, 25 Sep 44.

67. Memo, Capt William Griffin for Lt Col Bartley, 27 Oct 44, sub: Resupply of MARKET by B-24 aircraft. In FAAA 322 (MARKET). (Microfilm roll No. 3).

68. IX Tr Carrier Cmd, Supply by Air, 20 Nov 44 (lithograph), p. 7. 0101-66.2 (9829).

69. Ltr, Maj J. D. Hancock to CG FAAA, 14 Oct 44, sub: Rpt of Activities in Opn MARKET.

70. Ltr, Maj. J. D. Hannock to CG FAAA, 14 Oct 44. (British A/B Corps) Rpt of A/B Opns in Holland, pp. 18-19.

71. 101st A/B Div Rpt on Opn MARKET, Annex 4.

72. (1) Msg, SCAEF to EXFOR Main, for info to FAAA, 23 Sep 44. SHGCT FWD-15479. (2) Ltr, G-3 SHAEF to CofS SHAEF, – Oct 44, sub: U.S. A/B Divs in Opn MARKET. SHAEF/24571/Ops (A/B). (3) Ltr, G-3 SHAEF to CofS SHAEF, 4 Oct 44, sub: Release of A/B Divs from Opn MARKET, All in SHAEF SGS 38: (MARKET). (4) Msg, SHAEF Fwd to FAAA, 29 Sep 44. SHGCT. (5) Msg (Pers) CG FAAA to SCAEF, 8 Oct 44. V-25641. (6) Memo, Brig Gen Stuart Cutier, DCofS, Plans, FAAA, for CofS FAAA, 20 Oct 44. (7) Ltr, CofS SHAEF to CG FAAA, 2 Nov 44, sub: Release of U. S. A/B Divs from Opn MARKET. SHAEF/ 24573/Ops/(A/B). (8) Memo of tp msg, Col Eaton, CofS XVIII Corps (A/B), to Brig Gen Parkes, CofS FAAA, 8 Nov 1944, 1515 hours. All in FAAA 322 (MARKET) (Microfilm roll No. 3).

73. FAAA Rpt on Opn MARKET, p. 26.

74. *Ibid.*, p. 50.

75. *Ibid.*, p. 25.

76. FAAA Narrative of Opn MARKET, pp. 14-15.

77. Weather Summary, Opn MARKET, FAAA 322 (MARKET).

78. Hq Tr Carrier Forces FO No. 4, 13 Sep 44, Intelligence Trace No. 5.

79. Quoted in *The Brereton Diaries,* p. 354.

80. (British Airborne Corps) Allied A/B Opns in Holland, p. 23.

81. Draft ltr, CG FAAA to SCAEF, 13 Jan 45, sub: Lessons – Opn MARKET. 373.2 (FAAAC). In FAAA 322 (MARKET) (Microfilm roll No. 3).

82. (British Airborne Corps) Allied A/B Opns in Holland, p. 20.

83. Trans, Postwar German Study: Action in Belgium and Holland, Sep-Dec 1944. MS No. T-122.

84. (British Airborne Corps) Allied Airborne Operations in Holland, p. 22.

85. Ltr, Brig Gen James M. Gavin to Maj Gen P. L. Williams, 25 Sep 44. Reproduced in IX Tr Carrier Cmd Rpt on Opn MARKET, pp. 75-76.

86. Ltr CG XVIII Corps (A/B) to CG FAAA, 4 Dec 44, sub: Opn MARKET, A/B phase 370 (CG). Reproduced in XVIII Corps Rpt of Airborne phase of Opn MARKET.

87. *Ibid.*; ltr, CG 82d A/B Div to CG XVIII Corps (A/B), 3 Dec 44, sub: Lessons of Opn MARKET, Reproduced in Graphic History of the 82d A/B Div Opn MARKET.

88. Ltr, Maj J. D. Hancock to CG FAAA, 14 Oct 44, sub: Rpt on Activities in Opn MARKET.

89. Ltr, CG XVIII Corps (A/B) to CG FAAA, 4 Dec 44, sub: Opn MARKET, A/B phase. 370 (CG).

90. Ltr, Capt E. C. Thornton, observer A-3 sec. IX Tr Carrier Cmd to CG IX Tr Carrier Cmd, 29 Sep 44, sub: Observations on Aerial Re-Supply, Opn MARKET. E-ECT-19. In FAAA 322 (MARKET) (Microfilm roll No. 3).

91. Ltr, CG XVIII Corps (A/B) to CG FAAA, 4 Dec 44, sub: Opn MARKET, A/B Phase.

92. Trans, Analysis of A/B Landings at Arnhem issued by *Army Group B,* 1 Oct 44.

93. Ltr, CG FAAA to SCAEF, 22 Dec 44, sub: 1/B Opn in Holland, Sep-Nov 1944. AG 319.1 (Gen FAAAC). Reproduced in FAAA Rpt on Opns in Holland.

94. IX Tr Carrier Cmd Rpt on Ops MARKET, p. 80.

Chapter II

A New Approach in Warfare

1. Lt. Gen. Lewis H. Brereton, *The Brereton Diaries* (New York, 1946), p. 309; General H. H. Arnold, *Global Mission* (New York, 1949), p. 86.

2. Maj. F. O. Miksche, *Paratroops* (New York, 1943), pp. 7-10. See also B. H. Liddell Hart, *Europe in Arms* (London, 1937), p. 32.

3. Brig. Gen. E. G. Chapman, "American Divisions Take to the Air," *Command and General Staff School Military Review,* XXIII (Apr. 1943), p. 11.

4. Maj. Gen. William C. Lee in Introduction to Maj. Gen. James M. Gavin, *Airborne Warfare* (Washington, 1947), p. vii.

5. Lt. Col Bruce W. Bidwell to Maj. Gen. Orlando Ward, 17 May 50. Filed in Office of the Chief of Military History (hereafter referred to as OCMH).

6. (1) Rpt. No. 1987, Military Attache, Cairo, Egypt, 8 Sep 41, sub: A/B Invasion of Crete. MID 370.03 Germany. Mimeo copy in The National War College. (2) Great Britain, Ministry of Information, *The Campaign in Greece and Crete,* in *The Army at War* series (London, 1942), pp. 43-64. (3) Gavin, *Airborne Warfare,* pp. 29-72. (4) I. McD. G. Stewart, *The Struggle for Crete* (London, 1966).

7. AGF ltr GNTRG to CG's, 29 Apr 42, sub: German instructions for Crete Opns. 353/2.

8. FM 31-30, 20 May 42, par. 41-42; *see also* memo, CG AGF for CofS USA (Attn G-3), 2 Jul 42, sub: Policy re taf of A/B trs. 320.2/3 (A/B).

9. FM 31-30, par. 92-106.

10. *Ibid.,* par. 107.

11. Ltr, CO Airborne Comd to CO Tr Carrier Comd, 12 Aug 42, sub: Parachute Standardization Board, and 8 inds, 373 GNVOP. In AGF 353/108 (A/B).

12. AAF, I Tr Carrier Comd, The Operational Training Program, p. 285.

13. I Troop Carrier Comd Memo No. 60-3, quoted in *Ibid.,* p. 287.

14. Ltr, Gen Eisenhower to Gen Marshall, 19 Feb 44, OPD 381 case 217.

15. Memo, G. H. Dorr for the Secy of War, 2 Oct 43, sub: Air Borne Operations. Misc. Exec. file, Book 12, case 113. Copy in OPD 381 case 186.

16. FM 100-20, 21 Jul 43, para 14f.

17. Rpt of Airborne Operations Board, 6 Sep 43. 353/17 (A/B).

18. Ltr, Col Dalbey to Col F. N. Roberts, OPD, 4 Oct 43. ABC 322 (25 Sep 43).

19. OPD Note for Record 381 (9 Oct 43), 12 Oct 43, and WD ltr AG WDGCT 353 (11 Oct 43), 11 Oct 43, forwarding 10 copies. Both in OPD 381 case 187. Mimeo copy of circular in AGF 353/199 (A/B).

20. WD Tng Cir 113, 9 Oct 43, par 2b.

21. *Ibid.*, par 3.

22. *Ibid.*, par 5.

23. Ltr, CG Northwest African Air Forces to CG North African Theater of Operations, 18 Nov 43, sub: Employment of Airborne and Tr Carrier Forces. In OPD 381 case 186.

24. AFHQ 1st and AG 353-1 (A/B) GCT-AGM, 26 Nov 43.

25. Ltr, CG 82d A/B Div to CinC Allied Forces, 27 Nov 43, sub: Summary of Principles Covering Use of A/B Div. In AGF 353/6 (A/B).

26. FM 101-10, 10 Oct 43, paras 1001-1016.

27. *Ibid.*, par 1002.

28. CPS 91/1, 19 Oct 43, paras 9, 11. In ABC 322 (25 Dec 43) (TS).

29. Appendix A., par 21, *ibid.*

30. JPS 380, 24 Jan 44. In ABC 322 (25 Sep 43).

31. JPS 380/1, 3 Feb 44, sub: Policy as to the Organization and Employment of Airborne Troops. In ABC 322 (25 Sep 43).

32. CCS 496, 26 Feb 44, Policy as to the Organization and Employment of Airborne Troops. In ABC 322 (25 Sep 43).

33. *Ibid.*

34. Instructions from mins of JCS 149th mtg, 29 Feb 44, Item 6. In ABC 322 (25 Sep 43).

35. Instructions from minutes of GCS 148th meeting, 3 Mar 44, Item 3. In ABC 322 (25 Sep 43).

36. Notation, 6 Mar 44, in ABC 322 (25 Sep 43).

37. Ltr. G-3 COSSAC to Chief, Plans and Ops Sec G-3 COSSAC, 11 Dec 43, sub: S. A. C. Directive on Employment of Airborne Forces, and draft memo on Employment of Airborne Forces, 8 Dec 43. In SHAEF G-3 300.6-12/ops (A) (Op Memo No. 12, SOP for A/B and TC Units).

38. SHAEF Unnumbered Memo, 19 Jan 44, sub: Employment of Airborne Forces, par. 6 j. SHAEF/2297/4/Ops. In SHAEF G-3 300.6-12/Ops 'A' (Op Memo No. 12 SOP for A/B and TC Units).

39. *Ibid.*, par. 32.

40. *Ibid.*, par. 2.

41. SHAEF Op Memo No. 12, 13 Mar 44, Sub: SOP for A/B and TC Units. Mimeo copy in SHAEF G-3 300.6-12/Ops 'A' (Op Memo No. 12, SOP for A/B and TC Units.)

42. CG AAF to Exec Director, AAF Board, 22 Feb 44. Quoted in AAF, I Troop Carrier Command, The Operational Training Program, p. 393. Air Hist Off, 252-3, Vol. 2.

43. Rpt of AAF Board, Proj No. (T) 27, 29 Apr 44, quoted in *ibid.*, pp. 293-94.

44. Ltr, Col J. T. Dalbey to Brig Gen E. L. Eubank, exec director, AAF bd, 17 May 44. Copy in AGF G-3 A/B Br. (A/B Misc 1942-1945).

45. Ltr, Col J. T. Dalbey to Brig Gen F. W. Evans, 18 May 44. Copy in AGF G-3 A/B Br (A/B Misc (S) 1942-1945).

46. FM 100-5, 15 Jun 44, Ch. 14.

47. *Ibid.*, par. 988.

48. *Ibid.*, par. 998.

49. AGF, M/S, G-3 to RQT-2, 21 Apr 45, sub: Conf Publication, Airborne Assault on Holland. In AGF, G-3 A/B Br (A/B suspense Apr 35).

50. FM 71-30, July 1947, par 13.

51. *Ibid.*, par 12.

52. *Ibid.*, par 11.

53. WD Gen Council Min, 18 Mar 45.

54. (1) Memo for Record and AGF memo for CofS USA (Attn G-4) 30 Mar 45, sub: Introduction of Policy of "Air Transportability." 475/2230 1/2. (2) WD memo for CGs AAF, AGF, 3 May 45, sub: Incorporation of the term "Air Transportability" in AR 850-25. 300.3 (Ar 850-25).

55. *See* table and analysis in Greenfield, *et al, The Organization of Ground Combat Troops,* pp. 161-184.

56. Memo, CG AGF for ACofS OPD (Attn Col Nevins), 2 Apr 42, sub: Operations Plans – Western Europe. In AGF 381/12 (Preparation and Preparedness for War, Plans, Tables, Instructions), Binder No. 3.

57. *Ibid.*, Tab B. See *Biennial Report of the Chief of Staff of the United States Army, July 1, 1943, to June 30, 1945 to the Secretary of War,* pp. 8-9.

58. WD OPD D/F, 13 Apr 43, sub: Progress of Parachute Training. 322.54 (Para Trps) (25 Mar 42).

59. Air Transport Command Training Program, 29 May 42. Cpy in Air His Off 253.87-5.

60. AGF M/S Plans Div to CofS AGF, 6 May 42. AGF G-3 Plans Div (Bolero)/15.

61. Memo, Col L. L. Lemnitzer (Plans Div) for CofS AGF, G-1, G-3, Opns, Tng, Transp, Supply, Rgts, Mob., 17 June 42, sub: Airborne Divisions for Bolero. AGF G-3 Plans Div (Bolero)/31.

62. WD memo (C) WDGCT 320.2 for CGs AGF, AAF, SOS, 18 Apr 42, sub: Policy re Training of Airborne Divisions. 353/3 (A/B).

63. Memo, AGF Plans Div for CofS AGF, 3 Jul 42, sub: Bolero Conference, 2 Jul 42. AGF G-3 Plans Div/51 (Bolero).

64. *Ibid.*

65. Draft AGF memo for CofS USA (attn G-3), sub: Development of Specialized Combat Units, Troop Basis 1942 and 1943. Tab C with memo cited above.

66. Memo, OPD for Gen Giles, 22 Apr 43. In OPD 381 Case 144.

67. Quoted in *The Brereton Diaries,* p. 364.

68. *Ibid.*, p. 366.

Chapter III

Command and Control

1. (1) The Airborne Command and Center, AGF Historical Study No. 25, pp. 2-4. (2) See "The Role of GHQ in the Development of Airborne Training," K. R. Greenfield, R. R. Palmer, and B. I. Wiley, *The Organization of Ground Combat Troops* in THE UNITED STATES ARMY IN WORLD WAR II (Washington, 1947), pp. 93-98.

2. AGF Study No. 25, pp. 3-12, 21.

3. AGF Study No. 25, pp. 5-6.

4. *Ibid.*, pp. 12-13.

5. (1) *Ibid.*, pp. 13-23. (2) Memo, Gen. McNair for CofS USA, 17 Mar 42,/Airborne Command. 320.2/1 (A/B). (3) Memo, DCofS USA for CG AGF, 18 Mar 42, sub as in (2) above. 320.2/1 (A/B). (4) Ltr CG/AGF to CO Airborne Comd, 23 Mar 42, sub as in (2) above. 320.2/2 (A/B). (5) Ltr CG AGF to CO Airborne Comd, 24 Mar 42, sub as in (2) above. 320.2/2 (A/B). (6) Ltr CO Airborne Comd to CG AGF, 18 Apr 42, sub: Airborne Comd Trng Situation. 353/1 (A/B).

6. Ltr, CG AGF to CO Airborne Comd, 24 Mar 42, sub: Airborne Comd. 320.2/2 (A/B).

7. Ltr, CG AGF to CO Airborne Comd, 8 Apr 42, sub: Airborne Comd. 320.2/1 (A/B) (R).

8. AAF. I Troop Carrier Command, Vol. III: The Training of Troop Carrier Air Echelons. Part II: The Operational Training Program, pp. 7-9. Unpublished ms filed in Air Hist Off, 252-3, Vol. 2 (3379-2).

9. WD ltr AGO 320.2 (4-20-42) MR-M-AF, 30 Apr 42, in AFTCC 322 (Hq. AFTCC), quoted in *ibid.*, p. 238.

10. GO No. 8, CG AAF, 20 Jun 42, quoted in *ibid.*, p. 9.

11. Ltr, CG Airborne Cmd to CG AGF, 15 May 43, sub: Airborne Board. In 320.2/225 (A/B).

12. AGF Study No. 25, pp. 68-69.

13. AGF M/S, SG to G-3, 4 Oct 43, sub: A/B Cmd. 320.2/12 (A/B).

14. AGF M/S, CG to G-3, 23 Oct 43, sub: A/B Cmd. 320.2/14 (A/B).

15. *Ibid.*

16. Miksche, *Paratroops,* p. 20.

17. Ltr, CG A/B Cmd 354.2 – GNVGC to CG AGF, 3 Aug 43, sub: Equipment and Personnel to Conduct Large Scale A/B Ops, and AGF 1st ind, 20 Aug 43.353/195 (A/B).

18. Pers ltr, Col Dalbey to Col F. N. Robers, OPD, 4 Oct 43. ABC 322 (25 Sep 43).

19. *Ibid.*

20. *Brereton Diaries,* p. 223.

21. AAF, I Troop Carrier Command, The Operational Training Program, pp. 400-401.

22. Copies in AAF, I Troop Carrier Command, Vol. III: The Training of Troop Carrier Air Echelons, Part IV: Appendices (R), Appendix V, Air Hist Off 252-3 V 4 (3370-5).

23. FM 101-10, 10 Oct 43, para 1001.

24. WD memo for CG AGF, AAF, SOS, 18 Apr 42, sub: Policy re Training of Airborne Troops. WDGCT 320.2 In AGF 353/3 (A/B).

25. Memo, G-3 AGF for CofS AGF, 23 June 42, sub: Policy re Airborne Divisions. 320.2/4 (A/B).

26. Pers ltrs, Brig Gen W. C. Lee to Brig Gen Floyd L. Parks, CofS AGF, 27 Jun 42. 320.2/4 (A/B).

27. AGF Study No. 25, pp. 49-50. *See* Greenfield, *et al, The Organization of Ground Combat Troops,* pp. 339-341.

28. AGF M/S, CG to CofS, 25 Jun 42, and Tng to G-3, 29 Jun 42, sub: Policy re Training of Airborne Troops. 320.2/3 (A/B).

29. Memo, CG AGF for CofS USA (attn G-3), 2 Jul 42, sub: Policy re Training of Airborne Troops. 320.2/26 (Inf) GNTRG. In AGF 320.2/3 (A/B).

30. Memo of Plans for CofS AGF, 9 Jul 42, sub: Bolero Conference. Cpy in Plans File/49.

31. (1) Pers ltr, Brig Gen F. L. Parks to Brig Gen M. B. Ridgway, 29 Jul 42. 322.98 (2) Ltr CG AGF to CGs Third Army and A/B Comd, 30 Jul 42, sub: Activation of 82d and 101st A/B Divs. 320.2/9 (A/B). (3) Ltr CG AGF to CGs Second and Third Armies and A/B Comd, 21 Oct 42, sub: Directive for Tng A/B Divs. 353/11 (A/B).

32. Ltr, Maj Gen James M. Gavin to Capt John G. Westover, office of Theater Historian, USFET, 25 July, 45. (Sub: Reply to Questions submitted on 82d A/B Div in Opn MARKET) Annex No. 1. In Combat Interviews 171, 82d A/B Div.

33. Ltr, Col H. W. O. Kinnard to Capt Westover, 6 Aug 1945. In Combat Interviews 226-A, 101st A/B Div.

34. Extracts from Observer's Rpt on A/B Opns, ETO, Lt Col Frank E. Ross, 6 Dec 44.

35. Ltr, CofS FAAA to SCAEF, 16 Nov 44, sub: Recommended T/O and T/E for Standard A/B Inf. Div. 320.3 (FAAAC). In SHAEF G-3 24554/Ops (Prov Reorganization of A/B Divs).

36. Ltr, G-3 SHAEF to CofS SHAEF, 7 Dec 44, sub: Reorganization of A/B Divs. In SHAEF G-3 24554/Ops (Prov Reorg of A/B Divs).

37. T/O and 71T, 16 Dec 44, and related tables.

38. D/F, G-3 WD to TAG, 18 Dec 44, sub: Reorg of A/B Div. In AG 320.3 (1 Jan 44) (1) Part II-F.

39. SHAEF M/S, Col Twitchell, O&E sec, 22 Mar 45, sub: Attachments required by A/B Div in Ground Role. GCT 322 (A/B) O&E. In SHAEF G-3 24554/Opns (Prov Reorg A/B Divs).

40. USAFFE Rpt No. 270, 20 Apr 45, sub: Orgn of Para-Glider Inf. In OCMH files.

41. Memo, Col J. A. Hinton, A/B Sub-sec, for G-3 SHAEF, 20 May 44, sub: Airborne Forces. In SHAEF G-3 17281/1 (Formation of FAAA). See also Forrest C. Pogue, *The Supreme Command* in U. S. ARMY IN WORLD WAR II, (Washington: Office of the Chief of Military History, 1954), pp. 269-72.

42. Ltr, G-3 SHAEF to CofS FUSAG, CofS 21 AG, CofS AEAF, 2 Jun 44, sub: Establishment of a Combined US/British A/B Trs Hq SHAEF/24501/Ops (A). In SHAEF G-3 17281/1 (Formation of FAAA).

43. Ltr, CofS FUSAG to G-3 SHAEF, 8 Jun 44, sub: Establishment of a Combined US/British A/B Trs Hq 322 (G-3). In SHAEF G-3 17281/1 (Formation of FAAA).

44. Ltr, Brig R. M. Belcham to SHAEF, 4 Jun 44, no sub 21 A Gp/00/432/Ops (B). In SHAEF G-3 17281/1 (Formation of FAAA).

45. Ltr, SASO AEAF to G-3 SHAEF, 8 Jun 44, sub: Establishment of Combined US/British A/B Trs Hq AEAF/TS 22518. In SHAEF G-3 17281/1 (Formation of FAAA).

46. Ltr, G-3 SHAEF to CofS SHAEF, 17 Jun 44, sub: Airborne Troops. SHAEF/24501/Ops. In SHAEF G-3 17281/1 (Formation of FAAA)

47. Memo, CofS SHAEF for G-3 SHAEF, 20 June 44, sub: Airborne Troops. In SHAEF G-3 17281/1 (Formation of FAAA).

48. Ltr, Maj L. Gardner to Chief A/B Sub-sec G-3 SHAEF, 26 Jun 44, sub: Proposed A/B Hq. In SHAEF G-3 17281/1 (Formation of FAAA).

49. *Ibid.*

50. Ltr, Maj L. Gardner to Chief A/B Sub-sec SHAEF G-3, 27 Jun 44, sub: Suggested Combined A/B Hq. In SHAEF G-3 17281/1 (Formation of FAAA).

51. Ltr, ACM T. Leigh-Mallory to SHAEF, 17 July 44, sub: Orgn of a Combined US/British A/B Tr Hq. AEAF/TS 22518/Ops 3. In SHAEF G-3 17281/1 (Formation of FAAA).

52. Copy, Ltr, CofS SHAEF to ACinC AEAF, 31 Jul 44, sub: Org of a Combined US/British A/B Tr Hq. SHAEF/17281/Ops (A). In SHAEF G-3 17281/1 (Formation of FAAA).

53. Msg, Gen Marshall to Gen Eisenhower, 26 Jun 44. W-5 6294. SHAEF 75/8. In SHAEF G-3 17281/1 (Formation of FAAA).

54. Msg, Gen Arnold to USSTAF for Spaatz, SHAEF for Smith, 7 Jul 44. WX-61600. SHAEF 189/07. In SHAEF G-3 17281/1 (Formation of FAAA).

55. Msg, Eisenhower to Gen Marshall, 8 Jul 44. S-55194. In SHAEF G-3 17281/1 (Formation of FAAA).

56. Memo, Col Joe A. Hinton for Chief Plans and Ops Sec G-3 SHAEF, 30 Jun 44, sub: Personnel for A/B Hq. In SHAEF G-3 17281/1 (Formation of FAAA).

57. Msg, Marshall to Eisenhower for SHGCT, 8 Jul 44. W-62223. SHAEF 241/08. In SHAEF G-3 17281/1 (Formation of FAAA).

58. Ltr, AG SHAEF to CG ComZ ETOUSA, 1 Aug 44, sub: Establishment of a Combined A/B Hq and an A/B Corps Hq (U.S.) in the ETO. AG 322-1 (Comb A/B Hq) GCT-AGM. In SHAEF G-3 17281/1 (Formation of FAAA).

59. *Ibid.*

60. *The Brereton Diaries,* p. 309.

61. Ltr, Gen Brereton to Gen Eisenhower, 25 July 44, sub: Organization and Contemplated Operations of an Air Army. In SHAEF G-3 17281/1 (Formation of FAAA).

62. *Ibid.*

63. Ltr, CG Ninth Army to Maj Gen M. B. Ridgway, 4 Aug 44, sub: Assumption of Certain Command Functions Relating to A/B Units. In SHAEF G-3 17281/1 (Formation of FAAA).

64. Memo, Lt Gen Brereton for SCAEF, 4 Aug 44, sub: Designation of Combined Airborne Forces. In SHAEF G-3 17281/1 (Formation of FAAA).

65. Memo, G-3 SHAEF for CofS SHAEF, 9 Aug 44, sub: Redesignation of Combined A/B Forces. In SHAEF G-3 17281/1 (Formation of FAAA).

66. Ltr, AG SHAEF to War Office, CGS Army Groups, *et al,* 16 Aug 44, sub: Redesignation of Combined A/B Forces. AG 322-1 (First Allied Airborne Army) GCT-AGM. In SHAEF G-3 17281/1 (Formation of FAAA).

67. Ltr, AG SHAEF to Lt Gen Lewis H. Brereton, 8 Aug 44, sub: Directive. AG 322-1 (Combined Airborne H2) GCT-AGM. In SHAEF G-3 17281/1 (Formation of FAAA).

68. Ltr, CofS SHAEF to Air C-in-C AEAF, 18 Aug 44, sub: Reorganization of A/B Forces. SHAEF/17281/1 Ops (A). In SHAEF G-3 17281/1 (Formation of FAAA).

69. Ltr, G-3 SHAEF to CofS SHAEF, 22 Nov 44, sub: Reorganization of Hq, First Allied Airborne Army, and enclosed Study of Proposed Organization for First Allied Airborne Army. In SHAEF G-3 17281/1 (Formation of FAAA).

70. Ltr, TAG to CC USFETO, 10 Jan 45, sub: Reorganization of A/B Tr Basis for US Forces in ETO. AG 320.2 (4 Jan 45) OB-I-E-M. See T/O and E 210-IT, 26 Dec 44, and related tables.

71. 1st Ind. AG ETOUSA to CG First (Allied) Airborne Army (US Increment), 31 Jan 45, AG 322 Op CG, on ltr, TAG to CG USFETO, 15 Jan 45, sub: Constitution and Activation of First Airborne Army, AG 322 (12 Jan 45) OB-I-GNGCT-M. In FAAA 322 (Microfilm roll No. 1).

Chapter IV

The Machines: Quality and Quantity

1. Ltr, CG ASC to CG AAF, n.d. (circa 1 Apr 42), in AFTCC 322 (Plans and Programs), cited in AAF, I Troop Carrier Command, Vol III: The Training of Troop Carrier Air Echelons, Part II, The Operational Training Program, pp. 7, 11. Unpublished ms filed in Air Hist Off, 252-3, vol 2 (3379-3).

2. *Ibid.*, p. 13.

3. *Ibid.*, 00.14, 239-240.

4. AAF, I Troop Carrier Command. The Operational Training Program, p. 375. Air Hist Off, pp. 252-3, vol. 2. For carrying capacity of airplanes, see FM 100-10, *Staff Officers' Field Manual,* 10 Oct 43, par. 1016; *see also* TM 71-210, *Air Transport of Troops and Equipment,* 30 Apr. 45.

5. AAF, I Tr Carrier Cmd, The Operational Training Program, pp. 314-315. Air Hist Off, 252-3, vol. 2.

6. See WD Gen Council Min, 19 Mar 45. AAF, I Tr Carrier Comd, The Operational Trng Program, pp. 375-77.

7. Ltr, AGF Test Officer to CG Airborne Comd, 12 Dec 42. AFTCC 452.04 (Experiments, Tests and Trials), cited in *ibid.,* p. 376.

8. AAF, I Tr Carrier Cmd, The Operational Training Program, pp. 383-386.

9. Ltr, Brig Gen Josiah T. Dalbey to CG AGF, 7 May 45, sub: Rpt of O'seas Duty, ETO. Mimeo copy in AGF G-3 A/B Br (O'seas Obsrs Rpts.).

10. Draft of ltr, CG I Tr Carrier Cmd. to CG Continental AF, May 1945. Quoted in AAF, I Troop Carrier Command, The Operational Training Program, pp. 378-379. Air Hist Off 252-3, v 2.

11. AAF, I Troop Carrier Command, The Operational Training program, MD 390-91. Air Hist Off 252-3, v. 2.

12. AGF memo for CofS USA (Attn G-4 Div), 3 Nov 45, sub: Glider Requirements. GNRQT – 7/44168. 452.1/150 (Airplanes). For characteristics of all transport aircraft in use. See TM 71-210, "Air Transport of Troops and Equipment," 30 Apr 45, pp. 19-68.

13. AAF, I Troop Carrier Command, The Operational Training Program, pp. 382-385.

14. *Ibid.*, pp. 383-386.

15. *Ibid.*, pp. 388.

16. *Ibid.*, pp. 388-390.

17. *Ibid.*, pp. 386-387.

18. *Ibid.*, pp. 390-391.

19. AGF M/S, Tng (Spec Proj) to G-3, 24 Aug 44, sub: Troop Carrier Aircraft. In AGF G-3 A/B Br (A/B Suspense Aug 44).

20. AGF Study No. 25, p. 47.

21. See "The Role of GHQ in the Development of Airborne Training," in Greenfield *et al, The Organization of Ground Combat Troops,* pp. 94-96.

22. Memo, Gen Twaddle for CG AAF, 13 Mar 42, sub: Air Transports for Pcht Trp Tng. 452.1261 (A/B).

23. Ltr of Gen Lee to CG AGF, 18 Apr 42, sub: Airborne Comd Tng Situation. 353/1 (A/B) (C).

24. AAF, I Troop Carrier Command, The Operational Training Program, pp. 241-245. Air Hist Off 252-3, v 2.

25. AGF M/S (s) 452.1 (5 Sept 42) DCofS to G-3 AGF, 14 Sept 42, sub: Reqts for Glider and Trp Carrier Gps. 452.1/58 (Airplanes).

26. Draft ltr of Cg I Trp Carrier Cmd to Cos, 23 Nov 42. AFTCC 353.02 (Tng and Instr). Cited in *ibid.*, p. 247.

27. Wesley Frank Craven and James Lea Cate, eds, *The Army Air Forces in World War II* (Chicago, 1948) I, 347, 641.

28. *Ibid.*, II, 644.

29. *Ibid.*, II, 83.

30. *Ibid.*, p. 99.

31. *Ibid.*

32. Tactical Employment of the U. S. Army of Transport Aircraft and Gliders in World War II, (a study prepared for AAF Historical Office by Col Samuel T. Moore), I, 101. Photostat copy in Command and General Staff College Library. S-16464-A.

33. *Ibid.*, p. 15.

34. *Ibid.*, II, 389.

35. Craven and Cate, *The Army Air Forces in World War II,* I, 358-59.

36. *The Aircraft Yearbook for 1946,* p. 496.

37. *Ibid.*

38. Craven and Cate, *The Army Air Forces in World War II,* I, 623.

39. *The Aircraft Yearbook for 1946,* p. 474.

40. Craven and Cate, *The Army Air Forces in World War II,* II, 211-12.

41. *Ibid.*, p. 288.

42. (1) AAF Statistical Digest: World War II, p. 112; (2) *The Aircraft Yearbook for 1946,* p. 482.

43. Pers ltr, Gen Chapman to Gen. Parks, 30 Dec 42. 452.1./11 (A/B).

44. Rpt of Conf on Air Transport Requirements for Airborne Tng, Hq AGF, 14 Jul 42, 452.1/56 (Airplanes).

45. Memo, G-3WD for ACofS OPD 30 Oct 42, sub: Trp Carrier Rqmts for Airborne Tng. WDGCT 580.7. Copy incl no. 1 with memo, G-3, WD for ACofS OPD, 28 Jan 43, sub: Training of an Airborne Division WDGCT 353(25 Jan 43) In OPD 353 case 2.

46. Memo, G-3 WD for ACofS OPD, 13 Jan 43, sub: Attrition Rates for Aircraft. WDGCT 452.1 (28 Dec 42). Copy incl No. 2 with, *ibid.*

47. *Ibid.*

48. Memo, G-3 WD for ACofS OPD, 28 Jan 43, sub: Training of an Airborne Division, WDGCT 353 (25 Jan 43). In OPD 353, case 2.

49. OPD memo 353. (28 Jan 43) for ACofS, G-3, 1 Feb 43, sub: Training of an Airborne Division. OPD 353 case 2.

50. 2d draft, memo, CG AGF for CofS USA, 14 Jan 43, sub: Air Transport Reqts for A/B Tng. 452.1/11 (A/B).

51. Memo, Gen McNair for CofS USA, 14 Jan 43, sub: Air Transport Reqts for Airborne Tng 452.01/8-GNDCG. In 452.1/11 (Airborne).

52. *Ibid.*

53. (1) Memo, G-3 Spl Proj Div (Col R. Gaither) AGF for CofS AGF 18 Jan 43, sub: Rpt of Inspection of Airborne Installation. 353.02/7. (2) Ltr, AGF to CG Airborne Cmd. 18 Jan 43, sub: Visit to Airborne Cmd. Org. 353.02/7.

54. Memo, CG AGF memo for OPD WD, 21 Jan 43, Sub: Airborne Div for early Shipment Overseas 370.5 GNGCS. In 370.5/8 (A/B).

55. (1) Memo, G-3 WD to ACofS OPD, 4 Feb 43, sub: Tng of an Airborne Div WDGCT 353. In OPD 353 case 2. (2) AGF M/S, CofS to DCofS, 1 Feb 43. In 370.5/8.

56. Memo, CG AAF for G-3 WD, 22 Feb 43, sub: Tng of the 82d Airborne Div. In OPD 353 case 2.

57. (1) Memo, OPD for G-3 WD 4 Mar 43, sub: Tng of an Airborne Div. 353 (26 Feb 43). In OPD 353 case 2. (2) Memo, G-3 WD for CG AGF, 26 Feb 43, sub: Tng of an A/B Div., WDGCT 353, 22 Feb 43. In AGF 353/11 (A/B).

58. Memo, G-3 AGF for G-3 WD, 18 May 43, sub: Plans for Airborne Tng for Balance of 1943 353-GNGCT. 353/15 (A/B).

59. Memo, CG AAF for CofS USA (Attn G-3 Div), 3 Jan 43, sub: plans for Combined Troop Carrier-Airborne Training for Balance of 1943. AFACT-4. In AGF 353/15 (A/B).

60. Memo, G-3WD for CGs AGF and AAF, sub: Plans for Airborne Tng for Balance of 1943. WDGCT 353 (18 May 43). In AGF 353/15 (A/B).

61. Ltr, CG I Trp Carrier Cmd to CG AAF, 16 Jun 43, sub: Cooperation with Airborne Cmd. Incl, with AAF memo AFACT-4 for CofS USA, 19 Jun 43. Copy in 353/15 (A/B).

62. Memo, CG AGF for CofS USA, 22 June 43, sub: Plans for Airborne Tng for Balance of 1943 353-Gn GCT 353/15 (A/B).

63. WD memo MCGCT 353 (6 Jul 43) for CGs AGF and AAF, 23 Aug 43, sub: Plans for Airborne Tng for Balance of 1943, 353/15 (A/B).

64. 2nd ind, CG Airborne Cmd to CG AGF.

65. AGF M/S, G-3 to CofS AGF, 18 Sep 43 353/15 (A/B).

66. Rpt of the Board on Airborne Ops, 6 Sep 43. In AGF 353/17 (A/B). The Board generally was referred to as the Swing Board from the name of its chairman, Maj. Gen. Joseph M. Swing; the other members were Maj. Gen. Elbridge G. Chapman, CG of the Airborne Command, and Col. P. Ernest Gable, an Air Corps officer.

67. OPD memo for CofS USA, 17 Sept 43, sub: A/B Ops Bd. 334.8 (6 Sept. 43) In OPD 381 case 186.

68. WD memo for the CG's AGF and AAF, 24 Sept 43, sub: Schedule for Tr Carrier Unites. WDGCT 353.01. In OPD 381 case 186.

69. WD memo for CG AAF, 28 Oct 43, sub: Tr Carrier Units. WDGCT 334 (6 Sept 43). In OPD 381 case 186.

70. AAF, I Troop Carrier Command, The Operations Training Program pp. 264-265.

71. See FM 31-30, Tactics and Technique of Airborne Troops, 20 May 42, pars 129-136.

72. AGF Study No. 25, p. 10.

73. *Ibid.*, p. 11.

74. Airborne Comd 2nd ind to CG Air Serv Comd, 14 May 42, on Air Serv Comd ltr to CofInf, 14 May 42, sub: Activation of New Prcht Units. In AGF 320.2/5 (A/B).

75. Par 5b (2), AGF memo 320.2-GNTRG (4-24-42) for DofS USA (Attn G-3 Div), 20 May 42, sub: Activation of New Parachute units. In AGF 320.2/1 (Para Trps) (S).

76. Fld Serv Air Serv Comd 4th ind to Hq Air Serv Comd (Col J. T. Newberry), 6 Jun 42, on Air Serv Comd ltr to CofInf, 14 May 42, sub: Activation of New Pcht Units. In AGF 320.2/5 (A/B) (C).

77. Airborne Comd 7th ind to CG AGF, 1 Jul 42 on letter cited in note above.

78. Ltr CG AAF to CG AGF, 2 Sept 42, sub: Establishment of policy: (1) Pchts for Airborne Trps: (2) Responsibility for Loading of Transports and Gliders. 1st ind CG AGF to CG AAF, 20 Oct 42. 320.2/108 (A/B).

79. (1) AGF Study No. 25, pp. 65-67. (2) AGF M/S, G-3 to G-4, 18 Aug 44, sub: Quick Release Parachutes – Type T-7, and memo for record. In AGF G-3 A/B Br (A/B Suspense Aug 44). (3) AGF M/S, G-3 to RQTS, 28 Aug 44, same sub, and memo for record. In AGF G-3 A/B Br (A/B Suspense Aug 44).

80. FM 101-10, Staff Officers' Field Manual . . ., 21 Dec 44, par. 236.

81. Memo for record on AGF M/S, G-3 to RQTS, 13 Jul 44, sub: Parachute Aerial Delivery (Work Order DDM 3105). In AGF G-3 A/B Br (A/B Suspense Jul 44).

82. (1) OPD JEU – 3663. Capabilities of C-47 Transport and CG-4A Glider. In OPD 381 Case 186. (2) *See* Emanuele Stieri, *Gliders and Glider Training* (New York, 1943), pp. 65 ff.

83. Rpt of Maj Gen William C. Lee and Lt Col Silas R. Richards to CofS USA, 5 Apr 43, sub: Report of Discussions with British Authorities on the Subject of Gliders, Their Design, Manufacture, Procurement, Shipment and Use. 452.1/82 (Rpt. on Glider Developments to CofS).

84. Memo, Spl Projects Div G-3 Sec AGF to ACofS G-3, 28 Jan 43, sub: Transport Aircraft for Airborne Training. 353/10 (A/B) (S).

85. Ltr, Gen Chapman to Director Air Support, AAF, thru CG AGF, 31 Dec 42, sub: Proposed Cargo Glider. Cpy in 452.1/10 (A/B).

86. *See* Lewin B. Barringer, *Flight Without Power* (New York, 1942).

87. AGF M/S, TRG to CG (thru G-3), 2 Jul 42, sub: Assault Gliders. 452.1/52 (Airplanes) (S).

88. *Ibid.*

89. Ltr, CG AGF to CG AAF, 4 Jul 42, sub as above. *Ibid.*

90. Ltr, to CG Airborne Comd, 17 Jul 43, sub: Assault Gliders. 452.1/89 (Airplanes)

91. 1st ind. CG Airborne Comd to CG AGF, 4 Aug 43, on ltr cited above.

92. Ltr, CG Mtn Trng Cen to CG AGF, 19 Feb 43, sub: Gliders for Testing in Mountain Operations, and inds. 452.1/81 (Airplanes)

93. Glider Data, n.d. (c. 17 Apr 43) in OPD 381, Case 144.

94. Rpt of Maj. L. B. Magic, Jr., 121/1 GNVAS (C) to CG Airborne Comd, 16 Jul 43, copy Incl No. 2 with Airborne Comd 1st ind to CG AGF, 4 Aug 43, on AG ltr CNGCT to CG Airborne Comd, 17 Jul 43.

95. AAF, I Troop Carrier Command, The Glider Training Program, (C), pp. 176 ff. Air Hist Off 252 – 1 v 1.

96. AAF, I Troop Carrier Command, The Glider Training Program, pp. 96-97.

97. TM 71-210, 30 Apr 45, pp. 46-48.

98. *Ibid.*, pp. 236-239, 248-250.

99. *Ibid.*, pp. 49-52. OCMH Rpt of Col M. A. Quito on Visit in ETO, 5 May 45, para 4 c. OCMH file.

100. AGF memo for Chief, Rqts Sec. 13 Dec 44, Sub: Conf on Procurement of XCG-10A Gliders. 452.1/118.

101. AGF ltr to CG AAF (Attn ACofS, Material, Maintenance, and Distribution), 30 Jan 45, sub: Development of an Assault Type Glider to Replace Present CG-4 452.1/119 (Airplanes).

102. AAF memo (DC of Air Staff) for CG AGF, 21 Apr 45, Sub: Military Characteristics for New All-metal Gliders in AGF 452.1/119 (Airplanes).

103. AGF memo for CofS USA (Attn G-4 Div), 3 Nov 45, sub: Glider Requirements, Tab A AGF memo for CofS USA (Attn G-4 Div), 17 May 45, and WD D/F to CG AGF, 29 Dec 45, same sub, WDGS 7335. All in AGF 452.1/150 (Airplanes).

104. Speech of Capt J. W. Sharpe at Hq I Trp Carrier Cmd, Stout Field, 14 Jan 44. Copy filed in Air Hist Off 253.894.3.

105. AGF 1st ind, 25 Mar 42, on WD ltr to CG AGF (n.d.), sub: Mock-up of ICG-9 Glider, 452.1 (Airplanes).

106. AGF M/S (S), G-3 (Phillips for Lentz) to CofS, 12 Aug. 42, sub: Gliders for Airborne Tng. 452.1/58 (Airplanes).

107. Tactical Employment in the U. S. Army of Transport Aircraft and Gliders, II, 541.

108. Memo, G-3 AGF for CofS USA (Thru CG AAF), 16 Aug 42, sub as in note above. 452.1/58 (Airplanes).

109. AAF, I Troop Carrier Command, Glider Program, p. 28. Unpublished ms filed in Air Hist Off 252-1 v 1.

110. *Ibid.*, p. 29.

111. *Ibid.*, p. 106.

112. 1st ind, CG AGF to CG AAF on AAF D/F to CG AGF, 20 Jan 43, sub: Reqts for Pcht Pools for Airborne Tng. 353/8 (A/B).

113. *Ibid.*

114. AAF, I Troop Carrier Command, Glider Program, p. 119. Air Hist Off 252-1 v 2.

115. *Ibid.*, pp. 121-128.

116. Glider Data, in OPD 38 case 144.

117. Ltr, CG Airborne Cmd to CG AGF, 11 May 43, Sub: Glider Needs for Airborne Cmd 1943 and 1944, 452.1/85 (Airplanes).

118. I Trp Carrier Cmd R&R, CofS to CG, 19 Jun 43, in AFTCC 353 (Glider Training). Quoted in AAF, I Troop Carrier Command, The Glider Program, p. 57, Air Hist Off 252-1 v 1.

119. AAF, I Troop Carrier Command, Glider Program, pp. 74-75, Air Hist Off 252-1 v 1.

120. *Ibid.*, pp. 43-47.

121. Ltr., CG I Trp Carrier Cmd to CG AAF, 30 Dec 43, AFTCC 337 (Conferences, Military and Naval), Quoted in AAF, I Troop Carrier Cmd, Glider Program, p. 1 Air Hist Off 252-1 v 1.

122. Ltr, CG Airborne Cmd to CG AAF, 11 May 43, sub: Glider Needs of Airborne Cmd for 1943-1944. 452.1/85 (Airplanes).

123. Pathfinders, p. 2. Air Hist Off 251-4.

124. *Brereton Diaries,* p. 216.

125. Pathfinders, p. 21.

126. (1) WD Gen Council Min 28 May 45. (2) Memo for record on AGF M/s, G-3 27 to G-3 15, 8 Aug 45. In AGF G-3 A/B Br (A/B corresp Aug 45).

127. (1) WD Gen Council Min (S), 2 Apr 45 and 11 June 45. (2) Copy of reply to Questionnaire for Commanders Airborne Divisions, The General Board, USFET, n.d., unsigned. In AGF G-3 A/B Br (A/B Corresp Aug 46).

128. AGF M/S, G-3 to RQTS, 24 Nov 44, sub: Further Study of Radar Equipment and its Employment, and memo for record. In AGF G-3 A/B Br (A/B Suspense Nov 44).

Chapter V

The Men: Morale and Training

1. Statement of Col M. A. Quinto to Airborne Center Hist Off, Oct 45, cited in AGF Study No. 25, p. 6.

2. AAF, I Troop Carrier Command, The Operational Training Program, p. 171. Air Hist Off 252-3 v 2.

3. *Ibid.*, p. 172.

4. *Ibid.*

5. Suggested Points for Training Conference, Ft. Worth, 10 Jan 44, by Maj C. P. Hutchens, I Trp Carrier Comd, Asst A-3, Jan 44, A-3 Journal in AFTCC files, cited in AAF, I Troop Carrier Command, The Transition Training Program, p. 67.

6. Ltr, Col Reed G. Landis to Maj Gen Orlando Ward, 31 Jul 50. In OCMH.

7. Col J. J. Roberts, Jr., Individual Staff Study, 2d Command Class (1946), Command and General Staff College. N-13724.

8. R. R. Palmer, B. I. Wiley and W. R. Keast, *The Procurement and Training of Ground Combat Troops,* in THE UNITED STATES IN WORLD WAR II (Washington, 1948), p. 20.

9. (1) AGF Study No. 25; (2) WD Bull 19, Aug 44.

10. AAF, I Troop Carrier Command, The Glider Program, p. 7. Air Hist Off, pp. 252-1 v i.

11. Rpt on Prcht and Glider Fatalities, Injuries, and Glider Damage. A/B Misc 1942-1945/26. In OCAFF, Tng Sec (hereafter cited ATTNG), Joint Policy, Maneuvers, and Special Projects Div, Air and Airborne Br (Fort Monroe, Va.).

12. AGF Study No. 25, reproduced in App 22 of that study.

13. (1) *Ibid.*; (2) WD Bull 19, 26 Aug 44.

14. Commentson The Airborne Team,incl with memo, Lt Gen M. B. Ridgway for Chief of Military History, 29 May 50, sub: Airborne Team. In OCMH.

15. Ltr, Ridgway to Lentz, 14 Feb 43, copy in Lentz 201, Personal.

16. Tng Program, Air Transport Comd, 29 May 42 (s), copy in Air Hist Off 253.87-5.

17. CofS ATC to CO, Staff, and Trans Off, and to CO 50th Air Transp Wing, 9 Jun 42, in AFTCC 353.02 (Tng and Instr), quoted in AAF, I Troop Carrier Command, Vol. III: Training of Air Echelons, Part I: The Establishment of the Command Training Program, p. 7. Air Hist Off 25203 v 1 (2380-1).

18. Ltr, Col Reed G. Landis to Maj Gen Orlando Ward, 31 Jul 50. In OCMH.

19. AAF, I Troop Carrier Command, The Operational Training Program, pp. 290-292. Air Hist Off, 252-3 Vol. 2.

20. *Ibid.*, p. 291.

21. AAF, I Troop Carrier Command, The Glider Training Program, pp. 25-29, Air Hist Off 252-1 v 1.

22. (1) Ltr, Col D. M. Schlatter, Director of Air Support, to CG AGF, 16 Nov 42, sub: Inf Instructors for Glider Pilots. 353/5 (A/B). (2) 2d Wrapper ind CG airborne Cmd to CG AGF, 18 Dec 42. (3) Glider Pilot Training Survey by M. A. Quinto, Lt Col 88th Glider Inf, Ft Bragg, N. C., incl with Airborne Cmd 2d Wrapper ind. (4) AGF M/S G-3 to CofS, 23 Dec 42, sub as above, *ibid.* (5) 1st ind CG AGF to CG AAF, 27 Dec 42. (6) 2d ind CG AAF to CG AGF, 11 Feb 43.

23. "History of Liaison between Airborne and Troop Carrier Command," Maj A. B. Oldfield, Airborne Liaison Officer, Sep 43, in AFTCC hist files, quoted in AAF, I Troop Carrier Command, "The Operational Training Program," p. 268. Air Hist Off 252-3 v 2 (3379-3).

24. *Ibid.*

25. Memo, Co ATC for Col Philip R. Love, ATC Ln Off, 31 May 42, in AFTCC 322.01 (Ln Off), quoted in *ibid.*, p. 270.

26. Ltr, CO ATC to CG Airborne Comd 24 Jul 42, in AFTCC 353.02 (Instruction Visits). Quoted in *ibid.,* pp. 270-271.

27. Memo, ACofS A-3 Air Transp Comd for CofS Air Transp Comd, 10 Jul 42, in AFTCC 353.02 (Instruction Visits). Cited in *ibid.*

28. *Ibid.*, p. 274.

29. In general ltr, CG AGF to CG's Second Army, Third Army, Airborne Comd. 21 Oct 42, sub: Tng of Airborne Divs. Mimeo cpy in AGF 353/11 (A/B).

30. Brig Gen E. G. Chapman, "American Divisions take to the Air," *Military Review,* XXIII (Apr 1943), 13.

31. Ltr, Gen Arnold to CG AGF, 25 Jul 43, sub: Troop Carrier Tng. 353/193 (A/B).

32. WD Gen Council Min, 25 Oct 43.

33. (1) Rpt of Board on Airborne Operations, 6 Sept 43. 353/17 (A/B). Ltr, CG AAF to CO I Troop Carrier Cmd, 30 Aug 43, and I Trp Carrier Cmd 1st ind to CG AAF, 1 Oct 43, in AFTCC 322 (Airborne Command). (2) Cited in AAF, I Troop Carrier Command, The Operational Training Program, p. 293, Air Hist off 252-3 v 2. (3) OPD memo for CofS USA, 7 Oct 43, sub: Airborne Operations. 381 (2 Oct 43). In OPD 381 case 186. Also in AGF 353/311 (Air-Gnd).

34. WD memo for CGs AGF and AAF, 9 Oct 43, sub: Directive for Joint Tng of Airborne and Troop Carrier Units. WDGCT 353 (1 Oct 43) 353/199 (A/B).

35. AGF M/S, G-3 to CofS, 11 Oct 43, sub: Directive for Joint Training of Airborne and Troop Carrier Units. 353/199 (A/B).

36. CG to G-3, 15 Oct 43, *ibid.*

37. Memo, G-3 WD for DCofS USA, 19 Oct 43, sub: Airborne Operations Report. WDGCT 334 (6 Sept 43). In OPD 381 case 186.

38. OPD memo for G-3 WD, 28 Oct 43, sub: Airborne Ops Bd. 344.8 (19 Oct 43). In OPD 381 case 186.

39. Memo, G-3 WD for OPD, 28 Oct 43, sub: Airborne Ops. WDGCT 334. In OPD 381 case 186.

40. *Ibid.*

41. OPD memo 381 for G-3, 30 Oct 43, sub: Airborne Ops. OPD 381 case 186.

42. (1) Memo, G-3 WD for OPD, 28 Oct 43, sub: A/B Ops Board. WDGCT 334. (2) OPD memo for record 334.8 (19 Oct 43), 2 Nov 43. Both in OPD 381 case 186.

43. (1) OPD memo for record 334.8 (19 Oct 43). In OPD 381 case 186. (2) WD memo for CG's AGF and AAF, 5 Nov 43, sub: A/B and Tr Carrier Units WDGCT 334 (28 Oct 43). In AGF 353/15 (A/B).

44. Pathfinder Doctrine, Organization and Procedures, (Developed by 511th Prct Inf) incl no. 1 with ltr, CG AGF to CO Fifth Army A/B Tng Cen, 15 Aug 44, sub: Pathfinder Procedures. 353 (A/B) GNGCT-31. In A/B Suspense Aug 44, ATTNG, A/B Br.

45. AAF, I Troop Carrier Command, Vol III: The Training of Troop Carrier Air Echelons, part IV: Pathfinder Training within I Troop Carrier Command, pp. 16, 22, 24, 52. Typescript in Air Hist Off, 251-4.

46. AAF, I Troop Carrier Command, The Operational Training Program, pp. 313-314.

47. Ltr, Brig Gen Godfrey to Chief of Engrs, 14 May 42, sub: Airborne Aviation Engineers, Ag 321.7. In 353/4 (A/B).

48. WD 8th ind AG 321.7 MS-SPOPP to CG AGF, 14 Jul 42.

49. Notes of Conf on Airborne Avn Engrs held in Rm 4232, Munitions Bldg., Wash., D.C., 8 Jun 42, Mimeo cy in 353/4 (A/B).

50. AAF, I Troop Carrier Command, Vol V: Special Projects of I Troop Carrier Command, Part I: The Training of Airborne Engineer Aviation Battalions within I Troop Carrier Command, p. 4. Ms in Air Hist Off 251-1.

51. *Ibid.*, p. 14.

52. *Ibid.*, pp. 22-32.

53. Memo of I Trp Carrier Cmd, 12 Aug 43, cited in *ibid.*, p. 24.

54. T/O&E 17-55, 17-56, 17-57, 14 Jan 44.

55. Ltr Maj E. Bibb (CO, 28th A/B Tnk Bn) to TAG (thru channels), 28 Apr 44, sub: Classification of Airborne Tank Units. Copy in AGF G-3 A/B Br (A/B Suspense Apr 44).

56. Memo for record, on AGF M/S, G-3 to RQTS, 17 Aug 44, sub: Test of Airborne Tank. In AGF G-3 A/B Br (A/B Suspense Aug 44).

57. AGF M/S, G-3 31 to CofS, 26 Mar 45, sub: Aerial Delivery of Offensive Chemical Warfare Material, in AGF G-3 A/B Br (A/B suspense Mar 45), and AGF 6th ind, 14 Apr 45, on AGF ltr to CG A/B Cen, 8 Oct 44, same sub, 400.112 CNGCT-31.

58. AAF, I Troop Carrier Command, The Operational Training Program, pp. 305-307. Air Hist Off 252-3 v 2.

59. Ltr of Air Def Dept, AAF School of Applied Tactics, to CG AAF (Attn Director of Air Def), 9 Mar 43, sub: Request for Parachute Training, and AAF 1st ind thereon to CG AGF, 20 Mar 43, and subsequent AGF and Airborne Cmd inds. 353/18 (A/B).

60. AGF Study 25, p. 29.

61. WD Gen Council Min, 19 Jun 44.

62. AGF Study No. 25, p. 29.

63. AAF, I Troop Carrier Command, The Operational Training Program, p. 300-303. Air Hist Off, 252-3, v 2.

64. AGF M/S, G-3 to G-4 (Attn Col St. Onge), 16 Jul 44, sub: Air Transport Tng of Inf Divs. In AGF G-3 A/B Br (A/B Suspense Jul 44).

65. AGF M/S, G-3 to CofS, 17 Jul 44, sub: Air Transport Tng of Inf Divs. In A/B Suspense Jul 44/4. ATTNG, A/B Br. A month earlier AAF had requested data concerning the air movement of one infantry division a distance of 400 miles with airplanes carrying crews of five men. Passing the request along to Airborne Center, AGF interpreted the request as one not requiring the presentation of "specific loads and mass of details," but a general study which might form the basis for evaluating such an operation. – AGF 1st Ind, to CG A/B Cen 19 Jun 44, on AAF memo for G-3 AGF (Attn Lt Col F. E. Ross), 17 June 44, sub: Air Trans of Inf Divs. In AGF G-3 A/B Br (A/B Suspense Jun 44).

66. (1) AGF M/S, G-3 to CofS, 17 Jul 44, sub: Air Trans Tng of Inf Divs. (2) Ltr, CG AGF to CG XVIII Corps, 17 Jul 44, sub: Assignment of Personnel from the 13th A/B Div on Ty Dy at A/B Cen. In AGF 353 (A/B) GNGCT-31. (3) AGF M/S, G-3 to G-1, 18 Jul 44, sub: Air Trans Tng of Inf Div. In AGF G-3 A/B Br (A/B Suspense Jul 44).

67. Ltr, CG AGF to CG A/B Cen, 18 Jul 44, sub: Air Transp Tng of Inf Divs. In AGF G-3 A/B Br (A/B Suspense Jul 44).

68. Ltr, A/B Cen (CofS) to CG AGF, 1 Aug 44, sub: Outline for Air Transport Tng. In AGF G-3 A/B Br (A/B Mixc 1942-45).

69. AGF M/S, G-3 to CofS, 1 Aug 44, sub: Air Trans Tng of Inf Divs. 353 (A/B) (18 Jul 44) GNGCT-31. In AGF G-3 (A/B Suspense Aug 44).

70. (1) AGF M/S, Tng (Spec Proj) to G-3, 29 Jul 44, sub: Air Trans Tng – 84th Inf Div. (2) AGF M/S, Tng (Spec Proj) to G-3, 4 Aug 44, sub: Air Trans Tng – 103d Inf Div. Both in AGF G-3 A/B Br (A/B Suspense Aug 44).

71. AGF memo for CofS USA (Attn OPD, Lt Col M. S. Griffin, 9 Aug 44, sub: Air Trans Tng of Inf Divs. 353/105 (A/B) GNGCT-31.

72. AGF memo for CofS USA (Attn OPD, Lt Col Starbird), 27 Sep 44, sub: Air Trans Tng of Inf Divs. In AGF 353 (A/B) (21 Sep 44) GNGCT-31.

73. Col. H. L. Clark, Hq 50th Trp Carrier Wing, to CG I Trp Carrier Cmd. 6 Nov 42, in AFTCC 354.2 (Maneuvers). Quoted in AAF I Troop Carrier Command, The Operational Training Program, p. 321. Air Hist Off 252-3 v 2.

74. AGF Study 25, p. 22.

75. Brig. Gen. Fred S. Borum, "Here Come the Airborne Troops," *Air Force,* XXVI (Feb 1943), 8-9.

76. AAF, I Troop Carrier Cmd, The Operational Training Program, p. 322. In Air Hist Off 252-3 v 2.

77. Borum, "Here Come the Airborne Troops."

78. AAF, I Tr Carrier Cmd, The Operational Tng Program, pp. 322-23.

79. AGF study No. 25, p. 23.

80. Rad from Hq Second Army, 30 Mar 43, ref: Inspection of 82 Div. Incl with ltr, CG AGF to CG Airborne Cmd, sub: Training, Airborne Divs. In AGF 253/12 (A/B).

81. D/F, OPD to G-3 WD, 25 Jan 43, sub: Tng of an A/B Div, and Note for Record. In OPD 353 case 2.

82. AGF Study No. 5.

83. Comment: inclosed with memo, Lt Gen M. B. Ridgway for Chief of Military History, 29 May 50. In OCMH.

84. WD Gen Council Min, 3 May 43.

85. The Operational Training Program, p. 325. Air Hist Off 252-3 v 2.

86. WD Gen Council Min. 31 May 43, quoted in *ibid.*, p. 326.

87. AGF memo for Mr. McCloy, 12 Jun 43, sub: Maneuver, 101st Airborne Div. 353/2 (101st A/B Div).

88. I Trp Carrier Cmd, R&R, CofS to CG, 6 Jun 43, quoted in The Operational Training Program, pp. 328-29. Air Hist Off 252-3 v 2.

89. The Operational Training Program, pp. 327-31. *Ibid.*

90. Pers ltr, Gen McNair to Gen Fredendall, 2 Jul 43, 322.98/90.

91. (1) Report on Combined Airborne-Troop Carrier Maneuver, Camp Mackall, N. C., Dec 6-11, incl, 1943. Mimeo cy in AGF Special Projects file. (2) The Operational Training Program, pp. 331-38.

92. AAF, I Troop Carrier Command, p. 32. Air Hist Off 251-1.

93. A-3 Report on Opn BANDIT, to CG Comb Airborne-Trp Carrier Hq. 15 Dec 43. Incl in Report of maneuver cited above.

94. Ltr, CG Airborne Cmd to CG Air Serv Cmd thru CG AGF, 17 Dec 43, sub: Aerial Resupply in Command Airborne-Trp Carrier Maneuver. Cy and memo for record in 353/199 (A/B).

95. WD Gen Council Min, 13 Dec 43.

96. *Ibid.*

97. G-3 Report in Rpt of combined Maneuver cited above.

98. The Operational Training Program, pp. 337-338.

99. AAF, I Troop Carrier Command, The Operational Training Program, p. 338. Air Hist Off, 252-3 v 2.

100. *Ibid.*, pp. 338-41.

101. Rpt. of Combined Airborne-Troop Carrier Maneuver, January 5-9, G-3 Report. Mimeo copy in AGF Spl Projects file.

102. A-3 Rpt in Rpt of Combined Maneuver.

103. A-3 Rpt in Rpt of Combined Maneuver.

104. Rpt of Combined Airborne-Troop Carrier Maneuver. Quoted in AAF, I Troop Carrier Command, The Operational Training Program. p. 342.

105. AGF memo for CofS USA (Attn G-3 Div), 18 Apr 44, sub: Joint Tng of A/B and Tr Carrier Units thru July 1944. In AGF G-3 A/B Br (A/B Suspense Apr 44).

106. AGF M/S, G-3 to CofS, 29 Jun 44, sub: Joint Troop Carrier-A/B Tng, 13th A/B Div. In AGF G-3 Br (A/B Suspense Jun 44).

107. WD Gen Council Min. 21 Aug 44.

108. AAF, I Troop Carrier Command, The Operational Training Program, pp. 343-44. Air Hist Off, 252-3 v 2.

109. (1) Rpt of Combined A/B-Tr Carrier Maneuver, 24 to 29 Sept 44. Mimeo cy in AGF Spl Proj file (c). (2) WD Gen Council Min, 2 Oct 44.

110. AAF, I Troop Carrier Command, The Operational Training Program, pp. 344-46. Air Hist Off, 252-3 v 2.

111. (1) WD Gen Council Min. 2 Oct 44. (2) A-3 Rpt of Combined Maneuver.

112. AAF, I Troop Carrier Command, The Operational Training Program, p. 346.

113. A-3 Rpt and Combined A-2, A/B-2, G-2 Rpt in Rpt of Combined Airborne-Tr Carrier Maneuver.

114. A-3 Rpt in Rpt of Combined A/B-Tr Carrier Manuever.

115. Rpt of Combined A/B-Tr Carrier Maneuver. Quoted in I Troop Carrier Command, The Operational Program, p. 347.

116. Extract of ltr, AGF Board, Hq A/B Tng Cen, North Africa to G-3 Tng, AFHQ, 24 Aug 43, sub: Qualification of Parachutists, In AGF G-3 A/B Br, Overseas Observers Rpts (s) A9.

117. Memo, Williams (Spl Proj Div, G-3 Sec) for Gen Lentz, 11 Oct 43, sub: Overseas Observer Report. In AGF G-3 A/B Br, Overseas Observers' Rpts.

118. Comments incl with memo, Gen Ridgway for Gen Ward, 29 May 50.

119. AGF M/S G-3 to CofS, 1 May 44, sub: Prcht Repls. In AGF G-3 A/B Br (A/B Suspense May 44).

120.(1) Draft AGF memo for CofS USA (Attn G-3 Div), 9 May 44, sub: Prct Repls. 320.2 (O'seas Repls) GNGCT. In AGF G-3 A/B Br (A/B Suspense May 44). (2) AGF M/S Tng (Spl Proj) to G-3, 9 May 44 sub: O'seas Rpt re A/B. In *ibid.*

121. AGF memo for CofS USA (Attn – 3 Div), 9 May 44, sub: Prcht Repls. 320.2 (O'seas Repls) GNGCT.

122. AGF M/S G-3 to CofS, 24 May, sub: Prcht Repls, and memo for Record. In AGF G-3 Br (A/B Suspense May 44).

123. AGF M/S, G-3 to CofS, 12 Jun 44, sub: Prcht Repls. In AGF G-3 A/B Br (A/B Suspense Jun 44).

124. AGF M/S, G-3 to CofS *et al.*, 28 Jun 44, sub: Prcht Repls. In AGF G-3 A/B Br (A/B Suspense Jun 44).

125. AGF M/S, G-3 to CofS, 4 Jul 44, sub: Study of Prcht Repls, and Tabs A to O. In AGF G-3 A/B Br (A/B Suspense Jul 44).

126. Ltr, CG AGF to CG R&SC, 22 Jul 44, sub: Capacity of Prcht School. 341/7(A/B) GNGCT-12.

127. AGF M/S, G-3 to AG, 16 Aug 44, sub: Capacity of Prcht School, and memo for record. In AGF G-3 A/B Br (A/B Suspense Aug 44).

128. Draft AGF memo for CofS USA (Attn G-3 Div), N. D., sub: Joint Airborne and Troop Carrier Tng. AGF M/S, G-3 to CofS, 25 Sep 44, same sub. 353 (Air-Ground) 14 Sep 44 GHGCT – 31. In AGF G-3 A/B Br (A/B Suspense Sep 44).

129. (1) WD memo for CG AGF, 11 Nov 44, sub: Paratroop Repls. OPD 370.5. Copy, Tab D in AGF G-3 A/B Br (A/B Suspense Mar 45)). (2) Memo of Lt Col L. A. Walsh, Jr., for Gen Donovan, 14 Nov 44, sub: Prcht Repls (Tab A), memo for record, and AGF M/S, G-3 to CofS, 22 Nov 44, sub: Prcht Repl Rqts. In AGF G-3 A/B Br (A/B Suspense Nov 44).

130. WD memo for CG AGF, 15 Dec 44, sub: Paratroop Repls. WDGCT 200. Copy (Tab C) in AGF G-3 A/B Br in A/B Suspense (S) Mar 45/1.

131. AGF M/S, G-3 to CofS, 5 Mar 45, sub: Increased Production of Paratroops. In AGF G-3 A/B Br (A/B Suspense Mar 45).

132. AGF M/S, G-3 to CofS, 25 Sep 44, sub: Joint Airborne and Troop Carrier Tng. 353 (Air-Ground) (14 Sep 44).

133. WD memo for CG AGF, AAF, 28 Nov 44, sub: Joint Airborne and Tr Carrier Tng. WDGCT 452.1 (24 Aug 44). Copy in AGF G-3 A/B Br (A/B Suspense Nov 44).

134. Ltr, CG AGF to CG A/B Cen, 16 Dec 44, sub: Joint A/B and Tr Carrier Tng. 353/106 (A/B) (28 Nov 44 GNGCT – 31.

135. AGF M/S, G-3 to CofS, 3 Jan 45, sub: Inf Adv Rpl Tng Gen (Prcht), Ft Benning, Ga, and Tab I, Removal of Prcht Tng Bns from Ft Benning. In AGF G-3 A/B Br (A/B Suspense Jan 45).

136. Paraphrase of message from OPD to CG ETO, 28 Feb 45. Tab B in AGF G-3 A/B Br (A/B Suspense Mar 45).

137. Ltr, CG AGF to CG R&S Cmd, 5 Mar 45, sub: Increased Input into Prcht School, 353 GNGCT – 12, and WD memo for CG AGF, 27 Feb 45, sub: Capacity of Repl Tng Centers, WDGCT 320 (RTC) (Tab A). In AGF G-3 A/B Br (A/B Suspense Mar 45).

138. Draft M/S, G-3 to CofS, submitted by Col Ross to Col Pesek, 11 Oct 44, sub: 541st Parachute Regiment, in A/B suspense Oct 44 memo, Lt Col L. A. Walsh, Jr., for Colonels Pesek, Todd and Faine, 20 Oct 44, sub: Arrangements Necessary to Relieve 541st Inf of Present Mission with Prcht School to Enable it to be organized as a Regt on the Tr Basis, in A/B susp Oct 44; AGF M/S, G-3 to CofS, 9 Nov 44, sub: 541st Prcht Inf Regt, in A/B susp (S) Nov 44. In AGF G-3 A/B Br.

139. Cable, OPD WDGS to CA ETO, 18 Dec 44, Ex 71866. in OPD 353 case 60 (TS).

140. AGF M/S, Spec Proj to Tng Div, 12 Apr 45, sub: Status of A/B Units for Redeployment, with 1 incl. In A/B susp Apr 45/3 ATTNG, A/B Br.

141. AGF M/S, G-3 to CofS, 14 Aug 45, sub: A/B Units in Period II Tr Basis. In AGF G-3 A/B Br (A/B Corresp Aug 45).

142. AAF, I Tr Carrier Cmd, The Operational Training Program, p. 265.

143. *Ibid.*, pp. 265-66.

144. Memo for Record, 7 Jun 45. AGF G-3 A/B (A/B Corresp Jun 45).

145. Ltr, CG AGF to CG AAF, 10 Jul 45, sub: Joint A/B-Tr Carrier Tng. 320.2/2 (A/B) (10 Jul 45) GNGCT – 27.

146. AAF, I Troop Carrier Command, The Operational Training Program, pp. 266-27.

147. Ltr, CG A/B Cen to CG AGF, 19 Jul 45, sub: Aircraft Requirements. 452.01/1 = GNVDT.

148. AAF, I Troop Carrier Command, The Operational Training Program, p. 268.

149. Ltr, CG AGF to CG AAF, 31 Jul 45, sub: Aircraft and Glider Requirements for Airborne Training. 452.1 (31 Jul 45) GNGCT-27. In A/B Corresp. Jul 45/7. ATTNG, A/B Br.

Chapter VI

Trial by Battle

1. See George F. Howe, *Northwest Africa: Seizing the Initiative in the West,* U. S. Army in World War II (Washington: Office of Chief of Military History, 1957).

2. (1) Rpt of Lt Col Hugh P. Harris and Lt Col Gerald J. Higgins, incl with AGF 154 to CG's, 19 Feb 43, sub: Observers' Report. 319.1/9 (for Ops). (2) Rpt of Col Henry V. Dexter on Air-Ground Support in North Africa, incl with AGF memo for Ground, Gen and Spl Staff Sec, 11 June 43, sub: Rpt of Visit to the North Africa Theater of Opns. 319.21 (for Ops).

3. Preliminary draft of CinC's Dispatch, North African Campaign, Eisenhower. Geog. S. Africa 370.2, cy in OCMH.

4. Col Edson D. Raff, *We Jumped to Fight* (New York, 1944), pp. 16-18.

5. Rpt of Lt Col Harris and Lt Col Higgins, pp. 1-2.

6. Rpt of Col Dexter, p. 28.

7. Rpt of Lt Col Harris and Lt Col Higgins, p. 2.

8. *Ibid.*, pp. 2-4; Raff, *We Jumped to Fight,* pp. 30-46.

9. Rpt of Lt Col Harris and Lt Col Higgins, p. 4.

10. *Ibid.*, p. 3; Raff, *We Jumped to Fight,* pp. 182-86.

11. Rpt of Lt Col Harris and Lt Col Higgins, p. 9.

12. *Ibid.*

13. Draft Dispatch, CinC(Eisenhower), Sicilian Opns, p. 20. Mimeo cy in OCMH.

14. (1) *Ibid.*, p. 21. (2) Proceedings of Board of Officers Considering Airborne Opns, Rpt on Airborne Action in Opn HUSKY, n.d. (c. 29 Jul 43). Cy in OPD 381 ETO No. 77. (3) Gavin, *Airborne Warfare,* pp. 1-2. (4) Albert N. Garland and Howard McG. Smyth, assisted by Martin Blumenson, *Sicily and the Surrender of Italy,* U.S. Army in World War II (Washington: Office of the Chief of Military History, 1965), pp. 101-102.

15. Draft Dispatch, CinC, Sicilian Opns, pp. 3, 11.

16. Tactical Employment in the U.S. Army of Transport Aircraft and Gliders Vol. I, p. 111.

17. *Ibid.*, p. 112.

18. Fifth Army History, Vol I, p. 7.

19. Tactical Employment in the U.S. Army of Transport Aircraft and Gliders, Vol. I, p. 113.

20. Gavin, *Airborne Warfare,* pp. 4-5.

21. Tactical Employment in the U.S. Army of Transport Aircraft and Gliders, Vol. I, p. 114.

22. *Ibid.*, p. 120; Draft Dispatch, CinC, Sicilian Opns, p. 33.

23. *Ibid.*

24. Gavin, *Airborne Warfare,* p. 2.

25. (1) Min of conf held at Force 141, 22 Jun 43. Photostat cy in OCMH. (2) Rad, CinC, Med, to CG, F 141, CG, 82d A/B Div, AOC Med, 5 Jul 43.

26. (1) Draft Dispatch, CinC, Sicilian Opns, pp. 33-34; (2) Craven and Cate, *The AAF in World War II, Vol II,* pp. 446-49; (3) Tactical Employment of U.S. Army Transport Aircraft and Gliders, Vol I, pp. 121-124; (4) Proceedings of Board of Officers cited above; (5) Gavin, *Airborne Warfare,* pp. 6-15.

27. Draft Dispatch, CinC, Sicilian Opns, p. 35.

28. Rad, Patton, Eisenhower to CG's II Corps, 45th Div, 1st Div, 2d Armd Div, 3 Div, 6 Jul 43. Photostat copy in OCMH.

29. Garland and Smyth, *Sicily and the Surrender of Italy,* pp. 175-76.

30. (1) *Ibid.*, pp. 175-82; draft dispatch, CinC, Sicilian Opns, p. 35; (2) ltr, Maj Gen J. M. Swing to Maj Gen Orlando Ward, 5 May 1950; (3) Matthew B. Ridgway, *Soldier: The Memoirs of Matthew B. Ridgway* (New York: Harper and Brothers, 1956), pp. 69-73; (4) Wesley Frank Craven and James Lea Cate, eds., *The Army Air Forces in World War II,* Vol. II: *Europe: Torch to Pointblank* (Chicago: University of Chicago Press, 1949), pp. 454-54; (5) G. A. Shepperd, *The Italian Campaign 1943-45* (New York: Frederick A. Praeger, 1968), pp. 52-53; (6) Samuel Eliot Morison, *History of U. S. Naval Operations in World War II,* IX: *Sicily – Salerno – Anzio* (Boston: Little, Brown and Company, 1954), pp. 120-21.

31. Draft dispatch, CinC, Sicilian Opns, p. 35; Craven and Cate, *The Army Air Forces in World War II,* II, 454.

32. *Airborne Operations: A German Appraisal,* MS No. P-057, pp. 51-52.

33. Memo of Maj Gen J. M. Swing, 16 Jul 43, sub: Comments on Night Operation, 82d A/B Div, Night D plus 1-D plus 2. Photostat cy incl w/ltr, Gen Swing to Maj Gen Orlando Ward, 5 May 50.

34. Rpt (Personal and Secret) of Maj Gen F. A. M. Browning, 24 Jul 43, p. 5 Incl No. 6 with Proceedings of Board of Officers.

35. Ltr, CG 82d A/B Div to ACofS OPD, 6 Nov 43, in AFTCC 353 (A/B Tng), quoted in AAF, I Troop Carrier Command, The Operational Training Program, pp. 296-297, Air Hist Off 252-3 v 2.

36. Brief of Rpt of A/B Opn, HUSKY, 17 Sep 43, incl w/OPD memo 319.1 (15 Aug 43) for CofS USA, 20 Sep 43. OPD files. Quoted in AGF Study No. 25, p. 47. Also see extracts of Report of Lt Col C. Billingsea, A/B Opns – "HUSKY," 15 Aug 43, A/B O'seas Rpts. ATTNG, A/B Br.

37. Rpt of Gen Browning cited above, pp. 5-6.

38. *Ibid.*, p. 5.

39. *Ibid.*, p. 9.

40. Diary, WF St (Summer 1943) 13.7/5. In German Mil Docs Sec. OCMH.

41. Interrogation of Generaloberst Student by Col Moore and Maj French at Gockfoster, 27 Sep 45. Reproduced in US AAF in Europe, Air Staff Post Hostilities Intelligence Requirements on German Air Force: Tac Employment Tr Carrier Opns, App. 9. In Command and General Staff College archives, C-13600.

42. Ltr, Maj Gen J. M. Swing to Maj Gen Orlando Ward, 5 May 50.

43. Memo, CG AGF for CofS USA, 22 Sep 43, sub: Rpt of Board on A/B Ops. In 353/17 (A/B).

44. Pers ltr, Gen Eisenhower to Gen Marshall, 20 Sep 43, Misc Exec File, Book 12, case 80. Extracts in CPS 91/1, 19 Oct 43. ABC 322 (23 Sep 43).

45. Copy of extract from Rpt of Maj Gen Lucas, 26 Aug 43, incl with AGF lts 319.1 (NATO) (20 Sep 43) GNGCT to CG A/B Cmd, 20 Sep 43, sub: Overseas Rpt. A/B Misc 1942-1945/15. ATTNG, Joint Policy, manvrs, and Spl Proj Div; Air and A/B Br.

46. Ltr, Maj Gen J. M. Swing to CG AGF, 4 Oct 43, sub: Overseas Rpts on A/B Ops A/B Misc 1942-1945/15 (s), ATTNG, Air 2nd A/B Br.

47. Appendix A, CPS 91.1, 19 Oct 43. ABC 322 (25 Sep 43).

48. (1) Fifth Army History, Vol. I, pp. 23-24; (2) G. A. Shepperd, *The Italian Campaign 1943-45* (New York: Frederick A. Praeger, 1968), p. 103; (3) Gavin, *Airborne Warfare,* pp. 18-28; (4) Martin Blumenson, *Salerno to Cassino,* U.S. Army in World War II (Washington: Office of Chief of Military History, 1969), pp. 44-45.

49. (1) *Ibid.*, pp. 126-127; (2) Fifth Army History, Vol. I, pp. 39-41; (3) Gavin, *Airborne Warfare,* pp. 28-29; (4) Shepperd, *The Italian Campaign,* p. 131.

50. Fifth Army History, I, 41.

51. Brief of Rpt of Maj Mulcahy, w/memo of Col C. B. Ferenbaugh, C, N. African Sec, Theater Group, OPD for Gen Handy, 30 Sep 43, sub: Airborne Activities in the AVALANCHE Operation. In OPD 381, case 220.

52. *Ibid.*

53. (1) Gavin, *Airborne Warfare,* pp. 31-32. (2) Fifth Army History, Vol. I, p. 42. (3) Blumenson, *Salerno to Cassino,* pp. 131-32. (4) Shepperd, *The Italian Campaign,* p. 132.

Chapter VII

Invasion of France

1. OPD 381 case 217.

2. Lt Gen Sir Frederick Morgan, *Overture to Overlord* (Garden City, N.Y., 1950) pp. 203-205.

3. *Ibid.*

4. Memo of Brig Gen F. W. Evans and Col B. W. Bidwell for General Marshall, 1 Mar. 44. In WDCSA 381/2 (Drawer 145).

5. In OPD 381 Case 217.

6. Memo, Gen. H. H. Arnold for Gen G. C. Marshall, 29 Feb 44. In OPD 381 Case 217.

7. Draft of ltr to Gen Eisenhower and memo, Col B. W. Bidwell for ACofS OPD, 1 Mar 44. In OPD 381 Case 217.

8. *Ibid.*

9. Quoted in AGF M/S, Tng (spec Proj) to G-3, 7 Jun 44, sub: Summary of Action Taken and Trends noted from Rpts, May 1944. In AGF G-3 (A/B Suspense Jun 44).

10. (1) Report by the Supreme Commander to the Combined Chiefs of Staff, p. 4. (2) John C. Warren, *Airborne Operations in World War II, European Theater,* No. 97 (Maxwell AFB: USAF Historical Div, 1956), pp. 6-17.

11. Leonard Rapport and Arthur Northwood, Jr., *Rendezvous with Destiny* (Washington, 1948), pp. 32-46.

12. *Ibid.*, p. 55.

13. William G. Lord, II, *History of the 508th Parachute Infantry* (Washington, 198), p. 12.

14. *Ibid.*, p. 13. The 2d Battalion, 401st Glider Infantry went to the 82d Airborne Division in March 1944, so that each division had three glider infantry battalions thereafter.

15. Tactical Employment in the U.S. Army of Transport Aircraft and Gliders in World War II, pp. 182-86.

16. Comments incl with memo, Lt Gen M. B. Ridgway for Chief of Military History, 29 May 50, sub: Airborne Team. British authorities had complained that the docks and streets of Belfast were completely blocked with parachute boxes when the 82d Airborne Division debarked.

17. (1) ETOUSA G-3 Journal, 16 May 44. Adm No. 474. (2) Warren, *Airborne Operations in World War II, European Theater,* pp. 20-26.

18. (1) Tactical Employment in the U.S. Army of Transport Aircraft and Glider, pp. 187-88. (2) Warren, *Airborne Operations in World War II, European Theater,* pp. 20-23.

19. Rapport and Northwood, *Rendezvous with Destiny,* p. 56.

20. Appendix "B" to SHAEF Op Memo No. 12, 24 Mar 44. "Eureka" was the ground radar, and "Rebecca" the air radar.

21. (1) *Ibid.*, pp. 25-26. (2) W. A. Lord, *History of the 508th Parachute Infantry,* p. 14.

22. Ltr, Gen Brereton to Gen Arnold, 20 May 44, quoted in *The Brereton Diaries,* p. 267.

23. (Maj R. G. Ruppenthal), *Utah Beach to Cherbourg,* in the American Forces in Action Series (Washington, 1947), pp. 7-9.

24. *Ibid.*

25. Lt Col R. P. Carr, Troop Carrier Planning for Opn NEPTUNE (School of Combined Arms Monograph, 1945-47). Command and General Staff College Library. X-2253.80.

26. (1) F. O. Miksche, *Paratroops* (New York: Random House, 1943), p. 85. See Gavin, *Airborne Warfare,* p. 42.

27. Rapport and Northwood, *Rendezvous with Destiny,* p. 56.

28. Laurence Critchell, *Four Stars of Hell* (New York, 1947), p. 43. For more complete accounts of the airborne assault in Normandy see Gordan A. Harrison, *Cross-Channel Attack* in *The U.S. Army in World War II* (Washington, 1950), Ch. VIII, and (Ruppenthal,) *Utah Beach to Cherbourg,* pp. 14-42. For a full account of the action of the 101st Airborne Division see Rapport and Northwood, *Rendezvous with Destiny,* pp. 89-249. For a detailed and dramatic account of airborne troops in small unit actions on the ground in this operation, see S. L. A. Marshall, *Night Drop* (Boston: Little, Brown and Company, 1962).

29. First U.S. Army, Report of Operations, 20 Oct 43 – 1 Aug 44 p. 44.

30. Exhibit A, Rpt of Col Charles H. Coates, WD Observers Bd, ETO, sub: Operations of the 101st Airborne Division in the Invasion of France (AGF Rpt No. 116), 15 July 1944. In OCMH files.

31. Rpt of Col B. Conn Anderson, AGF Bd, ETO, sub: Employment of 75-mm. Pack Howitzers Dropped by Parachute in Airborne Divisions, 1 Aug 44. OCMH files.

32. First U.S. Army, Report of Operations, p. 44.

33. "It seemed more than ever that the Regiment was to carry 'the load of a mule with the speed of a fox.'" – Lord, *History of the 508th Parachute Infantry,* p. 16.

34. Marshall, *Night Drop,* pp. 10-11.

35. (Ruppenthal,) *Utah Beach to Cherbourg,* pp. 14-65.

36. (1) Airborne Operations: A German Appraisal, pp. 52-54. MS No. P-051. (2) Gavin, *Airborne Warfare,* p. 65. (3) First U.S. Army, Report of Operations, p. 119, (4) Rpt of 82d A/B Div, to SHAEF thru CG, FUSA, 25 July 1944, sub: 82d A/B Div – Opn NEPTUNE, SHAEF (A/B).

37. Interrogation of Generaloberst Student by Col Moore and Maj French at Gockfoster, 27 Sep 45. Reproduced in USAAFE, Air Staff Post Hostilities Intelligence Requirements on German Air Force: Tactical Employment Troop Carrier Operations, 15 Oct 45, Appendix VIII. In Command and General Staff College Library. C-13600.

38. Min GC, 3 July 44.

39. Ltr, Col Bidwell to ACofS, OPD, 1 Jul 44, sub: WD Observer's Report (Col Bidwell) – Airborne Phase – Operation NEPTUNE. In A/B O'seas Obsrs' Rpt. ATTNG, A/B Br.

40. *Ibid.*

41. Comments incl with memo, Gen Ridgway for Gen Ward, 29 May 50.

42. Ltr, Maj Gen Maxwell D. Taylor to SCAEF, 19 Jul 44, sub: Orgn of 101st A/B Div. in SHAEF G-3 (A/B) 24554/Ops (Prov Reorg of A/B Divs.)

43. Ltr, Maj Gen M. B. Ridgway to CG First Army, 10 Jul 44, sub: Orgn of A/B Div. In SHAEF G-3 (A/B) 24554/Ops (Prov Reorg of A/B Div).

44. AGF Board Report No. A-200, 4 Nov 44, MTO, Report on Airborne Operations in Dragoon, reported by Col. Paul N. Starlings (a reproduction of an AFHQ report). Mimeo copy in OCMH file.

45. *Ibid.*

46. (1) *Ibid.* (2) Rpt of 1st Airborne Task Force.

47. *Ibid.*

48. AGF Board Report C-511, ETO, Lessons Learned in Operation "Dragoon", submitted by Col Harvey J. Jablonsky, 5 Jan 45. Mimeo copy in OCMH file. For general appraisals see Studies of Recent Ops, Op ANVIL, 1st Command Class, Command and General Staff College, S-12846, and 2d Command Class, Op DRAGOON, R-13569.

49. Seventh U. S. Army, Report of Operations in France and Germany, 1944-45, I, 110-114.

Chapter VIII

Follow-Up in Europe

1. *Report by the Supreme Commander,* p. 49.

2. IX Tr Carrier Cmd Rpt on Opn MARKET, Air Invasion of Holland (litho) p. 8. In SHAEF SGS 5364.

3. First Allied Airborne Army Rpt on Ops in Holland Sep-Nov 1944, 22 Dec 44 (Mimeo), pp. 6-8. In SHAEF SGS 5364.

4. Rpt on A/B Opns ETO by Lt Col Frank E. Ross, 6 Dec 44, Tab E, pp. 1-2. Mimeo copy in files of OCMH.

5. *Ibid.*, pp. 2-3.

6. Quoted in *Ibid.*, p. 4.

7. *Ibid.*

8. *Ibid.*, pp. 5-6.

9. FAAA Opn Memo No. 1, 31 Aug 44. In FAAA 322 (LINNET).

10. Msg, CG FAAA to SCAEF, 2 Sep 44. V 25116. In FAAA 322 (LINNET).

11. Msg, CG FAAA to all interested commanders, 2 Sep 44. VX 25125. In FAAA 322 (LINNET).

12. Rpt on A/B Opns ETO by Lt Col Frank E. Ross, Tab E, p. 7.

13. *The Brereton Diaries,* p. 339.

14. Rpt on A/B Opns in ETO by Lt Col Frank E. Ross, Tab E, pp. 8-9.

15. *The Brereton Diaries* (entry for 11 Sep 44) p. 340.

16. *Ibid.*, p. 341; Rpt on A/B Opns in ETO by Lt Col Frank E. Ross, Tab E, p. 8.

17. *The Brereton Diaries,* p. 343.

18. IX Tr Carrier Cmd Rpt on Supply by Air 20 Nov 44 (lithographed). In FAAA 0101-66.2 (9829).

19. Rpt on A/B Ops ETO by Lt Col Frank E. Ross.

20. *The Brereton Diaries,* p. 309.

21. *Ibid.*, p. 339.

22. SHAEF Op Memo No. 29, 29 Apr 44. In SHAEF G-3 245 181/A/B (Supply by Air Policy).

23. IX Tr Carrier Cmd Rpt Supply by Air, pp. 2, 13, 21.

24. *Ibid.*, p. 10.

25. *Ibid.*, p. 22.

26. For the organization of this group see (British Airborne Corps) Allied A/B Ops in Holland, Part II, Appendix A.

27. IX Tr Carrier Cmd Rpt Supply by Air, p. 13.

28. Organization diagram attached to ltr, AG SHAEF to Lt Gen Lewis H. Brereton, 8 Aug 44, sub: Directive. AG 322-1 (Combined A/B Hq) GCT-AGM. In SHAEF G-3 1728/1/A/B (Formation of FAAA).

29. SHAEF Op Memo No. 29, 29 Apr 44, p. 3.

30. IX Tr Carrier Cmd Rpt Supply by Air, p. 14.

31. SHAEF Op Memo No. 29, 29 Apr 44, p. 4.

32. IX Tr Carrier Cmd Rpt, Supply by Air, pp. 4, 14-16.

33. SHAEF Op Memo No. 29, 29 Apr 44, p. 2.

34. IX Tr Carrier Cmd Rpt Supply by Air, pp. 9, 18, 24-25.

35. *Ibid.*, pp. 18-20.

36. Rpt on A/B Ops ETO by Lt Col Frank E. Ross, pp. 3-4.

37. First Allied Airborne Army, Resupply by Air Belgium Dec 44, 26 Apr 45, (Mimeo), pp. 1-2. In FAAA. 0101-66.2(14293) (1/2).

38. S. L. A. Marshall, assisted by John G. Westover and A. Joseph Webber, *Bastogne: The First Eight Days* (Washington, 1946) pp. 133-134, 139.

39. First Allied Airborne Army, Resupply by Air Belgium Dec 1944, pp. 2-3.

40. Marshall, *Bastogne: The First Eight Days,* p. 70.

41. *Ibid.*, pp. 135-38; First Allied Airborne Army, Supply by Air Belgium Dec 1944, p. 3.

42. First Allied Airborne Army, Supply by Air Belgium, Dec 1944, p. 3.

43. *Ibid.*

44. *Ibid.*, pp. 4-5.

45. *Ibid.*, p. 6.

46. Marshall, *Bastogne: The First Eight Days,* p. 138.

47. First Allied Airborne Army, Resupply by Air Belgium Dec 44, p. 6.

48. *Ibid.*

49. *Ibid.*, pp. 9, 19-21.

50. (1) Narrative of Operation Varsity, 24 March 1945, incl No. 1 with Rpt of Col M. A. Quinto, Observer, ETO, 5 May; First Allied Airborne Army Rpt on Opn VARSITY. Both in OCMH files.

51. Report by the Supreme Commander, p. 101.

52. Gavin, *Airborne Warfare,* p. 137.

53. FAAA Rpt on Opn VARSITY, p. 20.

54. First Allied Airborne Army, Rpt on Opn VARSITY, pp. 50-55.

55. Preliminary Planning Study for Airborne Invasion of Germany, Opn ARENA, FAAA, 6 March 45. In SHAEF G-3 24543 (A/B) (ARENA).

56. Notes of a conference at SHAEF forward, 12 Mar 45. In SHAEF G-3 24543 (A/B) ARENA.

57. *Ibid.*

58. Msg. CG FAAA to CGs XVIII corps and IX Tr Carrier Cmd, 15 Mar 45. V 27812. In FAAA (ARENA).

59. Ltr, Maj Gen H. R. Bull to CofS SHAEF 25 Mar 45, sub: Opn ARENA. GCT 370-44/Plans. In SHAEF G-3 24543 (A/B) (ARENA).

60. Msg, SHAEF to FAAA, 26 Mar 45, Fwd – 18204. In SHAEF G-3 24543 (A/B) (ARENA).

Chapter IX

Meanwhile, In the Pacific and Far East

1. (1) *Impact,* published by ACofS Intelligence AAF, Vol. I (Apr 1943), pp. 12-14. (2) *Papuan Campaign: the Buna-Sananada Operation,* American Forces in Action series (Washington, 1944), pp. 36-37. (3) Tactical Employment in the U.S. Army of Transport Aircraft and Gliders,

Vol. II, 274-79. (4) Capt Donaly Hough and Capt Elliott Arnold, *Big Distance* (New York, 1945), pp. 46-55. (5) Report of the Commanding General of the Army Air Forces to the Secretary of War (Washington, 1944), pp. 36-37.

2. Hough and Arnold, *Big Distance,* pp. 82-85.

3. (1) Rpt on Air Support by Col Henry P. Dixter, 10 Apr 44. In AGF 319.1/102 (For Obs). (2) "Paratroops Take Vital Strip," *Impact* (Oct 1943), published by AC of Air Staff, Intelligence, AAF, Vol. I, pp. 22-27. (3) 503d Prcht Inf FO No. 1. Photostatic cy in Command and General Staff College Library. S-6973. (4) Tactical Employment in the U.S. Army of Transport Aircraft and Gliders, Vol. II, pp. 25-28. (5) Hough and Arnold, *Big Distance,* pp. 86-93. (6) *General Kenney Reports,* pp. 292-93.

4. Tactical Employment in the U.S. Army of Transport Aircraft and Gliders, Vol. II, p. 30.

5. *Ibid.*, p. 31.

6. Rpt No. 1448, Joint Intelligence Collection Agency China Burma India (JICA/CBI), 29 Mar 44, sub: Burma, First Air Commando Invasion of; and Rpts no. 1449, 1 Apr 44, sub: Burma, Glider Ops in; No. 1883, 12 Apr 44, sub: Burma, Wingate Rpt on Airborne Invasion of; No. 1834, 15 Apr 44, sub: Burma, Supplemental Rpt on First Air Commando. Copies filed in Air Invasion-Burma, 1944, Command and General Staff College Library, S-9703. See Lowell Thomas "War-Adventure in Burma": *"They Called it Jungle Broadway," Collier's,* Sept 23, 1950, p. 13, "Glider Attack," *Collier's,* Sep 30, 1950, p. 27, "Wingate's Triumph After Death," *Collier's,* Oct 7, 1950.

7. *Merrill's Marauders,* in American Forces in Action Series (Washington, 1945), pp. 23-28. See also AGF M/S, Tng (Spec Proj) to G-3, 7 Jun 44, sub: Summary of Action Taken and Trends Noted from Rpts, May 44. In AGF G-3 (A/B Suspense Jun 44).

8. (1) *Merrill's Marauders,* pp. 93-113. (2) Rpt No. 477, JICA/CBI, 21 Jul 44, sub: Burma – Observations on Air Invasion of Myitkyina Airfield, In Air Invasion – Burma, Command and General Staff College Library. S-9703. (3) Narrative Rpt of Occupation of Myitkyina Airdrome by A/B MG Btry, by Capt J. H. Culbertson, 20 May 44. In Command and General Staff College Library. C-15212.

9. Ltr, Lt Col F. E. Ross to Col J. T. Dalbey, 9 May 44, sub: Glider Operations in Burma. In AGF G-3 A/B Branch (A/B Suspense May 44).

10. Tactical Employment in the U.S. Army of Transport Aircraft and Gliders, II, 310.

11. *Ibid.*, p. 306.

12. (1) *Ibid.*, pp. 42-44. (2) Ltr, Col G. M. Jones (Co, 503d) to CG US Forces, 1 Sep 44, sub: Noemfoor (Tabletennis). In AGF G-3 A/B Br. (A/B Misc 1942-1945). (3) Ltr, Col J. J. Ewell to Lt Gen M. G. Ridgway, 21 Jun 45, sub: A/B Ops in Pacific Ocean Areas. In AGF G-3 A/B Br. (A/B Corresp Jun 45).

13. Tactical Employment in the U. S. Army of Transport Aircraft and Gliders, p. 43.

14. Tactical Employment in the U. S. Army of Transport Aircraft and Gliders, II, 319-402.

15. (1) Unit Rpt, 503d RCT, 5 Mar 45, Photostat cy in Command and General Staff College Library, N-13251. (2) USAFFE Board Rpt No. 208, 16 May 45, sub: Corregidor Island Operation. Photostat cy in Command and General Staff College Library, R-10810-2.

16. Unit Rpt, 503d RCT, 5 Mar 45.

17. Ltr, Col J. J. Ewell to Lt Gen M. B. Ridgway, 21 Jun 45, sub: Airborne Operations in Pacific Ocean Areas. AGF G-3 (A/B Br Jun 45).

18. Extracts of WDCS Memo on the 11th A/B Div in the Leyte Opn, 17 Jan 45. In AGF G-3 A/B Br (A/B Lessons Learned).

19. USAFFE report No. 270, 20 Apr 45, sub: Organization of Para-Glider Infantry Units. Mimeo copy in Hist file.

20. (1) Ops Instructions No. 87, GHQ SWPA, 11 Jan 45. Mimeo copy in C&GSC Archives, R-5788.17. (2) Triumph in the Philippines 1941-1946 (prep by Combat Hist Div, AFWESPAC). (3) Narrative Incl with ltr, Lt Col L. A. Walsh, Jr., to CG POA, 30 Mar 50, sub: Rpt of A/B Ops Luzon Campaign Photostatic cy in C&GSC, R-11656. (4) Tactical Employment in the U.S. Army of Transport Aircraft and Gliders, II, 332-23.

21. (1) Combat Notes No. 7, Sixth Army, May 1945, pp. 31-39. Mimeo cy in C&GSC, R-8887.6. (2) Narrative of Lt Col L. A. Walsh cited above. (3) Ltr Col J. J. Ewell to Lt Gen M. B. Ridgway, 21 Jun 45, sub: A/B Ops in POA. (4) Triumph in the Philippines, IV, 70.

22. *Ibid.* II, 344-47; Triumph in the Philippines, IV, 89; Maj E. M. Flanagan, Jr., *Angels: A History of the 11th Airborne Division* (Washington, 1948) pp. 139-46.

23. Ops Instructions No. 5, GHQ USAFPAC, 15 Aug 45. Mimeo cy in C&GSC Archives R-12398.5.

24. (1) History of Air Cargo Sec A-3 54th Tr Carrier Wing Aug-Sep 45. Typescript in C/GSC archives, S-15433. (2) Flanagan, *The Angels,* pp. 147-55. (3) Tactical Employment in the U.S. Army of Transport Aircraft and Gliders, II, 347-49, 351-52.

Chapter X

The Airborne Effort

1. See Study of Recent Ops, Rpt of Committee No. 3, 1st Cmd Class, Command and General Staff School, 15 Jan 46, sub: Opn MARKET. G&GSC Archives, S-12847.

2. Trans, interrogation of Gen Student by Col Moore and Maj French at Gockfoster, 27 Sep 45. Reproduced in Air Staff Post Hostilities Intelligence Requirements on German Air Force, Appendix IX.

3. Ltr, Maj J. D. Hancock to CG FAAA, 14 Oct 44, sub: Rpt on Activities in Opn MARKET. In FAAA 322 (MARKET) (Microfilm roll No. 3).

4. Rpt on A/B ops ETO, Lt Col Frank E. Ross, 6 Dec 44, Tab E.

5. *Rpt by the Supreme Commander to the Combined Chiefs of Staff,* p. 49.

6. Gen H. H. Arnold, *Global Missions,* 521-2.

7. *Logistics in World War II: Final Report of the Army Service Forces* (Washington, 1947), p. 161.

8. IX Troop Carrier Command, Supply by Air, p. 2. The average daily expenditure of all items of supply, less 90 percent of gasoline and lubricants, in campaign amounted to approximately 45 pounds per man per day. (FM 101-10, Staff Officers' Field Manual: Organization, Technical and Logistical Data, 10 Oct 43, par 312). This would mean an average daily expenditure of about 320 tons for a standard, full strength infantry division.

9. *Rpt by the Supreme Commander to the Combined Chiefs of Staff,* p. 20.

10. See U.S. Strategic Bombing Survey, Over-all Report (European War), chart 4, p. 6.

11. AGF Equipment Review Board, (1945) Part I, pp. 116-117. Litho copy in Command and General Staff College library, S-10445-A.

12. Discussion AGF Reply to WD Questionnaire AG 322 (26 Jun 45) OB-S-WDSSP, incl with memo, CG AGE for CofS USA, 19 Oct 45, sub: A/B Forces in U.S. Postwar Mil Est. 370.01 (c) (19 Oct 45) GNPS. Photostatic copy in OCMH.

For further analysis of the logistical problems involved in establishing and maintaining an airhead, see studies proposed at the Command and General Staff College by Lt Col W. E. Harrison (x-2128.140), Lt Col Harry Balish (x-2128.139), Lt Col G. M. Hunt (x-2128.141-1), and Maj. R. L. Rowan (x-2128.142).

13. Airborne Operations: A German Appraisal, p. 50. Ms No. P-051.

14. Memo, CG AGF for CofS USA, 19 Oct 45, sub: A/B Forces in the U.S. Postwar Mil Est, 2nd Discussion incl.

15. USAFFE Board Rpt No. 208, 16 May 45, sub: Corregidor Island Operations 16 Feb – 8 Mar 45, par 19.

16. IX Troop Carrier Command, Supply by Air, p. 45.

17. Cf. B. H. Liddell Hart, *Europe in Arms* (London, 1937), p. 33.

18. AGF M/S, CG to CofS, 19 Jun 42, In AGF 320 2/3 (A/B) (S).

19. Discussion of Reply to WD questionnaire, incl with memo, CG AGF for CofS USA, 19 Oct 45, sub: A/B Forces in U.S. Postwar Mil Est.

20. *Ibid.*

21. (1) *Brereton Diaries,* pp. 217, 236. (2) First Allied Airborne Army. Army-ALAB-1-SU, Air Hist Off. (3) WD ltr to CG's, 1 Sep 44, sub: First Allied Airborne Army, CG, Memo for Info 229. AG 322 (29 Aug 44) OB-S-E. In AGF G-3 A/B Br, (A/B Misc 1942-1945) (S). (4) CGS Memo 229, sub: First Allied A/B Army. In ABC 322 (25 Sep 44). (5) Talk of Maj Gen Maxwell Taylor to AGF Staff, Army War College, 18 Dec 44. (6) AAF, I Troop Carrier Command, The Operational Training Program, pp. 396, 401-402. (7) AGF M/S, G-3 to CofS, 31 Jan 45, sub: Relationship of Air Transport and AGF Postwar. In AGF G-3 (A/B Br Suspense Jan 45). (8) Gen Board USFET, Reply to Questionnaire on the Postwar Mil Est. Copy in OCMH.

22. Memo, CG AGF for CofS USA, 19 Oct 45, sub: A/B Forces in the U.S. Postwar Mil Est.

23. Memo, Gen McNair for G-3 WD, 3 Jun 43, sub: Reduced Inf Div. 322/2 (Dirs). Quoted in Greenfield et al, *The Organization of Ground Combat Troops* in U.S. ARMY IN WORLD WAR II, p. 315.

24. See U.S. Strategic Bombing Survey, Over-all Report (European War).

25. Study, prep by Col J. J. Ewell for CG Airborne Center, 30 Nov 45, sub: A/B Forces in the U.S. Postwar Mil Est. In AGF G-3 A/B Br (A/B Classified Corresp Jun 45 – Aug 46). Photostatic copy in OCMH.

26. See Palmer *et al, The Procurement and Training of Ground Combat Troops* in U.S. ARMY IN WORLD WAR II, p. 258.

27. Expenditures for glider procurement alone amounted to over $375 million. *AAF Statistical Digest,* supp No. 1, p. 44 (table 203).

Index